# UNDERSTANDING MANAGEMENT CRITICALLY

SAGE has been part of the global academic community since 1965, supporting high quality research and learning that transforms society and our understanding of individuals, groups, and cultures. SAGE is the independent, innovative, natural home for authors, editors and societies who share our commitment and passion for the social sciences.

Find out more at: **www.sagepublications.com**

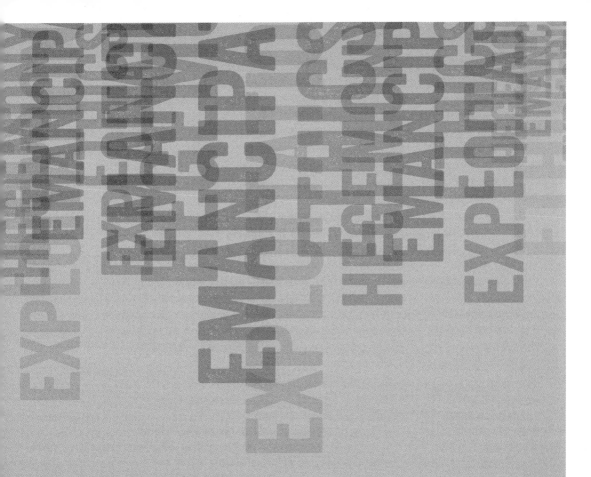

# UNDERSTANDING MANAGEMENT CRITICALLY

## A STUDENT TEXT

### SUZETTE DYER, MARIA HUMPHRIES, DALE FITZGIBBONS & FIONA HURD

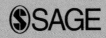

Los Angeles | London | New Delhi
Singapore | Washington DC

Los Angeles | London | New Delhi
Singapore | Washington DC

SAGE Publications Ltd
1 Oliver's Yard
55 City Road
London EC1Y 1SP

SAGE Publications Inc.
2455 Teller Road
Thousand Oaks, California 91320

SAGE Publications India Pvt Ltd
B 1/I 1 Mohan Cooperative Industrial Area
Mathura Road
New Delhi 110 044

SAGE Publications Asia-Pacific Pte Ltd
3 Church Street
#10-04 Samsung Hub
Singapore 049483

Editor: Matthew Waters
Editorial assistant: Nina Smith
Production editor: Sarah Cooke
Copyeditor: Sue Ashton
Proofreader: Derek Markham
Indexer: Judith Lavender
Marketing manager: Alison Borg
Cover design: Lisa Harper
Typeset by: C&M Digitals (P) Ltd, Chennai, India
Printed in Great Britain by Henry Ling Limited at
The Dorset press, Dorchester, DT11HD

**Library of Congress Control Number: 2013945184**

**British Library Cataloguing in Publication data**

A catalogue record for this book is available from
the British Library

MIX
Paper from
responsible sources
FSC
www.fsc.org     FSC™ C013985

ISBN 978-0-85702-080-2
ISBN 978-0-85702-081-9 (pbk)

# CONTENTS

# ABOUT THE AUTHORS

Dr Suzette Dyer lectures in Human Resource Management in the Department of Strategy and Human Resource Management of the Waikato Management School, University of Waikato, Hamilton, New Zealand. Her current research interests include globalisation, flexibility and work-place change, career management and development, women's experiences in complex organisations, and the settlement experiences of migrants. She also has a keen interest in developing critical pedagogy in the management classroom. Currently, she is collaboratively working on projects investigating the impact of changes to work in single-industry towns, the emotional experiences of skilled migrants living in New Zealand, and whether critical pedagogical teaching techniques improve students' critical reasoning.

Dr Maria Humphries is an Associate Professor in the Department of Strategy and Human Resource Management of the Waikato Management School, University of Waikato, Hamilton, New Zealand. She created and taught the first 'Business, Government and Society' course at the School in 1990. She co-initiated the early courses in 'Women and Management' that continue to be taught at both undergraduate and graduate levels. She was closely involved in the creation of a programme of studies focused on the development of indigenous management theories and practice. Various versions of the critical examination of management and civil society under the contemporary conditions of globalisation currently inform her leadership of the Social Enterprise Studies programme at the Waikato Management School. She takes a great interest in the United Nations' initiatives, such as the Global Compact and the promotion of the related Principles for Responsible Management Education. She brings a critical perspective to the training and mentoring of her doctoral students, as well as in all her post-graduate classes.

Dr Dale Fitzgibbons is an Associate Professor in the Department of Management and Quantitative Methods at Illinois State University, USA. He teaches strategy, corporate social responsibility and environmental management using a critical perspective. He is the Programme Director for the minor in Business, Environment and Society in the Department of Management and Quantitative Methods. His research interests are at the intersection of critical theory and sustainability, critical pedagogy, social/economic justice, corporate corruption, and indigenous knowledge and management education. He is a strong supporter of the United Nations' Principles for Responsible Management

Education. He publishes in a wide variety of scholarly journals and is a former editor of the *Journal of Management Education*.

Ms Fiona Hurd is a doctoral student in Human Resource Management in the Department of Strategy and Human Resource Management of the Waikato Management School, University of Waikato, Hamilton, New Zealand. Her thesis examines, through an identity lens, the impact of globalisation on work, workers and communities. Her wider research and teaching interests include critical management studies and pedagogy, gender and organisation, and critical perspectives on strategic management, organisational behaviour, and career management and development.

# ACKNOWLEDGEMENTS

We would like to thank the many people who have influenced our thinking, our teaching, and our writing. Among these are Rae André, Piet Kil, Margaret Bedggood, Richard and Rosie Bentley, David Boje, Suzanne Grant, Nina Gregg, John Kirton, David Steingard, Michelle St Jane, and Amy Verbos. Thanks is also extended to the numerous colleagues in the New Zealand and in the international Critical Management Studies community who have provided invaluable feedback on the content of our book in the form of conference papers and presentations.

We thank too, the many Post Graduate Students who have read segments and made such useful suggestions. To the students in all our courses who endured early versions of this text in the form of partial course readings, we thank you for your insights, and critical comments. Kahurangi Dey deserves a special mention for her thorough reading, editing and candid feedback.

We also thank Kiren, Ruth, Mark, Matt, Sue, Vanessa and all those members of the Sage team without whose good work we would not have a published manuscript.

# FOREWORD

## CRITICAL MANAGEMENT IN THE DESERT OF THE REAL – DAVID M. BOJE

I live in the Chihuahuan Desert in New Mexico. From a great distance the desert looks like a smooth space, rolling sands, dotted with green stuff you cannot quite make out in any detail. Get up close and look again and you see a very diverse space with lots of life: cacti, spiders, snakes, mesquite and other bushes; down along the arroyos, the desert willows. Up close it's all zigzagging and spiralling. The suburbs are consuming the desert. Each week some yoyo from the city hires a guy on a bulldozer to strip away all the soil and its life forms, leaving this smooth space of deadness. When the desert wind blows, the sod lifts up and blows away along with the topsoil. The dust devils kick up sand that scratches the paint right off your car. It disenchants what is on the license plate, 'Land of Enchantment'.

I stood in front of the bulldozer, 'Stop right there, leave the desert where it lies.' The desert is home for plants and animals. They live here too. Despite my efforts, the trend is clear. Each suburb takes a land full of life and turns it into deadness. The suburbs are getting dense. Strip malls, box stores and fast food joints are moving in. The suburbia sloth moves, tosses beer bottles and fast food wrappers onto any remaining desert patches. I volunteer to go pick up all that trash each year, and sometimes just pick it up as I hike.

Old school management education has assumed the right to own the planet, enslave workers, plants, animals, and even redesign life. That sort of management raises ethical concerns.

It's all about the storytelling. The worst managers only listen to one side of a story. Have you ever been called on the carpet and the manager already decided not to listen to your side of the tale? Old school managers spin a heroic tale of conquering nature, laying waste to the competition, cracking the whip to motivate workers by fear, or putting one over on the consumer.

Critical Management Studies (CMS) has a good side, a way of 'managing for goodness'. Managing for goodness means taking responsibility for the community, the environment, the way of life on the planet. It is an ethics of being answerable to intervene in the badness, to be responsible for bringing about goodness.

CMS is critical for good reasons. What organisations do and how they do it can harm the planet, its people, animals, plants, trees, rivers, air and soil. The financial collapse of the worlds' banking systems, the junk mortgage scandals, the ways Enron fibbed to investors, and how Arthur Anderson accounting executives looked the other way when their job was to tell it like it is … These events had consequences. You may be working for such organisations already, and if not, you perhaps soon may be. Beware or you will become the Storm Troopers of Empire, in service of the Emperor. CMS is the Jedi who sees through the logic of the Empire.

Another logic subtly woven through management education suggests that the survival of the fittest is all that matters. The rich are meant to be wealthy and the poor to remain poor losers of the big game of life. Each is the master of their own destiny. Critical management scholars detect a fib in that tale. There is a dimension woven through this tale: a logic – or logistics – of the necessary attention we must all give to increasing quality, continuous improvement, in the service in increased productivity and economic growth. All well and good, until you start looking at the social and environmental footprint all this productivity and economic growth has generated. All the 'reduce, recycle and reuse' you can muster will not make a dent in the corporate footprint. Take a look at the swirling plastic mass in our oceans, entangling and strangling life. Climate change is all about the effects of our footprints. CMS puts environmental concerns under close scrutiny, and then looks at who is accountable and who is avoiding responsibility for the consequences of footprints of Exxon, Shell, BP and the other big oil Empires. We each have a footprint too. The well-to-do have bigger footprints than others – or the means by which to 'off-set' their liabilities in some clever book-keeping kind of way.

Corporations are buying up water rights in every community with fresh clean drinkable water. Water is as expensive as beer. Water has been transformed into a commodity, something to buy and sell. This is such strange logic when looked at from the indigenous perspective. Water rights to lakes, rivers and springs were worked out to benefit everyone who lived there: the people, plants, and animals.

Why be a bystander? Do you watch and do nothing while life falls apart? You are the first generation that will live fewer years than your parents. Your children will live fewer years of life than you will. The fast and processed food, all those sugary drinks and the salty food, with all those genetically modified additives have consequences: heart disease, cancer, and diabetes. CMS questions the 'just loving it' fast food message.

Dyer, Humphries, Fitzgibbons and Hurd's book includes crucial reflection to prepare managers, students and teachers to go deeper into topics, get fired up, and take critical management action.

Try answerability ethics. Managers are guardians of the life world. Hear all sides of the storytelling and take action. Next time you pass a desert, take a walk while it's full of life. Ask yourself, however: 'For how long? What am I doing now, that will create the future?' Ask your friends, your family, your teachers – 'what are we doing now, to make a world worth living in for us, for our children and for theirs.' Pay close attention to the answers. Be alert to any contradictions in subtle seductive logic that suggests all will be well if we prioritise profit and growth with which to solve the problems besetting people and planet. Become more fluent in your responses. This book will help you do just that.

*David M. Boje*

# DEAR TEACHER

## WHAT IS IT TO STUDY MANAGEMENT CRITICALLY?

Scholars loosely grouped as critical organisational theorists approach their work in a variety of ways. The expressed purpose of critical theory is to serve human emancipation – sometimes defined as the elimination of any constraint on freedom. Within this aspiration, however, there are a variety of approaches. For libertarians, for example, we must be free to pursue our individually chosen ends. Some suggest we must be free for our actions to be considered moral or ethical. For them, freedom is a necessary condition for morality and is to be contrasted with compliance or complicity no matter how subtle. Others see the purpose of critical management studies as a contribution to the enhancement of justice for which we might choose to forgo some freedoms, but we must be free to forgo them rather than be forced to so. There are those who believe the exploitative impulse is so strong, that laws and constraints are necessary to prevent or publish the worst possible excesses.

A reflection on how much control managers may exert or be themselves constrained by might be generated from the question: "Must we be free to be good – or good to be free?" This question may be a good opening reflection when introducing students to this book. As with all examples in this book, you might contextualise the question in examples appropriate for the courses your students are enrolled in and the level of their studies. Invite students to see and challenge the ways over-simplification in management studies enter their 'taken-for-granted' world views. Theory X Theory Y propositions, the assumed validity and stability of personality traits, and right to control increasingly intimate aspects or our humanity while absolved from personal responsibility for wider social outcomes of their corporate fealty are just some examples. At most subtle, we are all encouraged to believe that market outcomes, if generally achieved within the boundaries of current law, will deliver justice. The very notion of 'justice' is itself a significant icon of western liberalism and democracy. Justice, a concept held by all peoples, is one however, that has a variety of interpretations.

None of the ideas or the reasons for engaging with critical theory has universal agreement. How to be responsible for their manifestation in practice must therefore generate open questions and resist overly simplistic responses. We raise some of these questions for investigation and their implications to management education. They inform what Boyce (1996) so usefully summarised as a 'critical pedagogy'.

> Beyond a casual reference to specific teaching practices, pedagogy concerns the way we construct relations between teachers and learners. How we understand processes of teaching and learning shapes our work as educators….Critical pedagogy, kin to critical theory, is theoretically grounded in the first generation Frankfurt school of critical theory, Gramsci's concepts of hegemony, subject, and counter-hegemonic practice, and a politics of ethics, difference, and democracy (Freire, 1970; Giroux, 1988; Giroux & McLaren, 1994; McLaren, 1993; McLaren & Lankshear, 1994; Misgeld, 1987; Shor & Freire, 1987). The first generation Frankfurt school emphasized attaining emancipation by the critique and social action of critically conscious persons. For Frankfurt School theorists the practice of de-reification, of personal and political emancipation, [is] through negative critique: that is, the negation of false consciousness through ideology critique (Luke, 1992: 27). As persons become aware of how social and political systems work and become conscious of themselves as agents, they can identify and critique domination (a process that Freire calls conscientization).

http://www.mngt.waikato.ac.nz/ejrot/Vol2_2/boyce.pdf

We have drawn inspiration from Clegg et al.'s *Managing & Organisations* to who advocate the support for students who really wish to understand their subject matter so that they can be "adept players in the language game of the subject" (p. 3). And to some extent we agree. More compelling for us in the creation of these supplementary resources is the observation by Clegg et al. that the ideas presented in the texts usually proscribed may not necessarily be accurate descriptions of actuality but that they must be "taken seriously because of the important effects they have on organisations…these ideas have a *performative* quality… the 'real world' begins to resemble the theory that describes it" (ibid) – or, rather, purports to do so. This way of thinking about what is in our teaching texts and styles is enhanced in this book with our orientation to the social constructivists in our field who make the study of purported structure and function of organisations a little less 'given' and invite greater focus on the ways these are formulated, enacted and embodied. Also compelling in the approach taken by Clegg et al., is the treatment of the subject matter in its various dimensions more critically "as a force within society in general". And with this too we are in agreement – understanding this 'force' to be evident in the effects of what some theorists might call the dominant 'institutional theories' (Thornton, Ocassion and Loundsbury (1012) and others might call the prevailing zeitgeist with all the various nuances among them. We also like the way Clegg et al. invite a reciprocal relationship between experience and theory – presented and balanced by the experience and theoretical sophistication of a specific class. Where experience is rich, examples can be used to illustrate theory. Where experience is less developed, abstract ideas need supplementing with diverse examples. Like us, these authors have found the internet to be a vast and useful realm to be drawn on. Aspects of the world beyond our immediate experience and beyond the bounty of our school library have become radically more accessible – and perhaps more problematic.

Along with *Understanding Management Critically* therefore, we have provided instructor resources on a companion website to explain further the ideas presented in each of the chapters. We offer teaching notes that may draw closer attention to background theory and we offer explanatory ideas and vignettes to begin or extend class discussions. For students we provide a parallel set of open resources that extends the material presented in the chapters through vignettes they can discuss and exercises that they can practice to deepen their insight into concepts and reasoning that either endorse or challenge the status quo. The examples we provide, are starting points only. They can be easily updated as more relevant, more regionally appropriate, or more easily understood examples come to light. Like Clegg et al., engagement with that world beyond the immediacy of our personal and organisational experience is important – because what we do (there) has a significant influence of what and who we become.

We hope you will enjoy using this book to enrich your classes. We hope the students will enjoy reading it because it is interesting and insightful and because it opens the way to increasingly critical engagement with the issues and the organisations we bring into focus – and eventually to influence their actions as managers, employees, consumers and citizens.

## Technical advice

YouTube may be more safely downloaded as PowerPoint Presentations – so as to be less reliant on secure internet feeds in your classroom.

# DEAR STUDENT

Never before in human history have such rich research resources as generated by the internet been so easily available to so many people. The student companion website for *Understanding Management Critically* that you find here offer you a vast range of materials to help you with your studies. Some are mere images or quotes to prompt some deeper research, some might motivate a change in direction of your thoughts, some might stimulate ideas for shaping essays and projects. We provide web-links to short or long films you may want to make the time to watch in a study group or on your own. Each companion webpage begins with a summary that explains the purpose of the Chapter it relates to. This will be followed by a variety of exercises and ideas to help you understand the chapter and to extend you thinking beyond what we have written. There is also a section called "People to Meet, [Web]Places to Visit, and Actions to Take". These are just examples of a rich world you can explore. You will no doubt come across many ideas we have not covered! Practice your growing critical thinking skills by asking yourself the classic questions that guide critical thinkers: "Who is speaking?", "What do they aspire to?", "What is in it for them?" "At whose expense?", "Do I want to get involved"? "How?" Use our ideas as starting points only. Surf around and begin to build your own Resource Bank to update and support your scholarly development, your political awareness and engagement, and your maturity in civil responsibility. From your initial investigation, build up your scholarly critique. We hope you enjoy the examples we have chosen. Even more, we hope that you will take our lead and research the issues and theories that are of most interest to you. Enriching your studies will enrich your life – and the lives of those you will necessarily touch.

# INTRODUCTION

Welcome to a way of thinking about human organisation(s) and management that is not typical of management education in general. We want to show you how this way of thinking may deepen your perspectives on the issues that are facing humanity as we enter the twenty-first century. Much management education has been based on assumed rights to take ownership of aspects of the planet that are thought to be useful to us and to control other people in their exploitation for profit. These very fundamental ideas are increasingly associated with the difficult issues of justice and sustainability that are now very widely discussed in many areas of political concern, ethical reflections, technical expertise and social and environmental activism. We want to help you unpack the ideas of management and organisation(s) that many people have come to believe are the normal ways to see the structures and processes of living in the 21st Century and to consider joining in some way with those who are seeking radical transformations to our way of being human.

Our book begins from an idea that the narrow focus on the instrumental and technical aspects of management helps to normalise the rhetoric of capitalism and shifts general attention away from its narrow ethical focus and its darker outcomes. This prevailing focus on technique over an examination of values and principles deflects deeper discussions about the embedded assumptions of capitalism and the ways in which these are being imposed on ever more spheres of what Husserl (1936) called the *Lebenswelt* or 'lifeworld': 'the world we live in and are absorbed by in our everyday activities' (Craig, 2005: 424). We are with Husserl! His concerns invite us to ask to what extent are people portrayed and treated as sovereign or emancipated beings? Can we observe examples of where people are treated as mere functionaries of the system or as cogs in the machine, whose energies can be instrumentally harnessed to serve 'the company', 'the economy' or the more ubiquitous ideas of 'economic growth'? What ethical frameworks would we need if people were defined ethically as free beings? How might this difference change how we think about, for example, human resource management practices? How would accounting practices and financial information be different? We are concerned in this book with the way in which these questions are examined in Western democratic societies, where Western capitalist organisational practices predominate and where ideas of democracy are given some but perhaps not enough critical significance. Critical theorists interpret their task as the identification and clarification of the necessary conditions for liberated living (Fleming, 1997). They are concerned with the assumptions, promised explicitly and implicitly, in the genesis stories of both capitalism and democracy as they apply to the study of organisation and management. These foundational assumptions have occupied many thinkers of the past and will continue to do so well into the future.

As authors of this book, we do not presume to offer specific truths and ready recipes for action from our own fixture in time and place. This does not mean we do not hold strong views. We share our views for discussion, development or challenge in the pages that follow and in the related companion webpages for each chapter. These companion pages provide extra notes and ideas to shape assignments, to explore cases that might expand our understanding, and to reflect on the ways in which we are engaged in the creation of the future in and beyond our participation in employment. We do not seek to provide 'facts' because we know that anything given as fact always requires interpretation. Rather, we aim to encourage life-long enquiry and action into and from a growing critical consciousness. This book thus has an aspirational focus. We aspire to contribute to the generations of future leaders and managers who will put their minds and efforts to managing for 'goodness', which we take to mean a concerted effort to challenge and transform harm to people and planet in the overt and subtle ways such harms are manifest.

Throughout this book, we argue and demonstrate that our collective enactment of the prevailing institutional logic is partially responsible for the seemingly intractable violations of human dignity and environmental degradation. This logic, uncritically endorsed, is insufficiently self-aware and far too instrumentally orientated to support meaningful efforts to transform the predominant and destructive attributes of our human being. The relationships between market activities, governmental action or inaction, and various forms of social responsiveness are not always clearly discernible. It is hard to tell how far clever public relations endorses organisational legitimacy by hoodwinking too many of us. Most of us will spend our lives in very ordinary circumstances – seemingly far from the system-creating decisions that are being made. But, we argue in this book, such disconnection between these macro-level actions and our daily lives is an illusion. The dynamics and the actions of much smaller organisations, work-teams, and the ordinary employees who are just doing their jobs, consumers purchasing goods and services, and citizens raising their families with more or less security of income are much harder to discern. Yet, discerning these connections is what we are encouraging you to do in this book. Flows and ruptures in the global financial system or the commercial opportunities variously afforded by war or peace affect the flows of investment capital, the potential contracts on offer, the availability of employees to meet these, and the consumer capacity and willingness to purchase the goods and services produced. In all spheres of human endeavour, from the boardroom to the pantry, from the political arena to the domestic sphere, in choices to save or to spend, in our commitments to donate or to accumulate, in our decisions to comply with or to resist authorities, we are all managing aspects of our personal and collective humanity.

In the chapters that follow, we will set out our understanding of the global context and influences of globalisation and our collective potential to influence its trajectory. In Chapter 2, we set out our orientation to critical management studies (CMS) and introduce some of the thinkers who have influenced our thoughts as critical management educators. In Chapter 3, we set out our views about globalisation and its reach into many aspects of our lives. In Chapters 4, 5 and 6 we explore some of the more subtle changes in the shaping of work, workers and their integration into, or alienation from, the means of a sustainable livelihood, a means made possible, ironically, by compliance with a system that destroys in order to remain sustainable. But it is not only as employees, managers or investors that we contribute to the maintenance of this system. Chapter 7 invites greater reflection on our activities as consumers, which have significant impact on systemic fluctuations and on the natural environment that generate issues we address more fully in Chapter 8. Chapter 9 invites a critical reflection on contemporary leadership and asks us to consider where and how the leadership for the transformation of the issues raised in this book is to be developed.

Participation in the deep discussion of managing for 'goodness' invites each of us to be alert to self-serving ideas about goodness, well-being, legitimacy and righteousness that cause harm to others and to take responsibility for transforming such ideas and practices. These are concerns that have occupied thinking people as far back as memory can serve us. The quest of ancient tribal leaders to ensure the well-being of their communities and their relationships with the spiritual realms can be contrasted with the priorities of those who terrorised others to protect their power, authority and privilege. These two extremes suggest that the questions we raise in this book are ancient, culturally diverse and of utmost contemporary relevance. We hasten to add that most situations are not one of two extremes, but a kind of messy mix, and we will discuss this mix in the diverse examples of human and corporate behaviours in the chapters that follow.

Our reach into this diversity, and our interpretation of the examples, are necessarily limited to our place in time and space, as authors and readers, teachers and students. This book reaches into English-speaking communities and cannot hope to represent the diverse cultural values and aspirations of each region, tribe and person who has come to study management – but we can try our utmost to use our language to open as many vistas as we can. We will provide a sample of the thoughts of accessible moral philosophers that demonstrate that questions that arise about 'goodness' still pulse with vitality and can drive curiosity and passion, and motivate us to revised action.

In this book, we are engaging primarily with you, students studying the management of human organisation(s). To understand the effect, effectiveness and significance of managers and management in the coordination of our common interests, however, invites a broad and deep reflection on who we are, on what we value, and how we go about our daily business as individuals and as organisations. There are many ways to undertake such reflections. In formal studies, such reflections are expressed through diverse theoretical approaches. CMS is one such approach. Scholars working from a CMS orientation focus on expressions of power and control. Where these are found to be destructive or exploitative, they are concerned with their transformation into dynamics that are deemed to be more just. Thus, studying the potentially exploitative or destructive tendencies of the capitalist system with a view to their transformation is an informative and responsible contribution to management education. Whether this system can be amended to address the issues of concern or whether a completely new form of human organisation must be invented is a point of controversy among scholars, practitioners and protesters alike. We hope you find our arguments compelling and enjoy the many examples we provide to encourage you to value a heightened consciousness about the world in which you must live, dream, work, play, raise families, care for elders, and will eventually die. That we should all have the opportunity to live and die with dignity underpins the orientation of this book.

In the next chapter, we introduce the ideas of some famous critical thinkers who have set about unsettling taken-for-granted ideas that they believe are part of the stories we tell ourselves to justify our ways of being, stories that may get in the way of believing that we can, if we will, transform injustice and exploitation. We will begin to examine the deep, underlying ideas that come to weave together our understanding of ourselves and our organisation(s). These are two ideas that cannot be treated separately. Both are figments of our imagination. Conscious attention to both is required. The consequences of each on the lives of all have concerned critical organisational scholars, some of whom we introduce in Chapter 2.

# REFERENCES

Craig, E. (2005) *The Shorter Routledge Encyclopedia of Philosophy*. London: Routledge.

Fleming, M. (1997) *Emancipation and Illusion: Rationality and Gender in Habermas's Theory of Modernity*. University Park, PA: Pennsylvania State University Press.

Husserl, E. (1936) The crisis of European sciences and transcendental phenomenology: an introduction to phenomenological philosophy. *Philosophia (Belgrad)*, 1: 77–176.

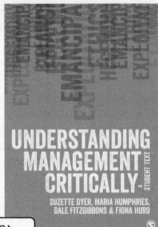

# 1 RAISING CRITICAL CONSCIOUSNESS IN MANAGEMENT STUDIES

---

## Learning Objectives

In this chapter, we encourage you to begin a sustained reflection on:

- how far you believe individual responsibility for universal and planetary well-being extends;
- whether management students (as potential and actual managers) have a specific duty to consider responsibilities beyond compliance with employer directives;
- whether ethical considerations can be compartmentalised, i.e., whether we can claim to hold personal values that we cannot uphold in our employment context;
- whether it is necessary or even possible to attempt to influence institutional values in some way to bring greater integrity between our worldviews and the values applied in the organisations we must engage with.

## CRITICAL CONCEPTS

*Consciousness (-raising)*, *legitimacy*, *authority* and *power* are central ideas in critical management studies (CMS). We introduce notions of *exploitation*, *compliance*, *domestication*, *subjectification* and *subjugation* so that throughout the book we can build up a progressive understanding of how such dynamics may be woven into the prevailing *institutional logics of capitalism*. We introduce the concepts of *hegemonic influence*, *transformation* and *emancipation* that are central to the concerns of *critical theorists* in contemporary organisational studies. Key to understanding the powerful influences we experience as the *system* is to comprehend the types of entities humans create and use to generate and sustain *social order*. The study of such entities is called *ontology*. The justification (or purported proof) of their existence is called *epistemology*. This chapter begins an ontological and epistemological enquiry into *capitalism* – a set of beliefs and practices that we present as an *ideology* and that, for radical critics, may be better thought of as a *dogma*.

All social systems of organisation are fabrications of the human mind. They are made up of a network of related concepts and values that are woven together as their institutional logics. Increasing awareness of our part in the fabrication and maintenance of the systems through which we organise ourselves is a necessary step in the shaping of an ethical life, a life of integrity that draws together our values in actions across the many spheres of our lives. Understanding our own logics is a proactive step towards shaping an integrated ethical life as student, teacher, manager, parent or citizen.

Artists and artisans, musicians and spiritual leaders, inventors and investors are all working to influence the way we human beings see ourselves and our place in the universe. So, too, are scholars in management studies. We, too, focus on how we individuals intuit or rationalise our way of being in (or through) what Husserl (1936) calls our 'lifeworld'. We are interested in the growing neoliberal reasoning we employ to justify our action or inaction. In this book, we will examine not only how this rationality is so prominent in contemporary organisational and management reasoning, but in so many spheres of our daily life. Our focus is on our common participation in the dynamics of the form of human organisation being intensified globally. This focus requires us to examine beliefs, values and attitudes, as well as systems and organisational processes in action. This focus requires us to grow in self-awareness. It requires us to become conscious of who we are and who we might yet become.

In keeping with the traditions of critical management studies (CMS), in this book we take as our task to detect and expose situations and processes of marginalisation, exclusion, exploitation and other harms to people and planet with the intent of contributing to their transformation. This task may be quite straightforward when we uncover explicitly corrupt behaviour. In such cases, we can use the law or various social and political pressures to achieve change. It is much more challenging, however, to detect the more subtle ways in which harm comes about. It is challenging to understand our own complicity with, tolerance of, or subjugation to harmful systemic influences and their outcomes for ourselves and others. This may be, in part, because any system may both reward and punish. There may be risks attached to being openly critical of any system of organisation we may rely on for our personal security. Exclusion from any personally significant system of organisation may be painful and perhaps even dangerous. It takes courage and stamina to explore the dynamics of systemic exclusion, exploitation and alienation in our own lives and the lives of others.

In the history of human thought, there has been much debate and little agreement on what a good society is. There is perhaps some traction in the idea that organised human activity must certainly not detract from human or planetary well-being. In this book, we encourage rigorous engagement in the shaping, protection and enhancement of this well-being for people the world over and for the planet that we must all share for our own immediate survival and for the thriving of our children and theirs. Such engagement with universal intergenerational well-being, however, is mindful not to privilege people unjustly or unwisely over other living species. Such mindfulness calls for an enlarged critical consciousness. Contributing to the enlargement of our critical consciousness and the engagement of our conscience in the organisation of our humanity is the stuff of this book. We invite you to join us in our enquiries and we hope to inspire you to some transformational action!

# WHY A MORE CRITICAL MANAGEMENT STUDIES?

The first two decades of the twenty-first century may be remembered for widespread protests by ordinary people against what they perceive to be the leaders and the systems that have not served them well and, in many cases, are believed to have harmed them directly or indirectly. Examples of such protests include the spring uprisings against despotic rulers in the Middle East and Africa and the uprisings by the people of Greece, Spain, Italy and Ireland against the austerity measures imposed on them by powerful external institutions. Growing perceptions in the United States that the decisions of a small group of elite were being made at the expense of the many became the flashpoint that fuelled the Occupy Wall Street Movement. This expression of discontent with the financially powerful soon spread to major cities around the world. Investment bankers, who appeared to be reaping vast profits, and seemingly overpaid executives in large corporations became the focus of attention. These protests and uprisings, however, are not the first and only expressions of frustration with the management of political, social, economic and environmental aspects of our common humanity. Nor can all frustration and tension be attributed to the same causes.

While each wave of protest to various forms of organisation has its unique and complex triggers, background and aspirations, the growing discontent now expressed in many parts of the world about the generation and distribution of wealth and the opportunity to flourish has generated both violent and non-violent action in many forms. In this book, we focus on the tension and discontent that we suggest are systemic in the form of development being intensified globally. Such tension and discontent warrant close attention from managers of corporations and from medium or small-scale enterprises. They warrant attention also from the future managers who will be mandated to manage aspects of the system of trade and exchange in all its dimensions: how raw materials are accessed, how the most attractive labour forces can be secured for the least cost, how the consumption of products and services can be maximised, and how the most competitive advantage can be negotiated for their organisation within given legal constraints.

The system of trade and exchange we are concerned with in this book is generally known as *capitalism*. The reach and strength of this system is growing the world over. It is frequently referred to as (economic) globalisation and is discussed more fully in Chapter 3. In this book, we examine the *prevailing institutional logics* that support and entwine the ideas that sustain the purported need for growth and the many political and social innovations that are generated from this form of logic and underpin its embedding and intensification globally.

# INSTITUTIONAL LOGICS

*Institutional logics* are 'taken-for-granted' beliefs that guide behaviour through legitimated identities, organisational forms and strategic behaviours (Thornton and Ocasio, 2008). We are interested in how such logics are involved in human *domestication*; that is, in the *disciplining* of populations as pliable *subjects* ready to obey market signals with regard to the prevailing *ideology* (Kockel, 2012), which more critical analysts might call a *dogma*. Butler (2011: 212) draws on Rose (1998) to explain *subjectification* as processes whereby 'forces outside of us come to determine the way we intimately relate to ourselves and so constitute us as subjects.' Of particular concern to us in this book is the seemingly naturalised and dominating institutional logic of the contemporary corporate capitalist *ideology* that is often uncritically reinforced in business education. Growing agitation with the prevailing ideology, however, is amplifying. There is an increasingly widespread association of this ideology with the exploitation of people and planet, with the mal-distribution of benefits, and with significant risk to the environment generated by the associated economic growth mentality.

The prevailing institutional logics informs identity formation and actions from the executives in the corporate boardrooms to economic and social policy-makers, and to the countless functionaries trained in our business schools. While Wang and colleagues (2011) depict this system as a system of greed, it may be better represented as a system of trade and exchange fuelled by fear as alternative systems of survival are increasingly diminished. Its institutional logics are encroaching deeply into our sense of self and the possibilities we may recognise as open to us. We question the intrusion of this logic on almost all aspects of human and planetary life.

The intensification of the institutional logics that sustain global capitalism warrants the critical attention of each of us as we are required to engage with it to feed our families, care for our health, educate our children, and care for our elderly and frail. Our engagement with this prevailing economic system consumes our time in finding and keeping employment. Many people are required to risk life and limb for access to the raw materials and the political and social organisation that will protect and intensify this system. We are each increasingly required to shape ourselves in its service. There seems little of human life that is now unaffected by this system of production and consumption. Despite some heavy costs, it has been almost universally legitimised (Bishop et al., 2011). When exposed, the recognition of such costs certainly invites a response. Part of our quest in this book is to invite you to explore whether you believe that such responses are robust enough to generate systemic change to the costs of such globalisation or whether they would be more accurately thought of as clever acts of system-protecting, population-placating window-dressing or public relations (PR).

The legitimacy of the capitalist system is undoubtedly under pressure. In our view, however, the system remains remarkably pervasive and persuasive. It may be that the protests and resistance that are now so explicit merely serve to strengthen its muscle! Is it a system 'for good'? Its advocates would claim so. In this book, we will examine their claims more closely because the globalisation of capitalism has been increasingly linked to some disturbing social and environmental outcomes. Among the many metaphors we have used to draw attention to the destructive outcomes of this system is an 'out-of-control juggernaut' (Steingard and Fitzgibbons, 1995) and a 'dance of death' (Humphries, 2010). These may seem extreme images of a system that we have been taught to accept as the best and perhaps only way we can organise people and planet in the creation and distribution of what each human being and the planet needs in order to live. We are all involved in this system. In this book, therefore, we assume that we all have a responsibility to assess it and its impacts.

Once, critics of the system we call capitalism were labeled as nay-sayers, destroyers, and perhaps as communists. They are labels intended to be reviled. Today, however, a much wider range of critics are turning their thoughts to the most macro and most micro of issues within which we must try to make sense of our everyday enactment of prevailing institutional logics. Many corporate and state leaders are now willing to consider that there may be a link between the intensification of this system of ideas in practice and the growing disparities between rich and poor, exacerbating environmental degradation related to our lifestyles and the increased social instability that comes with such mass alienation. There are now a number of calls for a re-visioning of capitalism; that is, for a greater attention to social (as contrasted with corporate) capitalism (Sennett, 2006), to shared values (Porter and Kramer, 2011) and to the rights and responsibilities of stakeholders (Russo and Perrini, 2010). Perhaps amongst the most radical of all such calls for internal adjustment of the ideology is the notion of 'conscious capitalism' promoted by Coates (2013) and Mackey and Sisodia (Mackey, 2011, 2013a, b and c; Mackey and Sisodia, 2013a and b).

Some critics suggest that Earth herself is calling us to caution. The work of Hart (2010) is one example. Another can be seen in the address to the Pacific Forum by the United Nations Secretary General Ban Ki-moon in September 2011. He stated: 'With waves rising ever higher ... the oceans are ... sending a signal that something is seriously wrong with our current model of economic development.' It is becoming increasingly, though not universally, agreed that intensifying floods, forest fires and droughts the world over are attributable to human activity. Regardless of the varied beliefs about the root causes of each concern, water tables are drying up or becoming too polluted for consumption; oceans are acidifying rapidly, deforming and depleting the food chain; and toxins in water, soil and air hold implications for the human immune system that affect rich and poor alike. Responses to these outcomes of the system are generating increasingly violent resistance to particular actions by some governments and to the very legitimacy of corporate activity in many parts of the world.

Perhaps because of the lack of agreement about the extent to which the system can be associated with the specific social and environmental concerns under scrutiny, who should be held accountable and where the price of remedies should be borne are up for debate. In many cases, the interests of investors or stockholders seem to be able to claim favourable priority and legitimacy when the costs of remedies are to be attributed. After all, if their investments are not protected (or maximised), specific companies, complete industries and maybe even whole nations may be destroyed. Or so we are asked to believe. The growth of the economy, through the actions of its avatar, 'the market', has drawn us all into believing in 'the market' as the (only) legitimate place through which to meet all social and political ideals. We will return to this point in Chapter 3. Fabricating the legitimacy of systems of human organisation is a complex process and such legitimacy is all the more robust the more natural it can be made to seem.

# LEGITIMACY

A central element of *legitimacy* is the meeting of a society's norms and values in the meaning we attribute to actions. Who shapes this legitimacy? Legitimacy implies that consent is granted by the governed (Warren, 2003). Organisational legitimacy is explained in the literature as an ongoing process, an activity that is continuously recreated through social enactment achieved and maintained through social dialogue and corporate communication (Suchman, 1995; Tilling, 2004; Tregidga et al., 2007). However, who is participating in the creation of legitimacy? Whose voices can be heard?

Historically, capitalism might have been attractive to a number of people as a means to lessen the grip of tribal leaders and feudal lords of all kinds. It might have been viewed as a force that might weaken papal clout in the Middle Ages. These powerful medieval institutions certainly had to grapple with new sets of ideas that placed both economic and conceptual opportunities into the hands of a much broader swathe of the population than had formerly been the case. In its early formation, the entrepreneurial and opportunistic spirit could be harnessed to the interests of European empires by providing a conduit connecting several seemingly disparate elements of the powerful. The elite of that time soon learned to protect their long-term interests by skilful assimilation of the most threatening of the newcomers. They opened the institutional logic of the day just enough to let in the new merchants and traders. Royalty, the Church, adventurers, scientists, preachers and investors all had a significant hand in creating the rhetoric and the practice that allowed for the extraction of wealth from many parts of the world and its consolidation in the coffers of individuals and the governments of Europe. Crafting legitimacy for these exploitative ventures was another matter. This task of crafting legitimacy for the processes of wealth creation and distribution remains to this very day. Legitimacy, however, is strongly linked to organisational reputation, a concept actively attended to by public relations specialists and spin doctors of various kinds.

Deephouse and Carter (2005: 330–3) highlight two key differences between legitimacy and organisational reputation:

(i)   organizational legitimacy involves the adherence to the expectations of social norms and values;

(ii)  organizational reputation concerns perceptions about an organization in comparison with other organizations to determine their relative standing.

Golant and Sillince (2007) suggest that individuals assess the value of an organisation according to the contribution of the organisation to their well-being within a set of given norms and expectations. The cognitive dimension of legitimacy, they suggest, refers to the way in which emphasis is placed on the idea that organisations and their operations and structures are made to appear part of the natural order within a given social context. Similarly, Lange and colleagues (2010) comment that there are three possible dimensions that can be attributed to organisational reputation: (i) being known, (ii) being known for something, and (iii) a generalised sense of favourability. It seems that so long as the populace can be led to believe that an organisation will (eventually) serve them, they are willing to overlook all kinds of aberrations of expressed ethics and tolerate in themselves all kinds of abrogation of responsibilities. Instrumental ethics prevail.

A feature shared by organisational legitimacy and reputation is that both are social achievements. It is this socially fabricated, therefore negotiated, condoned or contested aspect of both organisational legitimacy and reputation that we revisit time and again in this book. It is the socially fabricated dynamics of such achievements that invite us to look very closely at the ideas and values that are so entwined in these dynamics that they may have become invisible to the naked eye, so to speak. We posit in this book that each and every one of us is somehow implicated in the construction and legitimation of our way of being, in the prioritisation of the economic over all other considerations, and in the good and the harmful outcomes of the system by which we organise our humanity and our relationship with Earth.

Managers and students of management are not only generally implicated as persons, citizens, parents and playmates, but specifically so in their willingness to enact the directives of owners. Is this enactment merely a matter of 'following orders'? This question underlies many of the discussions and exercises we would like you to engage with in decisions about what representations of the world you accept as true or righteous and are willing to enact as just. Whose voices prevail in the decisions that are taken? In the prevailing institutional logics, only owners can mandate managers to take actions. There is some traction in the idea that the interests of investors or stockholders must take much greater account of the interests of stakeholders who are in a better position to express the need to respect shared value (Porter and Kramer, 2011). Stakeholders are demanding accountability beyond traditional firm responsibilities (Scherer and Palazzo, 2011). With increased scrutiny and more active stakeholders in a dynamic global marketplace, managers are urged to take action (or not) depending not just upon the regulatory framework of various regimes but also on the way they understand (or misunderstand) each person who is affected by the situation. It is an attractive theory that has spawned a number of very creative partnerships. Stakeholder theories invite an examination of the legitimacy of managers to act on behalf of the interests of others. Stakeholder influence, though, appears to remain constrained by the ultimate control of the owners.

Public–private partnerships (PPPs) between corporations and/or non-governmental organisations (NGOs) and governments are seen as the future for development. The government, civil society and stakeholders of various kinds, we are led to believe, would be the representatives of the people in these partnerships. Their wishes will be enacted by managers as their agents. Thus, the governed agree to allow corporations certain powers to act and trust that their managers will bear in mind their responsibilities not only to shareholders but to all stakeholders. Writing at a time when growth in the hopes expressed in stakeholder theories was gaining some reinvigorated interest, Andrew Weiss (1995) points to significant weaknesses in stakeholder theory as a conceptual framework capable of balancing investor/stockholder power. More recent authors call for global attention to sustainability as a framework through which to address social and environmental concerns, but, even here, the conversations are taking a more critical turn. As we will show in subsequent chapters, even the most enlightened of corporations are finding it difficult to track all aspects of their supply chain.

# SUSTAINABILITY

A focus on *sustainability* as a remedy for social and environmental problems has come under challenge from a number of researchers. Landrum and colleagues (2013), for example, propose that the growing interest in corporate social responsibility, when considered individually, is inadequate as an integral strategy (2013: 7) necessary for the personal and systemic transformation needed for short- and long-term sustainability (2013: 1). Sizoo (2010) points to the common practice of companies attaching themselves to calls for greater attention to sustainability projects through charitable donations to environmental causes, while engaging in blatant environmental abuses. Shell's forging of a partnership agreement with the International Union for the Conservation of Nature (IUCN) is given as a case in point by Steiner (2011). Critics point to the need for a radical rethinking of the underpinnings of enlightenment and liberal thought and our economic motivations and systems. It requires us to be more critically conscious of the economic priorities of contemporary capitalism and their consequences. Landrum et al. (2013) propose that successful companies in an era of 'conscious capitalism' (2013: 7) will be able to overcome the current impasse in the unification of the economic with ethical, ecological, 'and mind–body–soul considerations as organisations face the sustainability challenge' (2013: 1).

We agree with Landrum et al. (2013), but only to a certain degree and with some significant concerns that we will raise in the chapters that follow. We suggest that their analysis may not be robust enough to provide checks on corporate interests in the reshaping of the individual and collective consciousness. Their recommendation that the most significant transformations must occur and radiate from a transformed individual in the internal and external stakeholders may be a necessary change, but one not without risk of corporate co-option. We agree, however, that a relational ethics of responsibility for social, economic and environmental justice is required to respond to the pressing issues facing humanity. The United Nations is leading a number of initiatives to achieve such transitions, and we will examine some of these in various parts of this book.

# UNITING NATIONS IN THE MANAGEMENT OF THE GLOBAL ECONOMY

Saul (1997) argues that we are a dangerously unconscious civilisation, a society addicted to ideologies through which we reduce ourselves and others to the state of 'subject' or even 'serf'. He argues that, in its corporate form, the prevailing rationality requires people to deny or undermine the significance of citizenship beyond corporate interests. Corporate interests are seductively disguised as naturalised self-interest. The assumption is that, if each human being pursues self-interest within the boundaries of the law, this will result in the best outcomes for all. Critics of this ideology suggest that desirable outcomes have yet to be evident in the lives of most human beings and that the embrace of this ideology intensifies false hope in individual salvation and encourages an abdication of responsibility for the common good. The received wisdom is that 'economics' is at the heart of everything and everything flows therefrom. The effect of this ideology, argues Saul (1997), is passivity and conformity in the areas that matter, and opportunities and rejoicing in non-conformity in areas that do not matter that much. How can we begin to attend to matters that are not prominent in our consciousness or conscience? What do contemporary examples aimed at *consciousness-raising* bring to the legitimation, justification, concern, challenge and transformation of the system we call the globalisation of capitalism?

The beginning of such discussions can be seen in the United Nations Millennium Development Goals (MDG) and the Global Compact (GC), the Earth Charter, the Rio Plus forums, the meetings of powerful nations at Davos, the influence of the World Social Forum, the Global Ethic Foundation and similar organisations intending to have an impact on values and practices. Of growing influence on management education is the leadership of the United Nations through their initiative to promote Principles for Responsible Management Education (PRME), a vision fully described by Muff and colleagues (2013). These organisations are attempts to influence the development of ethical principles and guidelines for creating processes of human organisation that endorse and incarnate principles of justice and environmental responsibility necessary for human survival.

Authors as varied as Joseph Stiglitz (2010), Richard Branson (2011) and Graeme Maxton (2011) provide very readable summaries of the concerns now expressed by many and articulated so vividly by those participating in the uprisings of the people. While many may express similar concerns, their analysis of causes, and thus the sensible remedies, are not all the same. We will explore such challenges and the associated remedies throughout this book.

Beyond these global endeavours to guide human practice, how actively do you think individuals and communities engage in the endorsement or discipline of the capitalist system? Are all equally able to influence its governance? Those who initiated the protests against globalisation of corporate capitalism in Seattle in 1999 signalled their frustration and their anger at 'the system'. Subsequent protests and movements have become ever more heavily policed, but it appears that such policing of dissent cannot repress growing unrest and intentions to change the way we live – the way we produce and consume commodities and how we dispose of our waste. In this regard, we will discuss the Occupy Wall Street Movement and other such organisations that express and enact dissent with regard to the prevailing institutional logics.

The possibilities of sharing strategies, of calls to upcoming events, of promoting new production and consumption ideas and new distribution opportunities are all made more accessible through the general availability of the Internet and various social media. Our companion webpages for this chapter illustrate how much information (and potential action) is only the click of an icon away. It may seem ironic that the technologies so useful for activating protest against the very system that produced them are technologies that corrupt and disrupt as well as make the speed and reach of communication more intense than ever before in human history. These electronic gadgets may have been manufactured under the very conditions that many who use them are expressing concerns about. Those concerns may focus on the suspect methods of mineral extraction for the key components of our mobile phones and iPods or the manufacturing processes that are harmful to workers, their families, communities and even the planet.

## BLOOD-SOAKED PHONES

Valuable minerals are being extracted in hand-worked mines sometimes so deep that the miners stay there for days on end to make the trip down worthwhile. Men and young boys work slave-like in extremely dangerous, often life-taking, conditions for the base minerals essential to the electronics industries. Through the illegal extraction of these valuable minerals in the Democratic Republic of the Congo (DRC), for example, natural resources are being exploited, armed groups are financed, women are raped, and millions of innocent lives have been lost so that global corporates can bring gains to markets (Monbiot, 2013). Is the DRC the only place where such exploitations occur in the extraction of the ingredients of production? The companion webpages which supports all chapters in this book provide many leads for you to explore this question more deeply.

Just who has the right or the duty to control the means of life is a big question. Western ideas vest such rights and duties in the concept of (legalised) ownership. Privatisation of the means and proceeds of production is a fundamental act of faith in the prevailing institutional logic of capitalism. It is often portrayed as a necessary means to greater efficiency and a more just (user-pay) system of distribution. Water is a good example. Allocating ownership rights to springs, lakes, rivers and so on is deemed to be the fairest and most efficient way to govern water access and use. Yet, converting the source of life to a commodity to be traded and managed through the very markets we are expressing concerns about in this book has layers of problems if universal access to water is necessary for all living creatures. The work of Vandana Shiva is an example we find compelling for the integration and expression of the concerns we canvass in this book. As early as 2002, she proposed or prophesied that we will see wars over access to water just as we are now having wars over access to oil and minerals of all kinds (Shiva, 2002).

Regardless of warnings about impending violence and distress made by writers and activists, the privatisation of water is still being promoted as the best means to secure access to water, ensure the viability of industries and thus protect the investors' interests (see Hodges, 2012). This includes all of us whose pensions and thus assumed future well-being are directly or indirectly invested in everything from public utilities to privately owned hedge funds. And, of course, such investors create jobs, do they not? But what happens when people cannot afford to buy the water they need or have to choose between paying for water, heat, food or medical care? These concerns bring us very close to home. There will not be a country in the so-called developed world that does not struggle with these issues. Despite the havoc in the regions where this system has been long established (i.e., in the so-called developed nations), we are willing to insist that the so-called less developed countries follow the logic that is generating these difficulties. Ironic?

Paradoxical? Evil? Assessment of the morality as well as the efficiency and effectiveness of this logic is a responsibility we must each accept by virtue of our participation in it.

Critical management scholars focus on the processes of production, distribution and disposal of goods and services, and all the human and environmental relationships that are involved. It seems, however, that none but the very extremes of the free-market prophets have a confident vision for a pragmatic response to the issues of concern. They (want us to) believe that driving their battleship harder through current turbulence will somehow keep their ship on course. Some are willing to kill for this belief and, according to critics, such as Chomsky and Herman (1979) and Pilger (2007), will fuel and fund wars to ensure access to raw materials, water, land and labour. Others may close their eyes to, deflect their attention from, or diminish the significance of less visible, systemically related deaths, injury and destruction. Jobs are offered and withdrawn regardless of the effects on families, communities and even nation-states. For those who believe in the principles of neo-liberal development of the world, 'the market', a social fabrication which we will examine much more closely as the book progresses, will provide remedies through the logic of supply and demand. Advocates of this form of reasoning urge the rest of us to get better at demanding the supply of less destructive goods and services and their ethical and sustainable production, distribution and disposal. We take a closer look at this statement of faith in Chapter 7.

Those who believe that systemic issues cannot be addressed by 'the market' (alone) are willing to support greater political influence in shaping the conditions of trade and exchange, investment and spending, consumption and saving. There are global organisations at work to try to influence such changes. We will introduce some of these organisations in Chapter 3. There is also some controversy over what goods and services might be permitted to be offered through unpaid, community-generated activity. Social enterprise is attracting many people for whom the blatant pursuit of profit is abhorrent or who see a market opportunity personally to influence the direction of social and environmental organisation and outcomes. The growth and popularity of farmers' markets, the slow food movement, corporate responsibility (CR) activities within firms, and the marketing of fair trade and sustainable products to serve as fundraisers are just some examples of the growing interest in a more just and sustainable form of human organisation. These activities, however, are still situated within a macro-context in which managers must manage in their large or small organisations, government departments, small businesses, or contractual arrangements. How each of us responds to, lives with, resists or attempts to change these macro conditions are the micro conditions that together provide the outcomes we are witness to. Unchallenged, they will continue to harm our loved ones well into yet unborn generations. Can managers make a difference to this situation – or do they just follow orders? What, in this complex context, might we consider 'good management'?

# MANAGERS: AMORAL FUNCTIONARIES OR RESPONSIVE MORAL BEINGS?

It has long been the view that managers implement the vision and direction of owners. Managers are required to implement policy; they are expected to ensure that the activities undertaken, big or small, local or global, meet the aspirations of the owners. These owners may be clearly visible or only obliquely known through the more amorphous directorship of corporations, trusts and other legal fictions by which ownership responsibilities are diffused through a myriad of shareholders. Much organisation is driven by what we choose to call a 'factory model of production', despite much rhetoric about employee empowerment and purported emphasis on self-directed career trajectories that provide the freedom for people to work flexibly and creatively to meet their wider life desires. This is so even in the now corporately moulded public sector. Public universities are a good example of this. Researchers, the creative force in state universities, are increasingly managed as factory staff (Willmott, 2011). The 'outputs' are graduates and research papers. Factories for the production of graduates must compete with each other for grants and fee-paying students. In a more radical example, the creation of private prisons is worth a thought. A market for prisoners assumes a growing demand. Statistical indicators suggest such a demand is indeed growing and investors are taking note. Is a market-driven orientation to criminal production and containment a sensible or even just human enterprise?

## PROFITING FROM MISERY

Capitalism is promoted as an economic system that respects and enables individual liberty. It is said to reward those who invest their talents and make smart choices. Empirically, it has proved to create material wealth but this wealth has accumulated in the control of a relatively small percentage of the global population. As economic wealth concentrates in the bank accounts of fewer people, as downward pressures on middle incomes bite, as the social services that enhance the common good become increasingly accessible only by 'user pay', as philanthropic organisations are unable to meet the demands they are called on to meet, as individuals are seduced by consumer-driven identities, more desperate people turn to criminal acts to meet their needs. Debtors prisons are on the rise. Private prisons are devised to profit from the incarceration and containment of people. They are a growth industry. Even those courageous enough to protest the injustice of the system of production and distribution under scrutiny in this book can find themselves at risk of incarceration – as many leaders of justice movements can testify. You will meet some of these people in this book. What might happen to a portion of the student population, indebted with student loans, unable to access a job and having no income to repay their debts?

(*See articles at*: www.corpwatch.org/article.php?id=15784; retrieved 2 September 2013; and www.alternet.org/why-student-loans-are-even-bigger-sham-you-know; retrieved 2 September 2013).

The idea that our pursuit of an education may bind us into a systemic vice-like grip may seem far from the potential concerns of a student doing a business degree in an excellent university in Europe or the US. Yet, think again what might be learned from these examples and apply them to the administration of universities and their staff and students. To sustain their institutions, universities organise loans for students that saddle them with debt which many will find well-nigh impossible to repay and may land some of them in the proposed low-security, privately owned debtors' prisons. Student prisoners, like refugee prisoners, become the means for profit-making. The conditions of that profit-making become an issue of efficiency decided on financial returns, not on the morality of the enterprise deeply considered. Staff in universities, prisons, hospitals and charities are pressed to do more with less. Much the same might be said for large health systems, churches, schools, museums and art galleries.

Putting aside the complex issues of discerning culpability in criminal behaviour, many ordinary people may be more at risk of imprisonment than those who are hardened and intentional perpetrators of evil. Inadequate or fragile access to the means of a livelihood, the ever greater need to purchase the means of survival from 'the market', and the ever intensifying pressure to use credit to meet immediate survival needs is one line of enquiry you could pursue. There are many less obvious examples of the potential to reap profit from the frailties of others. The corralling of indigenous peoples, refugees, the frail and variously disabled, and the clinically diagnosed as insane or those judicially determined as criminal, is proving to be a goldmine for many entrepreneurs. This logic increasingly applies to local government and to whole nations. All seem to function more like the corporations once associated only with industrial mass production. Their researchers, doctors, artists, clergy and governors are managed by institutional logics that seem to pay little regard to the moral, creative and spiritual impulses that are the hallmarks of those with such professional or creative vocations. The cleaners and caretakers of their offices, homes and dependants are required to negotiate their contracts under ever greater competition and live with the same or perhaps intensified vulnerabilities.

A uniform economic rationality appears to rule all as if the production of cans of beans, the healing of the sick or the education of students is one and the same. Coordinating the activities of scholars was once a shared task of peers: teamwork. Over time, management was skilfully delegated to administrators with the idea that this would be more efficient and would allow researchers and teachers to get on with their scholarly work. Once separated from their self-organisation, together with the intensification of drone-like centrally devised and controlled templates, staff can be disciplined 'from afar' by faceless bureaucrats under the guise of 'self-management'. This provides an example of increased responsibility and diminishing resources not unique to academics employed in public universities. Principals of schools have been reframed as CEOs; public relations officers who manage the media releases for states and corporations appear to serve political or investor interests rather than provide accurate information to citizens. Police organisations the world over are monitoring and controlling populations at the direction of the state – states that are increasingly beholden to the might and power of corporate potential for investment or the threat of their divestment. This can and does at times put managers into situations of conflict: conflicts of interest, conflicts of moral and practical assessment, conflicts of ethical integrity.

## REPORT, COLLUDE OR BEAR SILENT WITNESS

Chris is working in a privately owned hospital that prides itself on its dementia care. Of late, the 'shifts' have been increased from 7 to 10 hours each. On this day, three out of seven staff called in sick. No replacements were found. Chris tried hard both to feed and toilet all the patients in need. One fell off the toilet. When Chris explained this in an incident report, the manager was furious. Disclosing the fall, let alone the shortage of staffing that explained the fall, would surely affect the quality rating, the attraction of investors, and thus risk everyone's jobs. Best for all if the incident report is not filed – or is it? Is this a good way to ensure that institutions of care act with integrity?

In the outcomes of conflicts of interest, managers may have privileged witness. Managers may also have significant influence. For example, in Chapter 9 we illustrate this point with a reflection on the actions of the deputy chief coroner in Cairo, Magda Helal. During the uprising in Egypt in October 2011, at some risk to herself, Magda spoke out to international media as the bodies she was examining were victims of assassins. She asked that these assassins be identified. This might be a question we could also ask of the real causes of death of the homeless boys of Rio de Janeiro, the rascals of Papua New Guinea, the employees burned or crushed in unsafe factories, or the countless un(re)marked deaths due to starvation, untreated illnesses of the poor and their lack of access to viable incomes. We could also ask this question of the deaths from workplace injuries, poisonings or stress, whether these manifest as slow or rapid deaths. So, too, we could ask the same question of alienation, despair and disheartenment manifest in the suicides of those who see no future, no respectable way to care for themselves or their dependants.

Managers have their part to play in the witness, exposure and transformation of what is 'unjust', however this notion of (in)justice is to be defined. To believe otherwise is to consign managers, administrators and professionals to a category of functionaries whose mindless compliance would not meet any notion of human agency and responsibility, a level of compliance dangerous in even the most regimented and loyal of armies. It would be to concede to a contemporary acceptance of what Hannah Arendt so aptly noted as the 'banality of evil'. Arendt attended the trial of Adolph Eichmann, accused of crimes against the Jewish people, crimes against humanity and war crimes (Assy, 1998). Her observations of Eichmann as an apparently 'unremarkable' character has generated much discussion. He did not seem particularly evil – as a kind of normal *but unthinking* man.

> The banality of evil which appeared through Eichmann made evident how superficial the phenomenon of evil could show its face [to be]. The evil could spread out as fungus under the surface, by a mass of citizens that did not reflect on events, did not ask for significance, nor made a dialogue with themselves about their own deeds. Arendt says: The greatest evildoers are those who don't remember because *they [have] never given the matter a thought*; nothing can keep them back because *without remembrance they are without roots*. (Assy, 1998)

The fascist regime of Nazi Germany was achieved through the millions of tiny decisions made by each person in 'the system'. While each little activity examined alone may diminish and dismiss culpability, when systemically woven together as they are, they allowed for a system that maimed and killed – just as, it seems, the justification of corporate profits appears to do in some of the cases we will examine in this book. Who is responsible? Arendt draws our attention to the apparent lack of capacity to think for, and in dialogue with, oneself (Assy, 1998).

## MAKING DIFFICULT MANAGEMENT CHOICES: WHO OR WHAT ARE WE RESPONSIBLE FOR?

The pressure on the principal of Midtown Primary School to cut the cost of running her school seems relentless. Already she had grown classes beyond what she thought was responsible practice. Many of the activities once deemed essential for a good education had been eliminated. Now she needed to reduce the cost of the cleaning and caretaking of the campus. A group of eight loyal employees had together, for many years, taken great pride in understanding the diverse needs of each teacher, and were motivated by the joy of teachers and students coming to a spotless class each day. They ensured that the toilets were not health hazards, and had kept the grounds beautiful and safe. Each member of this team and their families were as well known to the principal as they were to the teaching staff and their families. On hearing that the principal was being urged to contract out their services to a privately owned cleaning company, the cleaners got together. They offered to form themselves into a 'collective' and to bid for the contract. They searched for efficiency gains that would not compromise the quality of their service, and put together a proposal guaranteed to ensure all dimensions of the caretaking of the school would be met by them collectively. What issues might arise for the principal?

Today, management studies are at an interesting crossroads where a paradox appears to have developed. Perhaps the paradox was always there but is now more out in the open. The legitimacy of managers and the power they have in society are under greater scrutiny. At the same time, the spread of Western management techniques, education and training have infused management practice to a broader range of influences, both geographically and socially. Some of this 'management as control' has been reduced to mere monitoring of template compliance, an idea drawn from the work of Foucault, who we meet again in Chapter 2 and whose ideas we extend in Chapters 4 and 5. There we illustrate how this idea works in practice. There, too, we will see how some theorists moved the discussion of systems to discussions of discourses. By examining such discourses, it becomes possible to see how what were once processes of visible management control may have become so infused in who we are as much as what we do that such overt control is no longer required. Grey (1999: 577), for example, suggests that human life has become:

> something to be managed, and other forms of meaning or being in the world become marginalised, thus truncating the variety of human experience, while promoting a form of experience which ... is disciplinary, degrading and confining. This is not primarily because self-management is about the internalization of management control ... [but because] self-management [as it is being embedded in the prevailing institutional logic] entails a way of apprehending what it is to be human in managerial terms, and in that sense represents a diminution of the multiplicity of human potentials through the invocation of the one dimensional discourse of management ... The capacity of self-management to yield labour control is a second order effect ...

A simpler way of saying this is that once the discipline is internalised, the control of the asylum can be handed to the inmates. The inmates are so conditioned, drugged or demotivated that they will do what is desired by their controllers without too much overt or visible pressure. We explore this idea of mind control as the influence of power on the very formation of our identity further in Chapter 2. Jürgen Habermas (1987: 259) summarises this dynamic as the 'colonization of our life world'. The important contribution managers make to this dynamic is sometimes called *managerialism*. It refers to a way of managing that (i) preserves managers' personal interests, or (ii) the obligation of managers to meet pre-set outcomes, over and above all other interests. The two are usually entwined in a tight connection between performance requirements and rewards. Compliance is generally but not always secured through their service to the system or what they hope to extract from it. Concern about the colonising effect of such compliance is drawn to our attention by Deetz (1992). It is sharpened by Willmott's (2011) example of the contemporary management of academics in the subtle pressures on the substance of their scholarship, their vehicles of dissemination, and the processes of their organisation. Academics, he argues, appear to be increasingly corralled in corporate mentalities, and managed through a factory model of production, with all the nuances of instrumental control and output maximisation. Academics and students, employers and employees in all kinds of enterprises, seem to be increasingly treated as a plastic substance to be moulded to state or corporate value. This book rests on the premise that the extent to which a critical consciousness and conscience remain alive in the human spirit will determine the extent of this subjugation or its creative transformation into ways of being that enhance dignity and respect for others, for self, and for Earth on whom we all must rely. In this regard, we can take direction from Alvesson (2002) who invites the study of identity (re)formation, an issue we take up in Chapters 5 and 6.

Alvesson (2002: 638) recommends the study of theories that understand the processes of organisation to be 'fluid, unstable and reflexive … present[ing] opportunities for micro-emancipation as well as openings for "new" forms of subordination and oppression'. The more fluid social theories are of interest to us, not only for their potential to expose exploitative assumptions about human fixtures or malleability, but more particularly as potential streams of thought to enhance human emancipation as a more sophisticated notion than the neo-liberal market notion of freedom. Managers are central characters in the trajectories of our human organisation. The way each person understands their part in any situation will to a large extent be affected by their socialisation and education. It is for this reason that we invite the radical elaboration of management education beyond technical competencies into the broadest critical studies into context and self. We hope to contribute to the enlivening of a critical consciousness and conscience so that the decisions made are informed with wisdom not formulaic compliance. The aspiration for greater wisdom and responsibility in the organisation and management of human affairs is growing. A number of influential organisations are attempting to address the need to transform the ways we organise our human being. Such transformations will require the critical examination of long and deeply held truths.

# TRUTH TELLING AND TELLING TRUTHS

In this book, we invite reflection on the cumulative diminishing of espoused values of human dignity, of ourselves as ethical beings in the daily decisions we make – as employers, employees, producers, consumers, parents and citizens. The close relationship between sport, art, health, technology, military action, moral reasoning, news-generating media, the state and the corporations with vested interests must alert us to the need for the greater integration of our thoughts about these seeming discrete realms of operation. The recruitment of impoverished young people to become the cannon fodder for any regime, the loss and injury to military and civilian people in the preservation or extension of territorial or resource control, the recruitment and control of people for the myriad modes of commodity production and service delivery, and the resistance of regimes to care properly for those who are disabled, fragile or made vulnerable are radical examples. They are examples administered by countless well-functioning managers, team leaders and a myriad of empowered employees. This is so, too, of the police teams clearing the streets of 'Occupiers', the managers who oversee production processes that harm and even kill, and those organisations who outplace to uncertain and perhaps unsafe circumstances the employees who have served them well, and who have, through their loyalty or compliance, been made dependent on their wages for their very lives.

New empires are not achieved only on the battlefield. From the production of goods and services, such as the mobile phone, to the military drones that can destroy targets without the need for a human pilot, all are connected in a web of power and control. To see the links between the fun we can have playing a game on our phones, the convenience of instant communication, and the seemingly harmless constant upgrading of our gadgets, to the manufacture and use of 'drones controlled from a distance' is what we aim to do in this book. It is not so much the creation of the gadgets and services that we call into question. It is their mode of production and distribution in the context of a (perhaps distorted) ideology of neo-liberal-style profit maximisation that concerns us in this book.

# NEO-LIBERALISM: FROM THEORY TO DOGMA

*Neo-liberalism* is generated from a number of ideas about the assumed nature of human beings. These ideas are expressed in classic philosophical, political and economic assumptions about the functions of the state and markets in the achievement of desirable social outcomes. For example, from a selective reading of Adam Smith's early work, it is widely assumed that social well-being is best achieved by self-interested individuals making well-informed employment and consumption choices freely within the marketplace. The marketplace is deemed an avenue for human emancipation. Any government interference in the free flow of markets, argue modern proponents of this idea, denies people liberty and freedom and thus will ultimately result in an overall reduction in human social well-being.

While the early ideas of neo-liberalism can be located in European ideas about individual freedom, entitlements and property rights, they were taken up in specific ways in what was to become America, 'the Land of the Free'. The emergent 'American model' for development may come under challenge by ideals of a more controlled form of capitalism at times, but nevertheless it is still the model within which China, India, Russia and the rest of the world are competing for a higher ranking in the league table of dominating economies.

Critiquing the extent to which neo-liberal theories have infused our very sense of self requires us to stretch our minds from the most macro to the most micro of realms and back – and every position in between. In this book, we do this by beginning to challenge the very language through which we shape our understanding, organise our activities and assess our relationships with each other and with Earth. We suggest that the shape of social actions, including those of trade and exchange and the social relationships that support them, are an expression of our human imagination. The normalisation of these actions and relationships, so that they can be perceived as legitimate and taken for granted as reasonable, is in fact an amazing human achievement. Some ideas become so well entrenched in our thinking that they come to be experienced as natural, as real and as truth (Clegg, 2011: 195). We move easily from theory to dogma. Colignon (1989) warns against oversimplifying complex social behaviour as real things, and calls this a process of 'holistic reification'. We will incrementally unpack this view in subsequent chapters of this book.

The reconfiguration of people as objects such as 'labour units' or 'resources' is an example of important reifications that together support and enable systems of trade and exchange that are the brainchildren of capitalist-orientated economists, policy-makers and employers. These ideas reach their zenith in the prevailing neo-liberal expression the world over. Not only are people frequently thought of in this reified way by those who want to harness their energies and creativity, but increasingly so by the people themselves. It becomes good sense to seek ways to drive down their value and thus their cost. That is, what we come to see as significant and true (our conscious and unconscious awareness) takes on a market orientation. In extreme examples, human beings are encouraged to see themselves as mini-enterprises that reflect the capitalist values of competitive individualism and to adhere to a deluded faith in meritocracy as an explanation for unequal (but supposedly fair) market outcomes. To what extent we are groomed to see ourselves in this way will be further discussed in Chapters 4, 5 and 6.

Although the distinction between the individual and the collective is recognised in this process of oversimplification, the individual is collapsed into the collective through the notion of the organisation as a naturally occurring system. While it is not inherently wrong to simplify our understanding, Colignon (1989) cautions against misleading representations that oversimplify certain characteristics when trying to understand very complex interactions and/or relationships. In this book, we take a great interest in what established oversimplifications might be hiding. We take the view that the way we define our world and act on our ideas might be considered one of the most creative powers of the human species. We enact our ideas and values. We might choose to join the Occupy Movement and be branded as heroes or rebels. We may be named 'a manager' and expect to have 'authority'. What meanings are invested in these words? We may like or dislike rules and regulation or respect them as necessary for order and security. These rules and regulations, ideas about order and security, and the legitimate ways of achieving these, are all examples of meaning and sense-making. This process may be unique to humans. It is hard to think of an elephant telling a lie. Truth making appears to be a uniquely human capacity.

# MANUFACTURING TRUTH: REIFICATIONS – HANDY GRAMMATICAL SHORT CUTS OR TRICKY LITTLE TROJAN HORSES?

Truth telling is a tricky matter at any time. It is generally thought of as the right thing to do. This is particularly so in information about the way we organise society. 'Society', however, is a mythical beast! It may be better thought of as one of a number of conceptual constructs with which humans populate their reasoning. 'Society' is an excellent example of such a construct. We invest this construct (i.e., the concept 'society') with values that are manifest in all kinds of policies and practices. The values become incarnated in their out-working by people in a mostly unconscious way. The construct appears to become material. We can now use it to explain, organise and discipline behaviours in its service. This construct has found its way into our common sense and can be used to maintain a specific set of social relationships.

All 'societies' are conceptually constituted with other facilitating entities, such as families, communities, organisations and so on. The idea of 'society' (and its constituent entities) is made (seemingly) material through our very enacting of the invested relationships. It is a noun that refers to the way we group people. The concept might be more accurately thought of as an action, a decision regarding grouping, rather than a noun. It is a concept that we use to guide us in deciding who is to be considered as inside or outside our consideration. This idea helps us understand who has authority and entitlements and who does not. It is an idea through which we can reinforce our feelings of belonging or exclusion and thus our sense of identity. Real as this 'society' may feel to us, it is none the less a very different kind of entity from, for example, a chair or a tree. 'Society' is an idea. Precisely because it is a figment of our imagination, 'it' is what we call a fictive entity or social fabrication, a mental construct into which we can invest our values and through which we can organise our collective existence. Such mental constructs are wide open to manipulation. Examining what we take for granted when we talk about 'society' and its kin concepts is a powerful way that critical theorists can expose some of the more subtle constraints on our freedom and alert us to the watering down of our capacity to be responsible for change to the things than may disturb us.

In much common conversation, 'society' as an organising principle is now frequently reduced to another such social fabrication: 'the economy'. These concepts ('society' and 'the economy', along with their kin concepts of 'democracy', 'capitalism', 'the organisation', 'the family' and 'justice'), are so well established in our taken-for-granted mind maps that many personal sacrifices may be asked for and given in support of their protection. 'Jobs' and 'employment' are *entities* of the same kind. They are 'ideas' about how work is to be organised. To explore the transmutation of 'idea' to 'thing in the world' is a task of *ontology*. Fictive entities or social fabrications refer to 'ideas' made seemingly material by our collective enactment, embodiment or manifestation of those ideas in practice. In the prevailing institutional logics, the notion that employment is the only legitimate means to access a livelihood is a pervasive idea (see Figure 1.1). This idea is tightly woven into the common understanding of the supposed path to freedom. For many people, however, jobs and employment are rarely the means to liberation. In subsequent chapters, we will examine how jobs and employment may be better understood as a harness to a system of arrangements that often exploits and even kills. The vehicle of this exploitation is the depersonalised 'market', a character in the neo-liberal story of reality that we will meet again and again in this book.

**Figure 1.1**   'The most dishonest words in American politics: "Right to Work"'

*Source*: www.alternet.org/labor/right-work-unions-collective-bargaining. Photo credit: Flickr © 7 June 2013.

The impact of our jobs or lack of them on our lives is linked to the wider ideas we discuss in this book. All are influenced to some degree by the macro-principles used to shape the forms of capitalism and democracy being intensified the world over. These principles may reach also into the seemingly more personal decisions that we use to guide our relationships with others, to use our purchasing power, to navigate life's broader opportunities and, as we discuss in Chapters 5 and 6, perhaps even to shape our very identity. These principles offer a set of values we are asked to take as a given 'truth' and we are exhorted to live them as such: to work hard, be loyal and the rewards will be fairly distributed through the out-workings of 'the market' (perhaps now the most powerful character in the family of fictive entities). But truth telling is a complex matter. It is linked to the idea of legitimacy and our ideas about organisational reputation and the way these two constructs reinforce each other.

## CORPORATIONS: THE CONTEMPORARY FLAGSHIPS OF THE EVER MORPHING EMPIRE

Korten (2001), in *When Corporations Rule the World*, and Hertz (2001) in *The Silent Takeover*, discuss multinational corporations (MNCs) as having a hegemonic influence on the organisation of people and processes in the shaping of the global economy. Korten (2001) argues that by the end of the twentieth century approximately 70 per cent of global trade was controlled by just 500 corporations. Hertz (2001) shows how corporations manipulate and pressure governments. They argue that the MNCs' biggest success has been in homogenising a global, neo-liberal or free-market ideology that supports the capitalist aspirations. In *The New Rulers of the World*, John Pilger (2003) reports on the lives of hundreds of people, mostly women and children, living in slums with open sewers and unsafe disease-prone water. Many of the children were malnourished. His documentary shows how multinational corporations and the governments, and the myriad of institutions that back them, rule millions of people throughout the world. Their combined influence determines both the availability and conditions of employment for these people and can also make decisions at a global or local level that might eliminate their meagre jobs and livelihoods altogether.

Taking the analyses of Pilger as a starting point, we consider the darker side of the form of globalisation being intensified the world over. We see connections between the plight of exploited workers the world over and the attempts of the Ogoni people to restore their environment damaged by the Royal Dutch Shell company (Boele et al., 2001). Royal Dutch Shell has been a signatory to the UN Global Compact since the year 2000. Follow their story on the web all the way to the court decisions about their ongoing liabilities to the region. In 2013, the collapse of a factory in Bangladesh producing apparel for many well-known corporations was attributed to substandard building codes (Burke, 2013; Butler, 2013). It may be useful to explore how many of the investing companies in this location are Global Compact signatories and how far they are willing to accept responsibility and provide restitution.

The shift of Myanmar (Burma) towards democracy and, with it, the opening of opportunities for international corporations, and vice versa, invites us to think more deeply about the very principles of profit maximisation and economic growth associated with market liberalism. Together, these forces have infused much Western-style logic well beyond what might be considered the shaping and implementation of rules designed for the practical functioning of trade and exchange. Political unrest is not good for business – unless one's business is the control of political unrest. As we write this book, media attention has focused on the accusation of the cleansing of the Rohingya Muslim minority from the Rakhine State by Buddhist and Myanmar authorities. This unrest is closely watched by *The Economist* (2013), a clear indication of corporate interests in the region.

The claims of critics such as Korten, Hertz, Pilger and others stand as a marked contradiction to the claims by advocates of prevailing forms of capitalism that this is the most effective, efficient and just system for global economic growth, and, accordingly, for the assurance of national and individual wealth and well-being. Pilger writes that we are all being hoodwinked. Echoing Hardt and Negri (2000), the global system, he argues, is not about emancipation; it is about empire. Its façades cover the enduring struggle of people for their freedom. He offers his work as an antidote to authorised versions of contemporary history 'that censor by omission and impose double standards ... [and as] a contribution to what Vandana Shiva calls "an insurrection of subjugated knowledge"' (Pilger, 2007: 13). Pilger (2005) takes this idea further into an analysis of the media in global influence. Colonial assumptions, he argues, have not changed: 'to sustain them millions of people remain invisible and expendable …' (Pilger, 2007: 13). With what critical thinking skills can we assess Pilger's views? This book will provide many concepts you can use as lenses to examine opinions such as this, and to come to your own conclusions.

---

## TALK BOX

Corralling people into reservations has been one way to clear lands for corporate access to minerals, oil reserves, water, timber and so on to serve investment interests. 'Enclosure' of land in the UK is an example described in 'The Cheviot, the Stag and the Black, Black Oil' (www.youtube.com/watch?v=sb3qbFcLYZc). Land enclosure for conversion to private property or leasehold opportunities as a legal entity today still drive people away from their homes and livelihoods. The forest dwellers of India and Indonesia or the Sami people in northern Scandinavia provide contemporary examples. For some, this (re)moving was engineered as 'punishment' for 'resistance', most notably in the United States (see 'We Shall Remain' at: www.pbs.org/wgbh/amex/weshallremain/). Less dramatic are the countless small-holder farmers taxed off their land. Greece is a good example. Some such displaced people have been seduced into believing that new opportunities are awaiting them (or their children) in reservations or in sometimes dangerous urban labour markets.

Today, the form of removal may be undertaken in openly violent ways or be subversively seductive and draw us all into accepting what will be 'for the best'. For example, 'less than a dollar a day' is a phrase often used to gain public consent to the movement of indigenous people, forest and savannah dwellers, and river people into reservations with or without services to 'help them integrate into the modern world' where they can earn incomes and own property. Closer to home, small farms are sold up for more efficient agri-businesses, small businesses are pressured out of existence by super-stores, and families are forced from homes by opportunistic bankers or through the downstream effects of austerity measures imposed by those saving the global economy. What is wrong with this picture? Examine closely some of the cases made visible by Corpwatch (www.corpwatch. org/article.php?id=15674).

---

## Tricky Questions

- Why critical management studies (CMS)?
- What is it to enlarge our critical consciousness?
- Who are the stakeholders in the capitalist system? Are all equally served by it? Are all equally powerful in terms of influence?

- How is the legitimacy of corporate behaviour established and maintained?
- How are organisational legitimacy and good public relations (PR) related?
- Can managers make a difference or do they just follow orders?
- Is one human life more valuable than another?
- How important is it that consumers understand fully all the dimensions of a supply chain?
- Are the United Nations-led programmes, devised to strengthen ethical corporate behaviour, robust enough to counter consumer demand for ever more and cheaper consumer items?

# ADDITIONAL RESOURCES

Alvesson, M. and Deetz, S. (2000) *Doing Critical Management Research*. London: Sage.

Alvesson, M. and Willmott, H. (1992) On the idea of emancipation in management and organization studies. *Academy of Management Review*, 17 (3): 432–64.

Alvesson, M. and Willmott, H. (1996) *Making Sense of Management: A Critical Introduction*. Thousand Oaks, CA: Sage.

Berger, P. and Luckmann, T. (1966) *The Social Construction of Reality: A Treatise in the Sociology of Knowledge*. London: Sage.

Boje, D.M. and Al Arkoubi, K. (2009) Critical management education beyond the siege. In S.J. Armstrong and C.V. Fukami (eds), *The Sage Handbook of Management Learning, Education, and Development*. Thousand Oaks, CA: Sage. pp. 104–25.

Bower, J.L., Leonard, H.B. and Paine, L.S. (2011) Global capitalism at risk: what are you doing about it? *Harvard Business Review*, 89 (9): 104–12.

Boyce, M. (1996) Teaching critically as an act of praxis and resistance. *Electronic Journal of Radical Organisation Theory*, 2 (2) (www.mngt.waikato.ac.nz/ejrot; retrieved 5 September 2013).

Chomsky, N. (2013) Can civilization survive capitalism? *The New York Times* News Syndicate.

Coates, B.E. (2013) Embedding leadership driven conscious capitalism into corporate DNA. *Advances in Management*, 6 (4): 14–24 (http://ideas.repec.org/a/mgn/journl/v6y2013i4a3.html; retrieved 6 September 2013).

Dehler, G. (2009) Prospects and possibilities of critical management education: critical beings and a pedagogy of critical action. *Management Learning*, 40: 31–49.

hooks, b. (1994) *Teaching to Transgress: Education as the Practice of Freedom*. New York: Routledge.

Laszlo, C., Brown, J.S., Sherman, D., Barros, I., Boland, B., Ehrenfeld, J., Gorham, M., Robson, L., Saillant, R. and Werder, P. (2012) Flourishing: a vision for business and the world. *Journal of Corporate Citizenship*, 46 (www.greenleaf-publishing.com/productdetail.kmod?productid=3823; retrieved 21 September 2013).

Muff, K. (2012) Are business schools doing their job? *Journal of Management Development*, 31 (7): 648–62.

Munck, R. and O'Hearn, D. (1999) *Critical Development Theory: Contributions to a New Paradigm*. London: Zed Books.

O'Connor, J. (2010) Marxism and the three movements of neoliberalism. *Critical Sociology*, 36 (5): 691–715.

Rauch, D. (2011) Conscious capitalism: a better road map. *California Management Review*, 53 (3): 91–7.

Scanlon, T.M. (2008) *Moral Dimensions: Permissibility, Meaning, Blame*. Cambridge, MA: Harvard University Press.

Thornton, P.H., Ocasio, W. and Lounsbury, M. (2012) *The Institutional Logics Perspective: A New Approach to Culture, Structure, and Process*. Oxford: Oxford University Press.

Wolf, R. (n.d.) Capitalism hits the fan (www.capitalismhitsthefan.com/; retrieved 2 September 2013).

Young, W. and Tilley, F. (2006) Can businesses move beyond efficiency? The shift toward effectiveness and equity in the corporate sustainability debate. *Business Strategy and the Environment*, 15 (6): 402–15.

# REFERENCES

Alvesson, M. (2002) *Understanding Organisation Culture*. London: Sage.

Assy, B. (1998) Eichmann, the banality of evil, and thinking in Arendt's thought. Paper presented at the 20th World Congress of Philosophy, Boston, Massachusetts, 10–15 August (www.bu.edu/wcp/Papers/Cont/ContAssy.htm; retrieved 5 September 2013).

Bishop, T., Reinke, J. and Adams, T. (2011) Globalization: trends and perspectives. *Journal of International Business Research*, 10 (1): 117–30.

Boele, R., Fabig, H. and Wheeler, D. (2001) Shell, Nigeria and the Ogoni: a study in unsustainable development: I. The story of Shell, Nigeria and the Ogoni people – environment, economy, relationships: conflict and prospects for resolution. *Sustainable Development*, 9 (2): 74–86.

Branson, R. (2011) *Screw Business as Usual*. New York: Penguin.

Burke, J. (2013) Bangladesh factory collapse leaves trail of shattered lives. *Guardian*, 6 June (www.theguardian.com/world/2013/jun/06/bangladesh-factory-building-collapse-community; retrieved 22 September 2013).

Butler, N. (2011) Subjectivity and subjectivation. In M. Tadajewski, P. MacLaran, E. Parsons and M. Parker (eds), *Key Concepts in Critical Management Studies*. London: Sage. pp. 210–13.

Butler, S. (2013) Bangladeshi factory deaths spark action among high-street clothing chains. *Guardian*, 23 June (www.theguardian.com/world/2013/jun/23/rana-plaza-factory-disaster-bangladesh-primark; retrieved 22 September 2013).

Chomsky, N. and Herman, E.S. (1979) *The Washington Connection and Third World Fascism*. Cambridge, MA: South End Press.

Clegg, S. (2011) Power. In M.Tadajewski, P. MacLaran, E. Parsons and M. Parker (eds), *Key Concepts in Critical Management Studies*. London: Sage. pp. 194–7.

Coates, B.E. (2013) Embedding leadership driven conscious capitalism into corporate DNA. *Advances in Management*, 6 (4): 14–24.

Colignon, R.A. (1989) Reification: the 'holistic' and 'individualistic' views of organizations. *Theory and Society*, 18 (1): 83–123.

Deephouse, D.L. and Carter, S.M. (2005) An examination of differences between organizational legitimacy and organizational reputation. *Journal of Management Studies*, 42 (2): 329–60.

Deetz, S. (1992) *Democracy in an Age of Corporate Colonization: Developments in Communication and the Politics of Everyday Life*. Albany, NY: State University of New York.

*The Economist* (2013) Buddhism v Islam in Asia: fears of a new religious strife, 27 July (www.economist.com/news/asia/21582321-fuelled-dangerous-brew-faith-ethnicity-and-politics-tit-tat-conflict-escalating; retrieved 6 September 2013).

Foucault, M. (1980) *Power/Knowledge: Selected Interviews and Other Writings 1972–1977*, ed. C. Gordon. New York: Pantheon.

Golant, B.D. and Sillince, J.A.A. (2007) The constitution of organizational legitimacy: a narrative perspective. *Organization Studies*, 28 (8): 1149–67.

Grey, C. (1999) 'We are all managers now'; 'We always were': On the development and demise of management. *Journal of Management Studies*, 36: 561–85.

Habermas, J. (1987) *The Theory of Communicative Action*, vol. 2: *Life World and System: A Critique of Functionalist Reason*. Boston: Beacon Press.

Hardt, M. and Negri, A. (2000) *Empire*. Cambridge, MA: Harvard University Press.

Hart, S.L. (2010) *Capitalism at the Crossroads: Next Generation Business Strategies for a Post-crisis World*. Upper Saddle River, NJ: Wharton Business School.

Hertz, N. (2001) *The Silent Takeover: Global Capitalism and the Death of Democracy*. London: Heinemann.

Hodges, D. (2012) The coming water wars. *The Common Sense Show*, 11 December (www.thecommonsenseshow.com/2012/12/11/the-coming-water-wars/; retrieved 2 September 2013).

Humphries, M.T. (2010) Terror and organisation change: what does love have to do with it? Paper presented at the 26th EGOS Colloquium, Lisbon.

Husserl, E. (1936) The crisis of European sciences and transcendental phenomenology: an introduction to phenomenological philosophy. *Philosophia (Belgrad)* 1: 77–176.

Kockel, U. (2012) Being from and coming to: outline of an ethno-ecological framework. In L. Williams, R. Roberts and A. McIntosh (eds), *Radical Human Ecology: Intercultural and Indigenous Approaches*. Surrey, UK: Ashgate. pp. 57–72.

Korten, D. (2001) *When Corporations Rule the World*, 2nd edn. San Francisco, CA: Berrett-Koehler.

Landrum, N., Gardner, C. and Boje, D. (2013) A values-based and integral perspective of strategic management. *Journal of Value Based Leadership*, 6 (1) (http://scholar.valpo.edu/cgi/viewcontent.cgi?article=1079&context=jvbl; retrieved 6 September 2013).

Lange, D., Lee, P.M. and Dai, Y. (2010) Organizational reputation: a review. *Journal of Management*, 37 (1): 153–84.

Laszlo, C., Brown, J.S., Sherman, D., Barros, I., Boland, B., Ehrenfeld, J., Gorham, M., Robson, L., Saillant, R. and Werder, P. (2012) Flourishing: a vision for business and the world. *Journal of Corporate Citizenship*, 46 (www.greenleaf-publishing.com/productdetail.kmod?productid=3823; retrieved 21 September 2013).

Mackey, J. (2011) What conscious capitalism really is. *California Management Review*, 53 (3): 83–90.

Mackey, J. (2013a) It's not corporate social responsibility (video file). *Conscious Capitalism* (http://vimeo.com; retrieved 2 September 2013).

Mackey, J. (2013b) Higher purpose (video file). *Conscious Capitalism* (http://vimeo.com; retrieved 2 September 2013).

Mackey, J. (2013c) Marvelous, misunderstood, maligned (video file). *Conscious Capitalism* (http://www.wholefoodsmarket.com/blog/capitalism-marvelous-mis-understood-maligned; retrieved 2 September 2013).

Mackey, J. and Sisodia, R. (2013a) *Conscious Capitalism: Liberating the Heroic Spirit of Business*. Cambridge, MA: Harvard Business Review Press.

Mackey, J. and Sisodia, R. (2013b) 'Conscious capitalism' is not an oxymoron. *Harvard Business Review* (http://blogs.hbr.org/2013/01/cultivating-a-higher-conscious/; retrieved 23 September 2013).

Maxton, G. (2011) *The End of Progress: How Modern Economics Has Failed Us*. Hoboken, NJ: John Wiley and Sons.

Monbiot, G. (2013) My search for a smartphone that is not soaked in blood. *Guardian* 11 March (www.theguardian.com/commentisfree/2013/mar/11/search-smartphone-soaked-blood; retrieved 2 September 2013).

Muff, K., Dyllick, T., Drewell, M., North, J., Shrivastava, P. and Haertke, J. (2013) *Management Education for the World: A Vision for Business Schools Serving People and Planet*. Cheltenham, UK: Edward Elgar.

Pilger, J. (2003) *The New Rulers of the World*. London: Verso.

Pilger, J. (2005) A news revolution has begun, 25 November (www.antiwar.com/orig/pilger.php?articleid=8150; retrieved 2 September 2013).

Pilger, J. (2007) *Freedom Next Time*. London: Black Swan Press.

Porter, M.E. and Kramer, M.R. (2011) Creating shared value. *Harvard Business Review*, January–February: 62–77.

Rose, N. (1998) *Inventing Ourselves: Psychology, Power, and Personhood*. Cambridge: Cambridge University Press.

Russo, A. and Perrini, F. (2010) Investigating stakeholder theory and social capital: CSR in large firms and SMEs. *Journal of Business Ethics*, 91: 207–21.

Saul, J.R. (1997) *The Unconscious Civilization*. Melbourne: Penguin.

Scherer, A.G. and Palazzo, G. (2011) The new political role of business in a globalized world: a review of a new perspective on CSR and its implications for the firm, governance, and democracy. *Journal of Management Studies*, 48 (4): 899–931.

Sennett, R. (2006) *The Culture of the New Capitalism*. New Haven, CT: Yale University Press.

Shiva, V. (2002) *Water Wars: Privatisation, Pollution, and Profit*. London: Pluto Press.

Sizoo, E. (2010) General introduction. In E. Sizoo (ed.), *Responsibility and Cultures of the World: Dialogue around a Collective Challenge*. Berlin: PIE Peter Lang. pp. 13–44.

Steiner, R. (2011) IUCN Communication, 2 September (www.americandailyherald.com/20110906781/africa/niger-delta-leaders-accuse-dutch-government-and-shell-oil-of-conspiracy-to-persecute-activist; retrieved 2 September 2013).

Steingard, D.S. and Fitzgibbons, D.E. (1995) Challenging the juggernaut of globalization: a manifesto for academic praxis. *Journal of Organizational Change Management*, 8 (4): 30–54.

Stiglitz, J.E. (2010) *Freefall: America, Free Markets, and the Sinking of the World Economy*. New York: W.W. Norton.

Suchman, M.C. (1995) Managing legitimacy: strategic and institutional approaches. *Academy of Management Review*, 20 (3): 571–610.

Thornton, P.H. and Ocasio, W. (2008) Institutional logics. In R. Greenwood, C. Oliver, R. Suddaby and K. Sahlin (eds), *The Sage Handbook of Organizational Institutionalism*. Thousand Oaks, CA: Sage. pp. 99–129.

Tilling, M.V. (2004) Some thoughts on legitimacy theory in social and environmental accounting. *Social and Environmental Accountability Journal*, 24 (2): 3–7.

Tregidga, H., Milne, M. and Kearins, K. (2007) The role of discourse in bridging the text and context of corporate social and environmental reporting. Paper presented at the 5th Australasian Conference on Social and Environmental Accounting Research, Wellington, New Zealand, 22–24 November, and the 5th Asia-Pacific Interdisciplinary Research in Accounting (APIRA) Conference, Auckland, New Zealand, 8–10 July.

Wang, L., Malhotra, D. and Murnighan, K.J. (2011) Economics, education and greed. *Academy of Management Learning and Education*, 10 (4): 643–60.

Warren, R.C. (2003) The evolution of business legitimacy. *European Business Review*, 15 (3): 153.

Weiss, A. (1995) Cracks in the foundation of stakeholder theory. *Electronic Journal of Radical Organisation Theory*, 1 (1).

Willmott, H. (2011) Journal list fetishism and the perversion of scholarship: reactivity and the ABS list. *Organization*, 18 (4): 429–42.

# 2 INFLUENTIAL THINKERS AND THE CRITICAL DISCOURSE

## Learning Objectives

In this chapter, we introduce a selection of ideas and concerns expressed by some of the key people who have influenced critical management studies. You are invited to think about:

- truth and knowledge, not as set facts, but as slippery and contextually specific concepts;
- common sense as a skilful production in which each of us is always involved as an enabler, challenger or transformer;
- the make-up of the entities we assume to exist and which we go on to use in our reasoning and justification – thus adding to the false perception of their existence as material or concrete entities in the same way that physical entities such as cats, chairs, cars and buildings might be thought of.

## CRITICAL CONCEPTS

*Meritocracy*, *work ethic*, *docility*, *rationality* and a *circumscribed consciousness* are among the difficult ideas we tackle in this chapter. With our mind on the *emancipatory* ideals of *critical theorists*, we extend an invitation to *revolt* against the *uncritical* uptake of much management education by *deconstructing*, *de-reifying* and *interrogating* the *established order* or *truth* experienced as salient *discourses* under challenge by the authors we introduce in this chapter. This focus helps us to examine the extent of *hegemonic* influences on and through our ways of organising and managing human affairs and the potential of *management education* to contribute to their *transformation* in ways that enhance *liberation* from *exploitative control* and the abuse of *power*.

Beliefs and values expressed as *knowledge* or *reality* form the basis of all particular truth claims. What is to be understood as truth, however, varies among peoples, locations and historical epochs. What is deemed *truth* impacts what is considered to be right and proper under specific conditions. The routinisation of ideas about truth and reality are expressed as world-views. These ideas are generally framed as systems of reasoning that become institutionalised through their practice. In Chapter 1, we referred to the form of capitalist reasoning being intensified globally as the prevailing institutional logics of neo-liberal*ism*, a theory supporting systems of thought deemed by its critics to be an ideology. The widespread manifestation of this reasoning is raising deep concerns among its critics about attendant social and environmental degradation. Critical theorists make it their business to examine what comes to be routinely taken for granted as truth in specific situations by particular people. Critical management scholars believe that unsettling what we take for granted is a step towards rethinking what might become a more creative response to the future.

Without unsettling what we have always believed to be true, or the ways in which we have always behaved, it is difficult to imagine other possible ways to organise our humanity and our relationship with Earth. Critical management scholars seek to expose representations of situations, of relationships and of systems that they believe to be exploitative or unjust. They do this to make explicit what they think needs attention and transformation if acclaimed notions of justice and fairness of a given society are to be met. Their ideas invite us to question how our management textbooks and organisational practices portray and treat human beings, other species of life, and Earth who sustains us. Their ideas help us reflect on what we so often take for granted as reasonable, rational, good, right or true. In this chapter, we introduce some of the authors whose ideas have had an influential impact on critical management studies and on our thoughts.

# CRAFTING KNOWLEDGE, EXPLORING (UN)TRUTH

Men will fight for superstition as quickly as for the living truth ... but truth is a point of view, [and] as so is changeable.

Hypatia of Alexandria (370–415 BC; Bagenal, 2009)

What is now known as critical theory is a legacy of the questioning of conventional wisdom that made Socrates famous. It cost him his life. Take a leap forward. After the First World War, the most important representatives of such critical thinking would:

wage an unrelenting assault on the exploitation, repression, and alienation embedded in Western Civilization … [they insisted] that thought must respond to new problems and the new possibilities for liberation that arise from the changing historical circumstances … [They were] deeply sceptical of tradition and all absolute claims … [and they were] concerned not merely with how things were but how they might be and should be … [Their] ethical imperative led its primary thinkers to develop a cluster of themes and a new critical method that transformed our understanding of society. (Bronner, 2011: 1–2)

But a caution! Critical theory is not one theory. As a body of thought, it is informed by a number of theorists not all of the same persuasion. This body of work is most often associated with the writings of Immanuel Kant, Georg Hegel, Karl Marx, Antonio Gramsci, Georg Lukács and the scholars linked with the Frankfurt School of Social Theory. Their thinking has been added to by Jacques Derrida, Michel Foucault and by a range of postmodern thinkers and their critics of recent decades. You will notice as you progress through this book that we find the work of Jürgen Habermas important. We show how Slavoj Žižek has become better known in recent times through his engagement with the Occupy Movement. Among the modern-day authors who we think have made a significant contribution to bringing these ideas to contemporary critical management studies are Matts Alvesson, Bobbie Bannerjee, David Boje, Mary Boyce, Marta Callas, Stewart Clegg, Stanley Deetz, Gordon Dehler, John Jermier, David Korten, David Knights, George Monbiot, Vandana Shiva, Linda Smircich, Linda Tuhiwai-Smith Pushi and Anshu Prasad, Gayatri Spivack, Hugh Willmott and many more people whose ideas you will meet in this book.

Let us look at the 'seminal thinkers' first! Yes! They are nearly all 'Old Boys'. They are not, however, all of exactly the same school of thought! Our purpose in this chapter is to sample their similarities and their differences, and in this way enrich our reading of management studies and contribute to enlarging and perhaps even spicing up management education a little bit. Our focus is on describing how these particular theorists tackled the idea of human consciousness, reason and ethics and their manifestation of these in practice or perceived reality. We start by introducing Immanuel Kant, Georg Hegel, Karl Marx, Antonio Gramsci and Georg Lukács and some of their influential ideas.

# PILLARS OF CRITICAL THEORY: KANT, HEGEL, MARX, GRAMSCI AND LUKÁCS

## Immanuel Kant (1724–1804): Universalising the Dignity of All

Kant argues that people must never be treated as a means to an end. He posits that people are to be thought of as free entities. In his way of thinking, it is never ethical to harness a human being to the interests of others. Kant's philosophical contribution on ethics and morality is deemed by many as the foundation of universal rights and responsibilities (Ward, 2006). His thoughts were developed in an atmosphere of much intellectual ferment that included the ideas of David Hume (1711–1776), Jean-Jacques Rousseau (1712–1778) and Adam Smith (1723–1790). Kant argued that individuals hold their own distinct moral and ethical ideas. What is thus considered to be ethically or morally right or wrong differs from person to person. This diversity can lead to deep challenges for the way we live together.

Kant's position invites a deep reflection on the extent to which people in Western-style democracies oiled by capitalist-style economies can be thought of as free individuals, willing contractors, forced labour or duped functionaries. Kant urges us to look beyond narrow self-interest and to consider the well-being needs of wider society. But requiring people to subjugate their own interest to an abstract 'common good' is always going to be problematic! When we try to apply universal minimal standards to conditions of employment, all kinds of conflicts and controversies arise. Kant's opinion that no one is ever justified in using another human being as a means to an end becomes a thought-provoking idea if we think about the extent to which people are now often uncritically considered as 'human resources'; that is, just a part of the mechanical profit-generating system of ideas we prefer to call 'the market'. They may become known as 'the labour market', 'the workforce', 'staff', 'employees' and 'contractors' – each with subtly different connotations. Common to them all are the processes of categorising and objectification for functional purposes. To help the system, the machine or the organisation function efficiently to some predetermined specifications, human beings may be depicted as a unit in a team, as a cost-centre in a budget or as a necessary or expendable resource to be developed or deleted in the interest of an organisation, an industry, the economy or the nation.

Kant was concerned about the impact of diversity in freely formed individual freedom on the well-being of the wider society; the associated potential for a conflict of interest and the legitimate authority of the state in the resolution of such conflict was being heavily debated. Hegel drew on the work of Kant and his contemporaries to conceptualise individual identity, morality and ethics, and relations between individuals within civil society and the state.

## Georg Hegel (1770–1831): Fulfilling Self-consciousness

Hegel believed that each person constructs their own identity and defines their own moral and ethical codes. Individuals draw on these codes to decide how best to act in order to achieve fulfilled self-consciousness. Hegel recognised that tensions may arise between individuals' unique ethical and moral standards and the codified standards as set by state legislation in the form of basic rules that we must all comply with in order to live together. Individuals, he observes, are expected to modify their behaviour and subordinate their self-interest in accordance with codified moral and ethical standards. Such subjugation of oneself to the benefit of an abstract common good could get in the way of fulfilling one's full potential and for realising one's individual freedom. It was Karl Marx who helped to explain Hegel's concern with human alienation from each other and from their very recognition of themselves as free and creative beings under the conditions of the emerging capitalism of his time as he saw it.

## Karl Marx (1818–1883): Subordination to the Objectified World

Karl Marx, a student of Hegel, is most widely known for his philosophical analysis of capitalism and the capitalist mode of production. His ideas have contributed significantly to the development of critical organisational studies. Marx located the development of Western capitalism within specific historical, social, political and economic processes and believed that the capitalist economy must be understood as only one of many possible ways to organise society. He theorised that capitalism produces a distinctive class relationship between workers (or the proletariat) and the owners of capital (or the bourgeoisie). The bourgeoisie owns the means of production, such as land, factories, investment

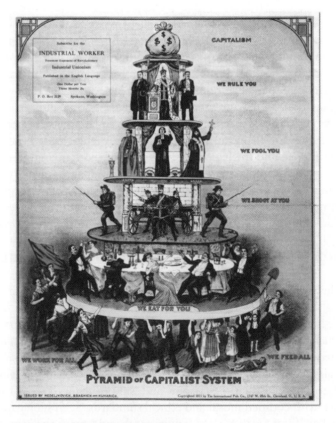

**Figure 2.1**   Pyramid of the capitalist system

capital and, increasingly, intellectual property. In contrast, the proletariat owns only its labour which it sells in exchange for wages. The relationship between the bourgeoisie and the proletariat within the capitalist production process, for Marx, is inherently exploitative and alienating (Figure 2.1).

Marx points out that, within the capitalist mode of production, all factors of production are treated as objects. In other words, nature, people and processes are reified. Experienced as 'things', they can be arranged into systems to be managed in order to maximise profit. Such things may include money, sale price, factories, land, water, minerals, institutions and investment capital. People become objectified as a unit of labour or, to use contemporary language, a 'human resource'. This resource, like any other, is to be managed in terms of 'its' productivity or cost – an ethical concern through the eyes of Kantian perspectives. Workers in a capitalist regime are exploited because the things they make or the services they deliver are sold for more than the workers receive in wages. Marx termed this devaluation of the human world, relative to the world of 'things', as 'the subordination of man [sic] to capital' (Marx, 1867) and to the world of things, or the objectified world. Similarly, the natural environment is treated in terms of the costs or contribution to profit, a point we explore more fully in Chapter 8.

Marx held that the capitalist mode of production rendered workers subordinate to time because they sell 'time' for 'wages'. Time and wages can now be equated on a table of comparable values. What workers do in a defined period of time is determined, measured and controlled by the capitalist. Time thus becomes a commodity that can be bought and sold. The worker as a human being becomes invisible in this process. The turning of 'time' into a 'thing' and then into a 'commodity' takes a particular turn in today's 24/7 society, involving workers employed in activities as diverse as international call centres, hospitals, manufacturing plants, supermarkets, fast-food restaurants or stock-exchange trading. Workers are increasingly faced with selling particular blocks of night-time as well as their day-time hours. Marx believed that an outcome of the capitalist production process is that people become alienated from the output of their work, the meaning they might make of work, in their social relationships, and from nature. Workers are alienated from the output of their own labour because they do not own the goods they produce or have control over the disposal of those goods. People become alienated from the meaning of work because all intrinsic value is removed from the process. Ultimately, they become alienated from their free and creative selves as authors of their own lives.

## FROM CRAFT TO GRAFT

Instead of work being an end in itself (e.g., I am making a chair to sit on), work becomes a means to another end (e.g., I am making a chair to 'make a living'). In

*(Continued)*

*(Continued)*

the context of mass production, I recruit, harness and train people for as little as I can get away with, under the most frugal conditions allowed by law, to make chairs that I can sell on the market for as much profit as I can muster. The chair's value is now determined by its ability to generate wealth for investors. Style, comfort and craft are now instrumental rather than intrinsic values. So, too, is the value of the crafter of the chair. The alienation in the work process extends into society as social relationships once embedded in the exchange process become fragmented and controlled by others. The direct interpersonal relationship between the producer of a chair and the customer who buys a chair is replaced by impersonal economic relationships of exchange: the worker (or 'grafter' in the colloquial of the English working class) exchanges labour for the capitalist for a wage. Having earned the money by making chairs, the worker as a consumer can exchange money for food, shelter or even a chair. Nature provides important contributions in terms of raw material and energy for the construction, transport and disposal of chairs. Much of that provision is still unaccounted for in contemporary environmentally conscious cost analyses.

The economic relationship under capitalist logic is measured in terms of how much workers earn and how much they can buy with their wage. We see this assessment being rehearsed and replicated in contemporary times in discussions about the desirability or otherwise of a required minimum wage in relation to cost of living calculations. This exchange of social relationships for economic relationships is embedded in Marx's analysis of 'commodity fetishism' (Dunne, 2011), an issue we return to in more detail in Chapter 7. As with the worker, the capitalist, too, is alienated by and subordinate to capital production processes. The capitalist's existence is dependent on their ability to acquire and own property, and to sustain their capital.

While Marx provides a powerful analysis of the capitalist production process, he suggests that analysis alone is not enough to achieve democratic participation for citizens. What is required is action. Here we see the development of the notion of praxis, the linking of theory to practice. In contemporary times, Marx's theory is complicated by the investment by many wage-earners in financial markets directly or indirectly through pension plans. The identity of individuals thus is not as uncomplicated as Marx's model might suggest. This is an issue we will return to several times in this book. What Marx did very well, however, was to draw attention to the way external conditions might influence the way we think about work and workers where capitalist ideas prevail. It was Antonio Gramsci who noted that where the conditions of work alienate people from their sense of sovereign being, and where they come to concur in their exploitation, the conditions of hegemonic control are achieved.

# Antonio Gramsci (1891–1937): Redressing Hegemony through Exposing False Consciousness

Antonio Gramsci extended Marx's analysis to develop his understanding of power in society (Adamson, 1980). He argued that philosophy, politics and social activity are intrinsically linked. Based on this belief, he began to analyse how elite groups gain and maintain power within society. 'His theorising about power relationships resulted in the articulation of hegemony as a form of power that is evident in society when one class and its representatives exercise power over subordinate classes by means of a combination of coercion and persuasion' (Simon, 1991: 22; see also Bottomore et al., 1983: 194). Hegemonic power is achieved when the elite group in society takes the interests of the subordinate classes into account and combines those interests with their own in such a way that the subordinate groups believe that the interests of the ruling class are, in fact, their own. Such hegemonic power is not achieved through explicit force or domination, but through gaining popular consent and through encouraging self-serving alliances between groups in society. To achieve this hegemony, the powerful or elite group offers or provides and secures popular consent and ideological leadership (that is, maintains hegemonic power) often but not only through the state apparatus.

Gramsci is able to argue this point because he views power as a social relation. The state apparatus reflects the bases of power developed in society (Simon, 1991). Gramsci (1971) recognised, however, that while hegemonic alliances and control are resilient, they are still provisional. Hegemonic control relies on forming coalitions with groups in society and making compromises with those groups to secure their allegiance. Hegemony is never complete as dominance and consent must be continually 'won, secured and sustained' (Schweitzer, 1991: 27). This means that while hegemony is difficult to change, it is not impossible. A counter-hegemonic challenge requires political consciousness-raising and forging alliances between varied and sometimes quite different subordinate groups (Gramsci, 1971). Consciousness-raising is therefore deemed necessary to redress false consciousness (as posited by Marx) by locating forms of domination within specific social, political, economic and historical contexts.

The exposure of arrangements suspected of supporting elite interests is to draw different groups together so they can work collaboratively to redress systemic domination within society. Such action, or praxis, serves the transformation or emancipatory intention of critical theorists. But how do we assess who is being served and who is being exploited, who is being harmed and who is being protected? Both Marx and Gramsci appear to present seemingly homogeneous categories of human beings arranged in tidy hierarchies that are not an actuality for most people. Most of us are complexly positioned in the social arrangements we call 'society', an issue explored more fully by Laclau and Mouffe (Klimecki and Willmott, 2011). The paradox of a system that sometimes simultaneously exploits and rewards the very same person will be a point we return to often in this book.

## JOB SECURITY AS DISCIPLINARY BOND

The Occupy Wall Street Movement, which came to media attention in 2010 and made a specific challenge to corporate greed, gained some initially favourable media representation. Replications soon spread around the world. There seemed to be a very wide cross-section of people overtly supporting the challenge to corporate greed. But, bit by bit, visible support diminished. Protesters were increasingly depicted as somewhat ridiculous, if not downright bad. Soon, it became very normal to see images of recalcitrant protesters being moved by police force. Potential sympathisers know well the consequences of a criminal conviction on one's record. Job loss might follow and all that flows from this acts as intuitive self discipline.

One way critical theorists bring our attention to the vested interests obscured in reifications is to 'deconstruct' the ideas we have come to accept and enact as real, true and good. Protesters who challenge the comfort zones of the powerful are redefined and categorised as 'disruptors'. If disruptors persist in their unsettling activities, they will be re-identified as sad, mad or bad people. If convicted as bad, their redefinition as criminals will have potentially lifelong consequences. If defined as sad or mad, a variety of therapeutic, disciplinary or other remedial pressures will be brought into play. Protesters, like people in debt, displaced people or surplus people, can all be reified as problems, statistics and cases. Decisions about them can then be easily made. They can then be managed more efficiently in systems devised to deal with such objects of systemic concern so that order can be maintained.

## MARVELLOUSLY MISCHIEVOUS OR MAD AND BAD?

Peter, Adrian and Sam have strong commitments to their Christian faith and to the duty of citizens to hold their governments to account. They believe that the justification for the state to spy on people to ensure their security is a lie that obscures elite interests. They set about drawing attention to their concerns by breaching the fence at the New Zealand government's Communications Security Bureau at Waihopai, a site they think of as a 'spy station'. They were, of course, arrested and charged. After an eight-day trial, they were acquitted by the jury. In response, the government lodged a civil claim and was awarded $1.2 million in damages. An appeal by Waihopai Ploughshares was heard by the Court of Appeal in May 2013 (www.converge.org.nz/pma/plshares.htm). The three men and their supporters found a novel way to keep the issue in public view. On the first day of the court of appeal hearing, they gathered at parliament dressed only in their underpants and carried their clothes to give to the prime minister in keeping with the teachings of Jesus: 'if any man will sue you at the law, and take away your coat, let him have your shirt as well' (Matthew 5:40; Scoop, 2013).

While reifications can be useful as shortcuts in thinking and communicating that make everyday life flow more smoothly and to make the management of systems more efficient, these shortcuts may also curtail our conscious awareness of what they represent. Once unconscious to the embedding of interests in these reifications, they may be useful to get a population to come to an agreement about how an elite group believes the world ought to be and the appropriate consequences of disruptive behaviour. Georg Lukács explains this process of reification more fully.

## Georg Lukács (1885–1971): Reifications as Repositories of Meaning (thus Power)

Georg Lukács's contributions to critical thought are embedded in his theorising of reification through his development of the Marxist concepts of alienation and false consciousness, and his development of the understanding of class consciousness. Reification (in this way of thinking) is defined as the 'moment in the process of alienation in which the characteristic of thing-hood becomes the standard of objective reality' (Berger and Pullman, 1965: 198). Jermier (1985: 75) further explains '[r]eified consciousness is characterized by a deprivation of awareness which prevents realization that the world is socially constructed, and can be remade.' One way to illustrate the process of reification is by examining the notion of organisational routines formalised in institutional(*ised*) rules. A reified understanding of organisational rules would have us believe that organisational rules tell us how to behave and we agree to obey. Obedience may perhaps be granted unconsciously, perhaps begrudgingly, perhaps strategically. Regardless, in this illustration, the organisational rules have been turned into a thing (perhaps a code of practice) that has the characteristic of authority and imposes standards of reality. Standards of required behaviour may be better thought of as the values, wishes and intentions of the rule-makers and our domestication by them may engender or maintain a form of hegemonic control that may be harmful to ourselves or others.

A de-reified understanding of the organisation's rules, codes and practices would be evident when we realise that these are the socially fabricated outcomes of people making countless decisions based upon their particular understanding of the efficacy of the rules and the rights of the organisation – be that the state, the corporation, the Church, unions, communities, families and so on, 'entities' that exist only as a conglomeration of humanly fabricated and sanctioned relationships governed by rules-for-being. In this way of thinking, organisations such as governments, corporations and their rules and codes of practice are historical social constructions, fictive entities or social fabrications that carry with them interests and power as we discussed these in Chapter 1. *Because* they are figments of the human imagination, they can be changed – no matter how entrenched they are 'as things' and no matter how hard and dangerous it is to expose them for what they are: the preferences of some imposed on others – a travesty of Kantian ethics.

There is always an opportunity to offer new ideas to replace those that support and justify processes that may be deemed unethical, destructive or unsafe when given a more critical analysis – no matter how seemingly dense the hegemonic influences at play. In the example where rules become things, and the things are made into systems, and the systems are so normalised we come to take them for granted (as 'natural' even), we can see the extension of the idea of false consciousness by including the notion of a reified consciousness. That is, reified consciousness is manifest (or incarnated) when we no longer recognise that rules, codes and customs are historically specific and are created, imposed upon and tolerated by people engaged in a complex web of power arrangements. We forget or choose not to remember that we can remake the rules.

Lukács further develops understanding of the Marxist analysis of class consciousness and Gramsci's analysis of hegemonic power (Pickford, 2001). For Lukács, hegemony can only be achieved when one class is able to assert its particular class consciousness on the rest of the population. The ability of one class to assert its dominance is dependent on the extent to which that class is aware of the actions needed to be performed to obtain power, and thus assert class consciousness. At the same time, this implies that all other classes, or the subordinate classes, are unaware of the actions required in order for their values to become dominant in society. Lukács puts it like this: class consciousness implies a 'class-conditioned unconsciousness to [their] historical social-economic conditioning' (Lukács, 1971: 52). Thus, the subordinate classes experience class-conditioned consciousness and accept the interests of the dominant class as their own and are unable to locate their lived experiences in wider sociopolitical and economic contextual factors. Instead, these contextual factors become taken-for-granted truths that inform and govern every aspect of life.

Lukács drew on his analysis of class consciousness to tease out the dialectic relationship between theory and practice. One hope of critical theorists is to transform social relationships through praxis for the benefit of all. Yet, Lukács suggests that as long as a challenge to hegemonic power remains theoretical, people with disparate views and interests can coexist peacefully. This is so because the antagonisms between social classes are expressed through theoretical discussions which do not directly challenge the prevailing social order, or the power of the dominant group, until unacceptable violence erupts. It is when the challenge shifts from a theoretical abstract argument to identifying problems that require action that hegemonic power is truly threatened. It is at this point that the relative power between the dominant class and the subordinate classes may inhibit or facilitate the achievement of transformative social change.

## MANAGING OUTRAGE

The extractive industries are under pressure from a variety of challenges to improve conditions for miners the world over. At times, some of the challenges come in the form of protests by outraged workers and their supporters. The media and the wider community become alerted. The protesters walk a fine line in the management of such expressions of conflict and the management of public opinion. Attempts to improve the circumstances of the miners at the Lonmin platinum mine in Marikana, for example, led to a strike in 2012. The police were sent out to disperse the protesters. Shots were fired, leaving 18 dead and many wounded. In a controversial use of an old law, many survivors were arrested for causing the death of their fellow protesters. Whose version of appropriate behaviour can be called into question in this example? Whose truth was to prevail? Many voices, using diverse forms of reasoning, have variously condemned or justified the police action. This example illustrates how the idea of 'ethical' behaviour can be viewed very differently by groups whose worldview is generated by a specific, but not the same, set of values and beliefs about the proper order of the world (Preston and Sinha, 2012).

The ideas that have concerned Kant, Hegel, Marx, Gramsci and Lukács find further extension in the work generated by the scholars of the Frankfurt School. We now turn our attention to some of this history.

# THE FRANKFURT SCHOOL AND CRITICAL THEORY

The term 'critical theory' often specifically relates to the scholarship originating from the Frankfurt School, founded in Frankfurt, Germany in 1923 (Cluley, 2011). The scholars most associated with the Frankfurt School include Max Horkheimer (the founding director), Theodor W. Adorno, Erich Fromm and Herbert Marcuse. Together, these scholars sought to revise the Marxist critique of capitalism and to develop the Marxist theory of social revolution. They attempted to explain why the predicted Marxist revolution had failed to occur, and to broaden the then emerging Freudian psychosocial analysis (Agger, 1991b). The term 'critical theory' was coined in 1937 as many of the founding members fled Germany for America in the lead up to the Second World War. They found a home at 'the university in exile' in New York, which in 2005 was renamed the New School for Social Research. The term 'critical theory' came into usage to mask the radical commitment of the scholars involved because of the sociopolitical dislike of Marxism and communism evident in America at the time. There was a real danger in trusting in the value of 'freedom of speech' even in this 'land of the free'.

## CONSTRAINTS ON FREE SPEECH IN MODERN DEMOCRACIES

Constraint on free speech in democracies is often justified for reasons of security or privacy. Defamation and hate speech are serious offences. These ought not to be tolerated in a just society. However, there are more complex pressures to silence populations. The West has made a virtue out of providing asylum for critics of some regimes, but has also found subtle ways to silence its own populations. The closing down of open academic conversations on the Internet at the time of the Twin Tower bombings in New York was a subtly imposed restriction of political commentary reminiscent of the 'reds under the beds' silencing of the McCarthy era in the US during the period of the Second World War. Today, laws passed to limit or criminalise the speech or protest actions of some are worthy of a closer investigation. The part of various states in Julian Assange's involvement in the WikiLeaks story needs closer critical scrutiny. In New Zealand, in 2013, there was a hot debate about whether protests on the high seas against deep-sea oil drilling were to be criminalised. The critics of this particular law under review, including high-ranking legal minds, suggest that this law is a deep incursion into democratic principles (Fairfax NZ News, 2013). Greenpeace activists redefined as Hooligans are at risk of imprisonment in Russia.

## Max Horkheimer (1895–1973) and Theodor W. Adorno (1903–1969): Unified Subjects

Horkheimer and Adorno share a particular concern with analysing the link between culture and society. They argued that, while at one time cultural pursuits enhanced individuality and social development, such pursuits may now be seen as one of many processes aimed at promoting conformity within the totally administered society (Kellner, 2001). Just as we are doing in this book, Max Horkheimer questioned the taken-for-granted aspects of what he saw as 'the society' of his day. His early work has been criticised for being *totalitarian* because he argued that society had the potential to be a unified subject with a unified will. Should this position of unitarism be realised, argue his critics, the 'unified subject' and 'unified will' would effectively marginalise considerations of social, cultural and *political pluralism* (Hoy and McCarthy, 1994) and a respect for human diversity deemed essential for the prevention of a Nazi-style attempt to homogenise the world of people and ideas.

**Figure 2.2**  Graffiti art. Photo credit: M. St Jane

To speak of ideology is to enquire into the relation between material reality and ideas, and to consider how particular discourses, forms of consciousness or practices might serve power (Beverungen, 2011: 143). Adorno, a leading figure in the Frankfurt School, provided the opening for the move from the prevailing structural metaphors for social and political analysis to an inclusion of interpretivist methods (Hancock, 2011). He was among those reluctant to advocate direct political action. Rather, he saw a need to explore the 'emancipatory moment' in philosophy and art, and, in particular, the moment of emancipation expressed through modern art (Berman, 2001; Figure 2.2). Adorno developed the notions of negative dialectics and dialectic consciousness. Negative dialectics involves illustrating how the dominant ideology within society does not reflect the actual material, social or economic conditions of society members (Pickford, 2001). Dialectic consciousness is a process that can help expose these contradictions and involves willingness and openness to examine actual experiences as they relate to the dominant ideology.

Adorno saw the purpose of praxis as a means of developing dialectical consciousness and the transformation of consciousness. Critical theorists therefore have a very strong kinship with the work undertaken by psychoanalysts concerned with consciousness. We introduce three examples below: Sigmund Freud, Erich Fromm and Herbert Marcuse.

# DIPPING INTO THE UNCONSCIOUS: FREUD, FROMM AND MARCUSE

## Sigmund Freud (1856–1939): Healing through Dialogue

Freud was a doctor of medicine at the University of Vienna in the early part of the twentieth century. There he was appointed a lecturer in neuropathology in 1885, and in 1902 he was made a professor. Freud's form of psychoanalysis was to become a significant clinical method for treating perceived mental illnesses through dialogue between a patient and a psychoanalyst. Among his interests are his ideas about mechanisms of repression as eventually energising the unconscious as a disrupter of conscious states of mind. These ideas about the out-working of this theory become helpful to critical theorists in attempts to understand the possibilities and denials in healthy or toxic organisational relationships. Carl Jung, an early collaborator, took a lot of this thinking into his own work, but dismissed Freud's conviction that so much of human well-being or otherwise could be so closely aligned with human sexuality. Jung's trajectory is significant for the way the ideas about the un/subconscious have come into the thinking of management. It is most evident in the personality theories we now know as the Myers Briggs model, used to match people and occupations, and Holland's matching of personality types and stereotypes of national character – issues we examine more closely in Chapter 5.

## Erich Fromm (1900–1980): Linking Theory and Practice

Fromm's contribution to critical theory is in his analysis and development of critical social psychology and his work on theorising the social construction of the individual (Bronner and Kellner, 1989). He was particularly interested in the interplay between instinct and subconscious and the development of society. He argued that the sociopolitical and economic context helped shape an individual's psychological state and their perception of reality. He stressed the importance of linking philosophy and analytical theory with psychoanalytic clinical data because to separate these 'is untenable in a science whose concepts and theories cannot be understood without reference to the clinical phenomena from which they were developed' (Fromm, 1989: 218). Fromm's analysis highlights the importance for organisation theorists to be more conscious of the theories they accept and embed in the management disciplines and the assumptions teachers and students bring to their work.

## Herbert Marcuse (1898–1979): Repressive Desublimation

Marcuse's contribution to critical theory and to critical scholarship lies in his analysis of why the Marxist revolution failed to occur. Marcuse conceptualised that, in late capitalism, new forms of domination and worker control would be needed to ensure compliance to the social order of capitalism and to maintain productivity and profit levels. He argued that the technological developments and the associated increased productivity and output witnessed in the period after the Second World War might lead workers to believe that the issue of scarcity had been resolved. This realisation might in turn lead to the potential decline in dependence on employment and, therefore, workers recognising the possibility of new forms of organising society. If this were to occur, Marcuse suggested, there would become a need to increase self-imposed control to ensure the continued domestication of society to the rules of capitalism.

Marcuse used the term *surplus repression* to describe this new form of self-imposed control that would ensure workers continue to accept the capitalist regime (Agger, 1991b). Surplus repression is an indirect process that relies on the individual controlling the self, by enticing the workers to continue to work productively in order to fuel an ever-increasing desire for consumer products and services. Surplus repression works through the process of repressive desublimation where individuals exchange their social, political and economic freedom for the espoused 'freedom' of consumer choice (Agger, 1991b), an issue we explore in greater depth in Chapter 7.

The process of repressive desublimation involves the capitalist economy as an organising principle that is supported by a group of thought-leaders (e.g., academics, economists, accountants, politicians) espousing one-dimensional thought and the simultaneous development of 'one-dimensional man' who is unable to form multi-dimensional understandings of the social, political and economic world (Marcuse, 1991). An example can be seen in the acceleration of the interest of neo-liberals in the 1980s. Margaret Thatcher, then prime minister of the UK, amplified the slogan 'there is no alternative' to the liberal preferences for a corporate friendly state and reduced state involvement in the well-being of citizens. This is the TINA principle ('there is no alternative') we explain more fully in Chapter 3. The market would fix all. She was backed up by economists who argued that the British economy needed to be liberalised. This particular political ideology became common sense to generations of management students. How these ideas are being intensified the world over is the subject of Chapter 3. Importantly, Marcuse helps us to understand the subtle yet powerful differences between an imposed power from above and the effects of their internalisation experienced as power from within. The 'one-dimensional man' of this type of theorising by both the Marxists and the neo-liberals came to be challenged by those who recognised that people were more complicated than these theories suggest. A number of authors, often categorised as postmodernists, set out to demonstrate the diversity of people, their relationships with each other and their influence on an unstable and re-definable social world.

# POST FRANKFURT SCHOOL: A SHIFT IN THE DISCOURSE

Postmodernists argue that there is a decline in the acceptability of a representation of a more or less uniform, standardised culture and shared sense of humanity (Lyotard, 1993) as presented in the positivists' search for universalising principles based on Eurocentric notions of progress and development. Instead, postmodernists view culture and values as diverse. Because of this, postmodernists claim that it is not appropriate to conceive society as a uniform mass or see it in terms of fixed class structures, as the early critical theorists portrayed them. Instead, from a postmodernist perspective, society is conceived as comprised of heterogeneous individuals with diverse values, needs and desires, which are in a constant state of change. Thus, many of the authors we discuss here, while influential critical thinkers, might also be considered as postmodernists.

## Jacques Derrida (1930– ): Powerful Signifiers

Jacques Derrida is most commonly associated with the post-structuralist thought emerging from France in the 1960s (Seidman, 2008). Post-structuralism has been described as the 'linguistic turn', with a focus on understanding how power is embedded in spoken and written language and in knowledge (Agger, 1991b). Derrida argued that words or sounds, which he called 'signifiers', do not have a fixed meaning; instead, people interpret meanings embedded in words in quite different ways. As such, what is understood is constantly being constructed as well as contested (Seidman, 2008). Derrida theorised that every text is embedded within particular political and social contexts, and these contexts inform the underlying assumptions embedded, concealed or suppressed within the text. Every text then contains and conceals undercurrents, tensions and conflicts. If the reader is unaware of the sociopolitical context or the underlying assumptions concealed and suppressed within the text, and if the interpretation upholds dominant power relationships in society, there is potential for reinforcing hegemony (Agger, 1991b). This is more likely if the reader is not fully aware of the implications that concealed assumptions have on presenting a particular viewpoint or 'truth claim'. This position is most easily illustrated in typical management textbooks that offer various ways to improve profit maximisation with little regard for the costs imposed and interests served. While particular political assumptions and the tensions surrounding profit might be embedded in these texts, they are very rarely made explicit.

Derrida was concerned about the preoccupation of Western scholars in developing a single, authoritative language or ideology to reveal truth, moral rightness and beauty (Seidman, 2008). He called this 'logocentricism'. He argued that this desire to uncover single truths about the world has resulted in the development of a series of binaries in Western thought and language; for example, male/female, feminine/masculine, soul/body, right/wrong and positive/negative. With the binaries, come assumptions that suggest one side of the binary is superior, while one is inferior. This binary system has led to the development of 'an order of truth and reality that could function as an authoritative basis for judging truth/falsity, knowledge/ideology, reality/illusion, or right/wrong' (Seidman, 2008: 161).

Instead of passively reading the text as a process and exercise to take up apparent truths, Derrida argues that reading should be considered a political act. From this perspective, the reader can be considered to be an active participant in the process of reading. The meanings and interpretations of readers continually change over time, reflecting the prevailing norms, rules and socially constructed roles evident at the time of each reading. Becoming an active reader is one way to expose the underlying assumptions and logocentric truth claims embedded in the text. Through a textual deconstruction, the reader actively looks to uncover gaps, underlying assumptions, political and cultural contexts or binary parings embedded in the text. The aim of deconstructive reading and analysis is to uncover the multiple meanings embedded in the text in order to destabilise exploitative power structures and relationships with the purpose of opening up the possibility for transformative actions (Seidman, 2008).

## Michel Foucault (1926–1984): Power is Knowledge

Michel Foucault's contribution to critical thought is embedded in his theorising of discourse, power and knowledge, and the creation of a disciplined society. To be able to manipulate the 'power from within' is really an internalised version of external influences on the formation of self, self-discipline and the disciplined society. Foucault explored some of the processes that facilitate the accepting of other people's ideas as our own. Traditional forms of discourse analysis focus on semantics and specific word construction. Foucault understood discourse as comprising written or spoken groups of statements and acts that made truth claims about social reality. He demonstrates that discourse is linked to power relationships, and discourse shapes knowledge, meaning, behaviour and what we assume we can know to be true. Knowledge claims, in this form of reasoning, are perhaps more accurately thought of as beliefs.

Foucault argued that any form of discourse is historically and contextually bound. In order to understand discourse and the embedded power relations, it is necessary to trace the creation of particular forms of knowledge back through time. He calls this process the archaeology of knowledge. The aim of Foucauldian discourse analysis is to locate groups of statements (referred to as 'discourse') in the historical context to uncover who developed the discourse and for what purpose and how discourses shape particular understandings of perceived 'reality' and understandings of our self and our identity. Through his recognition of the historical context of discourse and that discourse shapes meaning and behaviour, Foucault illustrates that power is (the capacity to shape and engage with what passes for) knowledge (at any given time and place). Among the many important contributions Foucault has made to the analytical strength of critical theorists is his theorising of the 'relations of power'.

Foucault argues that power is not simply located in hierarchical relationships (e.g., between manager and worker), or at the site of production (e.g., in the factory), or embedded in the relations of production (e.g., between the capitalist and the worker) in the way a traditional Marxist analysis might assume. Instead, he highlights that power is embedded in social relationships and is thus diffused throughout society. He illustrates this diffusion by uncovering the relationships between discourse, knowledge and the relations of power with the creation of the disciplined society where control of whole populations is achieved by controlling the behaviour, actions or attitudes of the individual through the application of specific disciplinary techniques that have the effect of creating the docile-utilisable body. In the process, the exercise of power becomes 'more anonymous and more functional' (Foucault, 1977: 193). From a critical position, the disciplinary process is problematic because political autonomy is reduced or lost as individuals become more (unquestioningly or unconsciously) obedient to the will of others. Truth, knowledge, meaning and our very identity become embedded in and shaped by others. Thus, human beings are what they are because they are in relation with others. It is our necessary (inter)relationship with each other that draws our mind back to Kant, and invites the examination of the work of Martin Buber.

## Martin Buber (1878–1965): I and Thou

Martin Buber proposes that it is through communication that respectful relationships can be formed. Echoing the concerns of Kant about the unacceptable objectification of others, he offers the I/thou relationship as expressing reciprocity between one subject and another through dialogue. From the work of Buber, we can ask: are our relationships with each other conducive to such dialogue? What about our relationship with the environment? The radical competitive individualism and exploitative values that infuse the discourses of capitalism can only occur through the objectification of others and of Earth and all her creatures. What other forms of 'relationship' can humans create? Jürgen Habermas suggests that the way to just relationships is achieved only through dialogue.

## Jürgen Habermas (1929– ): Communicative Action

Jürgen Habermas joined Adorno and Horkheimer and those at the Frankfurt School in the creation and development of critical theory. Habermas conceives critical theory as communicative, representing a significant shift from the original Frankfurt theorists, who he believes did not sufficiently further their critique of domination to include a paradigm of communication (Agger, 1991a). He argues that only through communication and interaction can people master society, form social movements and achieve power. He contends that communicative rationality suspends the domination of tradition and embedded power relationships. As freely participating equals, people engage in a communicative action which allows them to achieve consensus on contentious issues (Agger, 1991a; Tucker, 2007).

Of central importance to Habermas is the existence of a rich, vibrant public sphere which allows different voices to be heard in the context of egalitarian communication (Tucker, 2007). He contends that new social movements, such as environmentalism, feminism and post-colonialism, provide avenues for the development of new values and identities. Uprisings such as the Arab Spring and the Occupy Movement are examples. New social movements may represent the transition from an old politics based on economic and military might to a new politics involving the promise of an enhanced quality of life, equality and greater political and social participation (Tucker, 2007). Habermas offers that 'the communicatively produced power of common convictions originates in the fact that those involved are oriented to reaching agreement and not primarily to their respective individual successes' (1977: 6), but draws attention to the structural violence utilised by political and other institutions to provide the illusion of communicative action under the cloak of strategic actions. Strategic actions, suggests Habermas, have undoubtedly increased in scope and importance in modern societies. With the capitalist mode of production, this action type, which in pre-modern societies dominates above all in foreign relations, also became permissible within society as normal(ised) for economic relations. Let us understand the force exercised through strategic action as the ability to prevent other individuals or groups from realising their interests.

In this line of reasoning, structural violence does not manifest itself *as force*; rather, largely unperceived, it blocks those communications in which convictions effective for legitimation are formed and passed on.

## REPRESSING HER CONSCIENCE

Jen is exhausted. Her manager, for the umpteenth time, had drawn her attention to the fact that profits achieved by her branch were well below the agreed targets. This was true. All the graphs proved it. Already her staff works beyond the hours they are paid for. Perhaps, she thought, the targets were unachievable. She needs Jack to sell more loans. She hopes his health will hold out. She had been noticing his wheezing was becoming more laboured of late. She knows that he does not have any more sick-leave and his family could not cope with a drop in his income. The thought passed her mind that maybe she needed to leave this job. She noticed herself repressing her concerns. After all, if she did not hold this job, someone more ruthless might take her place. She would talk with Jack and inspire him to try harder. She knows he will agree.

Hypotheses about inconspicuously working communication blocks can perhaps explain the formation of ideologies. One can give a plausible account of how convictions are formed in which subjects deceive themselves about themselves and their situation. Ideologies are, after all, illusions of reality. They are reifications of ideas outfitted with the power of common convictions. In systematically restricted communication, those involved form a conviction subjectively free from constraint, convictions which are, however, illusionary. They thereby communicatively generate a power which, as soon as it is institutionalised, can also be used against them.

Habermas extended the notion of 'lifeworld' through the identification of two 'rationalisation processes':

i) lifeworld of social, cultural and personal dimensions of human relations which are produced and coordinated through communicative acts;

ii) a 'system of markets' and states where material reproduction has become apparently independent.

He considers that the system of markets reacts adversely upon the lifeworld as a colonising process and under conditions of crisis seeks to assimilate the social tensions that stem from this perceived crisis.

For Habermas, language is a means of achieving shared meaning. The 'ideal speech' situation is one where members reach a total consensus. But actors

> never have their situation totally under control. They control neither the possibilities for mutual understanding or conflict, nor the consequences and side effects of their actions; they are … 'entangled' in their (his)stories. A given setting presents a situation in which they orient themselves and which they seek to master, according to their insights and opinions. (Habermas, 1989: 149)

One thing all critical theorists have in common is their explicit or implicit call to humanity to become more self-conscious, to exercise their sovereignty over self and to revolt against those people and conditions that are exploitative. Julia Kristeva provides an explicit example of such a call.

## Julia Kristeva (1941– ): Revolting

Julia Kristeva may be remembered for her call for the freedom to revolt: a state of permanent questioning and transformation, of change that characterises psychic life and, in the best examples, art. Revolt, she argues, is not simply about rejection and destruction, but is a necessary process of renewal and regeneration (Oliver, 2002). Among the most difficult contexts in which to observe our own participation in the oppression of others is the colonisation processes in which we are a direct or indirect beneficiary. The taken-for-granted preferences of some (unwittingly or intentionally) imposed on those who are different can become the oppression, exclusion, demonisation and even the death of others (Lal, 2002).

Among the theories that suggest that people will not (only or always) allow themselves to be treated as 'objects' of other people's thought schemas are those that come out of a subset of critical theories called 'subaltern studies'. Gayatri Spivak helps us explore these kinds of ideas further.

### Gayatri Spivak (1942– ): Speaking Out from the Margins

Gayatri Spivak is perhaps best known for her challenge to the legacies of colonialism and the related marginalisation she articulates as subalterns. Her concerns are with the working class, women and others, particularly those who are not part of the privileged European empire. Taking these ideas forward, we can recognise that people 'at the margins' are no more homogeneous in their thoughts and ways of being than the mind set of each particular critical theorist who concerns themselves with their situation. What is of specific interest in this book is the focus on the exclusionary processes that marginalise people, but we need to be aware that these people may not desire merely to be let in if entry compromises their values. They may have very good reason for refusing entry – reasons we may do well to understand. This idea will be considered further in Chapter 6.

# POSTMODERN DEVELOPMENTS

Many authors we have introduced in this chapter, along with their many unnamed but perhaps equally influential peers, do not easily fit into one scholarly category. The desire to find tidy categories of thought is itself worth reflecting on. The preoccupation with classification and ordering, as Foucault so brilliantly explains, is part of the attempts to record aspects of the world as if they exist in some objective way that can be tabled and thus controlled and controlled by imputing value, incentives and punishments that are justifiable under the specific regime of truth in operation.

The imposition of an assumed order can lead to the imposition of a seemingly immutable truth that may hide selective interests. Scholarly attention to the rise in assertiveness of more diverse voices in the organisation of our common humanity has led to the emergence of a school of thought called postmodernism. Postmodernists argue that the era described as *modernity* is in decline. This was an era in which scholars of many denominations, including critical theorists, attempted to find a universal explanation for our humanity. There is greater acknowledgement of the many different ways people make sense of their existence. Conservative people may see this as a breakdown in what they think of as values and beliefs that *ought* to be universally held. Where their ideas are fuelled by wealth and power, those ways of being human are likely to be institutionalised and imposed. Those who were excluded from the prevailing way of depicting the world may see the greater diversity of allowable ideas as a window of opportunity to be heard, to be included or to be liberated from the constraints of the universalising views of some imposed on so many. This book suggests that we need to take a deeper look at this supposed respect for greater diversity. We suggest that, in this era, people the world over are increasingly at risk of being controlled through discursive methods that embed the institutionalised logic of the market – a cloak for the imposition of a rationality that maintains and intensifies the interests of a few at the cost of the well-being of many.

Ideas of modernity are linked with the political economy and technological changes associated with the industrial revolution (Best and Kellner, 1991). Historical events – for example, the rise and fall of Nazi Germany, the collapse of communism (Seidman, 2008) and the growth of global consumerism and corporate globalisation – lead postmodernists to assert that the era of modernity has given way to a postmodern era. What is particularly helpful from this development is that the search for understanding human organisation, particularly our understanding of power, control and exploitation, cannot be explained in a mono-toned representation of history – and critical theorists do run the risk of offering contrasting causal assumptions, but often assumptions that may still rely on universalisations and suspect one-way, causal arguments. In this way, we are attracted to Spivak's notion of subalterns, people who are seen by others as 'on the margins' – in need of assimilation or demonisation by some, as stalwart resisters by others. It all depends on your theoretical perspectives!

## SWORDS TO PLOUGHSHARES: SAINTS OR SINNERS?

And many people shall go and say, Come ye, and let us go up to the mountain of the *LORD*, to the house of the God of Jacob; and he will teach us of his ways, and we will walk in his paths: for out of Zion shall go forth the law and the word of the *LORD* from Jerusalem. And he shall judge among the nations, and shall rebuke many people: and they shall beat their swords into ploughshares, and their spears into pruning hooks: nation shall not lift up sword against nations, neither shall they learn war any more. (Isaiah 2: 3–4)

Peter, Adrian and Sam were pleased they had succeeded in breaching the fence to the government's Communications Security Bureau at Waihopai. They had successfully spiked the inflatable plastic dome that covered one of the special satellite dishes. They hoped that they had achieved a disruption to the flow of information they believed was serving war. They erected an altar and sang hymns of thanksgiving. They were arrested (follow their story at http://ploughshares.org.nz). Are they to be thought of as heroes or criminals/saints or sinners?

Because, argue postmodernists, society is a concept that groups heterogeneous individuals with very different needs, desires and values, the state seeks to control whole populations by generating and imposing assumed shared cultural norms and values through a universal set of social principles that shape thought and conduct. Among those with a critical orientation derived from the traditions introduced above, some critical theorists concern themselves with the extent to which control of this heterogeneous population is now exerted directly or indirectly in the marketplace. The marketplace is purported by its neo-liberal advocates as the means to emancipation.

The reconfiguration of the organising principles for humanity – individual needs, desires and identities – become shaped not through culture, class or other socially defined norms, but through the supposedly free-market opportunities to shape (and earn) one's status in life. Social conformity, or loyalty to work, for example, is now to be achieved not through disciplines of the family, tribe, church or state, but through seduction to the belief that freedom is to be found through market participation. Particular lifestyles, dreams and identities are marketed through advertising campaigns and the achievement of which is simply a matter of buying the right products, or engaging in the right leisure activities, or decorating your home and dressing yourself in the latest fashions. Unequal outcomes, unless demonstrably linked to structural impediments, are deemed to be the outcome of diligence and commitment to the work ethic.

We are not positing that market forces are the *only* disciplinary force at play. The state still has a controlling function. The forms of disciplinary control used by the state to organise whole populations associated with the modern era are now, however, reserved largely to manage specific members of the population who cannot be controlled through the market: the poor or those who are not sufficiently seduced to engage in preferred lifestyles; for example, those who persist in bad eating habits or act as criminals (Seidman, 2008). However, when examined more closely, even here the institutionalised logics of markets are widely applied. 'Bad' eating habits, smoking or refusing (unacceptable) employment are represented as costly drains on the rest of us – and the stretch of concerns is quite elastic. In one era, mothers supported by welfare payments may be deemed a drain on the public purse and pressed to take up any employment – no matter how stressful. In an era of high unemployment, however, they may be viewed as 'taking the jobs of men' (implicitly categorised as family breadwinners). Special opprobrium is reserved for single mothers or other welfare recipients who resist taking up the most inappropriate of employment. They risk being cast adrift to fend for their family in whatever way they can muster.

Because postmodernist theorists point out that multiple values, beliefs, desires and lifestyle choices coexist, they argue that it is not possible to use a single universal authoritative theoretical standpoint to analyse social conditions. Instead, postmodern research is based upon a case-by-case, localised analysis of an individual's perception of a situation. Postmodernist researchers draw on discourse and text analysis to understand the experiences and perceptions of the individual (Alvesson and Deetz, 2000). This is because postmodernists hold that individual identity and experience is discursively constructed, and therefore how an individual experiences their own reality must also be understood through discursive techniques. From a postmodernist perspective, the concept of a single, easily defined self is deemed to be an illusion that has been crafted through dominant discourses expressed through seductive messages in the marketplace, enticing people to conform to certain ways of being. These dominant discourses suppress power relations in society. Individuals normalise themselves to dominant discourses when they purchase the right products and design the self in accordance with the seductive messages.

Postmodernists are concerned with uncovering dominant discourses that privilege certain groups' experiences, while silencing the voices of marginalised groups and therefore devaluing their lived experiences. They do so by deconstructing text and language (as described above) in order to expose the politics embedded in language and text and in the processes of constructing and validating particular identities over others. It is through exposing the politics in dominant discourses, and enabling the voices of the marginalised to be heard, that resistance to more powerful discourses is to be achieved (Alvesson and Deetz, 2000).

# INFLUENTIAL RADICALS: HUMAN LIFE AS OPEN-ENDED STORIES: ŽIŽEK, BOJE AND SHIVA

## Slavoj Žižek (1949– ): Violations and Violence

Slavoj Žižek is concerned with violations and violence – or violations as a form of violence. He argues that ever-increasing, 'new' categories/labels of sociological thought are being constructed in order to provide individuals with a sense of security and order. He further posits that these new categories of 'reality' (postmodern, post-structural, post-colonial and so forth) are just new labels placed on existing ideas. Žižek asserts that activism/critique paradoxically acts to reinforce the predominant ideology, by acting as the 'necessary critics' of any ruling class. He further asserts that, although this critical element may be effective enough to 'convince' the population of its 'right', it will never be enough to move the population to act.

Žižek argues that in order to expose the contradictions of the predominant group, you must act according to the principles of the dominant group, exaggerating these principles to the point that the contradictions/ridiculous nature become obvious. This argument is not incongruous with critical analysis, but is contradictory to the way in which this analysis has traditionally been presented by critical theorists. Žižek insists on the possibility of a space 'outside ideology, an empty space whose boundaries must be continuously redrawn' (Beverungen, 2011: 145). Scholarly activists David Boje and Vandana Shiva provide some great examples of what might be done in those empty spaces to invigorate our consciousness and our conscience.

## David Boje (1947– ): The Drama in the (Ante) Narrative

David Boje is a contemporary management educator who has created many examples of how contradictions can be exaggerated in order to bring our minds to focus. (In)Famous for his story-telling, Boje opens critical pragmatism to scholars in critical theory. He recasts the American pragmatists (particularly the work of James Dewey) in a more critical way. Boje's interest in the application of the insights of quantum physics to the understanding of organisations and work is a way into the contribution of Bakhtin and Nietzsche and other theorists rarely but perhaps usefully read more in management studies.

## Vandana Shiva (1952– ): An Exemplary Practitioner

Critical theory is concerned with the amplification of praxis. Of the many scholarly activists in contemporary times, Shiva's creativity is matched only by the power of the corporations she challenges. We will meet her many times in this book, sometimes directly, and sometime indirectly. The culmination of the exposure of corporate power and the extent to which we are all at risk in this contemporary form of colonisation are demonstrated in her courageous works.

Žižek, Boje and Shiva are among many contemporary critical thinkers whose work demonstrates the emancipatory ideals of critical theorists. The out-workings of these ideas in praxis, however, are not (yet) widespread enough to address the significant issues of injustice, insecurity and environmental degradation facing humanity that critical theorists link to the system of development intensifying the world over. What *use*, then, is this engagement with the ideas of critical theories if their intent is to transform the world, but so many people on Earth do not enjoy a sustainable way of life and the environment for many is dangerously toxic?

# CONCLUSION: PULLING IT ALTOGETHER

This chapter has introduced some of the people who have influenced the growing discipline of critical management studies. We have introduced some of the complex ideas that can be examined for insights into our organisational practices. Some of these will be developed further in the chapters to come. Our own preferred style is a focus on meaning making and the critical deconstruction of the 'taken for granted' in organisational contexts as we understand them. Mary Boyce and Stanley Deetz are among those who point to the usefulness of *de-reification* as a tool for taking a critical position on values deeply naturalised in the common acceptance of capitalism and democracy as primary organising principles for humanity. These principles have been reified into an ideology and some might suggest taken as dogma. For better or worse, these principles are being intensified the world over as discussed more fully in Chapter 3. Sometimes, perhaps paradoxically, the intensification of capitalism and the imposition of democracy as ideologies of freedom are achieved through some very violent means. These means are resourced through a complex web of organisational interactions involving police, armies, confiscations, taxes (imposition or evasion) and the administrative functionaries that empower them. Corporations are in the thick of it.

The analysis of organising and organisations undertaken by critical management scholars contrasts significantly with the conventional and long-held functionalist and positivistic approaches to these topics. Functional and positivist analyses of organisation, for example, are based on improving organisational outputs and profits, which in turn are often based on narrow definitions of humanity, efficiency and effectiveness (Alvesson and Willmott, 1992). In contrast, critical scholars question these assumptions about human nature, efficiency and effectiveness, and locate existing relationships in the historical, sociopolitical and economic context. The basic critical premise is that overarching structures impose societal control in such a way as to reinforce the position of privileged groups in society at the expense of all others, and increasingly the environment that sustains us. The hope of critical theorists is that, through critical examination and action, the disempowering social relationships and the structural manifestations of these relationships can be changed to be fairer and more just. A simplified explanation is that critical theorists look beyond taken-for-granted assumptions and question whether accepted practices are working towards equitable outcomes for all stakeholders in society. In the following chapters, we draw out and elaborate the terms introduced in this chapter to explore the wider sociopolitical and economic context that managers and employees now negotiate in their working lives.

## TALK BOX

Workers must work. They must work under the conditions provided. If they do not, the power of the state, the force of the police and the silence or anger of the citizens can be turned against them – or so we will see in the many stories we tell in this book. Employers can expect a ready supply of employees. Much effort of the state supports the fabrication of employees that can fill the labour needs of employers. Institutions for management education are a significant part in this process of producing reliable functionaries and robust processes through which we organise our relationships with each other and with Earth. Critical theorists provide many tools and insights to enhance our understanding of these dynamics. Exploring these ideas is hard work and can unsettle the ideas about the world we take much for granted. Some, starting with Socrates, suggest that it is our obligation to live an enquiring life. If directly or indirectly, we are implicated in the injury or death of others, if only through our (wilful) ignorance, for whom is this, or ought it be, a concern?

## Tricky Questions

- Humans order their ideas in categories: rocks, trees, animals, people, companies, economies and angels, for example. Can you detect the defining boundaries of their 'categories'?
- We can re-think the meaning or the use of some things. A chair can be a throne. A table can be an altar. A rock, a tree, a table or a person can be re-thought as a marketable product. By and large, these entities exist as material things. We can invest the material object with a variety of meanings and values. Can you think of other examples where 'a thing' can be given many meanings? How are actions influenced by the meanings we invest or accept?
- 'Social fabrications' or 'fictive entities' are not 'real things' in the way rocks, tables, trees or people are – no matter what meaning we invest in them. They are 'ideas' that come to be experienced as real things by our enactment of them. They 'feel real' because we have learned to treat them as such. They become seemingly real as we enact them. 'The economy' feels real as 'it' can demand job losses for 'its' very survival. But, no matter how real it feels, the economy is an idea only. The idea is manifest only through other ideas – ideas about what can be owned and traded and how, ideas that become the rules for trade and exchange. Can you name and explain other organising principles that 'feel real'?
- What 'values' and 'disciplines' are invested and exerted in and through these ideas? What (un)truth is hidden in these ideas?
- Why is it useful or tricky to ask: *what* are 'managers'?
- To what extent are students of management encouraged to think historically and politically?
- Who benefits from designing management education and management degrees that are ahistorical and apolitical?
- Why does management education concentrate on narrowly focused profit or commercial goals? Who benefits from producing this kind of graduate?
- Why might critical theorists take issue with the phrase 'the organisation thinks' or 'the market demands'? What is this an example of?

# ADDITIONAL RESOURCES

Berger, P. and Luckmann, T. (1966) *The Social Construction of Reality: A Treatise in the Sociology of Knowledge*. New York: Anchor.

Breen, R. and Goldthorpe, J.H. (1999) Class inequality and meritocracy: a critique of Saunders and an alternative analysis. *Psychology and Health*, 50 (1): 1–27.

Burr, V. (2003) *Social Constructionism*, 2nd edn. East Sussex, UK: Routledge.

Forester, J. (1985) Introduction. In J. Forester (ed.), *Critical Theory and Public Life*. Cambridge, MA: MIT Press. pp. ix–xvii.

Giddens, A. (1971) *Capitalism and Modern Social Theory: An Analysis of the Writings of Marx, Durkheim and Weber*. Cambridge: Cambridge University Press.

Giroux, H.A. (2007) Utopian thinking in dangerous times: critical pedagogy and the project of educated hope. In R.J.F. Day, G. De Peuter and M. Cote (eds), *Utopian Pedagogy: Radical Experiments against Neoliberal Globalization*. Toronto: University of Toronto Press. pp. 25–52.

Herman, E.S. and Chomsky, N. (1994) *Manufacturing Consent: The Political Economy of the Mass Media*. London: Vintage Press.

Honneth, A. (2008) *Reification: A New Look at an Old Idea*. Oxford: Oxford University Press.

Mannheim, K. (1959) *Ideology and Utopia: An Introduction to the Sociology of Knowledge*. New York: Harcourt Brace.

Marshall, G. (1998) *Oxford Dictionary of Sociology*. Oxford: Oxford University Press.

Mullard, M. (2004) *The Politics of Globalisation and Polarisation*. Cheltenham: Edward Elgar.

Ogbor, J. (2001) Critical theory and the hegemony of corporate culture. *Journal of Organizational Change Management*, 14 (6): 590–608.

O'Neill, J. (1977) *On Critical Theory*. London: Heinemann.

O'Neill, J. (1986) The disciplinary society: from Weber to Foucault. *British Journal of Sociology*, 37 (1): 42–60.

Pozo, L.M. (2007) The roots of hegemony: the mechanisms of class accommodation and the emergence of the nation-people. *Capital and Class*, 31: 55–88.

Rasmussen, D.M. (ed.) (1996) *Handbook of Critical Theory*. Oxford: Blackwell.

Ritzer, G. (2013) *Contemporary Sociological Theory and its Classical Roots: The Basics*, 4th edn. St Louis, MO: McGraw-Hill.

Saul, J.R. (1997) *The Unconscious Civilization*. Melbourne: Penguin.

Steingard, D.S. and Fitzgibbons, D.E. (1995) Challenging the juggernaut of globalization: a manifesto for academic praxis. *Journal of Organizational Change Management*, 8 (4): 30–54.

Vroom, V.H. (1964) *Work and Motivation*. New York: Wiley.

Wee, C. and Pelczar, M. (2008) Descartes' dualism and contemporary dualism. *Southern Journal of Philosophy*, 46 (1): 145.

# REFERENCES

Adamson, W.L. (1980) *Hegemony and Revolution: A Study of Antonio Gramsci's Political and Cultural Theory*. Berkley, CA: University of California Press.

Agger, B. (1991a) Critical theory, post structuralism, postmodernism: their socio-logical relevance. *Annual Review of Sociology*, 17: 105–31.

Agger, B. (1991b) *A Critical Theory of Public Life: Knowledge, Discourse and Politics in an Age of Decline*. London: Falmer Press.

Alvesson, M. and Deetz, S. (1999) Critical theory and postmodernism: approaches to organizational studies. In S.R. Clegg and C. Hardy (eds), *Studying Organization: Theory and Method*. London: Sage. pp. 185–211.

Alvesson, M. and Deetz, S. (2000) *Doing Critical Management Research*. London: Sage.

Alvesson, M. and Willmott, H. (1992) On the idea of emancipation in management and organization studies. *Academy of Management Review*, 17 (3): 1–20.

Bagenal, F. (2009) Teaching as Hypatia of Alexandria. AAS Committee on the Status of Women (www.aas.org/cswa/status/2009/JANUARY2009/Hypatia.html; retrieved 7 October 2013).

Berger, P. and Pullman, S. (1965) Reification and the sociological critique of con-sciousness. *History and Theory*, 4: 195–208.

Berman, R. (2001) Adorno's politics. In N. Gibson and A. Rubin (eds), *Adorno: A Critical Reader*. Malden, MA: Blackwell. pp. 110–31.

Best, S. and Kellner, D. (1991) *Postmodern Theory: Critical Interrogations*. New York: Guilford Press.

Beverungen, A. (2011) Ideology. In M. Tadajewski, P. MacLaran, E. Parsons and M. Parker (eds), *Key Concepts in Critical Management Studies*. London: Sage. pp. 143–6.

Bottomore, T., Harris, L., Kiernan, V.G. and Miliband, R. (1983) *A Dictionary of Marxist Thought*. Oxford: Blackwell.

Bronner, S.E. (2011) *Critical Theory: A Very Short Introduction*. Oxford: Oxford University Press.

Bronner, S.E. and Kellner, D.M. (eds) (1989) *Critical Theory and Society: A Reader*. New York: Routledge.

Cluley, R. (2011) Critical theory. In M. Tadajewski, P. MacLaran, E. Parsons and M. Parker (eds), *Key Concepts in Critical Management Studies*. London: Sage. pp. 92–5.

Dunne, S. (2011) Commodity fetishism. In M. Tadajewski, P. MacLaran, E. Parsons and M. Parker (eds), *Key Concepts in Critical Management Studies*. London: Sage. pp. 50–3.

Fairfax NZ News (2013) Sea protest law challenged (www.stuff.co.nz/national/politics/8527204/Sea-protest-law-challenged; retrieved 27 September 2013).

Foucault, M. (1977) *Discipline and Punish: The Birth of the Prison*, trans. Alan Sheridan. Harmondsworth: Penguin.

Fromm, E. (1989) Politics and psychoanalysis. In S.E. Bronner and D.M. Kellner (eds), *Critical Theory and Society: A Reader*. New York: Routledge. pp. 213–18.

Gramsci, A. (1971) *Selections from the Prison Notebooks*, trans. Q. Hoare and G. Nowell-Smith. London: Lawrence and Wishart.

Habermas, J. (1977) Hannah Arendt's communications concept of power. *Social Research*, 44 (1): 3–23.

Habermas, J. (1989) *The Theory of Communicative Action*, vol. 2: *Lifeworld and System: A Critique of Functionalist Reason*, trans. T. McCarthy. Cambridge: Polity Press.

Hancock, P. (2011) Dialectics. In M. Tadajewski, P. MacLaran, E. Parsons and M. Parker (eds), *Key Concepts in Critical Management Studies*. London: Sage. pp. 100–103.

Hoy, D.C. and McCarthy, T. (1994) *Critical Theory*. Cambridge, MA: Blackwell.

Jermier, J. (1985) When the sleeper wakes: a short story extending themes in radical organization theory. *Journal of Management*, 11 (2): 67–80.

Kellner, D. (2001) T.W. Adorno and the dialectics of mass culture. In N. Gibson and A. Rubin (eds), *Adorno: A Critical Reader*. Malden, MA: Blackwell. pp. 86–109.

Klimecki, R. and Willmott, H. (2011) Hegemony. In M. Tadajewski, P. MacLaran, E. Parsons and M. Parker (eds), *Key Concepts in Critical Management Studies*. London: Sage. pp. 131–2.

Lal, V. (2002) *Empire of Knowledge: Culture and Plurality in the Global Economy*. London: Pluto Press.

Lukács, G. (1971) *History and Class Consciousness: Studies in Marxist Dialectics*, trans. R. Livingstone. London: Merlin Press.

Lyotard, J.F. (1993) *The Postmodern Condition*. Minneapolis, MN: University of Minnesota Press.

Marcuse, H. (1991) *One Dimensional Man: Studies in the Ideology of the Advanced Industrial Society*. London: Routledge.

Marx, K. (1867) *Capital*, vol. 1 (www.marxists.org/archive/marx/works/1867-c1/ch07.htm; retrieved 27 September 2013).

Oliver, J. (2002) *The Portable Kristeva*. New York: Columbia University Press.

Pickford, H.W. (2001) The dialectic of theory and praxis: on late Adorno. In N. Gibson and A. Rubin (eds), *Adorno: A Critical Reader*. Malden, MA: Blackwell. pp. 312–340.

Preston, J. and Sinha, S. (2012) Video shows South African police shooting miners. 'The Lede Blog', *The New York Times* (http://thelede.blogs.nytimes.com/2012/08/16/video-of-miners-shot-by-south-african-police/; retrieved 27 September 2013).

Schweitzer, D. (1991) Marxist theories of alienation and reification: the response to capitalism, state socialism and the advent of postmodernity. *International Journal of Sociology and Social Policy*, 11 (6–8): 27–42.

Scoop (2013) Waihopai Ploughshares' Court of Appeal hearing (www.scoop.co.nz/stories/PO1305/S00096/waihopai-ploughshares-court-of-appeal-hearing.htm; retrieved 27 September 2013).

Seidman, S. (2008) *Contested Knowledge: Social Theory Today*. Oxford: Blackwell.

Simon, R. (1991) *Gramsci's Political Thought: An introduction*. London: Lawrence and Wishart.

Tucker, K.H. (2007) Ideology and social movements: the contribution of Habermas. *Social Enquiry*, 59 (1): 30–47.

Ward, A. (2006) *The Classic Thinkers: Kant, the Three Critiques*. Cambridge: Polity Press.

# 3 NEO-LIBERALISM, GLOBALISATION AND THE GLOBAL ECONOMY

## Learning Objectives

In this chapter, you are invited to reflect on:

- the form of reasoning that is encouraged in your readings of globalisation;
- the extent to which any discussion of globalisation reaches beyond economic expression in your other studies;
- the extent to which growth of the (global) economy demonstrates the trickle-down effect promised by its advocates;
- how we, as managers, employees, customers, consumers and citizens, are being invited or required to manage our organisations to support the growth of the global economy;
- how far we ourselves will go to serve the global economy, and under what circumstances and at whose expense;
- how responsible you believe you are for ensuring organisational success is achieved without human or environmental sacrifice.

## CRITICAL CONCEPTS

*Globalisation* of the *neo-liberal* model of development is argued as a form of domination that engenders and intensifies a form of *hegemony* that requires *transformation* if the values of *emancipation* promoted in *democracies* are to be realised universally. Globalising *techniques* of system-preserving *control* are generated from *prevailing institutional logics* packaged into an *ideology* that more critical readers might call a *dogma*, while non-critical readers simply consider these 'normal'.

# INTENSIFYING CAPITALISM GLOBALLY: WHAT NEED FOR DEMOCRACY?

If the global financial crises [2008 onwards] put any development model on trial, it was the free-market or neoliberal model [of capitalism], which emphasises a small state, deregulation, private ownership, and low taxes. (Birdsall and Fukuyama, 2011: 52)

Birdsall and Fukuyama (2011) suggest that, in the first decade of the twenty-first century, the free-market or neo-liberal model of capitalist development was put on trial. They write that the financial crisis that was thought to have peaked in 2009 underscored the instability of capitalist systems that regularly produces faultless victims. For many people of Cyprus, Greece, Spain, Portugal and Italy, however, the repercussions of this particular crisis for capitalists are a long way from being over. For these people, as for many people bereft of a reliable or safe livelihood under the specific conditions of capitalism of their time and place, capitalism *is* their crisis. This is not to say that only capitalist systems of trade and exchange generate exploitation of people and planet. It is the type of exploitation endemic in the form of capitalism intensifying globally that we are concerned with in this book.

Despite the systemic injustice and environmental degradation associated with this form of global development, the system of free markets is still widely promoted as the most effective and efficient means of generating wealth. Its underlying principles continue to inform the related disciplines of organisation, management and control. These values and principles are rarely made explicit in functionally oriented management classrooms. Instead, students are generally invited to explore structures and functions for ways of improving organisational efficiency and economic growth through their chosen management field of study, be it human resource management, marketing, accounting, auditing, economics or finance. The economy or the market is largely conceived of as a mechanical object – a bit like a well-wound clock. The hands of this clock appear to be moving humanity towards what Kivisto (2011: 45) sees as 'a single economic entity supported and sustained by a shifting group of strong nation states that constitute the wealthy core'.

## TICKING ALONG TO JUST REWARDS

'We are now enthralled by a new all-powerful clockmaker god – market place – and his archangel, technology. Trade is the market place's miraculous cure for all that ails us. And globalisation is the Eden or paradise into which the just shall be welcomed on judgment day' (Button, 1997).

The ever greater integration of nations and economies associated with the term 'globalisation' is often presented as a recent phenomenon and as the inevitable trajectory of the march of progress that will bring salvation to all based on freeing markets, knocking down trade barriers and ensuring the easy flow of capital. Fasenfest (2010: 630) warns that this may be one of the 'greatest misconceptions of this era', concerns shared by Barton (2011), Hart (2010) and many more. Thus, we are left with an interesting paradox at the heart of the globalisation debates (Cohen and Kennedy, 2007). Powerful universalising trends appear to exhort humanity to greater expressions of freedom – and yet implementation appears to curtail the opportunities to flourish for many.

# GLOBALISATION: ONE WORLD READY OR NOT – BUT WHOSE WORLD?

We are on the verge of a global transformation. All we need is the right major crisis and the nations will accept the new order.

David Rockefeller

David Rockefeller, businessman and philanthropist of significance, is the grandson of oil tycoon John D. Rockefeller. In his education, and in his adult professional and private life, he was well integrated into the powerful economic and political networks of the USA. He was given many platforms from which to express his visions, platforms that not many less well-endowed citizens could hope to grace. Critical analysts might ask: what is it to build a new world order as Rockefeller hopes to achieve? Whose interest might be implicitly promoted, protected or enhanced in a 'new order' led by the economically supreme of the world? Whose interests are at risk of being sacrificed and how are such sacrifices justified?

The success of wealthy Americans is often attributed to the universal achievability of the 'American Dream': the opportunity to generate and control vast amounts of personal wealth, and with it greater political and social influence than any mere voter in a democracy. This idealised 'American Dream' is often assumed by many people in America and beyond as a desirable blueprint for a 'universal dream'. It is a dream expressed in part as the American entrepreneurial economic model that stresses free trade and uninhibited competition. It is a dream, however, that for many has been a nightmare and, according to Slater (2008: 48), sets the scene for a 'seemingly consensual American hegemony'. The displaced indigenous peoples, the imported slaves of the nineteenth century and the exploited wage labour of the twentieth century can testify to the dark side of this dream (Lal, 2002). This dream does have its critics. American novelists, such as Harriet Beecher Stowe in *Uncle Tom's Cabin*, F. Scott Fitzgerald in *The Great Gatsby*, John Steinbeck in *The Grapes of Wrath* and Upton Sinclair in *The Jungle*, provide disturbing insight into the exploitation of others in the creation and consumption of wealth in a period from early settlement leading up to the most famous economic depression of the 1930s, known as the 'Great Depression'. This 'Great Depression' exacerbated the already significant poverty and distress of many people. It is a form of poverty and distress that has resulted from an opportunistic economic system purported to be a beacon of freedom and opportunity.

At the beginning of the twenty-first century, a series of financial crises for the poor and vulnerable has generated a variety of protests at different times, but such protests have not driven the neo-liberal agenda off the boil. Rather, the principles and values of the neo-liberalists have intensified in their scope and reach to what can only be described as an ideology that represents a positive and transformative process for all involved (Quiggan, 2005; Tiemstra, 2007; Raffer, 2011). It may be argued that the preferences of the neo-liberals have been elevated to the point of being a dogma to which all of humanity is required to subject itself. People the world over are bombarded with pressure to cut costs and improve efficiency in order to attract investment or International Monetary Fund (IMF) loans. This pressure is an exhortation for a worldwide ordering of the opportunities and struggles for most beings on the planet (Stiglitz, 2010; Maxton, 2011; Rickards, 2011; Hiscock, 2012). It is this pressure or force that we are calling 'globalisation'. It is depicted by Barkin (2002: 132) as a 'crusade to shape a single international economy'. The intensification of this crusade remains an influence on the lifeworld that Husserl (1936) was concerned with in his work. It is an influence we are expressing as the intensification of the *prevailing institutional logic* of capitalism now dominated by giant corporations whose power and influence eclipse that of many a nation-state (Stiglitz, 2010; Chomsky, 2013). It is not a new world order as such, but an intensification of the trajectory towards the world order that the elites, such as the Rockefeller family, still worship. If the Rockefellers, Duponts and Rothschilds represent the 'old' money supporting this crusade, they have now been joined by 'new' money such as the Walton family, the Koch brothers, the Mars family and individuals such as Sheldon Adelson and Rupert Murdoch, all of whom are influencing legal and political institutions through funding mechanisms that are pressing a radically conservative business agenda.

Interestingly, there is a movement afoot among a subset of the super-rich who seem to recognise an alternative use for at least some of their amassed fortunes. Starting in 2010, the Gates, along with Warren Buffet, have begun to coax, goad or cajole at least 90 of their wealthy brethren into signing a pledge to give away at least 50 per cent of their wealth during their lifetimes or upon their death to 'better the world' (*Forbes Magazine,* online). The 'market' is seen as both 'the place' and 'the leader' for emancipation. Furthermore, the commitment of much smaller investors may also be harnessed, where each of us can donate to programmes of aid or invest in the financing of small entrepreneurial businesses seen as the remedy to endemic poverty the world over.

The story of the globalisation of wealth and power is a long one. The reach beyond one's own patch, however, may be traced through many histories. Many such narratives have entailed violence, destruction, the confiscation of land and the enslavement of people. We do not have space in this chapter to cover the pillage and control that can be traced, for example, to the activities of the Vikings, the Romans, the Visigoths and others before and since them. We are keeping in mind the ancient and contemporary tribal wars on all continents over access to land, water and labour and the external interests in them. We do not dismiss these histories in our thoughts, and we will revisit them in various parts of this book. We are concerned in this chapter, however, with the many ways current corporate wealth has been enriched in the long established process of globalisation with its alliances in various imperial and colonising epochs, and how this story is now being projected forward.

Do corporations have any fealty to governments or nations? Are the governors of our nations mere handmaidens to corporate interests? Are the corporations now so powerful that a form of global governance is necessary? Would such governance be formed to serve the well-being of all people and the planet or simply a new, perhaps more sophisticated way to oppress? Would such governance be disproportionately guided by corporate interests thinly disguised as stakeholder interest, an illusion of control dressed in diffused and fragmented influence and offered as a substitute for citizen control of the lifeworld? Asking such questions expands our consciousness and provides exercise for our conscience as students of the disciplines of critical enquiry. These questions 'sit behind' the more specific investigations into the global intensification of the system of neo-liberalism we introduced in Chapter 1, an institutional logic that gives material expression to a system that does not serve all people equally well and is generating great risks to the viability of Earth's capacity to support life.

We take up the story of capitalist expansion in the main as it developed after the Second World War. This history itself is, of course, but one of many ways to slice and dice the past. As an already given story, it might be told through many perspectives. We posit that the predominant version of this story is formalised through an Anglo-American orientation to the institutions, techniques, systems and methods that have come to dominate the direction and control of national, corporate and individual interests the world over. This Anglo-American orientation is no longer as pure as it was during the past century. China, India, Africa, Latin America and the Middle East are regions which have committed to vigorous engagement with this form of globalisation and the outcomes of their engagement cannot yet be properly assessed (Sennett, 2006; Rickards, 2011). The principles and values of this form of globalisation are gaining a foothold in many places where previous regimes or traditional lifestyles have become unsettled. We can think of Burma and Mongolia among others. We thus open this chapter with a US/Eurocentric start. We think this beginning is justifiable in light of the origins of charters that enabled the activities of corporations in these jurisdictions.

The reach, grip and impact of increasingly powerful corporations on the lives of people and on the planet are the reason for choosing this as our starting point for our discussion about globalisation. The increasing integration of other influences that support and endorse the reach of the logic that sustains these corporations and insinuates them into all aspects of human organisation is of significant concern to those who value universal emancipation. Ultimately, it may not matter if these corporations fly the flag of American, European, Asian or African identities if their operating logics are largely the same.

# NEO-LIBERALISM: A NATURALISING TURN IN THE DISCOURSE OF POWER

In 1944, nearing the close of the Second World War, 730 delegates representing all 44 Allied nations met at the Mount Washington Hotel in New Hampshire at what is known as the Bretton Woods Conference. The deliberations resulted in the formation of the General Agreement on Trade and Tariffs (GATT), the IMF and the World Bank. The GATT was designed to encourage international trade. The IMF was devised to develop and manage an international monetary system to facilitate such international trade and to assist nations with balance of payments issues (Fritz-Krockow and Ramlogan, 2007). The World Bank was mandated to facilitate the reconstruction of Europe and to focus on long-term economic development and structural issues (Del Castillo, 2008). At their outset, these institutions were proactive in developing the Keynesian macro-level framework that many democratic Western nations adopted after the Second World War and up until the 1980s. This system is frequently described in the literature as the Keynesian-welfare compromise (Giddens, 1998).

In their application of Keynesian styled macro-level management, many governments increasingly regulated the activities of the marketplace. They involved themselves in various forms of wealth redistribution, such as state-provided healthcare services and partially or wholly subsidised incomes for the unemployed. They sought full employment policies, linked real wage rises to productivity gains, and stimulated the economy through *fiscal* and *monetary* policies (Drache, 1996). Until the early 1970s, continued economic growth and prosperity were attributed to this form of macro-level economic management. By the mid-1970s, however, the world economy was in recession. Interest rates were in the middle to high teens, price increases were rampant, and world economies were slowing down to a crawl. Many nations experienced trade and budget deficits, rising inflation and unemployment, falling profits and productivity, and a decrease in consumer demand (Boyer, 1988).

A number of events were thought to have caused this recession. Most often named are the 'oil shocks' of the 1970s when Middle Eastern oil countries formed a cartel (the Organisation of Petroleum Exporting Countries or OPEC) in order to control the price of their oil better. In response, calls for wage increases were placed alongside claims about decreasing employee productivity, concerns about increased competition from newly industrialised nations, and a fear that mass markets had reached saturation point (Piore and Sable, 1984). Critics of such analyses argued that these concerns were highlighted, discussed and presented in the media in such a way as to create a sense of economic crisis, a crisis that would need urgent attention, a crisis that could only be addressed through the radical structural adjustment of Western economies. A new type of politician was to emerge in the form of Ronald Reagan in the US and Margaret Thatcher in the UK (Grady and Harvie, 2011).

So emerged the Washington consensus: a group of economists, politicians and journalists who argued for less government involvement and more freedom for the market. Global institutions such as the International Monetary Fund and the World Bank joined the chorus. All of them provided a renewed sense of energy to US foreign policy, which encouraged other countries to adopt the American model of democracy and freedom, with liberalised markets (Maxton, 2011: 14).

'There Is No Alternative' became an often-used refrain. This mantra became known as the TINA principle and was skilfully established in the minds of the public. It helped embed ever more deeply the now generally taken-for-granted logic of global development, a development seen almost solely in economic terms. Most recently, in the US, we have seen the looming 'fiscal cliff' where unpaid national debt would leave the country bankrupt and wreak havoc among world banking centres. In only the past two years, we have seen 'austerity measures' sweeping across Europe and South America, resulting in millions of poor and working-class citizens taking to the streets in protest against their own government's actions.

What now seems like a particularly radical historic change in the economic direction of the major capitalist nations, however, warrants a deeper enquiry, and it is to this we now turn our attention. It requires us to take a step back in time to think about the influence of the neo-classical economists who were about to become very attractive to policy-makers the world over. It now seems remarkable that a small group of men could wield such a powerful turn in the direction of global affairs. But influence the turn of events they did. These scholars were drawing upon the classic economic theories to critique the then prevailing Keynesian-welfare state ideas of management and public policy. They sought to understand how government macro-level monetary and fiscal policies, legislative frameworks, and the way industries organise their labour-management policies affect individual behaviour. Among the group of influential thinkers of that time were Milton Friedman and Friedrich Hayek.

Friedman had already been developing and publishing his theories during the period following the Second World War when governments in many industrial-ised countries were putting much effort into rebuilding the countries so devas-tated by war. Many social programmes had been devised to cope with the need for employment, to care for the ill and the injured and to provide for the education of the generations of workers that would be needed for the rebuild-ing of the economy and the management of its supporting infrastructure. The welfare of the people was expressed as 'social security' and was to be seen as the hallmark of a democratic society. Much of this development needed to be paid for through taxation. The wealthy and elite, many of whom had profited handsomely from supplying war materials, saw this as a direct theft of the wealth they had earned. Friedman's ideas provided strong support in formalis-ing such concerns in the mind of the public and the hands of policy-makers.

Hayek helped consolidate such ideas by *naturalising* the concerns of critics of the welfare costs. He made a distinction between fundamental laws of nature and government initiated laws that set rules of behaviour. He believed that people naturally take advantage of opportunity for personal gain. When they apply this natural inclination to generate wealth within the boundaries of the law, they have the right to the resulting proceeds. Hayek advocated that gov-ernment laws and policies aimed at redistributing wealth to those who did not generate it contravened the fundamental individual rights to own and control what one could legitimately gain through market activities. At the political/ pragmatic level, these efforts were embodied in Roosevelt's New Deal in the US and the Marshal Plan in Europe.

It is more than likely that the political and social preferences and prejudices of European liberal philosophers influenced Friedman's argument for the idea of a free market as a logical extension of the individual freedom so prized in eighteenth-century Europe and in the modern USA – the 'Land of the Free' – an escape from the various political and ethical considerations framing European entrepreneurs experienced as constraints on their activities. The Land of the Free offered a fresh start, too, for many disenchanted, disenfranchised or undesirable Europeans who could be seduced or exiled to make a new life on its chain gangs, production lines or in the fields to be broken in for future agricultural expansion.

Friedman makes explicit linkages across the concepts of free markets, democracy and individual freedom. He advocates a seamless pursuit of both economic and individual freedom to achieve his view of 'true' political freedom. His socioeconomic approach draws on Adam Smith's theories through his references to individual self-interest and the workings of 'the invisible hand' of markets. However, Friedman remarkably ignores the guiding moral philosophy that was the cornerstone of Smith's work in *The Theory of Moral Sentiment*. Smith's theories were largely about moral philosophy infused with 'principles of justice, tolerance, and fairness that needed to be upheld' (Maxton, 2011: 6). The invisible hand worked only when predicated on a set of shared values. After all, Adam Smith was a Professor of Moral Philosophy at the University of Glasgow, Scotland. His writings reflect that economics must be built upon a firm foundation of shared values. Most of the 'free market capitalists' we see today have conveniently overlooked this fact. For example, Friedman's work too contains what might be considered 'moral principles', but they look little like those of Smith's. He assumes that under his prescribed conditions the market will inherently benefit the majority of society economically, while manifesting democratic ideals for all its citizens and that the free flow of the markets will distribute just rewards according to contribution.

While Friedman and Hayek were generating theories that revived and amplified the liberal economic values and principles of the earlier Europeans, the political elite of Europe and the US were identifying a new threat on the horizon. A communist global take-over was feared. After the Second World War, the US and the USSR came to represent two opposing economic and political perspectives of what is best for the common good. As a result, in the 'West', any policies that even remotely related to government influence on social welfare were often demonised, particularly in American society (Stiglitz, 2010).

By the latter half of the twentieth century, Friedman had a commanding influence in macro-economics. He received a Nobel Prize in Economics in 1976. In a 2006 tribute, *The Economist* described him as 'the most influential economist of the second half of the 20th century' (para. 3). In his seminal book, *Capitalism and Freedom* (1962), Friedman details his theory and logic for *laissez-faire* economics: a neo-liberal theory that ties individual freedom to the free market. He argued that economic and personal freedom, along with minimal government intervention (*laissez-faire*), were the necessary conditions under which true capitalism would flourish. In subsequent years, this model for development served the military *junta* regime of Pinochet in Chile and was implemented alongside the structural adjustment conditions across Latin America, Africa, China, Russia, more or less voluntarily, as 'free market fundamentalism'. Most recently, it was 'ordered in Iraq by Paul Bremer, head of the US-appointed Coalition Provisional Authority' (Grady and Harvie, 2011: 173–4).

The liberal notions of competitive individualism as a natural condition of humanity and private ownership of property as a fundamental human right are now deeply embedded in the development theories that flow from this ideology. The underlying belief is that 'the market' is, or ought to be, a level playing field. As such, it is deemed to provide equal opportunity for all individuals to engage actively in the competitive game of earning a living, to spend or save their incomes, to invest or to divest, and thus, within the boundaries of the law, to enjoy the benefits of their labour as they see fit. Rewards achieved in the game are deemed 'just' and based on 'merit'. Thus, liberalism does have an associated ethic of responsibility. Unequal social and financial outcomes are, however, not necessarily a cause for concern. If inequalities are not generated from illegal actions, then they may be seen as the fair returns for unequal participation, investment or commitment – thus 'just'. This notion fuels the belief that social justice and the allocation of society's resources ought to be left to market forces. Taxing the rich to fund the poor is seen as unjust as well as self-defeating. Perkin (1996: 191) explains the assumptions of individuality embedded in this view:

> the poor are victims of their own inadequacy and not of the system, and welfare will only encourage them to be idle and to breed, and so increase their poverty. The rich see themselves as the benefactors of society: the more they consume, the more good they do to the rest by providing work and income.

The Chicago School of Economic scholars argued that the 1970s' recession was an outcome of Keynesian macro-level political and economic policy and the development of the welfare state, which, they claim, resulted in creating welfare dependency, overly regulated markets and inflexible labour practices (Giddens, 1998). Their solutions were that governments should deregulate markets, reduce the size and role of the state, decrease government spending, especially on welfare provision and trade subsidies, and remove trade tariffs to open up local markets to international free competition. Together, the principles for global development and the solutions to what are seen as costly redistributions of wealth and an encouragement to become dole-bludgers are now known as neo-liberalism. It is a set of ideas, values and principles made selectively solid in the policies of many governments the world over. It promulgates their theories as a truth, necessity or even an expression of the natural order. And it is this that suggests that it is reasonable to call it an *ideology*, no longer a mere theory. Where this ideology is uncritically followed, we claim the theory has become a *dogma*. Where even those harmed by the manifestation of the dogma concur in their oppression, we claim that the conditions of *hegemony* have been achieved. Such conditions of *subjugation* are counter to the emancipatory values of democratic societies – values often promoted to underpin the *freedom* of corporations.

Giddens (1998: 14) suggests that 'neo-liberalism is a globalizing theory. The neo-liberals apply at world level the philosophy that guides them in their more local involvements.' They have gained specific support for their political and economic perspective from the institutional leaders operating in the IMF, the World Bank and the World Trade Organization (WTO), and from politicians in a number of nations who have selectively applied neo-liberal principles to varying degrees in the pursuit of regional trading blocs and alliances, as well as from the heads of multinational corporations ostensibly concerned with issues such as rural development and poverty reduction (Pechlaner and Otero, 2010).

By the 1980s, the GATT, the IMF and the World Bank had shifted their perspective from a Keynesian focus to one that supported neo-liberal ideals and they have continued to work together to extend neo-liberalism globally (Simmons and Elkins, 2004). As an outcome of the 1986–93 GATT Uruguay round, the WTO was created. The WTO deals with the global rules of trade between nations in a multilateral trading system. Its main function is to ensure that trade flows as smoothly, predictably and freely as possible between member nations of the system. The WTO negotiations have come to include free-trade talks involving goods and services, agricultural products and the protection of intellectual property rights. WTO negotiations, conducted between governments and their representatives, are held largely in secret, with the outcome of binding trade agreements between signatory nations. The expressed purpose of these negotiations and ensuing trade agreements is to 'help producers of goods and services, exporters, and importers conduct their business, while allowing governments to meet social and environmental objectives' (WTO, 2011a).

The neo-liberal intentions were made explicit and their implementations are continuing and expanding. They are manifest in the negotiations to reduce or remove tariff and non-tariff trade barriers, to remove government support for various industries and farmers, and in the implementation of legislative frameworks that enable businesses to set up operations, sell services and move personnel and money between host nations. Strategic economic partnerships, previously closer economic relations and free-trade agreements, under WTO, IMF and World Bank influence, now operate on an unprecedented scale. Neo-liberal values and principles have now been adopted in a number of regionally based trade agreements, regional alliances and trading blocs. Some of these regional organisations and agreements include the Organisation for Economic Cooperation and Development (OECD), the Asia Pacific Economic Community (APEC), the Association of Southeast Asian Nations (ASEAN), the North American Free Trade Agreement (NAFTA) and the European Union (EU). Membership in these organisations is often geographically based. The WTO (2011a, b) continues to promote trade liberalisation based on the belief that firms operating under competitive advantage at the national and international levels will result in mass production of better quality but less expensive goods, and that the creation of new global mass consumer markets, new industries and jobs will result. This model of development covers everything from the production of shelter, food and clothing to the delivery of human services now commodified as market goods.

Increasingly, in the context of neo-liberalism, the role of the state acts as the facilitator of business interest. States leaders and policy-makers have changed national policy agendas to meet WTO and global trading arrangements or the loan conditions set by the IMF and the World Bank (Stone, 2008). National policies deemed to hinder international trade have been targeted, especially those relating to protecting employment conditions, the environment or the welfare of citizens, and monetary and fiscal policies. While the degree of liberalism differs between trading blocs, alliances and member nations, the underlying philosophy remains the same: that of liberalising trade and domestic policies to enhance free trade between member nations (Ravenhill, 2001). Governments are expected to decrease market interference while, at the same time, increasing protectionist legislation for capital (Stiglitz, 2003). One effect of this is that decisions that directly affect society are increasingly the outcome of confidential negotiations, whether as part of free-trade negotiations or under the guise of commercial sensitivity (Kim, 2010).

## THE (IN)EFFICIENCIES OF GLOBALISATION

'The mass production of food to feed more people at less cost has been seen as one of the many ways industrialisation has raised the level of wellbeing of millions of people. Putting aside an historical critique of this proposition, we question this form of food production for the future as neither just nor efficient. Globalized industrialized food is not cheap. It is too costly for the Earth, for the farmers, and for our health. Earth can no longer carry the burden of groundwater mining, pesticide pollution, disappearance of species and destabilization of the climate. Farmers can no longer carry the burden of debt, which is inevitable in industrial farming with its high costs of production. It is incapable of producing safe, culturally appropriate, tasty, quality food. And it is incapable of producing enough food for all because it is wasteful of land, water and energy. Industrial agriculture uses ten times more energy than it produces. It is thus ten times less efficient. Regardless, food production, transport, consumption, and disposal continues to rely on large scale operations and interlinked corporate interests' (Shiva, n.d.).

The IMF and World Bank have had such faith in the ideas of neo-liberals that they continue actively to promote them globally and impose them on member and borrowing nations. Initially, neo-liberal policies were promoted globally by the IMF and the World Bank and imposed on member nations. This imposition was frequently framed as assistance to Third World and impoverished borrower nations. The wisdom was offered to nations with more centrally controlled economies as strong advice and assistance to liberalise their economies (Stiglitz, 2003, 2007). The IMF continued to exert moral pressure on member countries to pursue neo-liberal values. Both the IMF and the World Bank now require borrowing nations to implement neo-liberal policies as a condition of gaining loans (Stiglitz, 2003). To examine the charmed run of this seemingly contradictory proposition of enforcement or imposition of neo-liberal ideas, it is necessary to return to history, again, to remember the way in which the corporations that are driving this form of development gained their mandate.

# THE UNITED NATIONS: VANGUARD OF JUSTICE OR GLOBAL HEGEMON?

Outspoken criticism of prevailing economic conventions is no longer the sole domain of radical activists. Various organisations with far-reaching tentacles into the leadership of corporations and of governments are creating disruption to the prevailing views of development. The United Nations is an important example of an organisation amplifying the alarm bells. It expresses a commitment to human emancipation. It advocates and acts to embed universal human rights. It promotes the principles of democracy and the rule of (Western) law. It works to enhance a global understanding that social and environmental degradation poses a risk to all. In 2002, for example, Kofi Annan, then Secretary General of the United Nations, was keen to:

> bring home the uncomfortable truth that the model of development that has prevailed for so long, has been fruitful for the few but flawed for the many ... The world today, facing the twin challenges of poverty and pollution, needs to usher in a season of transformation and stewardship, a season in which we make a long overdue investment in a secure future. (*Washington Post*, 3 September 2002, p. 6)

It is a view echoed a decade later by Annan's successor, Ban Ki-moon. Their expressed concerns have resulted in the United Nation's commitment to the Global Compact (GC), a 'strategic policy initiative for businesses that are committed to aligning their operations and strategies with ten universally accepted principles in the areas of human rights, labour, environment and anti-corruption' (United Nations, 2013). At the time of writing, more than 10,000 signatories have committed themselves to its principles. Only just over 500 of these are listed as US corporations. You can examine the list of signatories and their espoused intentions by surfing the related websites. The principles underpinning the GC are affiliated with the Millennium Development Goals (MDGs), a set of eight targets adopted by a number of world leaders in the year 2000 with a commitment to achieve them by 2015. These goals are said to be:

> the most broadly supported, comprehensive and specific development goals the world has ever agreed upon ... [and they] include goals and targets on income poverty, hunger, maternal and child mortality, disease, inadequate shelter, gender inequality, environmental degradation and the Global Partnership for Development. (United Nations, n.d.)

Governments are urged to play their part at a time 'when investing in development is more vital than ever to ensure social stability, security and prosperity' (United Nations, n.d.). To that effect, 'donor governments are called upon to renew rather than revoke their commitment to reaching the MDGs.' Corporations who commit to these recognise 'business, as a primary agent driving globalisation, [and] can help ensure that markets, commerce, technology, and finance advance in ways that benefit economies and societies everywhere'

(United Nations, 2013). How are managers to be educated to meet such wide-reaching ideals? Directly linked to the initiatives of the MDGs and the GC are the Principles for Responsible Management Education (PRME). These are seen as a means to entwine United Nations' ideals into the education of future leaders and managers. The PRME are an implicit invitation to engage with marginalised voices that are generally excluded from consideration in business classrooms. At the time of writing, almost 500 organisations, including many business schools, have signed up to the PRME. The support of these principles is an opportunity to bring ethical reflections on corporate governance, the rule of law and the expression of human rights in general to the heart of management education.

Do we think the United Nations will be able to bring its ideals to fruition? Through the influence of the IMF, the WTO, the World Bank and even NATO (the organisation mandated as a peacekeeper),we alert ourselves to the possibility that their emphasis might be more on making the world safe for capitalism than on securing the well-being of the poorest people on Earth. The United Nations, through the explicit activities associated with the IMF, the WTO and the World Bank, is implicated in a model of development in which corporate interests appear to dominate (Munck and O'Hearn, 1999; Lal, 2002). Its critics suggest that these bodies are responsible, at least in part, for creating the conditions that exacerbate the exploitation of children, migrant labour, human trafficking, underpaid or overworked employees, and workers made redundant and set adrift to care for themselves and their families as best they can. Somehow, their plight is entwined in the fortunes made on stock markets, on the free flow of the consumer items many take for granted, on the social and economic exploitation embodied in our food chain, along with the many chemical toxins of mass production and long-distance distribution of food and other commodities. For the many people negatively affected by the prevailing form of development, capitalism is not *in* crisis. Capitalism *is* the crisis! And yet, more capitalism, particularly in its most radical, neo-liberally inspired form, is posed as the means to their salvation. Einstein would invite us to rethink such a remedy (see Figure 3.1).

When do the poor become of strategic interest? When evaluated purely in terms of monetary income, indigenous peoples the world over are counted among the poorest on Earth. We notice, however, that many indigenous people are located in geographical areas of increasing interest to the corporations of capitalism. This interest bears the seed of some interesting conflicts of values and worldviews. Many indigenous people are steeped in, and committed to, traditional values that have held together their societies for hundreds, if not thousands of years. Recently, an increasing number are also highly trained in Western professions (e.g., law, accounting, economics). And, of these, many have the intention of attending to their perceived care-taking obligations to people and planet in the face of rapacious or seductive corporate self-interest. Common to indigenous worldviews is the belief in the interrelationship of all life and the dependency of such life on the energies of the cosmos.

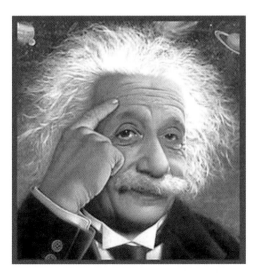

**Figure 3.1**  Albert Einstein: 'The significant problems we face cannot be solved at the same level of thinking we were at when we created them'

The notions that all human beings are equal and have rights to self-determination are central to United Nations-inspired work. In December 2012, the United Nations circulated a draft of a Business Reference Guide (the 'Draft Guide') to advance the United Nations Declaration on the Rights of Indigenous Peoples (the 'Declaration') through the auspices of the Global Compact. This document recognised that indigenous peoples are affected by global business and are entitled to human rights, cultural rights and labour rights as one aspect necessary to create an inclusive and sustainable global economy. We agree, but with a cautious alert to the potential subtle embedding of an uncritical victimisation mentality. Yes, dreadful things were done and are being done to the indigenous peoples of the world. However, many are now situated in positions of strategic interest to investors – East and West alike. Are we to witness a new chapter of intensifying rapacious and devious thefts? To remain alert to these risks, we interweave the ideals of the United Nations Global Compact and those generated from the Declaration with the aspirations of the PRME for universal inclusion in the processes that sustain human life and the responsibility for the sustainability of the life forces all depend on.

Principle 1 of the PRME is a fruitful opportunity to integrate the PRME with the United Nations Declaration on the Rights of Indigenous Peoples and, through this confluence, contribute to a manifestation of the espoused aspirations of the UN Global Compact , i.e. the transformation of poverty and environmental degradation to universal human and environmental thriving. By dovetailing with the insights generated in the United Nations Universal Declaration of Human Rights and the Declaration of the Rights of Indigenous Peoples, we are encouraged to examine more closely the experiences of indigenous peoples, displaced and trafficked people, the young and the fragile and the issues more notably addressed by the ILO, union movements, and the NGOs who work for justice in and through employment-related considerations. For an excellent example to understand the entwining of these institutions, follow the work of the Bench Marks Foundation (www.bench-marks.org.za), a faith-based organisation that works for justice in the mining industry in South Africa and has reverberations for the mining industry the world over. Their work has implications for all the goods and services that rely on the extraction of Earth's minerals, the use of water, air, land and human energy.

We can see from the various challenges to the organisations and systems of capitalism that explicitly exploitative practices are increasingly censured and sometimes punished. Corporations who have signed up to the MDGs, for example, but who transgress their commitments, can be struck off. Organisations, large and small, can be fined significant amounts of money for misleading the public, for causing environmental damage or for having inadequate safety conditions in place for their employees. Do these measures go far enough? Excommunication from the UN or the imposition of fines by various courts does not restore damaged lives and the livelihoods of those affected. Such damage must be prevented as well as punished. Prevention and punishment, however, suggest that we can locate cause and allocate blame with precision. This is not always the case in outcomes that have their origin in diffused and obscured systemic processes. These processes can be thought of as the institutionalisation of ideas and practices that are mutually reinforced through the network of relationships formed in market, state and broader social activities that manifest these ideas into practice. Are these ideas to be judged on some societally shaped set of values or by self-serving public relations specialists trained to craft clever stories and reassuring images of their paymasters? How might experts in corporate legitimacy and reputation be implicated in misleading or attention-deflecting good news stories, as discussed in Chapter 1?

While a commitment to the Global Compact is not the only way to address the issues we concern ourselves with in this book, the corporations who have expressed allegiance to the principles are among those who have made an explicit commitment to honour the values promoted by the United Nations. There is much good work that can be legitimately managed into action through these values. But how do we assess the integrity of the participants? How far reaching is the impact of their influence? We have noted with interest the small number of current signatories that are identified as US companies. This is an observation worth exploring in light of the deeply held notions about responsibility for leadership of the world claimed by the US and the extent it will go to preserve the power of the US globally. It will certainly go to war to exert it, be that in a claim to expand democracy or in the securing of territories for its corporations to practise (capitalism) freely. This claim to leadership will be explored further in Chapter 9.

Many examples of expressed corporate concern and action, which we have brought to the discussion in many chapters, invite just such an exploration. What is important, in our view, is that the very foundations of Western capitalist rationality are not challenged deeply enough by the global institutions purporting to lead change. We thus persist in asking radical and wide-ranging questions about the system of capitalism to be managed by graduates of business schools the world over who appear to remain embedded in the prevailing institutional logics. Thus, the embedding of this destructive logic persists by their uncritical enactment of capitalist processes of production that cause the systemically generated degradation we are concerned with in this book. When pressed to address the most undeniable of harms, the remedies they are willing to enact are generated by the same logic.

# THE RISE OF THE CORPORATION: A ROYAL ALLIANCE

Corporations are not new inventions. They are the creations (or creatures) of nation-states. In the seventeenth century, a charter would be granted by the reigning monarch of a territory in order for the company to set forth some type of venture, typically an exploration by sea. For example, in the year 1600, the British East India Company received a royal charter from Queen Elizabeth I to pursue trade with the East Indies. Wealth-holders were able to purchase shares or stocks in a chartered company, and received a share of the returns from the venture; most often, cash in divisions according to the proportion of investment they had made, but possibly ship's cargo. In this way, capital has been commodified into a tradeable thing – in the form of shares or stocks – where ownership is made transferable through the market.

From these humble beginnings, corporations now dominate globally. Big Business is now the most powerful institution on the planet, and concentration within some key industries is approaching grave levels. Much of the global trade in goods and services is controlled by fewer, yet more powerful multinational corporations. Corporate power has grown to such extent that it might be said that these Frankenstein-like creations now call the tune their creators must dance to. According to Hatch and Cunliffe (2006), corporate power is more insidious than state power because it is inherently non-democratic, pervades our everyday experience and is regarded by many as normal.

Perkin (1996: 18) demonstrates this concentration pattern: 'the largest 100 manufacturing companies in 1909 produced 15 per cent of the national output; by 1930 they produced 26 per cent; by 1970 45 per cent; [by the mid-1990s] the largest 200 firms produce about 85 per cent of total manufacturing output.' Similar concentrations of ownership and profits were evident in service industries throughout the 1990s, including media, banking and insurance, and food. By 1996, five companies controlled 40 per cent of the global oil, personal computers, and media markets (Mander, 1996). In 2000, the ten largest food corporations controlled half of the food and beverage sales in the United States (Lyson and Raymer, 2000; see Figure 3.2).

**Figure 3.2**  American flag with corporate logos

By 2005, five 'Gene Giants' – multinational corporations Monsanto, Dupont (Pioneer), Syngenta (Novartis and AstraZeneca), Aventis (acquired by Bayer) and BASF (Dow) – had global control of the world's seed supply (Hendrickson and Heffernan, 2002; Oligopoly Inc., ETC Group Report, 2005 as cited in Shiva, 2009) and five 'Food Giants' – multinational corporations Cargill, Conagra, ADM, Louis Dreyfus and Binge – had control of the processing and trade of food (Dan Morgan, 1980, as cited in Shiva, 2009). Hendrickson and Heffernan (2002) discuss how joint ventures and strategic alliances through vertical and horizontal integration between these already globally significant food organisations, such as those between Cargill/Monsanto, DuPont/Conagra, and Novartis/ADM, are blurring the corporate delineation between gene and food giants, further concentrating the power and control of these goliaths.

# CONTEMPORARY CORPORATIONS: INTENSIFIED OR DIFFUSED RESPONSIBILITY?

Of the parties that benefit most under the current trajectory of globalisation, multinational companies appear to have a form of privilege and power that seems to undermine the very ideal of universal emancipation held central to their liberal ideals. Their presence in a community as producers or retailers appears to skew the purportedly level playing field for competing smaller businesses. They are able to capture ever more dependent groups of wage-earners and to relegate thousands of individuals to the vagaries of casualised labour or employment at will. Global corporates appear to have formal or informal access to the power-brokers within various nations. This access provides easy influence on explicit government actions to liberalise their political economies or to see their allegiance to these corporations as wealth-creating opportunities through creating attractive conditions for their presence in their jurisdictions.

There seems to be little difference in the alliances between the European royals and their entrepreneurial elite of the seventeenth century and the elite individuals and families (as listed above) and the business and philanthropy of the twenty-first century corporations that produce the goods and services we consume on a daily basis. As you can see on the companion webpage for this chapter, John Pilger (2003) wastes no words. He sees the corporate form of capitalism as a form of neo-imperialism.

## A FAMILY OF COMPANIES: A COMPANY FOR FAMILIES?

De Beers, established in 1888, is today the world's leading diamond company with 'unrivalled expertise in the exploration, mining and marketing of diamonds'. The company expresses its commitment to addressing sustainability issues 'openly and honestly', whether it is the development of sustainable post-mining economies, the global challenge of climate change or ensuring that the global supply is free of conflict diamonds. 'We are committed to living up to diamonds in all we do' (De Beers Family of Companies, *Report to Society*, 2010). Managing the size of the workforce is a key success factor. In 2010, the aspiration of a 'leaner workforce' was achieved through a restructuring that enabled a 23 per cent reduction in the workforce in 2009. 'By the end of the year non-permanent employees made up a larger proportion of the workforce' (De Beers, *Report*, p. 34). Union participation is high but 'relationships become stressed when worker reductions become imminent' (De Beers, *Report*, p. 34). Certainly DeBeers self-report to society is detailed, beautifully presented and very reassuring to shareholders and stakeholders alike. We read, too, that, in the interests of all, De Beers Group has sold 40 per cent of its business to Anglo American, a corporation whose activities you can examine more critically at www.bench-marks.org.za/.

As initiators, multinational companies have used their growing financial strength to lobby and pressure their own and other governments to implement political, economic and social infrastructures that meet or enhance company profits. This strength has grown significantly since the late 1970s, with a number of multinational corporations earning more per annum than many nation-states earn in GDP (Perkin, 1996; Kaplinsky, 2005). Multinational corporations lobby their own governments to represent their interests in global international negotiations; this is particularly evident with the inclusion of services and intellectual property rights in WTO negotiations, a process that began in the 1996 GATT Uruguay round (Weissman, 1996; Kelsey, 1999; Salokannel, 2006). It is the combined activities of the WTO, the IMF, the World Bank, regional trading blocs and alliances, and multinational companies that have resulted in the development of global neo-liberalism.

While there is debate about the extent, form, benefits and outcomes of global neo-liberalism, there is agreement that a number of features in the current global market differ from past international trade patterns. For example, since the 1970s, an exponential growth in international financial trade has been documented, with the growth of managed funds by 1,100 per cent (Giddens, 1998), the majority of which is invested in the stock exchanges (Kasemir et al., 2001). In this environment, wage-earners, through their investment in the stock market, have, in Marx's terms, become capitalists; they, too, now have a vested interest in the profit maximisation of the firms that increasingly operate in the global arena. Similarly, countries are involved in the global goods trade. In 2013, the WTO had 159 members and 25 observer governments from a total of 196 countries globally (WTO, 2011a, b).

# GLOBAL NEO-LIBERALISM AS IMPERIAL FORCE

In the late 1970s and early 1980s, Margaret Thatcher, then prime minister of the UK, Ronald Regan, then president of the US, and the 1984 New Zealand Labour government were among the first voluntarily to adopt neo-liberal political and economic policies at the nation-state level (Kelsey, 1995/1997; Perkin, 1996). By the 1990s, free-market ideology had replaced welfare-state ideology in many industrialised nations, developing countries, Eastern Bloc and Asian economies to varying degrees (Perkin, 1996; Crane, 1999; Simmons and Elkins, 2004). As part of these structural reforms, governments implemented domestic market and trade liberalisation, reduced the size and scope of state activities, deregulated labour markets, and focused on price stability and market access predictability (Perkin, 1996; Kelsey, 1995/1997; Larner, 2000). This approach has resulted in reductions in health, education and welfare payments (Kelsey, 1995/1997), and a renewed focus on satisfying consumer demands for affordable goods, business needs for affordable wages and unrestricted market access, and the terms of international free-trade agreements.

Under this regime, citizens are deemed responsible for caring for themselves. Government responsibility is reserved for those deemed to be the most deserving or the most dangerous. In times of fiscal restraint (i.e., when governments want to bail out corporations and the corporations are dropping unprofitable business aspects or offloading employees), there is nothing for the most vulnerable to do but fend for themselves. The state cannot be seen to be encouraging bludging, and corporations cannot be expected to carry deadwood. We all agree. Or, at least, it seems that enough of us agree with enough of the story to let it continue not unchallenged but also not fatally disturbed.

Throughout the 1990s, a number of political responses were being developed to the growing criticisms of global neo-liberalism voiced from multiple public spheres, national policy-makers and some business leaders. One of the most significant political changes was the adoption of a 'Third Way' political ideology. The political movements and politicians most commonly associated with Third Way politics are the US administration led by the then president Bill Clinton (1993–2001), the British prime minister of that time, Tony Blair (1997–2007), and the then German Chancellor, Gerhard Schroeder (1998–2005). A number of contemporary writers now argue that these systemic issues associated with the intensification of global corporate capitalism had been better understood and lessons had been learned (Stiglitz, 2003). The espoused goal of the Third Way was to achieve social prosperity and well-being through state-negotiated (free) global economic growth, and individual responsibility for communal well-being, embodied by the phrase 'No rights without responsibilities' (Giddens, 1998: 65). The Third Way was to adhere to the underlying principles of neo-liberalism, but its proponents sought to soften the harsh policies implemented from the mid-1980s. In particular, the Third Way was deemed a political approach that could address the challenges that neo-liberalism posed to democracy, the changes to the nature of work and income distribution, and welfare provision (Latham, 1998). Indeed, proponents of the Third Way argued that it is possible to reconcile free-markets with social well-being (Giddens, 1998).

The Third Way is associated with such terms as 'neo-Keynesianism'; however, one aspect which marks the 'post' stance is the role of government. Under Keynesianism, the state took an active role in regulating and coordinating all realms of society. The diminished role of the state applied in neo-liberalism remains entrenched in Third Way politics, instead of regulation. Discussions become centred on forming partnerships with private sector and non-profit organisations (Rose, 2000; Etherington, 2006). Moreover, the underlying premises regarding globalisation, economic centrality, meritocracy, individual responsibility and acceptance of the new forms of work remain intact. The Third Way might be better read as an attempt to soften the extreme inequalities associated with neo-liberalism within given conceptual boundaries created by the advocates of neo-liberal market ideals.

In attempts to preserve the system by softening the response to some of its harshest consequences, we might be seeing skilful leadership in renegotiating consent with the concerned public. From a Gramscian perspective, hegemonic control may have been preserved, or even intensified. Some accommodations and concessions were made in response to the growing discontent of subordinate groups throughout the global society. Hobsbawm (1998) suggests that the Third Way is traditional neo-liberal policy under a different disguise, while Hall (1998) argues that the Third Way political agenda merely provides the rationalisation for formally left-wing political parties to move their political agenda towards right-wing neo-liberalism. The espoused values of the Third Way were certainly more appealing to critics of neo-liberalism than the hard economic determinism of the 1980s and 1990s. The fundamental assumptions remained unchallenged. The fundamental social relations between the hegemonic leaders within the global system and the rest of society remained intact (Egan, 2007).

# CHALLENGING NEO-LIBERALISM: A GLOBAL GROUNDSWELL OF RESISTANCE

Advocates of global neo-liberalism argue that the prevailing system of development will result in economic growth, employment, affordable quality goods and service, and a reduction in world poverty. However, not all commentators and citizens are convinced, as indicated by systematic opposition to global neo-liberalism occurring throughout the 1990s and into the twenty-first century. Highly publicised protests include those held at the 1999 Seattle World Trade Organization summit, with simultaneous protests occurring in London, the 2001 Quebec NAFTA summit, the 2001 Genoa G8 summit and the Occupy Movement of 2011.

During the latter part of 2011, the Occupy (Wall Street) Movement that took shape initially in New York soon spread to many cities of the world. So, too, did the means by which the authorities eventually dispersed them. Protesters were dealt with – swiftly in Seattle, more carefully with regard to the 'Occupiers' – to a point. By mid-2012, their campaign was no longer visible in the media. The ideas of this vanguard, however, have not gone away. They call for no less than a radical overhaul of the system of capitalism. And they are well supported in their aspirations by numerous critics of 'the system'. Prominent among the outspoken intellectuals are Slavoj Žižek, George Monbiot, Vandana Shiva, Jane Kelsey and Noam Chomsky. Award-winning authors such as John Pilger bring the theory to dramatic illustration. Whose interpretation of the principles and out-workings of this economic system so pervasive in our lives are to be believed: Žižek and like-minded intellectuals; the Occupy Movement; the high priests and functionaries of Wall Street and the like; or the apologists who recognise systemic harm – but want to explain and justify that harm – and amend it only if, in doing so, sustainability (of the system) is not compromised?

The official state response to protests against apparently unbridled corporate control by the Occupy Movements, the miner uprisings in South Africa and China and the indigenous resisters to rainforest felling in South America is unequivocal. It includes the use of riot police and tear gas to disperse crowds (Dube, 1999; *The Economist*, 1999). Poisonous gas and bullets aimed to kill are not limited to use in Burma, China or South Africa. In general, the media portrays protesters as violent and anti-capitalist unless there is media mileage to be made in portraying African, Burmese or Chinese governments as particularly backward or draconian and in need of Western-style democratisation so that responsible investors can safely enter those markets and provide decent opportunities for their citizens through their emancipation to engage in the free employment market. This portrayal helps to divert attention away from the many concerns any protesters have about the real conditions under which they suffer or the combined effects of global neo-liberalism.

In Gramsci's terms, the state and the media show a willingness to protect the interests of the growing elite capitalist class and the handmaiden state (e.g., multinational corporations and their empowering governments), and to uphold and extend their hegemonic position in the global arena. As we write, it remains to be seen whether the corporate response to the Bangladesh factory collapse (where over 1,200 died) and the commitment to more stringent building codes continue to be resisted by many corporates. The people of Singapore obligingly wore masks, stayed indoors and tolerated the closure of schools to avert the dangerous effects of the smoke drifting in from the forest fires illegally lit in Indonesia to clear more land to develop as palm plantations. The prime minister had the courtesy to apologise. But will he stop the burning while corporations are in such need of land cleared of forests (Associated Press, 2013)? While capital may flick around the world with a click of a computer icon, most of humanity is much less mobile, much less able to exert the threat of withdrawal. Can the call to democracy reduce the power of the corporates (see http://reclaimdemocracy.org/about/)?

## (NO LONGER) TRAPPED ON THE ROCK OF FREE ENTERPRISE: FREE TO GO!

Bermuda epitomises the development of a jurisdiction based on the early expansion principles of the British empire. It is now the hub for corporate activity in the (re)insurance industry. Unemployment for locals is high and so is the cost of living. Many residents are now living in growing poverty. The recommended remedy for their plight is to compete for non-existent or poorly paid jobs to pay for housing and food that has become increasingly out of reach. Homelessness in this land of commercial success is the reality for a growing number of people. Increasing social/civil unrest, drug-related violence and mental health issues are on the increase. This unrest provides jobs for police, prosecutors and the security industry. It provides opportunities for philanthropists to enact their charity. More recently, there is policy talk of making it easier for still legally anchored Bermudans to leave the islands to seek their fortune elsewhere. Keeping angry young men trapped on this idyllic island is putting tourism at risk. Best they go and seek their fortunes elsewhere. But where? Is there space in your community for an influx of economic refugees to compete with the locals for available jobs, homes, services and space to play?

The outcome of the decisions made to ensure the future of corporations affects the way we live, employment conditions, the environment and indigenous rights, and determines what products are produced and where, and who has access to welfare provision, including access to health and elder care. Yet, often the criteria applied to determine which policies to pursue increasingly reflect narrowly defined corporate goals associated with efficiency and profitability (Alvesson and Deetz, 2000). This is problematic in democratic societies where the assumption is that citizens ought to be able to influence the direction that their nations take as a necessary framing of the conditions of their personal life-chances and the futures they want for their children. Instead, many Western nations have adopted various forms of liberal democracy that limit meaningful input from citizens (Green, 1993), and rights and freedom are reframed as better achieved through producer and consumer markets. We return to this issue in Chapter 7. Democracy becomes reduced to the election-day politics of choosing representatives, which, Deetz (1992) contends, merely creates the appearance that voting is an act of democratic participation. Once the election is over, citizens are excluded from further participation in the direction their elected leaders take. This makes it difficult for meaningful participation to occur (Ehrensal, 1995; Kelsey, 1995/1997).

Green (1993: 9–10) suggests that there is nothing new about this contradiction. Moreover, he suggests that the liberal democratic tradition does not take into account the unequal starting points of citizens: historically, the greatest obstacle to widespread citizen equality has been the existence of social and economic inequalities that render access to democratic institutions – the vote, the press, communication with representatives, the right to organise – either difficult or meaningless (Green, 1993: 9–10). Nor does this take into account the many various competing responsibilities, disabling tragedies and systemic expulsions that are beyond the capacity of individuals to control. There are fewer places to meet the necessities of life outside 'the market,' an issue we shall illustrate in Chapters 4 and 5. As such, the system of global neo-liberalism undermines the very premise of individual freedom and liberty that proponents claim to uphold. This is especially evident as it relates to the assumption that informed individuals making self-interested choices in an unregulated market will benefit all of society. The very practices of business and government not only obscure information, but prevent individuals from gaining access to meaningful information on which to base any decision.

# CONCLUSION: GLOBALISATION – WE ARE ALL IN IT TOGETHER

As early as 1977, McCullough and Shannon predicted that in a world economy 'alignments and power blocs continuously emerge and it is these which globally determine the organization of organizations' (cited in Clegg and Dunkerley, 1980: 461). Many critics of global neo-liberalism are concerned about the impact of this system on democracy. John Pilger (2003) calls it a form of neo-imperialism. That citizens might turn the tide on this neo-imperialism would require a recognition of the extent to which the institutional logics that permit the current form of corporate existence and the legal and policy endorsement of such permissions have infused our lifeworld. It is these issues of embedded logic that we discuss more fully in the following chapters. Whether the values and processes of democracy can overcome the embedded hegemony is the constant question that underpins this book as a whole, and the companion web-pages offer many leads to explore for yourself. What part we each play in endorsing, tolerating or transforming this system and its hegemonic grip invites deep self-reflection – a hallmark of a critical thinker and responsible human being. More people than ever, from more sections of society than ever, are deeply concerned about the impact that the intensification of global neo-liberalism has on the structure and conditions of work, the particular form of global redistribution of employment and income, and the widening of income inequality and the means to life. It is the conceptualisation and value of work that we turn to in the next chapter.

## TALK BOX

David Rockefeller was committed to achieving a 'one world order'. He believed various types of crises could usefully accelerate this goal. Speaking at the Bilderberger meeting in Baden, Germany, in June 1991, he had this to say: 'We are grateful to the *Washington Post*, *The New York Times*, *Time Magazine* and other great publications whose directors have attended our meetings and respected their promises of discretion for almost forty years.' He went on to explain: 'It would have been impossible for us to develop our plan for the world if we had been subjected to the lights of publicity during those years. But, the world is more sophisticated and prepared to march towards a world government. The supranational sovereignty of an intellectual elite and world bankers is surely preferable to the national auto-determination practiced in past centuries' (Escobar, 2005). If bankers and media moguls are to be midwives to a new world order, would you have any concerns about that? If not, why not? If so, where could you put your energies and talents?

## Tricky Questions

- How is globalisation discussed in your other studies?
- Are the discussions of the global context robust enough to prepare you for future decisions you will be required to make in your personal and professional life?
- How are you (dis)engaging from the shaping of the wider context that will set the parameters of your life opportunities and those of others, the vitality of the natural environment and the political stability of your region?
- How responsible do you feel in the achievement of security for all people, their access to food, water, income, health and peace in their region?

# ADDITIONAL RESOURCES

Ardalan, K. (2010) Globalisation and global governance: four paradigmatic views. *American Review of Political Economy* 8 (1): 6–34.

Bremmer, I. (2011) *The End of the Free Market: Who Wins the War between States and Corporations?* New York: Penguin.

Buckley, P. (2009) The impact of the global factory on economic development. *Journal of World Business,* 44 (2): 131.

Centento, M. and Cohen, J. (2012) The arc of neoliberalism. *Annual Review of Sociology,* 38 (1): 317–40.

Hiscock, G. (2012) *Earth Wars: The Battle for Global Resources.* Singapore: John Wiley.

Mir, R. and Mir, A. (2009) From the colony to the corporation: studying knowledge transfer across international boundaries. *Group and Organization Management,* 34 (1): 90.

Moore, M. (2009) *Capitalism: A Love Story* (www.imdb.com/title/tt1232207/; retrieved 6 September 2013).

Rachman, G. (2011) *Zero-sum World: Politics, Power and Prosperity after the Crash.* London: Atlantic Press.

Van Oosterhout, J. (2010) The role of corporations in shaping the global rules of the game: in search of new foundations. *Business Ethics Quarterly,* 20 (2): 253.

Worth, O. and Buckley, K. (2009) The world social forum: postmodern prince or court jester? *Third World Quarterly,* 30 (4): 649.

Yeates, N. (2002) Globalisation and social policy: from global neoliberal hegemony to global political pluralism. *Global Social Policy,* 2 (1): 69–91.

# REFERENCES

Alvesson, M. and Deetz, S. (2000) *Doing Critical Management Research.* London: Sage.

Associated Press (2013) Indonesian president apologises to Singapore and Malaysia for forest fires. *Guardian,* 24 June (www.guardian.co.uk/world/2013/jun/24/indonesian-president-singapore-malaysia-fires; retrieved 6 September 2013).

Barkin, D. (2002) Globalisation: love it or leave it. *Latin American Perspectives,* 29 (1), 132–5.

Barton, D. (2011) Capitalism for the long term. *Harvard Business Review,* March: 85–91.

Birdsall, N. and Fukuyama, F. (2011) The post Washington consensus. *Foreign Affairs,* January/February.

Boyer, R. (1988) The evolution of wage/labour relations in seven European countries. In R. Boyer (ed.), *The Search for Labour Market Flexibility: The European Economies in Transition.* Oxford: Clarendon Press. pp. 3–25.

Button, J. (1997) The market of Eden (www.civilization.com.au/civilization-articles/1997/5/2/the-market-of-eden/; retrieved 6 September 2013).

Chomsky, N. (2013) *Can Civilization Survive Capitalism?* New York: New York Times News Syndicate.

Clegg, S. and Dunkerley, D. (1980) *Organization, Class and Control*. New York: Routledge and Kegan Paul.

Cohen, R. and Kennedy, P. (2007) *Global Sociology*. Hampshire, UK: Palgrave MacMillan.

Crane, G. (1999) Imagining the economic nation: globalisation in China. *New Political Economy*, 4 (2): 215–32.

Deetz, S. (1992) *Democracy in an Age of Corporate Colonization: Developments in Communication and the Politics of Everyday Life*. Albany, NY: State University of New York.

Del Castillo, G. (2008) Economic reconstruction of war-torn countries: the role of the international financial institutions. *Seton Hall Law Review*, 38 (4): article 3.

Drache, D. (1996) From Keynes to K-Mart: competitiveness in a corporate age. In R. Boyer and D. Drache (eds), *States against Markets: The Limitations of Globalization*. London: Routledge. pp. 31–61.

Dube, J. (1999) The curfew comes down: protests rock Seattle, disrupt WTO meeting. ABCNEWS.com, Seattle, 30 November (http://more.abcnews.go.com/sections/business/dailynews/wto¬_protests991130.html; retrieved 25 February 2000).

*The Economist* (1999) The battle in Seattle (www.economist.com/editorial/freeforall/current/sa8436.html; retrieved 26 November 1999).

*The Economist* (2006) Milton Friedman: a heavyweight champ, at five foot two. The legacy of Milton Friedman, a giant among economists, 23 November (www.economist.com/node/8313925; retrieved 8 October 2013).

Egan, D. (2007) Globalization and the invasion of Iraq: state power and the enforcement of neoliberalism. *Sociological Focus*, 40 (1): 98.

Ehrensal, K.N. (1995) Discourses of global competition: obscuring the changing labour processes of managerial work. *Journal of Organizational Change Management*, 8 (5): 5–16.

Escobar, P. (2005) Bilderberg strikes again (www.atimes.com/atimes/Front_Page/GE10Aa02.html; retrieved 6 September 2013).

Etherington, S. (2006) A new third way. *Public Finance*, 24: 24–5.

Fasenfest, D. (2010) Neoliberalism, globalisation, and the capitalist world order. *Critical Sociology*, 36 (5): 627–31.

Friedman, M. (1962) *Capitalism and Freedom*. Chicago: Chicago University Press.

Fritz-Krockow, B. and Ramlogan, P. (2007) *International Monetary Fund Handbook: Its Functions, Policies and Operations*. Washington, DC: International Monetary Fund.

Giddens, A. (1998) *The Third Way: The Renewal of Social Democracy*. Cambridge: Polity Press.

Grady, J. and Harvie, D. (2011) Neoliberalism. In M. Tadajewski, P. MacLaran, E. Parsons and M. Parker (eds), *Key Concepts in Critical Management Studies*. London: Sage. pp. 173–6.

Green, P. (ed.) (1993) *Key Concepts in Critical Theory: Democracy*. New Jersey: Humanities Press.

Hall, S. (1998) The great moving nowhere show. In M. Jacques (ed.), *Marxism Today, Special Issue*, November/December.

Hart, S.L. (2010) *Capitalism at the Crossroads: Next Generation Business Strategies for a Post-Crisis World*. Upper Saddle River, NJ: Wharton Business School.

Hatch, M.J. and Cunliffe, A. (2006) *Organisation Theory*. Oxford: Oxford University Press.

Hendrickson, M.K. and Heffernan, W.D. (2002) Opening spaces through relocalization: locating potential in the weaknesses of the global food system. *Sociologia Ruralis*, 42 (4): 347–69.

Hiscock, G. (2012) *Earth Wars: The Battle for Global Resources*. Singapore: Wiley and Sons.

Hobsbawm, E. (1998) The death of liberalism. *Marxism Today* (November/December): 4–8.

Husserl, E. (1936) The crisis of European sciences and transcendental phenomenology: an introduction to phenomenological philosophy. *Philosophia (Belgrad)*, 1: 77–176.

Kaplinsky, R. (2005) *Globalization, Poverty and Inequality*. Cambridge: Polity Press.

Kasemir, B., Suess, A. and Zehnder, A.J.B. (2001) The next unseen revolution. *Environment*, 43 (9): 8–19.

Kelsey, J. (1995) *The New Zealand Experiment: A World Model for Structural Adjustment*. Auckland: Auckland University Press.

Kelsey, J. (1997) *Economic Fundamentalism: The New Zealand Experiment – A World Model for Structural Adjustment?* London: Pluto Press.

Kelsey, J. (1999) *Reclaiming the Future: New Zealand and the Global Economy*. New Zealand: Bridget Williams Books.

Kim, S.Y. (2010) *Power and the Governance of Global Trade*. Ithaca, NY: Cornell University Press.

Kivisto, P. (2011) *Key Ideas in Sociology*. London: Sage.

Lal, V. (2002) *Empire of Knowledge: Culture and Plurality in the Global Economy*. London: Pluto Press.

Larner, W. (2000) Neo-liberalism: policy, ideology, governmentality. *Studies in Political Economy*, 63: 5–26.

Latham, M. (1998) *Civilising Global Capital*. Sydney: Allen & Unwin.

Lyson, T.A. and Raymer, A.L. (2000) Stalking the wily multinational: power and control in the US food system. *Agriculture and Human Values*, 17 (2): 199–208.

McCullough, A. and Shannon, M. (1977) Organizations and protection. In S. Clegg and D. Dunkerley (eds), *Critical Issues in Organisations*. London: Routledge and Kegan Paul. pp. 41–71.

Mander, J. (1996) The dark side of globalization: what the media are missing. *The Nation*, 15–22 July: 9–32.

Maxton, G. (2011) *The End of Progress: How Modern Economics has Failed Us*. Hoboken, NJ: John Wiley and Sons.

Munck, R. and O'Hearn, D. (1999) *Critical Development Theory: Contributions to a New Paradigm*. London: Zed Books.

Pechlaner, G. and Otero, G. (2010) The neoliberal food regime: neoregulation and the new division of labor in North America. *Rural Sociology*, 75 (2): 179–208.

Perkin, H. (1996) *The Third Revolution: Professional Elites in the Modern World*. London: Routledge.

Pilger, J. (2003) *The New Rulers of the World*. London: Verso.

Piore, M.J. and Sabel, C.F. (1984) *The Second Industrial Divide*. New York: Basic Books.

Quiggan, J. (2005) Interpreting globalization: neoliberal and internationalist views of changing patterns of the global trade and financial system. United Nations Research Institute for Social Development, Programme Paper no. 7.

Raffer, K. (2011) Neoliberal capitalism: a time warp backwards to capitalism's origins? *Social Economics*, 40 (1): 41–62.

Ravenhill, J. (2001) APEC adrift: implications for economic regionalism in Asia and the Pacific. *Pacific Review*, 13 (2): 319–33.

Rickards, J. (2011) *Currency Wars: The Making of the Next Global Crisis*. New York: Penguin.

Rose, N. (2000) Community, citizenship and the third Way. *American Behavioral Scientist*, 43 (9): 1395–411.

Salokannel, M. (2006) Global justice and intellectual property rights: reforming the international IPR regime for balanced development. *E-Learning and Digital Media*, 3 (3) (www.wwwords.co.uk/pdf/freetoview.asp?j=elea&vol=3&issue=3 &year=2006&article=17_Salokannel_ELEA_3_3_web; retrieved 2 February 2011).

Sennett, R. (2006) *The Culture of the New Capitalism*. London: Yale University Press.

Shiva, V. (2009) Women and the gendered politics of food. *Philosophical Topics*, 37 (2): 17–32.

Shiva, V. (n.d.) Vandana Shiva quotes (www.goodreads.com/author/quotes/144748. Vandana_Shiva; retrieved 6 September 2013).

Simmons, B.A. and Elkins, Z. (2004) The globalization of liberalization: policy diffusion in the international economy. *American Political Science Review*, 98 (1): 171–89.

Slater, D. (2008) Imperial powers and democratic imaginations in a global era. In E. Kofman and G. Youngs (eds), *Globalisation: Theory and Practice*. New York: Continuum. pp. 40–56.

Stiglitz, J.E. (2003) *Globalization and its Discontents*. New York: W.W. Norton.

Stiglitz, J.E. (2007) *Making Globalization Work*. New York: W.W. Norton.

Stiglitz, J.E. (2010) *Freefall: America, Free Markets, and the Sinking of the World Economy*. New York: W.W. Norton.

St Jane, M. and Humphries, M.T. (2013) The Victorian–Dickens era: in the name of capitalism; colonies, convicts, charities, and royals-in-training. *Journal of Academic Perspectives*, 1 (www.journalofacademicperspectives.com/back-issues/ vol-2013/no-1/; retrieved 8 October 2013).

Stone, R.W. (2008) The scope of IMF conditionality. *International Organization*, 62 (4): 589–620. Reprinted in M. Tadajewski, P. MacLaran, E. Parsons and M. Parker (eds), *Key Concepts in Critical Management Studies*. London: Sage, 2011. pp. 589–620.

Tiemstra, J. (2007) The social economics of globalization. *Social Economics*, 36 (2): 143–59.

United Nations (2013) Overview of the UN Global Compact (www.unglobalcompact.org/AboutTheGC/; retrieved 6 September 2013).

United Nations (n.d.) MDG strategies (www.undp.org/content/undp/en/home/our-work/povertyreduction/focus_areas/focus_mdg_strategies/; retrieved 6 September 2013).

Weissman, R. (1996) Long, strange trips: the pharmaceutical industry drive to harmonize global intellectual property rules, and the remaining WTO legal alternatives available to Third World countries. *University of Pennsylvania Journal of International Economic Law*, 17: 1069 (http://heinonline.org/HOL/LandingPage? collection=journals&handle=hein.journals/upjiel17&div=43&id=&page=; retrieved 8 June 2011).

Willock, R. (1988) *Bulwark of Empire*. Bermuda: Bermuda Maritime Museum Press.

World Trade Organization (2011a) Understanding the WTO: what is the World Trade Organization? (www.wto.org/english/thewto_e/whatis_e/tif_e/fact1_e.htm; retrieved 8 June 2011).

World Trade Organization (2011b) Understanding the WTO: principles of the trading system (www.wto.org/english/thewto_e/whatis_e/tif_e/fact2_e.htm; retrieved 8 June 2011).

# 4 ORGANISATIONAL STRUCTURES AND THE IDEA OF WORK

## Learning Objectives

In this chapter, we invite you to reflect critically on:

- the notion that work makes us free;
- the restructuring of work as paid employment and its implications;
- the implication of work in the exacerbation of hegemonic control of populations;
- the paradoxical transformation of life-sustaining activities into paid employment as the means to purchase life-sustaining and life-enhancing products and services;
- the centrality of work in the achievement of universal justice and environmental restoration;
- the usefulness of being able to use different theories in the analyses of your observations of work in your own context.

## CRITICAL CONCEPTS

What is considered as work or *employment* can be shown to vary over time. *Full, un(der)- and over-employment* are slippery concepts. *Employee empowerment discourses* linked to *accelerated productivity* may contribute to the strengthening of *hegemonic control*. *Structural functionalists* and *social constructivists* go about their analyses of these dynamics in different ways. *Critical theorists* may use these and other *theoretical paradigms* to expose and challenge *exploitation* and *injustice* with the intent to change these.

*Arbeit Macht Frei*: Work Brings Freedom. These were the words on the sign over the gates of Auschwitz, one of the notorious human extermination sites of the Nazi regime in the Second World War (Figure 4.1). The sign was placed

**Figure 4.1**  Sign over the gate at Auschwitz: Arbeit Macht Frei: Work Brings Freedom

there by Major Rudolf Höss, commandant of this labour camp. He seems not to have intended it as a mockery, nor as a false promise to those who worked to exhaustion that they would eventually be released. Rather, the sign stood as a kind of mystical declaration that self-sacrifice in the form of endless labour brings a kind of spiritual freedom. The attribution of mystical qualities to activities called work is not unique to Höss. It is an intuitively held truth that is co-opted by many regimes. The link made between work and freedom is very persuasive and pervasive in Western liberal societies. Perhaps more subtly, the duty to engage in a selective set of activities deemed worthy work can be required of people no matter how damaging to their health and well-being, or how destructive to their families, communities and the environment.

In this chapter, we challenge the link made between work and freedom under the conditions of capitalism. We examine some of the changes in the patterns and labelling of activities we call work in contexts where capitalism is well established. In Marxist-style analyses, this work is frequently referred to as 'labour'. In management education, it is more usual to talk about 'employment': discussions of employment are linked to considerations of productivity gains or expanded opportunities for profit-making. In these contexts, the connection between ways of working and the generation of profit has been elevated to a science. Frederick Taylor is among the influential thinkers who believed that the scientific study of labour as a means to achieve greater efficiency is a good thing. Just what was allowed to come into the equation of the cost of these achievements remains a live issue to this day. Max Weber was another author who contributed to the idea that work can be managed by well-trained specialists who would use rational ideas to improve organisational efficiency and effectiveness, as well as enhancing fairness and justice.

The dominant form of rationality or reasoning that we are calling the institutional logics of capitalism shows a preference for mechanistic or naturalistic metaphors in the conceptualisation of work *as* employment, jobs, contracts, careers or vocations. Together, these subtly diverse notions of work, and how they are expected to function in the interest of economic growth, populated the myth of 'work makes (one) free'. The cumulative effect of such a collective focus on work is deemed to benefit all and becomes a myth to be materialised locally and globally. We argue that under the regime of market-led, competitive capitalism, such a dream of universal benefits cannot materialise. There is a built-in logical inconsistency – a win-lose dynamic that not even the most sophisticated of consultants offering 'win-win' scenarios can overcome.

We begin this chapter with a brief coverage of employment patterns associated with Taylorism. These ideas still explicitly or implicitly influence notions of work efficiency, sometimes in unexpected places and in ways that may be very difficult to notice. We examine the influence of the experts related to the Human Relations School whose ideas were intended to address the perceived shortcomings of Taylorist approaches to managing work. Examining these strands of the direction and control of work as employment is a precursor to a closer look at claims that appear to endorse and value employee empowerment framed in the lexicons of human resource management (HRM) – a development we will turn more specific attention to in Chapter 5.

In most recent years, corporate leadership is coming under increasing pressure to take responsibility on issues of justice, human rights and environmental restoration (Muff et al., 2013). These responsibilities are expressed through the corporate social responsibility (CSR), corporate responsibility (CR) and corporate sustainability (CS) movements that have attracted many followers over recent decades. These movements are given more specific focus in later chapters in terms of thinking about them as potentially radical systemic transformations or as system-preserving responses. In this chapter, we note them in relation to the growing influence of the Principles for Responsible Management Education (PRME) in the shaping and control not only of work but of 'good works' of many kinds.

In this chapter, the claim that employment is a means to human emancipation is examined through the prevailing ideas of work and employment under the conditions of capitalism. These are the conditions that are being intensified the world over in the neo-liberal versions we are asked to think of as 'free trade' – a market determination of outcomes of work and investment that are deemed fair so long as participation is free and unencumbered.

# UNIVERSAL EMANCIPATION THROUGH PAID WORK

What is work? Who does it? How is it organised and valued? How are the benefits and risks of the contemporary arrangements of work distributed?

Neo-liberals view work in the form of paid employment to be the path to freedom. Freedom includes the opportunity to select our occupations and our levels of commitment to employment. Our income from this work gives us the freedom to purchase what we need or what we want. We can choose to save or invest our surplus income to make more money. Does work offer a path to emancipation for everyone in the way neo-liberals propose? To what extent might the shape and control of work be considered as a means to the oppression and exploitation of many, as critical theorists warn us about?

In this chapter, we examine the way in which we shape our work and the organisation through which we conduct and control that work. Perhaps it is more accurate to think of the dynamics of work the other way around. Do the ways in which we choose to organise work somehow provide the frame for how work itself is to be thought of and valued? Is there perhaps a kind of symbiotic relationship of mutual endorsement between the way we conceptualise, name, organise, control and value the activities we now call 'work' or, more specifically, 'employment'? For example, if all highly paid medical specialists and all garbage collectors went out on strike at the same time, perhaps for a year, what would be the relative impact of the withdrawal of their work on whole communities? What if parents refused to parent? Think about the activities at ever-accelerating assembly lines, in self-managed teams pressed to meet increasing outputs, in secured jobs, in casualised contracts, at hot-desks or as vocations when driven by the pressure for ever-greater productivity or efficiency euphemistically represented as the need for organisational or economic growth. Think about all the tasks associated with the care of the young and the frail, and with ensuring the well-being of families and communities. Think of the efforts needed for the task of remaining encouraged and motivated enough to take on the challenges of each day to find the wherewithal for life. For many unemployed people, such work occupies much of their day, often under the strict guidance of a government official or a state-contracted employment service. In almost all OECD nations, full-time caregivers who do not have an independent income, or access to someone else's independent income, are being pressed into employment – often with little regard for the real cost of that employment to the parent, the family and the community.

Ideas of 'work' and how it is to be organised, controlled and valued are deeply entwined. In any given historical time or geographical place, what is deemed as a rightful way to ensure that life is sustained will be deeply embedded in the collective unconscious of that time and place. Such rightful activities may not always be known by the word 'work', but whatever these activities are, the meaning, value, responsibilities and entitlements vested in them cannot be disassociated from the wider social context in which such meaning is made, imposed, valued and policed. Complex beliefs about the right use of time can be harnessed as motivation and as discipline to establish and maintain order. These beliefs can be culturally represented as duties, economic needs or in the fulfilment of ego aspirations. This motivation and discipline are more easily achieved where populations are well socialised into supporting norms. Where the order does not serve all equally well and where the population concurs in unequal outcomes even by those who are disadvantaged by the prevailing arrangements, the conditions of hegemonic control are established. Such conditions of control are more robust and sustainable than power exerted by direct violence or its threat. Chomsky (2013) notes that these subtle forms of control are at their most powerful in realms where freedom is a purported value, in societies that claim to be the most free.

Hegemonic control is, by definition, difficult to see in all societies. In societies that claim to value freedom, the very embeddedness of ideas about worthy work and its connection to well-being in the collective (un)conscious makes them difficult to bring to view for explicit consideration. Many of the theorists we introduced in Chapter 2 tackled the notion of unconscious influences on our understanding and actions. The unconscious commitment to various values applied to work, livelihoods and justice are under scrutiny in this chapter. The link between employment, management and productivity gains to serve company profitability, national incomes statistics and the indicators of the growth of the global economy are common concepts in the interweaving of work and the assessment of just outcomes in OECD associated nations. In other words, where capitalism and democracy are influential organising principles, productivity gains and assumed positive social outcomes are embedded in the naturalised taken-for-granted views that drive many ordinary and everyday decisions.

**Figure 4.2** Who are the real beneficiaries of the system?

Such work is deemed to serve the so-called trickle-down benefits of capitalism promoted by both classical economists and many politicians. Corporations and states work together to shape the conditions of service that provide the opportunities (or otherwise) for the employment now so necessary for human survival. Wider populations who concur in and (tacitly) support this logic may condone explicit discipline or exert subtle pressure in various expressions of approval or disapproval. The extent of violence tolerated in the pressure to drive single mothers 'to work' is an example. The cartoon shown in Figure 4.2 has been on an academic's office door since 1990. It has never seemed out of date. In the current climate of pressure on all unemployed people, some person has taken the trouble to find a number of pins to stab into the heart of the single mother – perhaps the butt of their anger. Such rage may be expressed in many forms and be directed at people who have not been able to find work, or who refuse work that is typically unsafe, unfairly paid or degrading.

Despite the demonisation of many who cannot find suitable paid employment, we are all vulnerable to finding ourselves in this very situation. As the use of robots, drones and electronic control of work(ers) intensifies, automation replaces ever more jobs. At the same time, alternative means of life are being destroyed. The move from a land-based existence in self-sustaining communities organised through minimal specialisation and little need for money, to a much greater dependency on paid employment as the means to survival is now a global phenomenon. This move is heralded historically and in contemporary times as a step towards greater emancipation from what are often (pejoratively) called subsistence economies. It might be thought of as a change from activities that sustain life to systems of paid employment that are supposed to generate the income with which to purchase the means to live.

In Europe and its colonies, this transition has been in progress for many generations. In other parts of the world, the process is merely beginning. The implied argument for this move is that goods and services are more efficiently (and profitably) produced in formalised organisations of increasing size. The promised increase in productivity will trickle down to all contributors. Thus, argue the neo-liberals, economic growth will benefit all, not equally, but according to their input. The market will mete out rewards and discipline according to assumed merit. Justice has been achieved. Or so the neo-liberal story goes. Yet, being forced from one's subsistence ways of life to earn a living in substandard conditions of service, attempting to keep one's job in the tensions and stress-riddled boardrooms, or working at dangerously placed and paced assembly lines, are all part of the patterns of paid employment experienced by many people. From a more critical orientation, these patterns of employment appear to harness people to markets in order to maximise profits rather than to facilitate their emancipation – or the achievement of a transcending spiritual freedom, as the gates to Auschwitz suggested.

## DANGEROUS WORK

Work can be dangerous. Countless lives have been lost in the building of dams and railways in the relentless expansion of empires. Lives continue to be lost in the mining of precious metals and minerals, not only under the conditions of capitalism. Limbs continue to be amputated by unguarded machinery. Workers the world over ingest toxins and suffer stress that eats away at their health. Work in unsafe factories make the headlines around the world for a few days, as did the collapse of the clothing factory in Bangladesh in 2013 in which more than a thousand workers were killed. Does the discourse of human rights (to work) both seed the duty to work and offer an attempt to ameliorate the unsafe or unjust conditions of such work? Would you assess the influence of the United Nations through such instruments as the Global Compact as a friend and ally of the powerful corporations or as a beacon of hope for the (economically) oppressed? Whose responsibility is it to make the conditions of work safe? What power might various individuals have to resist employment under unsafe conditions? The student companion webpage associated with this chapter provides you with some good starting places to explore these questions.

As the processes of market distribution of goods, services and justice have intensified, so too have the criticisms of the conditions of life for many people brought to dependency on such arrangements. Charles Dickens and Upton Sinclair are examples of authors from two different eras and two different geographical regions of the world who graphically illustrated the inhumane conditions of labour they witnessed in their time. Today the Internet gives us more direct witness to the dire conditions under which many people must labour. There are many examples from across the globe where the control of mechanisation, industrialisation and innovation has been a significant part of the rearrangement of societies, communities, families and personal identities. These conditions exist in the widely published examples of contemporary sweat-shops globally and more subtly in the tension-filled lives of many people secured in employment in factories, corporations, schools, hospitals, NGOs and other institutions the world over, be they executives, middle managers, technicians or cleaners. Even more vulnerable are the lives of those who must rely on short-term contracts that do not generate reliable or life-sustaining incomes.

There is much more to be said about many forms of work, its control and the distribution of its benefits and risks. For this chapter, we take the starting point of our discussion from the 1970s. At this time, a specific crisis for capital was made a crisis for all – and thus the responsibility for each of us to overcome it. The remedy was to be the restructuring and devaluing of work: a task that required the diminishing of the influence of worker organisations, such as unions, and the transfer of worker concerns to employer-sanctioned worker support services. Careers for guidance counsellors, work-station re-designers and workplace-based pastors were in the ascendant.

In the 1970s, ideas about development and productivity gains were developed in ways through which neo-liberals could harness governmental support and public opinion for cost cuts in one region and investments in others. In some places, specialised job designs and bureaucratic organisational structures were being unsettled (Lipietz, 1997). Mass production with dedicated long-run plant and machinery was considered too rigid to respond to increased global competition and an increasingly sophisticated consumer market. The associated deskilled workforce was believed to be too inflexible to meet the demands of increased international competition (Piore and Sabel, 1984; Cappelli and Rogovsky, 1994). Scientific rules that were designed to increase productivity and managerial control over workers were now being viewed as creating too many structural benefits for employees in terms of creating influential internal labour markets and personally enriching career paths for low-level workers. Bureaucratic rules governing promotion, sick pay, leave entitlements and layoffs were increasingly perceived to provide unions with too much bargaining power that could restrict management prerogative and create high fixed costs affecting international competitiveness and profits (Thompson and McHugh, 1990).

Contests to the rigidity of the scientific rules governing work and the bureaucratic rules governing workers were to come. Throughout the 1970s and 1980s, many employer groups and some governments wanted to create greater organisational and labour flexibility to meet the challenges posed by the 1970s' crisis, and to increase international competitiveness, productivity and profits. The theme of the need for greater organisational and labour flexibility continued throughout the 1990s. However, the discourse of 'crisis' could not be sustained indefinitely. It was to be morphed into a universal exhortation to contribute to the necessary productivity improvements that were to safeguard jobs, firms, industries and whole nation's economies. Organisational and labour flexibility ideas and practice were widely established as a necessary dynamic for global competitiveness (Ehrensal, 1995), a race we must all enter to safeguard the future of capitalism and thus our own future and that of our children's children. The free-trade musketeers were on a roll!

Since the 1980s, multinational companies have lobbied governments to implement structural reforms to facilitate access to international goods and services trade. These structural reforms and the removal of trade barriers and the deregulation of finance markets have been central to enabling large organisations to restructure and relocate production and increasingly service operations to make use of cheaper labour and less restrictive labour and environmental standards (Pollert, 1991). This offshore relocation of multinational companies involved downsizing local workforces, de-layering management levels, as well as entering and withdrawing from foreign countries as served corporate interests (Reich, 1992; Perkin, 1996; Sussens-Messerer, 1998; Gandolfi, 2007). The precursor of this pattern of investment and divestment was the deregulation of the labour markets and the destabilisation of unions. There seemed little real concern about the emancipation of individuals that work was supposed to bring. It was an assumed truth. Improved conditions of employment, hard won by many workers' organisations, were being both actively and subtly undermined. To explore this undermining, we turn to the work of Braverman (1974) and the theorists who took up his analysis to examine this dynamic.

## ORGANISING FOR INCREASED PRODUCTIVITY

Throughout the 1970s and 1980s, governments, employers, behavioural scientists, unions and employees were raising concerns about the effects of Taylorist mass-production methods and bureaucratic administrative systems on workers and productivity, but not all with the same motivation or anticipated outcomes. Drawing upon Marx, Braverman (1974) argued that Taylorist work designs prevalent in the period following the Second World War led to the dehumanisation of the workforce. This dehumanisation, he argued, was achieved through the process of dividing work into small, specific tasks that required minimal training, thus deskilling jobs and people and enabling workers to be easily replaced. It entailed separating what is often referred to as the 'doing' and the 'thinking' components of work. For Braverman (1974), these Taylorist production and control methods reduced the worker to an appendage of the plant and machinery and are perhaps usefully reconsidered through Marx's notion of alienation introduced in Chapter 2. Many contracting firms continue to organise workforces and production processes based firmly around Taylorist hierarchical manufacturing processes (Crowley et al., 2010) with demonstrable benefits for successful players, but devastating consequences for the most vulnerable in this rearrangement of work.

## FLEXING FLEXIBLE NOTIONS OF FLEXIBILITY

By the 1980s, a number of employee groups and some critically orientated behavioural scientists were raising concerns over specialised job designs, arguing that these designs did not fulfil workers' psychological needs, as well as preventing them from participating in decision-making and meaningful contributions that might help address workplace issues (Cappelli and Rogovsky, 1994). In keeping with the ideas generated from the Human Relations School (HRS) of thought, specialised jobs were believed to be linked to low morale, low job satisfaction and high absenteeism. The separation of conception from execution and the inflexibility of jobs were believed to lead to poor communication between workers and managers, thus preventing workers from contributing their work knowledge to help improve the functioning of the organisation. Combined, these negative impacts were believed to be linked to decreased productivity and even some examples of deaths caused by inadequate understanding of effective organisation as well as specific technical issues. Employee groups and behavioural scientists holding these views argued that the productivity issues evident throughout the 1970s could be addressed by widening the skill bases of jobs, improving worker flexibility and increasing worker participation in decision-making to enable employee contributions to workplace improvement.

# FROM TASK SPECIALISATION TO FLEXIBILITY OF SKILL, TIME AND LOCATION OF WORK

Braverman's (1974) conceptual framework invites us to think about workers as objects of class control. The consciousness that arises from this depiction of the relationship between the ways Marx framed the relationship of capitalism as two classes with conflicting interests can explain the associated ideas of class warfare as a response to unsatisfactory conditions of work. As Gramsci pointed out, this is an inefficient and expensive way to control employees (Burawoy, 2012). Burawoy (1979) helps us see that gaining the consent of workers to their situation is a more effective form of control (Beverungen, 2011: 153). These ideas were to filter into much management theory about the desirability of certain types of work(er) flexibility.

As well as implementing increased skill flexibility, changes in job design were also to transcend previous notions of working time (Allvin, 2008). Once tightly linked to the notion (if not the actuality) of a standard 40-hour week and embedded within national boundaries, exploiting time has come to include over- and under-employment. Working across international time-zones may mean an employee will do double duty just to get a cross-time-zone project completed. Service or contract staff may be attempting to patch together inadequate and unstable work arrangements to meet their costs of living. More recently, employee groups and some academics are arguing for a need to improve work–life balance. Part of this argument is that the standard working day does not reflect the needs of an increasingly diverse workforce; in particular, the growing proportion of women in the labour market. More flexible arrangements – for example, part-time work – are considered one response that will enable employees to balance their multiple responsibilities and various desires to achieve balance between work and other life commitments and interests. Selectively articulated and valued, 'flexibility' became the new buzzword, and the characteristic most desired in a workforce, in policy and in legislative regimes. Such flexibility, it was implied, would empower the worker by cutting their shackles to outdated ideas about work and destructive unions. It would place the responsibility for employment and employability squarely on the individual – the centrepiece of the neo-liberal mythology.

The 1980s and 1990s might be variously reviewed as the era of 'employee empowerment' or their delusion, depending on your perspective. Framed in their earlier formats, these orientations were promulgated as the effective importation and adaptation of 'Japanese management practices' into the car-manufacturing industries – promising to make US workers safe from growing Japanese competition. Employee vulnerability and fears were skilfully melded with ever more sophisticated organisational rhetoric to bring about a much greater interest in the 'flattening of hierarchies' achieved, for example, through the introduction of quality-control circles that were later to be variously strategically re-named with less reference to their origins in Japanese management practices. Managerially driven ideas of teamwork became the new means to generate worker cooperation and collaboration.

In contrast to the dramatic examples of both draconian and enlightened Taylorist work arrangements in factories all around the world, we also want to consider some other groups of workers who are part of the functionally flexible workforce. These are the seemingly secure and often well-paid workers in 'the core' of this segment of the workforce. A number of metaphors have been used to describe the apparently flexible ways of organising work in that context. The 'matrix firm', the 'shamrock firm' and the 'virtual organisation' are three examples. These metaphors share common themes captured by the notions of 'the boundaryless organization' (Ashkenas, et al., 1995) and the 'boundaryless career' (Briscoe and Hall, 2006; Allvin, 2008; Zeitz et al., 2009). In the arrangement of work and organisation depicted in these metaphors, workers are supposed to be able to transcend all kinds of boundaries assumed to be more porous: work and home, organisation and the nation-state, and the private-self and the public-self. The individual is charged with balancing their time across work and non-work activities.

Rather than emancipating employees in processes of self-direction, this change in the way employees are managed is strikingly depicted by Barker (1993) as a particularly powerful form of concertive control applied by workers to themselves. The employee empowerment rhetoric that was promoted actually resulted in the deconstruction of the skill-based power built up by the unions after Taylorism took hold. The weakening of employee influence was achieved under the ever more skilful demonisation of the unions as being too confrontational and destructive in an era of accelerating competition. Workers and managers needed 'to pull together' in the interests of all. The prevailing ideology was shifted from an explicit recognition of plural interests that needed careful management to a (deluded) rhetoric of unitarism in which workers and citizens were to believe that the global intensification of production and consumption was for the benefit of all. The analyses of the consequent weakening of the unions can be better understood through the analytical approach of Foucault and the critics of modernism who track this shift of power from external to internal control (Humphries, 1998). Where such consent is gained despite conditions of injustice to which the oppressed become normalised, we can call on Gramsci's work to test to what extent the conditions of hegemony have been achieved under the conditions of neo-liberalism.

One important policy change embedded through the promulgation of neo-liberalist ideas has been the abandonment of full employment which dominated political thinking under Keynesian agendas in favour of Milton Friedman's (1968) theorising of the natural rate of unemployment. This adaptation of Friedman's notion of natural rates of unemployment was to argue and to justify the idea that policies of greater labour market flexibility were the only way to increase employment (Palley, 2010). As part of the neo-liberal agenda, Ronald Regan and Margaret Thatcher began the process of deregulating the US and UK labour markets and, in doing so, undermined the power of unions, reduced employment protection and employee rights, downgraded social welfare nets, including unemployment benefits, and placed downward pressure on the incomes of workers (Palley, 2010; Grady and Harvie, 2011). Moreover, by the mid-1980s, business leaders and governments were being supported by a growing body of academics offering a number of organisational flexibility frameworks (Atkinson, 1984). The idea occupying many minds was not whether this was a *good* move for the universal emancipation of people but 'how to do it'. In other words, a once normative theory can now be read as a descriptive theory – and as such can be read to seek the means to intensify a manifest reality.

# THE FLEXIBLE FIRM AS NEW AND DESIRABLE ARCHETYPE FOR HUMAN ORGANISATION

In his depiction of the 'flexible firm', Atkinson (1984: 29) proposed that new organisational structures would involve the break-up of the labour force into increasingly peripheral, and therefore numerically flexible, groups of workers, clustered about a numerically stable core group of employees who would conduct the organisation's key, firm-specific activities (Figure 4.3). Numerical flexibility relates to the ability of organisations to alter the number of employees rapidly, and is achieved through policies such as part-time and temporary, casual or contingent workers, and flexible working hours. The number of periphery workers can expand or contract rapidly to meet the staffing needs of the organisation. For Atkinson, the core workforce is comprised of people whose skills are deemed essential to the firm's operations; and they gain job security and high wages in exchange for becoming functionally flexible. Functional flexibility relates to a worker performing a variety of tasks as required by the employer, and is generally associated with practices such as teamwork, job rotation and remote working (van der Meer and Ringdal, 2009).

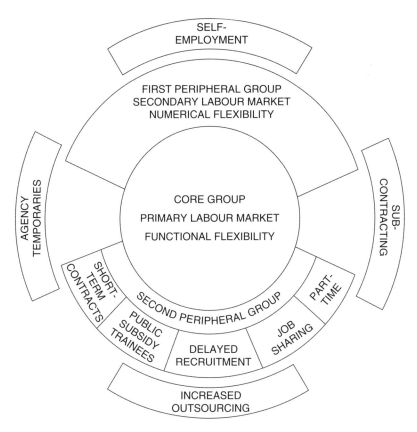

**Figure 4.3** Atkinson's diagram of the flexible firm

*Source*: Atkinson (1984: 29)

Well into the second decade of the twenty-first century, Atkinson's (1984) depiction of the workforce made structurally, functionally and numerically flexible can be seen in actuality the world over. Atkinson illustrates the interconnections of the labour market segments. We ask you to imagine this diagram with constant pressure on the most expensive or most readily replaced employees – and the related outward and inward movement of employees. Perhaps spare an extra thought for those pressed completely out of the diagram, the unemployed, the frail and those deemed un-useful to 'the system'.

Atkinson's flexible firm model can be usefully adapted to depict the relationships that are developing in the global economy between multinational corporations and outsourced firms and their sub-contractors and the complex supply chain arrangements developing within the global economy. This depiction can also be applied to the government sector where many public services have been contracted out to the private sector (including locally owned and multinational companies) and/or to NGOs. Exceptions to this way of organising may well thrive in various parts of the world. There may be some fabulous showcase alternatives in your region. These are not significant enough, however, to invalidate the depiction presented by Atkinson, to mop up its outfall around the globe or to address the dangerous environmental and health issues increasingly associated with this system of production and consumption. How can we support our view of this as a systemic outcome?

Palley (2010) and Scott (2011) demonstrate the combined effect of these processes on the job losses in the American manufacturing sector since the signing of the free-trade agreement known as NAFTA, one of the many regional versions of these agreements we introduced in Chapter 1. The US manufacturing sector job losses have often been explained away in terms of improvements in productivity, and, therefore, fewer workers are required for the same level of output. Palley (2010), however, demonstrates that, in the United States, manufacturing job loss is a result of the NAFTA agreement and outsourcing to Mexico (Atkinson et al., 2007). Importantly, between 1991 and 2007, manufacturing employment fell regardless of whether the US economy was expanding or retracting. Scott (2011) suggests that, on average, 40,200 jobs have been displaced per annum from the US to Mexico since NAFTA took effect. Of these, 60.8 per cent were in the manufacturing sector. Moreover, in Mexico, an estimated 1.3 million jobs were lost in the agricultural sector as a result of cheap and subsidised US corn imports.

Since China joined the World Trade Organization (WTO) firms have further relocated from Mexico to China to access even less expensive labour. Thus, the development of these agreements has enabled multinational corporations to develop offshore productions plants, while consumption has been supported by asset value inflation and credit (as discussed in Chapter 3) rather than improvements in the income levels of workers (Palley, 2010). Perhaps use this example to examine the various free-trade commitments in your region, or regions of interest to you. PACER Plus (OCTA, 2011) is an example of what critics are calling 'free trade on steroids'! Vanguards for change, such as the Sierra Club (2013), want to transform this free-trade process into one of responsible trade. Do you agree with them? If not, why not? If you agree, what kind of management education should we be aiming for? How would 'responsible management' look in practice?

The restructuring of work according to neo-liberal principles is not limited to the corporate sector. Government agencies are frequently restructured and reduce their labour forces in line with commitments made within multinational and bilateral agreements (e.g., free-trade agreements) to reduce government spending (Kelsey, 1995). These restructurings in the local markets are being facilitated by the deregulation of the labour market, enabling the erosion of the strength of unions and the dismantling of the labour relations frameworks associated with Keynesian macro-level employment practices. Restructuring and downsizing and the changes to the shape and conditions of employment are collectively referred to as necessary for the achievement of organisational and labour flexibility. Despite such urgent and creative calls as can be found in the Sierra Club's appeal for responsible trade and the more conservative United Nations, the G8 appears to remain firmly harnessed to an American Dream that is a nightmare for many – inside and outside the US.

## EXPOSING THE FALLACIES: THE TRICKLE DOWN OF BENEFITS? YEAH, RIGHT!

Joan has worked at the light-bulb assembly line for many years. The work has been boring, but the support in hard times generated among her fellow workers continued to motivate her to come to work. Over recent months, Joan and her workmates have been advised that unless they increase their outputs per hour, the factory might be moved offshore. The women put their mind to the matter. Sure enough, they found ways to up the outputs. The improved profit their company was making was reported in the local paper. How pleasing. Not long ago, the team was again asked to put on their thinking-caps to see if they could find further improvements to their outputs. Again, efficiencies were found. Record profits were reported. Confidence in the security of their incomes grew. The women were proud to record their new processes in the employee manual so that future employees could continue the good work. As their confidence in the security of their jobs grew, Joan and her friends enjoyed comparing the increasing numbers of purchases they had made in the village – from more frequent visits to the local bakery to the upgrading of household appliances. Joan found that she could now afford to employ a helper around the house from time to time. The efforts of Joan and her friends to increase outputs were generating a satisfying growth in the village economy.

You can well imagine that Joan was especially gutted to read in the local paper that the company had decided to move offshore. Labour rates in the offshore plant would be more competitive and the government there was not so stringent on the occupational health and safety requirements Joan and her friends were used to. The factory would be closed within the week. 'The productivity manuals we have made will be an excellent "how to" guide for the new workers', thought Joan angrily. So much for their capacity to spend their wages in the village! Joan's helper would need to be let go. Her helper would need to curtail her own household spending. The thriving little bakery in the village would close. Joan is looking for another job but there are few to be found. Many of her friends need them as much as she does. She thinks about the village women in some far-off land who will soon be packing light-bulbs to pay for the food that they will no longer have time to grow in their village gardens. She thinks of the hope these women will feel as the fruit of their new job opportunities trickle into their village. She knows this hope will last only until such time as the corporation has discovered a new place to expand profits. That is global development. There's no stopping it, she thinks.

As a result of the structural adjustment and deregulation of global finance and the labour markets that occurred during the 1980s and 1990s, employers from diverse nations have implemented various forms of organisational and labour flexibility strategies that can be depicted through the Atkinson model. The international trends associated with various forms of organisational and labour flexibility include organisational re-engineering and downsizing, increased outsourcing and the emergence of an international division of labour, and the creation of a more localised periphery workforce (Rodgers, 1992; Brenner et al.,

2004; Fletcher, 2009). Since then, the process has only been intensified and can be almost seamlessly implemented across nations and within organisations as diverse as corporations, government departments and NGOs. Ironically, perhaps, community start-ups and various social enterprises intending to address the issues we are concerned about in this book also have an impact on the downward pressure of wages when the work they undertake is performed by unpaid or poorly paid volunteers.

# DOWNSIZING, RESTRUCTURING AND RE-ENGINEERING THE CORE

Various forms of work reorganisation and reduction have become increasingly prevalent since the 1980s. Justified as a way of cutting costs and implementing more flexible organisation of the workforce, restructuring involving mass redundancies has become a common and normalised part of organisational life (Gandolfi, 2007). During the 1980s, organisational restructuring and mass redundancies were mostly associated with blue-collar jobs, poorly educated workers and the low skilled. The blame was pinned on people deemed unproductive or ill prepared for the jobs on offer. During the 1990s, layoffs occurred even in profitable organisations, disproportionately affecting white-collar workers, and often involving outsourcing jobs once performed by full-time workers (Ehrensal, 1995). Metaphors used to describe redundancy included 'pruning the deadwood' and 'cutting the fat', portraying the downsized staff as lacking in 'value' to the organisation, or as being too old, having outdated skills or just being an expendable resource. It was the duty of corporate office-bearers to eliminate them in the interest of their mandate to maximise corporate profit. Managers in the government sector were charged to find efficiencies in the use of taxpayer money. In the philanthropic sector, business notions of efficiency began to influence notions of effectiveness in the use of charitable donations.

In the early part of 2000, layoffs could be attributed to a new looming crisis for capital and could be framed as a (naturalised) global recession. Approximately one million jobs were lost in the United States in 2001 (Herring, 2001). Redundancies were affecting both the local core and periphery workers and the international labour markets of multinational companies. For example, in one week, three Japanese firms between them announced 37,400 job cuts, of which 11,400 were in international operations and 2,000 were local subcontractors (CBS News, 2001a, b). The seeming inevitability and the continuation of the pressures on workers have become exacerbated in the first decades of the twenty-first century as employees jostle for position in the model in order to sustain or enhance their life. Even more recently, global job losses have occurred as an outcome of the 'Great Recession' or, as others describe it, the 'Financial Crisis' of the late 2000s sparked by the housing market collapse in the US (these more recent statistics are presented below).

How do we explain the tolerance of populations to this situation? One explanation offered by critical theorists is to be found in the pervasiveness of neo-liberal ideas. These ideas, however, are theories. These theories and their constituent social fabrications have been elevated to an ideology. They have been manifest in practice with such fervour that their principles could be called a dogma. They have been normalised to such an extent that they might be considered as well naturalised. Where these conditions are exploitative and pass as a normal or natural way of being, the conditions of hegemony have been achieved. Such an achievement is a significant achievement of power, but, as Foucault is good at explaining, such power is never exercised in a one-dimensional track; or, as Gramsci argued, consent to hegemony is never complete: the elite must continually negotiate consent with subordinate groups, as such hegemony can be challenged in these negotiations.

One way that hegemonic situations can be challenged and transformed is through the exposure of systemic injustices and exploitations. This means noticing and working with the paradoxes and contradictions within a given order and demanding that these be addressed (Seo and Creed, 2002). To do this in our own contexts requires us to revisit our ideas about ethics and 'the good society' with which we began Chapter 1. We can explore this issue more with a closer look at the generally wide acceptance of outplacement/outsourcing strategies. Based on using the Atkinson model as a normative theory, outplacing people is not deemed a moral issue as much as a mechanical function of a well-functioning, self-regulating economy. In the more recent rescue of capitalist interests, most intensely experienced in Cyprus, Greece, Italy and Spain, national economies are required to 'take a radical haircut' – a metaphor cavalierly distracting attention from the actual workers who will lose jobs and livelihoods. Other nations are already committed to more regular and perhaps less overtly visible trims! This normalisation of the needs of capital by controlling work deserves a closer look.

# OUTSOURCING WORK

Atkinson (1984) argues that organisations should outsource functions that are not essential to the core business of the firm (profession, industry, government department or national interest). Initially, this outsourcing involved contracting out functions to local firms. However, this practice has come to include international outsourcing, resulting in an intensification of the international distribution of labour (Harzing, 2004; Lincoln, 2009). Citizens in host nations gain employment, while firms gain access to relatively less expensive labour markets. Combined, this is believed to lead to lower priced yet higher quality goods available to consumers.

## MOVING GOODS ABOUT

Jamie is a builder. He is surprised to find that to be competitive in his bid for the contract to build the new school in the forested region where he lives, it is more economic to purchase timber from abroad. Ironically, the timber he is importing originated in the very region in which he lives. 'How can that be right?' he wonders! Across the ocean, in a town some way from his village in the Pacific, Sione is shopping for food. He sees the wonderful fresh fish in the refrigerated section of the supermarket. It would have been caught and cleaned by the big trawlers off the coast of his island. The price for the fish is too high for Sione. He settles for a can of imported tuna. Just as well his cousin has a job on the fishing fleet. He will surely remember to send some of his wages back to the village. Sione will make sure to ring and remind him – if the woman who makes the phone connections from some far-off land can understand his language that is! How he misses Ani who used to run the telephone exchange in the village. She was such a hoot. Pity about her diabetes! Thank goodness for the new nurse, though. She is bringing great medicines to help keep Ani comfortable. 'I wonder who pays the nurse?' he thinks, but does not stay with the thought. The kids are waiting for the shopping. Pity for them that it will be tinned corned beef for dinner again and not that yummy looking fish! Best he hurries back to the village. He best not miss the bus! 'That bus! Belching beast! What a joke!' Nothing like those air-con jobs he has seen on TV! 'Maybe one day I will have a car of my own and I will not even need a flash bus!' For this to happen, Sione knows he would need a job.

Evidence suggests that, although outsourcing was initially deemed most suitable for low-skilled work, a variety of functions, at all skill levels, are now being performed externally to the firm, including in offshore locations (Miller and Mukherji, 2010). Low-skilled positions are often outsourced to factories and call centres which operate employment conditions reminiscent of an intensified Taylorist manufacturing process. High-skilled and semi-skilled service work is also being outsourced. Information technology, medical tourism, engineering and dental work is moved to Asia, film production work to New Zealand so long as the actors' unions do not make waves. This mobility of work has led to the classification of the outsourcing of skill based on locations where appropriately skilled labour is available. Repatriation is the latest of these moves of work. As Asian contexts such as Singapore become saturated, and office and factory rents rise, the scorched lands of past work-exits begin to look like green fields with a relatively well-educated and suitably domesticated workforce to make the move there attractive.

Despite variances in national definitions of full- and part-time work, the creation of a localised peripheral labour market to meet the numerical interests of organisations is evident in the international rise in non-standard forms of work; for example, part-time employment, temporary and casualised work. There has been a marked increase in the part-time workforce, for both males and females (ILO, 2004). Workers in the periphery do not have job security, and often have fewer benefits compared to full-time, permanent employees; for example, periphery workers are much less likely to have sick leave or holiday entitlements, and frequently receive lower hourly wages (Lee et al., 2007). Both outsourcing and the creation of periphery work transfers business risk and responsibility from organisations and the state to the newly contracted firm or the individual worker (Lambert, 2008).

# OUTCOMES OF ORGANISATIONAL FLEXIBILITY

The adoption and extension of flexible work practices have been accompanied by contradictory trends of over-employment, under-employment and the growth in numbers of the structurally unemployed (McBride, 1999) and of the non-voluntary volunteer (O'Shea, 2010).

## The Over-employed

'Over-employment' is the term used to describe people who are working more hours than they would ideally like to, or are working significantly more than the standard working week. Although figures on official contracted hours are available, there appears to be a paucity of comparative global figures on actual hours worked (Lee et al., 2007). High, officially legal hours of work are most often associated with developing countries. Over-employment, however, appears to affect every category of worker the world over as they relate to the flexible firm model. Long hours are associated with core salaried workers. Outsourced workers, piece workers and small contractors are required to work ever-increasing hours to meet price and delivery date obligations. Often, family members will contribute un(der) acknowledged support. Low-paid hourly workers and the periphery causalised workers are seeking paid over-time or multiple job holdings to earn enough to survive. These trends have been found in countries as diverse as the US (Hymowitz, 1997), Australia (van Gallecum et al., 2008), New Zealand (Bain, 2001) and China (Huang, 2010). While men are more likely to work extended hours, more women are also working more than the hard-won notion of a 40-hour week.

## Under-employment and Involuntary Part-time Work

'Under-employment' is the term used to describe the portion of the workforce that is employed part-time, is needing, willing and able to work more hours, but is unable to find additional hours of work. This is termed 'involuntary part-time work' (Walling and Clancy, 2010). Such workers have been recorded in Australia (van Gallecum et al., 2008), the UK (Walling and Clancy, 2010) and New Zealand (Statistics New Zealand, 2010) but are evident the world over. More recently, shorter working hours have been associated with family-friendly practices and portrayed as a method of creating a work–life balance. This benefit is often associated with the increased proportion of women in the labour market and offered as one solution to enable them to engage actively in paid employment while simultaneously caring for their family. We critically address this issue in Chapter 6. However, this argument assumes that women, or any individual, can choose the type of hours that meets their personal preference. Walling and Clancy (2010: 17) note that in 'the real world, hours are not this flexible ... the employer, institutions like trade unions, economic conditions and the degree of labour mobility, all determine the actual hours offered to workers.' Additionally, Lee et al. (2007) demonstrate that practices such as flexi-time are often viewed as fringe benefits for valued employees, and so a trade-off is made with longer hours in return for flexible conditions. These examples have some commentators questioning the degree of tangible worker benefit realised by these flexible practices (Skorstad, 2009).

## STRETCHING HOMEWORK

Shelley was relieved to read a memo from her manager in which he suggested that, instead of returning to the office full time when baby Emma turns ten weeks old, she might like to consider coming in only three days a week and to work the other two days from home. Shelley was pleased. This meant she could spend more time with Emma and at the same time reduce the cost of childcare. The first few weeks seemed to go well, though Shelley remained exhausted from Emma's many unsettled nights. Emma seemed also to need more attention during the day than she had in the first few weeks they were at home together. Soon Shelley was choosing not to go back to sleep after Emma's 4 a.m. breast feed. She felt she could better use that time catching up on work emails. It seemed to her that the tasks embedded in the emails coming from the office were becoming bigger and more complex. Perhaps she was imagining it. She would ask Emma's Dad to take Emma for a few long walks over the weekends so she could be sure to stay on top of the workload. She did not want to risk being asked to come into the office five days a week. It was, after all, a privilege to be able to work from home.

# STRUCTURAL ADJUSTMENT: UNEMPLOYMENT AND UNEMPLOYABILITY

Restructuring programmes throughout the 1980s and 1990s led to rising unemployment for most Western nations, up until the latter part of the 1990s when unemployment began to fall (*The Economist*, 2000). Throughout the 2000s, employment and unemployment rose and fell along with economic growth and recession. In response to the fall in unemployment in the mid-2000s, many commentators believe that structural unemployment is a permanent fixture of the neoliberal labour market policy because those who are unemployed help to keep real wages down and help to discipline those in the workforce to accept poorer working conditions and wages than they would otherwise agree to (Lee et al., 2007).

In the first two decades of the twenty-first century, significant job losses have been attributed to the bursting of the US housing market. In their report, the ILO (2011) details the extent of changes to employment between 2007 and 2010. In 2010, there were an estimated 205 million people unemployed globally, a rate of 6.2 per cent, up from 5.6 per cent in 2007. This is despite indications of a recovery in the latter part of 2010, including increased private consumption, GDP, investment and trade at higher pre-crisis levels and 'it is clear that the ongoing economic recovery is not yet leading to a sufficient expansion in employment opportunities in many countries' (ILO, 2010: ix). Global youth unemployment (those aged between 15 and 24 years) was 12.6 per cent in 2010, up from 11.8 per cent in 2007 (but slightly down on 2009 figures of 12.8 per cent). However, there is evidence that there is significant youth discouragement, with an estimated 1.7 million youth not in the labour market, and as such are not counted in unemployment figures.

For the same period, real wages have yet to match productivity increases. This is likely to extend the crisis as workers are still unable to purchase the items that keep the consumer dynamic of this system moving – an issue we turn to in Chapter 7. An estimated 1.5 billion workers, or 50.1 per cent of workers, were in vulnerable employment in 2009; this figure is up on pre-crisis levels, which was showing a steady decline in this group. For the extreme working poor (those earning US$1.25 a day), figures for 2009 were estimated at 20.7 per cent up from pre-crisis predictions by 40 million people. Workers earning below US$2 per day are estimated at 1.2 billion workers worldwide, or 39.9 per cent. Regional differences show that 55 per cent of the unemployed are concentrated in developed countries and the European Union region, yet these regions only make up 15 per cent of the world's population; moreover, in these regions, part-time employment grew considerably throughout the crisis and continued to grow in the recovery phase of 2010. Moreover, male-dominated jobs and industries were significantly affected by the crisis, leading to more men than women losing employment.

Statistical indications of the generally very high rates of unemployment in Europe, the US, Asia and the Pacific do not make clear the specific ways this unemployment manifests itself in particular communities. Take some time to explore the way (un)employment is distributed in your communities. In New Zealand, for example, over 20 per cent of youth identifying as Pacific Islanders were reported to 'not be in employment, education or training' (NEET). In the far North, over 50 per cent of youth do not have paid work. Some say, then, that they should move to where the jobs are. Easier said than done! As the location of available work changes, so then too must people move? Current patterns of migration show that many people do move to find work. Many people have always needed to do so. Family disruption by the type of work now on offer has its own characteristics. Explore, for example, what the impact of the mining boom in Australia is generating in terms of social patterns. Rough and dangerous work still undertaken by undocumented workers in the US ensures a wall of silence around conditions of work on offer. Prostitution as a form of work is undertaken as a necessity by many women, men and children. Unemployment is no picnic. When your life depends on employment and you cannot find it, you will be ripe for the pickings of any unscrupulous employer or the well-meaning agency mandated to mop up the unemployed locally and internationally. The creation of an international division of labour, coupled with deregulated finance markets, enables organisations to draw upon the unemployed from across international boundaries to replace localised workers. Alternatively, organisations can discipline localised workers to accept lower conditions of work simply by threatening to relocate.

Along with structural unemployment, there is a growing recognition of a group of workers who are now deemed unemployable. Core unemployment refers to the section of the workforce that has been rendered unemployable due to a mismatch between job skills and job demand. This is often attributed to a structural change in the local labour market. In a recent study of rural counties in Pennsylvania, for example, Julian and colleagues (2010) reported that, in rural counties, the majority of unemployed fell into the core unemployable category, and in only one case was the percentage of those deemed unemployable less than 50 per cent of the total unemployed. In most cases, the number of unemployable people was assessed as well over 50 per cent of the total unemployed.

# ALTERNATIVE FORMS OF WORK: NON-VOLUNTARY VOLUNTEER

In addition to changes in paid employment, neo-liberal policy changes have led to the (re)emergence of a new form of worker – the 'non-voluntary volunteer' (O'Shea, 2010) – a group of workers that were once described as unfree labour such as slaves, bonded serfs and enforced prostitutes. These practices are still prevalent today and involve women, men and children (Miles, 1987; Kerr-Ritchie, 2002).

## CONTEMPORARY SLAVERY

Women, men and children are at risk of being drawn into slavery by force or seduction. For some, the conditions of their bondage may not be overtly named as slavery, but their lack of freedom to leave their place of work is tantamount to the same thing. This makes it difficult to put an actual figure on contemporary slavery. The available statistics can only be thought of as the 'tip of the iceberg' (Hardy, 2013).

But work-as-slavery might be considered also in a more seemingly benign context. The non-voluntary volunteer has been created as a joint outcome of increased unemployment and the reduction on welfare expenditure associated with neo-liberalism and a renewed emphasis on individual responsibility to care for the self. Along with the renewed emphasis on user-pays systems for services and notions of 'active citizenship', previous state welfare entitlements to unemployment benefits have been transformed into various work-for-the-dole policies. The unemployed must enter a contract and perform volunteer duties in exchange for a welfare payment (Ramia, 2002). The non-voluntary volunteer workforce supplements capitalism by being forced to accept work that was once paid for either by the state through government employment or by employers through an assumed just wage.

Thus, this new workforce helps to discipline those in paid employment to accept lower conditions of employment as the alternatives for everyone are far less acceptable. One way this is achieved in the lives of those who already have paid work is to encourage or require non-voluntary unpaid overtime. Many will accept this work for fear of losing their own job. Such informal job expansion is a practice that is heralded as adding to productivity and as enhancing employment flexibility. This requirement to work extra unpaid hours could equally be described as a form of slavery. It puts workers at greater risk of exhaustion, stress and related workplace accidents. It causes distress in families. The practice produces unpaid work by some that could provide the paid work for those who need it.

# THE GLOBAL REDISTRIBUTION OF WORK, INCOME AND TAX TAKE

Palley (2010) argues that the neo-liberal growth model relies on redistributing income from lower income earners to high income earners and corporate profits. Combined, the above practices have been accompanied by a global redistribution of income and wealth on a global scale. There are growing income disparities between and within nations. The incomes of the highest paid workers, for example CEOs, have grown exponentially since the 1970s. Meanwhile, other groups of workers have experienced downward pressure on their incomes; specifically, real incomes have eroded since the 1970s for those with low skills, those in the periphery and those reliant on welfare provision. At the same time, the gap between poor and rich nations has also grown (Mander, 1996; Perkin, 1996).

Between the early 1990s and the mid-2000s, despite a period of rapid economic growth and strong job creation in many countries, the income for high-income households rose faster than for low-income households, the wage share between workers and capital declined, and the gap between the top and bottom 10 per cent of wage-earners grew in most countries (ILO, 2008). In the same period, the ILO report that, as a result of performance-based systems (which ironically have not necessarily led to improved performance), there has been an exponential growth in earnings of CEOs coupled with slow wage growth for workers in many countries. The ILO (2008: 3) illustrates the effect of this in the US:

> between 2003 and 2007, executive managers' pay grew in terms by a total of 45%, compared with a real pay increase of 15% in the case of the average executive, and less than 3% for the average American worker. Hence by 2007 the average executive manager in the 15 largest US firms earned more than 500 times the average employee in the United States, compared with over 300 times in 2003.

Palley (2010) points out that, between 1979 and 2006, the share of income for the bottom 40 per cent of Americans decreased significantly; at the same time, the income share for the top 20 per cent increased, and significantly so for the top 5 per cent. More dramatically, the bottom 80 per cent of Americans' income share fell from 58.6 per cent in 1979 to 51.5 per cent in 2006, and, conversely, the top 20 per cent had an income share growth from 41.4 per cent in 1979 to 48.5 per cent in 2006. Moreover, the top 1 per cent of income share in the US grew significantly from the early 1970s (Pons-Vignon, 2010) and continued to grow throughout the 'Great Financial Crisis', amidst corporate bailouts with money that Pons-Vignon (2010) argues was never available for health or welfare spending prior to the 'Great Financial Crisis'.

Outsourcing was initially deemed most suitable for low-skilled work; however, now a variety of functions, at all skill levels, are being performed externally to the firm, including in offshore locations (Miller and Mukherji, 2010). Low-skilled positions are often outsourced to factories which operate employment conditions reminiscent of an intensified Taylorist manufacturing process. In comparison, high-skilled and semi-skilled service work is being outsourced; for example, information technology and engineering workers in India and film production workers in New Zealand. This leads us to suggest that companies seek access to appropriately skilled and relatively less expensive workers in the global arena.

To compete with increased global competition, nationally based firms and industries have frequently responded by also restructuring and downsizing the labour force, and reducing wages and conditions (Brunhes, 1989; Ehrensal, 1995; Kelsey, 1995; Perkin, 1996). Those unable to compete have closed operations. Similarly, government agencies have restructured and reduced their labour forces in line with commitments made within multinational and bilateral agreements (e.g., free-trade agreements) to reduce government spending (Kelsey, 1995; Scott, 2011).

While many Western countries celebrated falling unemployment in the latter part of the 1990s, job creation was often in the low-paid periphery sector or in smaller companies that offered lower pay, fewer (if any) benefits and part-time or insecure temporary positions (Uchitelle and Kleinfield, 1996; McBride, 1999). Although in full-time employment, inadequate wages and salaries reduce people to living in or marginally above poverty level (Kossek et al., 1997). When all aspects of human survival are to be 'earned on the market', is a living wage a moral obligation?

## CEOS OUT OF TOUCH? LIVING WAGE CLAIM 'WRONG'

Napier Council staff have hit back at the mayor's claims they were paid well. Council staff contacted *Hawke's Bay Today* after reading that Napier's mayor Barbara Arnott would be 'very surprised' if any council employees were not receiving a 'living wage' in Hawke's Bay. A council-employed lawn mower, who asked not to be named, said Ms Arnott was 'not in touch with reality'. 'She would be very surprised if she found out how many people there were [paid under the living wage].' (Hawke's Bay Today, 25 February 2013)

# WORK THAT ENABLES EMPLOYMENT

While in this chapter we have focused mainly on work that is now called 'employment', we began the chapter with an alert that this in itself is a capitalist conception. There are many other types of activities that might equally be thought of as work but are harder to notice. We have space only to note the developments in this area of study.

## Immaterial Labour

Lazzarato (1996: 13, cited in Beverungen, 2011: 148) reviews the concept of immaterial labour to include 'the labour that produces the informational and cultural content of a commodity'. You might like to think about what work has gone into creating Coke as a 'life-enhancing' soft drink.

## Emotional Labour

Emotional labour is the display of specific emotions that is deemed to be required for a job. Cheerfulness is expected at McDonalds and a calm demeanour would be thought appropriate in a hospital. Maintaining emotional expressions that are not authentic can be 'hard work'. Bryman (2011: 171) suggests that, when applied to the employees at Disneyland, such employees 'are enjoined to exhibit positive emotions in order to create more uplifting experience for visitors'.

## Performative Labour

According to Bryman (2004: 103), there is 'a growing trend for work, particularly in service industries, to be construed as a performance, much like in the theatre. The employee becomes like an actor on a stage'. Performative labour is 'the rendering of work by managements and employees alike as akin to a theatrical performance in which the workplace is construed as similar to a stage' (Bryman, 2004: 103).

## Aesthetic Labour

In the *World English Dictionary*, 'aesthetic labour' is defined as 'workers employed by a company for their appearance or accent, with the aim of promoting the company's image'. Hancock (2011: 13) reviews the critical concern with the managerial manipulation of the sensuous values that might or might not be conducive to the organisation's interests.

## Domestic Labour

What is done in the home is a hot topic in many families. It has begun to be recognised in the organisational literature as significantly impacting upon the career opportunities of those who do it and those who seem to be able to avoid it.

## Community Labour

Community work is what we do when we involve ourselves in our community as formal volunteers, or the myriad of tasks we undertake as a matter of course to ensure our life together has some form of cohesion, character and trustworthiness. You might think about parent help at the local school, the clearing up after disasters while insurers and governments sit on their hands. However, the non-voluntary volunteer in the form of court-commanded service could also be considered.

These many types of work are made less visible in the bright lights given to employment as *the* most significant work and the need for such work to be flexible in terms of place, space, time and skills.

# CONCLUSION

Atkinson's flexible firm model, along with the forms of teamwork associated with the employee empowerment movement, were proposed as means to respond to the crisis of the 1970s and to improve productivity and profits in light of increased international competition. The organisational flexibility strategies inherent in the flexible firm model continue to be employed to the present time. The persistence of unequal or inequitable outcomes would suggest a structural flaw in the stated aspirations of advocates of both democracy and the free market as organising principles for our humanity. However, implementing flexible organisational practices depends upon a number of prerequisite macro-level conditions being evident in the political, economic and social realms (Skorstad, 2009).

At the political level, the mobility of capital and the repatriation of profits and labour laws allowing for managerial prerogative must be assured. This structural analysis must be complemented with the insights of critical psychologists, cultural analysts and artists of all kinds. In the economic realm, implementing flexible organisational practices that downgrade work conditions is often associated with high unemployment and/or poor union strength, enabling labour forces in diverse nations to discipline each other. Barker (1993) demonstrated how this works at the level of the firm and is as relevant today as it was 20 years ago. The analysis is quite useful applied to whole industries and economies. Change in the very notions of work and workers in the social realm also becomes evident (a point we discuss in Chapter 5). Within the global neo-liberal context, these conditions offer greater power to multinational companies and employer groups to determine policies that affect work and workers, as well as citizens and their families and the environment. Addressing these concerns becomes increasingly difficult because, in the global context, the outcomes often remain invisible until the most negative effects gain public attention. Deetz (2003: 30) writes that:

> While new forms of resistance are made possible, they are also made less likely by the complicity [of workers in the systems that control them] and new form of surveillance ... Systems such as these do not lend themselves well to ideological criticism. They are not filled with false needs or hidden values. Rather, it is the [perceived] truth and naturalness of the domination, the *free* acceptance, that make it so powerful.

## STEVE'S JOBS: WORKING AT FOXCONN

Foxconn is the world's largest contract manufacturer of electronics and supplier to such companies as Apple, Sony, Dell, Nokia and Hewlett-Packard (Huang, 2010). In the first six months of 2010, ten Foxconn employees committed suicide, and another three attempted suicide (Huang, 2010; Standing, 2010), mostly by jumping off company buildings, reportedly over despair generated by the extensive working hours and inhumane conditions. The response from the company was

*(Continued)*

*(Continued)*

an increase in workers' pay from US$130 per month to US$176 per month, with another promised pay rise to US$270 per month in October of that year. This pay rise was to be available only to employees who had satisfactorily completed a 'trial period' based on the employer's assessment of whether the worker was at risk of suicide. Only those found to be a limited risk would be eligible for the pay increase. Additionally, the organisation is installing safety nets around the buildings. In May of 2011, a fire was reported at the Foxconn factory in Chengdu City, three workers were killed and another 15 were injured. This fire was reported under the heading: 'Foxconn Factory Fire Puts iPad Supply in Jeopardy' (GamePolitics, 2011). In contrast to the working conditions at Foxconn, Apple Inc. boast that 'whatever you do here, you play a part in creating some of the best-loved technology on the planet. And in helping people discover all the amazing things they can do with it. You could call it work, or you could call it a mission. We call it a blast' (Apple Inc., 2010). In July 2011, Apple Inc. reported that profits had doubled since last year, mainly due to sales of iPads and iPhones (Milroy, 2011; see also Duhigg and Barboza, 2012).

The exploitation of labour we are concerned with in this book occurs not only in the manufacture of electronic devices but also in many of the items we all buy, items such as food, clothes, cars and gadgets of all kinds. Examining the processes and relationships of their production can become the focus of our alerted conscience. The Foxconn story above is just one example. Does the addition of safety nets to the Foxconn buildings to prevent death by suicide absolve the responsibility of consumers who maintain market efficiency by seeking the best product for the lowest price? Is the use of psych-testing to weed out potentially unstable employees a fair part of the selection process? These are important and practical questions.

Some people take their concerns more deeply. They may focus on the fact that more people than ever are pressed into jobs that cannot sustain life. Some may be concerned that, for some people, there may be no job whatsoever. Others integrate these important social concerns with environmental awareness. For example, water is being increasingly diverted from communities of small farm holdings the world over to generate electricity to power the factories and to irrigate crops on corporate estates. Work in factories, in offices, at hot-desks, in fields, in wards and in mines is increasingly undertaken by robots. Robots, farm machinery, transport vehicles and supplies of fuel all rely on the manufacture of electronics. All manufacture produces waste. Water is needed in both the production process and the disposal of waste. Waste management of humans and of mechanical and natural componentry seems to be attracting attention to the institutional logics that produce and attend to such waste – and whole new realms of employment are being invented. The control of such work, as the control of all work in the context of capitalism, requires tailor-made employees. It is to the reshaping of the worker that we turn our attention in Chapter 5.

## TALK BOX: CASUAL CASUALTIES

One of New Zealand's largest employers, Fletcher Building, has shed 600 workers in the past three months and has warned that another 200 jobs could go at PlaceMakers if the economy continues to deteriorate. But it says its policy is to take a compassionate approach and shed its casual and temporary staff initially, followed by reducing the amount of overtime worked by permanent staff, then relying on natural attrition before being forced to resort to redundancies (*Weekend Herald*, 2008).

## Tricky Questions

- How do the various vignettes in this chapter illustrate the achievement of employment (in)flexibility, globally and locally?
- What aspects of the flexible firm model does each of these examples illustrate?
- Who does this supposed employment flexibility serve best in each example?
- What issues are evident that relate to outsourcing as illustrated in the Foxconn case?
- How much control do individuals have to act in their own best interest when attempting to address any concerns they may have about this form of labour market structure?
- Is anyone 'safe' in this work environment?

# ADDITIONAL RESOURCES

Chan, J. and Pun, N. (2010) Suicide as protest for the new generation of Chinese migrant workers: Foxconn, global capital and the state. *Asia Pacific Journal*, 37: 2–10.

Clegg, S. and Dunkerley, D. (1980) *Organization, Class and Control*. London: Routledge and Kegan Paul.

Farndale, E. and Paauwe, J. (2007) Uncovering competitive and institutional drivers of HRM practices in multinational corporations. *Human Resource Management Journal*, 17 (4): 355–75.

Fink, L. (2006) When community comes home to roost: the southern mill town as lost cause. *Journal of Social History*, 40 (1): 119–45.

Fox, M. (2011) *The Reinvention of Work: A New Vision of Livelihood for our Time*. San Francisco: Harper.

Geoghegan, M. and Powell, F. (2009) Community development and the contested politics of the late modern agora: of, alongside or against neoliberalism? *Community Development Journal*, 4 (4): 430–47.

McBride, S., McNutt, K. and Williams, R. (2007) Tracking neo-liberalism: labour market policies in the OECD area. In S. Lee and S. McBride (eds), *Neo-Liberalism, State Power and Global Governance*. Netherlands: Springer. pp. 79–93.

Nayyar, D. (2006) Globalisation, history and development: a tale of two centuries. *Cambridge Journal of Economics*, 30 (1): 137–59.

OECD (2011) *Working Party on Employment and Unemployment Statistics*, ch. 5. Paris: OECD.

Sewell, G. (2005) Nice work? Rethinking managerial control in an era of knowledge work. *Organization*, 12 (5): 685–704.

# REFERENCES

Allvin, M. (2008) New rules of work: exploring the boundaryless job. In K. Näswall, J. Hellgren and M. Sverke (eds), *The Individual in the Changing Working Life*. Cambridge: Cambridge University Press. pp. 19–45.

Apple Inc. (2010) Jobs at Apple: less of a job, more of a calling (www.apple.com/jobs/us/welcome.html; retrieved 18 September 2010).

Ashkenas, R., Ulrich, D., Jick, T. and Kerr, S. (1995) *The Boundaryless Organization: Breaking the Chains of Organizational Structure*. San Francisco: Jossey-Bass.

Atkinson, J. (1984) Manpower strategies for flexible organizations. *Personnel Management*, 16: 28–31.

Atkinson, S., Ibarra, M., Assunção, J. and Verhoogen, E. (2007) The effect of Mexican workforce migration on the Mexican *maquiladora* labor market (with comments). *Economia*, 8 (1): 179–210.

Bain, H. (2001) Why short week is tall order. *The Dominion*, 17 January, p. 13.

Barker, J.R. (1993) Tightening the iron cage: concertive control in self-managing teams. *Administrative Science Quarterly*, 38 (3): 408–37.

Beverungen, A. (2011) Immaterial labour. In M. Tadajewski, P. MacLaran, E. Parsons and M. Parker (eds), *Key Concepts in Critical Management Studies*. London: Sage. pp. 147–50.

Braverman, J.R. (1974) *Labour and Monopoly Capital: The Degradation of Work in the Twentieth Century*. New York: Monthly Review Press.

Brenner, M.D., Fairris, D. and Rusher, J. (2004) 'Flexible' work practices and occupational safety and health: exploring the relationship between cumulative trauma disorders and workplace transformation. *Industrial Relations*, 43 (1): 242–66.

Briscoe, J.P. and Hall, D.T. (2006) The interplay of boundaryless and protean careers: combinations and implications. *Journal of Vocational Behavior*, 69: 4–18.

Brunhes, B. (1989) Labour market flexibility: trends in enterprises. *Organisation for Economic Co-operation and Development*, pp. 11–36.

Bryman, A. (2004) Performative labour. In *The Disneyization of Society*. London: Sage. pp. 103–31 (http://knowledge.sagepub.com/view/the-disneyization-of-society/n5.xml; retrieved 24 September 2013).

Bryman, A. (2011) McDonaldisation. In M. Tadajewski, P. MacLaran, E. Parsons and M. Parker (eds), *Key Concepts in Critical Management Studies*. London: Sage. pp. 168–72.

Burawoy, M. (1979) *Manufacturing Consent: Changes in the Labour Process under Monopoly Capitalism*. Chicago: University of Chicago Press.

Burawoy, M. (2012) The roots of domination: beyond Bourdieu and Gramsci. *Sociology*, 46 (2): 187–206 (http://burawoy.berkeley.edu/Marxism/Roots%20of%20Domination.Sociology.pdf; retrieved 10 September 2013).

Cappelli, P. and Rogovsky, N. (1994) New work systems and skill requirements. *International Labour Review*, 133 (2): 205–20.

CBS News (2001a) Fujitsu to cut 16,000 jobs. CBS News, 20 August, Tokyo (www.cbsnews.com/stories/2001/08/20/world/main307240.shtml; retrieved 17 March 2002).

CBS News (2001b) Toshiba to slash 17,000 jobs. CBS News, 27 August, Tokyo (www.cbsnews.com/stories/2001/08/27/world/main308272.shtml; retrieved 17 March 2002).

Chomsky, N. (2013) *Can Civilization Survive Capitalism?* New York: New York Times News Syndicate.

Crowley, M., Tope, D., Chamberlain, L. and Hodson, R. (2010) Neo-Taylorism at work: occupational change in the post-Fordist era. *Social Problems*, 57 (3): 421–47.

Deetz, S. (2003) Disciplinary power, conflict suppression and HRM. In M. Alvesson and H. Willmott (eds), *Studying Management Critically*. London: Sage. pp. 23–45.

Duhigg, C. and Barboza, D. (2012) In China, human costs are built into an iPad. *The New York Times*, 25 January (www.nytimes.com/2012/01/26/business/ieconomy-apples-ipad-and-the-human-costs-for-workers-in-china.html?pagewanted=all; retrieved 7 September 2013).

*The Economist* (2000) The great American jobs machine. *The Economist*, January 15: 35–6.

Ehrensal, K.N. (1995) Discourses of global competition: obscuring the changing labour processes of managerial work. *Journal of Organizational Change Management*, 8 (5): 5–16.

Fletcher, D.R. (2009) Social tenants, attachment to place and work in the post-industrial labour market: underlining the limits of housing-based explanations of labour immobility? *Housing Studies*, 24 (6): 775–91.

Friedman, M. (1968) The role of monetary policy. *American Economic Review*, 58: 1–17.

GamePolitics (2011) Foxconn factory fire puts iPad supply in jeopardy (http://game-politics.com/2011/05/23/foxconn-factory-fire-puts-ipad-supply-jeopardy; retrieved 7 September 2013).

Gandolfi, F. (2007) Downsizing, corporate survivors, and employability-related issues: a European case study. *Journal of American Academy of Business*, 12 (1): 50–6.

Grady, J. and Harvie, D. (2011) Neoliberalism. In M. Tadajewski, P. MacLaran, E. Parsons and M. Parker (eds), *Key Concepts in Critical Management Studies*. London: Sage. pp. 173–6.

Hancock, P. (2011) Aesthetics. In M. Tadajewski, P. MacLaran, E. Parsons and M. Parker (eds), *Key Concepts in Critical Management Studies*. London: Sage. pp. 11–14.

Hardy, Q. (2013) Global slavery, by the numbers. *The New York Times*, 6 March (http://bits.blogs.nytimes.com/2013/03/06/global-slavery-by-the-numbers/; retrieved 7 September 2013).

Harzing, A.W. (2004) Internationalization and the international division of labour. In A.W. Harzing and J. Van Ruysseveldt (eds), *International Human Resource Management*, 2nd edn. London: Sage. pp. 9–32.

Herring, H. (2001) A year of layoffs. *The New York Times*, 30 December, D2.

Huang, A. (2010) iPad maker raises pay 30% after suicides at China plants. *Toronto Star*, 2 June (www.thestar.com/business/companies/apple/article/817849–ipad-maker-raises-pay-30-after-suicides-at-china-plants on 21/08/2010; retrieved 7 September 2013).

Humphries, M.T. (1998) For the common good? New Zealanders comply with quality standards. *Organisation Science*, 9 (6): 737–49.

Hymowitz, C. (1997) Stop the world, it may be time for some parents to get off. *The Wall Street Journal*, Interactive Edition, April: 2.

ILO (International Labour Organization) (2004) *Labour Market Trends and Globalization's Impact on Them*. Geneva: ILO.

ILO (International Labour Organization) (2008) *World of Work Report 2008: Income Inequalities in the Age of Financial Globalization*. Geneva: ILO.

ILO (International Labour Organization) (2010) *Global Wage Report 2010/11: Wage Policies in Times of Crisis*. Geneva: ILO.

ILO (International Labour Organization) (2011) *Global Employment Trends 2011*. Geneva: ILO.

Julian, Jr. J., Hall, C. and Yerger, D. (2010) Estimating core unemployable and workforce non-participants: a study of rural Pennsylvania's labor force. *Journal of Business and Economics Research*, 8 (2): 11–18.

Kelsey, J. (1995) *The New Zealand Experiment: A World Model for Structural Adjustment?* Auckland, NZ: Auckland University Press.

Kerr-Ritchie, J.R. (2002) Gender, unfree labor, and globalization. *Nature, Society, and Thought*, 15 (3): 347–57.

Kossek, E., Huber-Yoder, M., Castellino, D. and Lerner, J. (1997) The working poor: locked out of careers and the organizational mainstream? *Academy of Management Executive*, 11 (1): 76–92.

Lambert, S.J. (2008) Passing the buck: labor flexibility practices that transfer risk onto hourly workers. *Human Relations*, 61 (9): 1203–27.

Lazzarato, M. (1996) Immaterial labour, trans. P. Colilli and E. Emory. In P. Virno and M. Hardt (eds), *Radical Thought in Italy: A Potential Politics*. Minneapolis, MN: University of Minneapolis Press. pp. 133–49.

Lee, S., McCann, D. and Messenger, J.C. (2007) *Working Time around the World: Trends in Working Hours, Laws and Policies in a Global Comparative Perspective*. New York: Routledge.

Lincoln, D. (2009) Labour migration in the global division of labour: migrant workers in Mauritius. *International Migration*, 47 (4): 129–56.

Lipietz, A. (1997) Economic restructuring: the new global hierarchy. In P. James, W. Veit and S. Wright (eds), *Work of the Future: Global Perspectives*. Melbourne: Allen and Unwin. pp. 45–65.

McBride, S. (1999) Towards permanent insecurity: the social impact of unemployment. *Journal of Canadian Studies*, 34 (2): 13–30.

Mander, J. (1996) The dark side of globalization: what the media are missing. *The Nation*, 15 (22): 9–32.

Miles, R. (1987) *Capitalism and Unfree Labour: Anomaly or Necessity?* London: Tavistock.

Miller, V. and Mukherji, A. (2010) Offshoring sectors: a critical comparison of Mexican maquiladora plants with Indian outsourcing offices. *Advances in Competitiveness Research*, 18 (1/2).

Milroy, A. (2011) Apple profits sustainable, fueled by demand (www.youtube.com/watch?v=eXdvXrwtuJc; retrieved 7 September 2013).

Muff, K., Dyllick, T., Drewell, M., North, J., Shrivastava, P. and Haertle, J. (2013) *Management Education for the World: A Vision for Business Schools Serving People and Planet*. Cheltenham: Edward Elgar.

OCTA (Office of the Chief Trade Adviser) (2011) PACER Plus (www.octapic.org/trade-negotiations/pacer-plus/; retrieved 7 September 2013).

O'Shea, P. (2010) Are community organisations losing their way when they may be most needed? Paper presented at the 9th Organizational Discourse Conference, Vrije University, Amsterdam, 10–12 July.

Palley, T. (2010) America's exhausted paradigm: macroeconomic causes of the financial crisis and the great recession. *New School Economic Review*, 4 (1): 15–43 (http://newschooljournal.com/files/NSER04/NSER4-1.pdf#page=15; retrieved 9 December 2012).

Perkin, H. (1996) *The Third Revolution: Professional Elites in the Modern World*. London: Routledge.

Piore, M.J. and Sabel, C.F. (1984) *The Second Industrial Divide: Possibilities for Prosperity*. New York: Basic Books.

Pollert, A. (1991) The orthodoxy of flexibility. In A. Pollert (ed.), *Farewell to Flexibility?* Oxford: Blackwell. pp. 3–31.

Pons-Vignon, N. (2010) Introduction: beyond neoliberalism. In N. Pons-Vignon (ed.), *Don't Waste the Crisis: Critical Perspectives for a New Economic Model*. Geneva: ILO. pp. xv–xx.

Ramia, G. (2002) The 'new contractualism', social protection and the Yeatman thesis. *Journal of Sociology*, 38 (1): 49–68.

Reich, R. (1992) *The Work of Nations*. London: Vintage Books.

Rodgers, C.S. (1992) The flexible workplace: what have we learned? *Human Resource Management* (1986–1998), 31 (3): 183–99.

Scott, R. (2011) Heading south: US–Mexico trade and job displacement after NAFTA. Economic Policy Institute Briefing paper, no. 308. Washington, DC.

Seo, M.G. and Creed, W.E.D. (2002) Institutional contradictions, praxis and institutional change: a dialectical perspective. *Academy of Management Review*, 27 (2): 222–47.

Sierra Club (2013) NAFTA-on-steroids! Replacing 'free trade' with 'responsible trade' (http://lospadres.sierraclub.org/santabarbara/calendar/e008.html; retrieved 7 September 2013).

Skorstad, E.J. (2009) The ambiguity of flexibility. In E.J. Skorstad and H. Ramsdal (eds), *Flexible Organizations and the New Working Life: A European Perspective*. Surrey: Ashgate.

Standing, J. (2010) Another Foxconn worker dies, family blames overwork. *Reuters*, 3 June (www.reuters.com/article/2010/06/03/us-foxconn-china-idUSTRE6520K420100603; retrieved 7 September 2013).

Statistics New Zealand (2010) *Labour Force Survey*. Auckland: Statistics New Zealand.

Sussens-Messerer, V. (1998) Globalization and jobs. *Finance Week*, 76 (70): 20–2.

Thompson, P. and McHugh, D. (1990) *Work Organisations: A Critical Introduction*. London: Macmillan.

Uchitelle, L. and Kleinfield, N.R. (1996) The downsizing of America. *New York Times*, 3 March.

van der Meer, P.H. and Ringdal, K. (2009) Flexibility practices, wages and productivity: evidence from Norway. *Personnel Review*, 38 (5): 526–43.

van Gallecum, Y., Baxter, J. and Western, M. (2008) Neoliberalism, gender inequality and the Australian labour market. *Journal of Sociology*, 44 (1): 45–63.

Walling, A. and Clancy, G. (2010) Underemployment in the UK labour market. *Economic and Labour Market Review*, 4 (2): 16–24.

*Weekend Herald* (2008) Casual casualties: justice and compassion in a market economy. *Weekend Herald*, 1 November, Section C: 1.

Zeitz, G., Blau, G. and Fertig, J. (2009) Boundaryless careers and institutional resources. *International Journal of Human Resource Management*, 20 (2): 372–98.

# 5 POLITICS, POWER AND CONTROL WITHIN ORGANISATIONS

## Learning Objectives

In this chapter, we encourage you to continue a sustained reflection on:

- the fit between neo-liberal ideas of freedom and democratic notions of emancipation of all humanity;
- Braverman's (1974) discussions of the labour process;
- how employee empowerment rhetoric can be used to facilitate the manifestation of the 'panoptic gaze';
- the extent to which the 'panoptic gaze' is a useful metaphor for understanding the disciplining of self and populations;
- Rose's (1988) ideas about the (self) governance of the soul;
- the difference between variously implied doctrines of unitarism and pluralism in the context of employer/employee orientations to work;
- whether management students (as potential and actual managers) have a specific duty to consider responsibilities beyond compliance with employer directives in relation to work.

## CRITICAL CONCEPTS

The shaping of populations to meet the needs of *markets* was intensified by focusing on how the body moves in relation to work through an application of *Tayloristic control* of *behaviour*. Over time, this form of control was modified by the Human Relations School (HRS) of thought to include a greater influence on human attitudes and emotions. Opportunities for *resistance* are reduced where employees see their *interests* in harmony with that of employers, rather than where overt *conflicts of interest* are openly acknowledged. *Unitarist* or *pluralist* orientations underlie this difference in orientation. The next development in *concertive*

*(Continued)*

*(Continued)*

*control* was to attempt a more sophisticated indirect management of the *soul*, skilfully produced through a discourse of *employee empowerment*. Most recently, the duty of employees also to contribute to the restoration of damage resulting from the systemic harm associated with the very forms of production that pay their wages is being normalised. We are all in the mess together we are reminded. But are the remedies on offer equally beneficial? Sobering employment statistics and worrying environmental indicators should keep us cautious. What if you notice something of real concern in your place of work? Would you tackle it?

# WORKERS

Survival and prosperity for most human beings on the planet are increasingly to be attained through paid employment in a competitive market. The necessity of being in paid employment appears to override all other obligations we may believe we have to ourselves and to others. We are taught that this is *the way* we meet our obligations to ourselves and to others. Wherever the neo-liberal market model is introduced or amplified, however, it can be shown that not all people have access to this means to meet their needs. Some are systematically driven into certain types of paid or unpaid work that may not be safe, fairly paid or even paid at all. For most people on Earth, many of whom are still children, the need to compete for employment is increasingly harnessed to the necessity to earn money to purchase our means of survival. Paid employment is a subset of work. What work is to be paid through employment and how employment is to be controlled and valued cannot be merely thought of as the natural outcome of markets. Access to the means of life ought to be open for debate. Changes to the meanings, structures and values of work that we have discussed in Chapter 4 have radical implications for the meanings, identities and values we invest in workers. We intend to dig more deeply into the meanings we have invested in workers and how people are encouraged to think about themselves and others.

Survival of the fittest is an idea that has become deeply embedded in the now widely normalised expressions of neo-liberalism. The idea seems to suggest that corporate closures or employee displacement are processes of nature and are somehow linked to the equally naturalised fluctuations of markets. Reshaping the employment relations under the prevalence of neo-liberalism draws us to examine the reshaping of workers to fit the restructuring of work that we have discussed in Chapter 4. Harvey (2006) argues that neo-liberalism is a political enterprise that has the aim of restoring power to capital by shifting the economic resources back to the owners of capital and by weakening the power of workers to challenge or resist workplace or public policy changes. Who will have access to these jobs if we are to take seriously Hiscock's (2012) question that implies that the means to survival is unlikely to be universally available?

What would it mean to accept paranoia as the best motivator to work? In functionalist, mechanical or naturalised ways of thinking about work and workers, these types of questions can be largely avoided.

According to the prevailing ideology or truth-vesting myth, people are allocated an identity to be expressed in metaphor. Organisations, work and people are represented in metaphorical terms. In time of economic progress or growth in regions where suitable workers are difficult to find and retain, workers may be positively depicted as small but necessary cogs in a well-oiled machine or as new shoots in a reviving economy that must be tended to no matter how difficult, demanding or paranoid they may seem. In times of economic contraction or stagnation, or in a decision to move all or parts of an organisation abroad, local workers may be depicted as out of date or overly expensive cogs in a machine that needs re-engineering. They may be depicted as a piece of deadwood to be cut from the trunk to save the tree. Each dehumanising metaphor used to depict employees brings subtle disciplinary logics justifying inclusion or exclusion from what is to be welcomed or tolerated as reasonable employment by individuals, communities and governments.

This chapter explores the disciplinary contribution of human resource management (HRM) theory and practice in the processes of fabricating desirable workers, eliminating those who are no longer desired, and the (re)-engaging of potential workers in the vagaries of globalisation in an emerging process seductively called 'repatriation'. We question whether there is any place for dissent where poverty predominate or where the rhetoric of employee empowerment and participation discourses predominate, despite unsatisfactory or even dangerous terms of engagement. Desperation and unmet desires can be significant silencers.

# MOULDING WORKERS

In Chapter 3 we argued that many governments actively participate in the creation of a global economy based on neo-liberal ideas about individual freedom to participate in markets. A good life is to be achieved through the capacity to buy the necessary and desired goods and services according to one's individual preferences and earning capacity. As the rewards of market participation are deemed to be based on merit, inequality of outcomes in terms of life attainments can be dismissed as merely the fair outcomes of energy committed to earning. Thus, so long as there are no demonstrable structural impediments in markets, inequality of outcomes are indicators of fair returns. For people of this faith, observable inequality does not equate to unfairness. Where obstacles can be demonstrated, policy pressures can be brought to bear to remove them. Based on this reasoning, governments have implemented economic, social, political and legislative frameworks to achieve greater free-trade agreements between nations. It can be deemed acceptable to craft social policies that are thought to equalise individual opportunities to compete fairly and to spend freely. Surplus cash can be spent or reinvested in markets according to individual preference. Investments are encouraged, as this provides the fuel for further development and growth of the economy. Spending is necessary, too, as the market relies for its life-blood on the trading of goods and services.

The drive to deregulate labour markets in the interest of investors is consistent with the belief that underpinning the interests of investors will generate the fuel that energises the global market and thus grow the opportunities for the human race to survive. The idea(l)s of neo-liberalists are deemed to serve the expansion and mobility of global free trade and thus human emancipation and thriving. Critical theorists take a less benign view of this ideology. In Chapter 4, we argued that political changes that embed neo-liberal ideals in employment enable forms of flexible labour practices to be implemented at the organisational level, which, in many nations, have undermined the collective power of employee unions to challenge employer control over the conditions and processes of work. Critical theorists are interested in the deeply assumed ideas and the pervasive processes that generate the fabrication, normalisation and policing of competitive individualism as the natural or necessary nature of human beings. Individual responsibility and flexibility are key watchwords in this ideology. People must learn that no company or government owes them a living. Change is inevitable. Employees should enhance their flexibility to meet the needs of organisationally determined change.

In Chapter 4 we detailed the characteristics of organisational flexibility, epitomised by Atkinson's (1984) flexible firm model, witnessed since the 1980s. These outcomes included mass redundancies throughout the 1980s and 1990s, and the creation of core and periphery forms of work and workers, much of which has been achieved through the outsourcing of jobs. One community's loss is another community's gain. The critique of that model is as apt today as it was when it was depicted. The situation just seems to have become even more difficult if one needs a job. At the end of the twentieth century, over eight million Americans were unemployed. The situation globally was estimated at 205 million (ILO, 2010). That is a lot of people needing jobs! The remedy, as always, is for various calls to grow the economy and for the unemployed to make themselves employable and to find a job.

## WORK AS EMPLOYMENT: WHO IS IN CHARGE?

'The total number of unemployed and underemployed Americans at the end of 2009 stood at over 25 million men and women. Every one of those 25 million Americans has a face, a name and a family', says James Rickards (2011: 111), investment banker and risk manager. As, of course, does every human being, whether they are the displaced of Asia or of Europe, trafficked sex slaves, undocumented labourers, vulnerable urbanised or the indigenous peoples corralled in transition camps because they have been required to leave their homelands. Is anyone more or less deserving than another for a sustainable livelihood?

In the first two decades of the twenty-first century, we have witnessed the debate about the efficiency and fairness of the capitalist system intensify. The people of Cyprus, Greece, Spain and Portugal are required to accept austerity measures and their protests are being controlled not only by the threat and actuality of police presence, but more subtly by the impervious influence of policy pressure. In other parts of Europe and in the US, austerity measures, the exacerbation of poverty and the growing gap between the rich and the poor are also evident. Compliance with the disciplines of the regime in those regions of the world, however, may not yet have required police enforcement – unless, of course, one is an active member of the Occupy Movement.

The issues now in the media are not unique to the places in the spotlight. Unemployed people everywhere are urged to get off their butt and go out to compete for the jobs that are assumed to be there, to see even unpaid labour as a step to future employment opportunity and thus personal security, regardless of what other family, community or health issues they may be facing. Success or failure in job terms is deemed to be the outcome of merit. Merit is defined as benefits earned by way of investing energy into paying and training for occupational success, chasing and winning jobs, and performing in those jobs as required. Out-performing one's competition generates new and better opportunities for firms and nations. Cumulatively, this competition enriches the individual and thus society. Or so the story goes. It will remain difficult to compete for jobs in countries where conditions of service have incrementally improved and are now deemed to have become too costly to retain, when the hopeful people of Burma may be willing to work for less than the people of Thailand, for example. In this situation, as elsewhere, mighty corporations are waiting in the wings for the conditions of human need and the achievement of employment readiness to come into balance with sufficient political stability to make the investment worthwhile. Flexible workers and organisational flexibility are the required ingredients for all business. The effects of organisational flexibility on work and workers, however, have not been uniform. Instead, the movement away from what has been termed the standard working day and secure employment arrangements has resulted in employment insecurity, and over-, under- and unemployment for many. It has also led to the creation of the unemployable and the non-voluntary volunteer.

## TAKING PERSONAL RESPONSIBILITY FOR EMPLOYABILITY

Jake has a masters degree in human resource management. With an astute eye on the volatility of the job market, he managed also to get a taxi driver's licence and a barista certificate. For many months after his graduation, Jake not only

*(Continued)*

*(Continued)*

responded to every job in his field, but for any employment at all – from driving taxis to making coffee. He spent good money he could not really afford to enlist the services of a career consultant. Her advice was to bolster his CV by doing some voluntary work. Currently, he drives the mini-bus for a local rest-home funded by a faith-based organisation. This 20-hour week commitment once provided a small income for Jennie, a local woman raising children on her own. When the funding of the service came under pressure, the job was outsourced to a volunteer recruitment centre. Jake felt lucky to be appointed. Fortunately, the small wage he makes at a trendy café where he has found work on a Saturday morning pays for the interest he is paying on his credit card with which he meets his most pressing bills. He does not know about Jennie, or that he now performs what was once her job for free. He does not know how she and her children are doing.

Changes in the way work is framed and paid (or not) have a significant effect on people's hopes and aspirations. The neo-liberal doctrine would celebrate as much flexibility in this process as can be achieved. Such ideals, however, do not account for the significant imbalance of influence between individual people who need the income only employment might bring them and the powerful corporations that frame possibilities and opportunities. Within the global framework, significantly more manufacturing processes and service work have been deemed non-core business, and many multinational corporations have outsourced this work to contractors operating locally or in the still so-called developing countries. There are signs that some jobs are being repatriated to regions deemed fertile for fresh exploitation – much like a field left fallow for a season or two. Regions that have high unemployment, basically well-educated and docile populations, and low social welfare safety nets, can offer corporations attractive tax deals and lower compliance standards than in other places.

Neo-liberals would see this as the effective working of the markets which are evidently bringing job opportunities to those who need them. Many of these contracting firms continue to organise workforces and production processes based firmly around the Taylorist hierarchical manufacturing processes discussed in Chapter 4. Clothing, electronics, car and food manufacturing plants use these processes in urban and suburban factories, on ships and in private domestic garages the world over. Many workers continue to be treated as expendable components of the production line. In principle, most are 'free to leave' – unless, of course, the manager is minding their passport or other work documents. Unless, of course, their identity, their security or their apathy has been firmly harnessed to the particular rhetoric of necessity that prevails at a given time and place where capitalism has become triumphant.

Min and her parents were so proud on the day she came top of her class in the village school. As a result, she and five similarly bright girls from the surrounding villages were chosen by the recruiter to go to the big city to earn money her parents needed so badly to educate her two younger brothers. The recruiter was a kind lady. She explained that Min and the other girls would live in a hostel. She would be encouraged to come home for big celebrations, like Chinese New Year. 'But', cautioned the kind recruiter, 'Min would have to work hard to earn this privilege, as export orders must be met for the security of the firm, and thus the employment of all.' Min went off with high hopes and great determination. She worked long days. Sometimes she worked two shifts in a row. She missed her family and her village. She thought about the extra money the long hours were storing up for her visit home. She was very frugal with her spending. Ten months later, Min realised that no matter how many hours she worked, or how careful she had been with her wages, she just could not spare the money for her fare home. How sad! Perhaps she should have left the factory for work in the massage parlours of the tourism sector as two of her friends had done. She had seen them on one of her rare visits to the city. They did not see her. They looked even more lethargic than Min felt. It was very hard work to stay feeling positive.

The work arrangements associated with the neo-liberal political and economic environment intensifying the world over require a different kind of worker compared with that required under the Keynesian political economy that was linked to the Human Relations School of thought (Crane, 1999). The neo-liberal individual must accept responsibility for taking care of the self through attachment to paid employment, or through attachment to someone who is in paid employment. Government welfare support for individuals is viewed as counter-productive, leading to dependency and social decline. People are to be 'set free' to earn their living, and their capacity to purchase goods and services necessary for life will be allocated to them through the workings of the labour market according to their merit: that is, their commitment to educate and train themselves appropriately and their dedication to finding and retaining a job. The path to freedom through work seems to hold a number of obstacles. Overt shaping of work and the controlling organisations were discussed in Chapter 4. In the next section, we will look more closely at how the consent of individuals to accept less than desirable or even unsafe work is achieved and justified. Better *a* job than no job! Yeah, right.

# COERCION AND CONTROL OF THE SELF

In Chapter 4, we showed how Braverman (1974) argued that Taylorist work production methods control workers through deskilling jobs and by removing knowledge from workers and locating this with managers, engineers and other specialists. This process of deskilling ensures that any single worker has little control over the work process and is easily replaced should the worker prove unproductive, uncooperative or undesirable in some way. Worker productivity could be monitored through direct shop-floor supervision, automated clocking in and out systems, and through pacing the speed of machinery. More recent examples of monitoring and control have taken the form of CCTV surveillance systems and publicly displayed productivity charts. One aim of these monitoring and control measures is to ensure continued acceleration of worker productivity, in part by the display of outputs and by employing the explicit or implicit doctrine of competition based on pride in winning or fear of losing contracts, jobs, market dominance and so on. Each individual must play their part.

The labour process characterised by Taylorism and theorised by Braverman (1974), however, only partially explains the coercion and direct control of workers. In an environment that enables the cross-national movement of finance and production facilities, combined with the existence of the structurally unemployed, the peripheralised workforce and diminished welfare provision, an entire workforce that is deemed unproductive can be replaced by any suitably skilled and attitudinally compliant workforce. In this environment, discipline to accept decreased working conditions is achieved through fear of job loss or of being replaced by people in distant places who are willing or forced to accept conditions of service that might not be acceptable in other domains. The outsourced work can be managed from a distance using modern technology, expat managers and local supervisors.

Changes associated with the mobility of work are not associated only with factory jobs. Increasingly, technological inventions allowing 'management from a distance' affect middle to upper management jobs also. Templated and electronic means of control can now allow smaller, elite managerial labour forces to be motivated through rewards presented as privileges and lifestyles that do not require them to live in places where distress and political volatility will unsettle their families or expose them to an environmental quality that they do not wish to endure. Just who will be able to hold those jobs may be a bit of a lottery.

## COMING HOME

Jill has worked hard to ensure that their time spent as a family in Shanghai served everyone well. Daniel, her husband, was able to work the long hours required of him by the firm, while she ensured that the children were well cared for. Daniel excelled in his work. He trained locals to do aspects of his job that could soon be managed just as well from afar. His work in Shanghai was done. Jill and Daniel were relieved to hear that at some time in the next six weeks Daniel might be recalled to the head office in New York, the city that was still home for them. There

were friends and family awaiting them! The climate suited them better. Less settling, however, was to notice the talk of layoffs being proposed to ensure head-
office profitability. Jobs were being 're-scoped', 're-framed' and 're-valued'. Surely
Daniel would fit one of them? Hearing that the family was free to come home had
felt so good. A tinge of worry was creeping into their joy.

Braverman's (1974) articulation of labour process theory and the existence of
a potential replacement labour force helps us to understand certain dynamics
of control and coercion. Other analysts consider the more subtle processes
involved in gaining consent and hence in reducing resistance to managerial
control and the prerogatives of the owners of capital. These more subtle forms
of gaining consent to intensifying conditions of work rely on assimilating and
domesticating individuals to wider political and economic agendas through
creating the self-governed and self-disciplined individual. It is to those processes we now turn our attention.

# SELF-DISCIPLINED AND SELF-GOVERNING INDIVIDUALS

The way human beings are invited to believe the rhetoric of freedom explicitly
and implicitly promised in the ideology of neo-liberalism often requires people
to think of themselves as atomised individuals required to compete on the
employment market for life's necessities. In doing so, they serve the competitive advantage of the firm, the industry, the nation and the global economy –
and thus their own self-interest (in survival). The global economy promises to
reward all fairly, according to the doctrine of meritocracy, and all as equally as
possible, according to the supporting doctrine of democracy. Yet, this doctrine
is patently untrue for many human beings.

In Chapter 2, we provided an insight into the hierarchical arrangements of
capitalism that allowed power and control to be institutionalised and intensified. We noted, too, however, that Foucault (1977) demonstrates that power
and control need not be and are not always expressed hierarchically but may
be embedded in social relationships. He termed this process the 'relations of
power'. Foucault demonstrates his idea of the relations of power through an
historical analysis of the changes in the notion of crime and the forms of
punishment that occurred throughout the seventeenth and eighteenth centuries. Of particular interest to critical management scholars are his observations of the shift from publicly punishing the body (for instance, in public
floggings and hangings of wrongdoers) to working on the minds of individuals. In Foucauldian style, an analysis of this shift in the focus of punishment

from the body to the mind represents the beginning phases of the development of the *disciplinary society*.

In the disciplinary society, whole populations are controlled by controlling single individuals within the population by winning and reinforcing their compliance. Weber, too, noted this capacity of ordering populations. Gramsci's (1971) use of the concept of hegemony helps us understand how such compliance can be retained even when it harms the compliant, their loved ones or the people and planet they have been successfully alienated from in the process that Marxists call 'atomisation'. This compliance is achieved by creating a population of docile and useable bodies that can be controlled through the establishment and application of the 'panoptic gaze' – an external and even internal monitoring system that we began to illustrate in Chapter 2.

# CREATING DOCILE BODIES

Foucault argues that to create docile, utilisable bodies requires a disciplinary organisational space and the application of particular disciplinary techniques. Foucault draws on Jeremy Bentham's ideal panoptic prison as a metaphor to illustrate the principle of a disciplinary organisational space. Bentham designed his ideal panoptic prison to maximise surveillance of prison inmates. The architectural design of the prison had a central watchtower surrounded by prison cells. The cells were placed in such a way that prisoners could not see other inmates or the overseer in the tower. Meanwhile, from the central watchtower, it was possible for the overseer to observe any prisoner at will, simply by glancing around the tower. Prisoners cannot tell whether they are being observed or not. They must act as if they are. Foucault (1977: 245) calls the possibility of being held under surveillance the 'panoptic gaze'.

Critical management theorists argue and demonstrate that the disciplinary organisational space is supported by the application of panoptic techniques of training, surveillance, hierarchical observation, comparisons, normalising judgements and examination. The combination of these techniques makes the individual visible, comparable, changeable and docile. For Foucault (1977), the primary function of disciplinary power is to train individuals to become useful, whether to the trainer, organisation or the economy. Once appropriately trained, the individual becomes an instrument for achieving the goals of the institution by acting in desirable ways – in utilisable ways.

Training is assessed through a combination of hierarchical observation, comparison, normalising judgements and examination. Hierarchical observation involves someone in a position of authority observing a person in a subordinate position; for example, managers and workers, teachers and pupils, prison wardens and inmates or doctors and patients. Hierarchical observation is the process of making the subordinate visible to the observer. While the object of the gaze is the individual, what is being observed could be anything of interest to the observer; for example, the activities, skills, knowledge or attitudes of the worker or pupil, or the symptoms and ailments of the sick patient. These observations are recorded and coded and given a score. Through statistical analysis, each individual score can be mapped and presented in any number of ways deemed useful to the observer; for example, on bar or linear graphs, tables or bell curves. These statistical representations aggregate all individual observations and, at the same time, enable a single observation to be located on a continuum. As a result, each individual observation can be compared against the continuum as well as against other specific individuals. Comparing individuals, whether it is in relation to their skill, attitudes or symptoms, becomes a mathematical process of comparing scores.

The process of comparing scores is the basis for making normalising judgements. An individual can be judged in relation to where their score is located on the continuum; for example, as above, at or below average, or as exceptional, normal or abnormal. Foucault (1977) argues that disciplined individuals constrain their own behaviour in a desire to be, or at least to appear to be, normal or to avoid being labelled abnormal. In this way, individuals behave in a manner that will either result in achieving the rewards associated with normality or avoiding the sanctions and punishments associated with abnormality. Such a person is now rendered docile. Hence, the creation of a docile, utilisable individual is complete.

The examination, which combines hierarchical surveillance and normalising judgements, represents a new form of power because the individual provides information about themselves and, in turn, receives a statement or picture of his or her own individuality. The observer's power and knowledge over the individual is strengthened with each new disciplinary round. At the same time, the political autonomy of the observed weakens. This occurs because the examination links a certain type of knowledge formation with a particular exercise of power. Disciplinary power is exercised by the invisibility of the controller; at the same time, the individual who is the object of disciplinary power becomes completely visible. The examination at once objectifies the individual through gazing at them as an object and at the same time subjects the individual to the power of the gaze of the examination. Disciplinary power is achieved through the visibility of the examination as opposed to the visibility of the power-holder. The docile subject responds to disciplinary power by doing things to themselves to improve future examination scores. It is because of this that individual autonomy is weakened with each new disciplinary round, as docile individuals learn more fully what it means to present themselves as normal, and then unquestionably change their behaviour to meet this prescribed normality or risk the consequences of being deemed abnormal or disobedient.

## THE UNIVERSITY AS FACTORY: REDEFINING QUALITY AND ACCELERATING PRODUCTIVITY

Jess has been a successful professor for 20 years; her teaching and research evaluations and publications are amongst the highest of scores within the school. At a recent performance appraisal, Jess was told that the university was coming under increasing pressure to compete against newcomers in the education industry. Staff productivity would need to be improved. Unfortunately, resources were increasingly hard to come by. Incomes for the university would only be improved if professors attract more external funding. The best place to find this funding would obviously be from the large, multinational companies that were locating their head office in the city. Jess felt depressed. The corporations settling in the city were hardly likely to be interested in a critique of their activities! But Jess has a mortgage to pay. There were also the medical bills that have come about through little Jonnie's food allergies. A large chemical company was offering a substantial research grant that would support research that would show that their products do not harm the food chain. It seems an ideal fit. Bringing in a big research grant would surely mean a great performance appraisal next year and job security for Jess in the time ahead. There might even be enough funding in the budget to re-employ the tutors who had been so great with the students before they lost their career-entry jobs in the decision not to reappoint tutors in the latest round of institutional cost-cutting. Teaching quality, sadly, would need to take a back seat for a while, as an excellent proposal was in everyone's interest, was it not?

# GOVERNMENTS, GOVERNANCE AND CONTROL

As the governors of public institutions seek to find and implement measures to accelerate productivity, and as the stakeholders in private companies press their boards, executives, managers and employees to increase profitability or productivity, the interests of investors are being cared for. That is the stated intent and ethic of the capitalist system. Competition is the fuel of the engine. Governments have their part to play to ensure that the machine is well oiled and that the appropriate policies and populations that will enhance profitability are in place.

## MAIDS TO ORDER

'There is a large shortage of maids in Singapore and the region. The Indonesian government will prepare 25,000 for export ...' (*Straits Times*, June 2011). Practise your understanding of reification on this headline! The opportunity to train as a maid may be very attractive to a woman who feels constrained by village obligations or has not found satisfying work in the urban areas of Indonesia. In meeting their commitment to manufacture maids, does the Indonesian government have any obligation to (i) the communities from which these women are withdrawn; (ii) the safety of the maids in their new contexts. How far will the maids need to re-think their identity when they become formalised servants with perhaps few options to leave their employment?

Rose (1990) builds on the work of Foucault and examines how modern governments attempt to assimilate and control populations, not by coercion or force but through gaining their compliance and consent to wider government policy initiatives. Rose (1990) maintains that governments do this by indirectly managing individuality and the subjective capacities of citizens through two complex and interrelated processes which he calls 'technologies of the self' and 'techniques of the self'. The maids who service expat communities the world over, the 'factory girls' who variously claim emancipation or oppression in industrial China (Chang, 2008), or the men who believe that the on-sea fish factories will bring them and their families the necessary income to live, serve as good examples. In some ways, their stories are no more or less insightful than the stories of career expats, corporate executives or local contractors who can see how to morph themselves to fit with the changing needs of their paymasters.

*Technologies of the self* are the outcome of the combined activities of governments, organisations and various 'experts in subjectivity'. Governments develop policy initiatives and set up and charge organisations, bureaucracies and institutional webs to gain individuals' compliance and consent to the policy initiatives. Examples of such policy initiatives include military efficiency, the methods of raising and educating children, public health, divorce rates, fertility rates, productivity, fitting people to jobs, welfare provision and motivating workers. The organisations act as intermediaries between government and individuals, and because of this, Rose argues, governments control populations 'at a distance'. In this sense, Rose (1990: 2) suggests that managing 'subjectivity has become a central task for the modern organisation'. Organisations have come to fill the space between the private lives of citizens and the public concerns of rulers.

Foucault (1976: 61) termed the information-gathering process of these 'experts in subjectivity' as the 'ritual of confession'. The confessor is required to provide certain information, whether through an interview, observation or a written questionnaire. The ritual of confession is a power relationship because, as a result of the information gathering, the expert makes comparative and normalising judgements about the individual. This power relationship is further strengthened as experts in subjectivity draw on the information gathered to create new language and vocabularies to talk about whole populations, and therefore individuals within those populations.

*Experts in subjectivity* lend their diagnosis of individuals to other experts in the chain of control. The diagnosis may be explicitly conveyed by the candidate of the diagnosis and become or be subtly entwined in the choices they think they have. The experts in the chain of control draw on the panoptic techniques of examinations, surveillance and normalising judgements in their day-to-day work to gather and use information gained from individuals. How often have you heard an individual explain that they would be good or bad at a particular task or occupation because an 'expert' some time in their past has allocated them a personality type? Put together the typecasting of people with the typecasting of occupations and we have an example of Foucault's tables of equivalences. More recently, there is a suggestion that blood-testing and DNA characteristics can not only tell prospective employers information about the physical health of a candidate, their drug and alcohol intake and their potential life ailments as ticking clocks, but that blood samples may provide personality indicators also (International Biosciences, 2013).

New languages and vocabularies of self-responsibility, self-care and personal obligation to meet institutional outputs are increasingly drawn on to inform the creation of governable knowledge which enables individual subjectivity to become 'amenable to management' (Rose, 1988: 184). Experts in subjectivity seek compliance by offering images of a desired self and lifestyle, and then intervene by providing advice on how to achieve this, and by acting upon the 'choices, wishes, values, and conduct of the individual in an indirect manner' (Rose, 1990: 10). Rose (1990: 8) maintains that such 'a citizen subject is not to be dominated in the interests of power, but to be educated and solicited into a kind of alliance between personal objectives and ambitions and institutionally or socially prized goals or activities.' The entire intervention is based on mindsets reconceived as 'knowledge' or 'truth' about what is to be considered normal, a normality that has been produced by these experts in the first instance. Yet, the creation of this knowledge requires certain features of a population to be highlighted and certain features to be ignored. Therefore, only partial information is ever gathered through the ritual of confession, and entered into the calculations of managing the self. Because of this partiality, the new languages created by experts both legitimate power and mystify domination (Rose, 1988). Government objectives and the control of populations become hidden behind a veil of legitimised expertise. Thus, for Rose (1988: 193), the application of technologies of the self transforms the 'panoptic gaze' of the manager, warden, teacher or doctor to the 'psychological gaze' of the expert in subjectivity.

Rose recognises that it is not sufficient for individuals merely to seek the advice of experts in order to fit the mould of available employment opportunities; they must also be willing to do things to themselves to appear normal. It is this willingness to do things to the self that he terms *techniques of the self*. These techniques are evident when people change themselves or follow advice to match the criteria offered to them by experts to become normal, acceptable or desirable. Integral to this process is the notion of disciplining difference (Rose, 1988). It is the gaps, or variance, between the individual and the defined normal behaviour that become the target of discipline and the subject of change. Advice can be given, along with the design of personalised action plans that have the aim of helping individuals change themselves to meet normalised values and sanctioned behaviours. If employees find the workload too heavy or too stressful, there are personal remedies they can undertake. The guidance and uptake of spiritual disciplines – for example, the now fashionable treatment of work-related stress with meditation and yoga – is an example of the deflection of attention by individuals from systemic exploitation to personal responsibility by employers and employees alike. What is not often encouraged is a close examination of the work processes causing the stress.

Those who internalise and accept the prescribed norms or values as their own and act upon the self to achieve normality are deemed to have become 'docile objects' by critical theorists (Lynch, 1985) rather than, and in direct contradiction to, the emancipated beings that populate the capitalist mythology. Such a subject is not controlled through force or coercion, but seemingly through their own choice to comply and consent to the advice given. Those who act in accordance with prescribed norms without internalising them are controlled through their decision to avoid punishments or sanctions of non-compliance. Regardless of the motivation, the outcome is the same: the subject has become self-governed and self-disciplined. The system is stabilised. The deviant and the abnormal may become the target of coercive control or further rounds of intervention. The government's role in managing citizens at a distance to behave in ways consistent with wider sociopolitical and economic policy initiatives becomes obscured within an array of complex intermediary relationships that exist between the individual, experts and organisations. The concern is that disciplinary techniques fabricate particular notions of what it means to be normal and, thus, fabricate a society of individuals who unwittingly change their behaviour to reflect and fit into a particular, and possibly invisible, political economy and ideology. Our even seemingly free actions may unwittingly uphold ideological systems that undermine our material circumstances as our focus is diverted to become a desirable self.

Garsten and Grey (1997) suggest that the majority of people are unlikely ever to seek the services of Rose's 'experts in subjectivity'. Many of the world's workers are still controlled by a Tayloristic focus on their behaviour. More privileged and literate populations gain exposure to expertise through the media and 'self-help' books. The self-help book industry in the US was reported to be worth around $US600 million in 2007 (Loomis, 2008, cited in Hancock, 2009). As with counsellors or psychologists, 'self-help' and 'how-to' books offer techniques and strategies to come to know oneself, and advice on how to change this 'self' (including behaviour, attitudes and values) to become more effective in the world as depicted in neo-liberal ideals. The authors of such books claim to provide individuals with the means to control or improve themselves and to some degree their environment. Typically, however, they ignore the constraints of the contextualising environment within which people live their lives. In this way, argue Garsten and Grey (1997: 223), self-help books guide individuals to manage their soul in terms of Rose's (1990) analysis. The disciplinary impact of these books becomes clear in a Foucauldian sense because the particular version of the self to be fabricated is one that 'is congruent with demands of organizational life'. In the context of employment, it is seen to be largely associated with helping people to accept, adjust and even naturalise organisational restructuring and the labour flexibility practices associated with them.

While Garsten and Grey (1997) focus on managerial self-help and how-to books, their argument is equally compelling in relation to career management self-help books. Carson and Phillips-Carson (1997) found over three thousand such books published on career guidance in the ten years to 1997, arguably the period of rapid transition to a liberalisation of economies. The specific form of career guidance offered in such self-help books, and in the more recent and equally prolific career guidance websites, has remained constant and is aimed at fabricating individuals to change themselves to fit the ever-changing landscape of employment associated with the insecure forms of work available.

The process of managing the subjective capacities of citizens at a distance, we have suggested above, involves employing 'experts in subjectivity' (Rose, 1990: 2). Examples of such experts include psychologists, social workers, personnel or human resource managers, probation officers, occupational psychologists and vocational and careers guidance advisers. Have a look at the website of the world-class career services of the government of New Zealand (www.career.govt.nz/), a little country that might be said to be punching well above its weight in terms of its global influence.[1] We turn now to the question of what norms are being normalised, and in whose interest, in these skilful and far-reaching forms of expert help.

## WHOSE NORMS ARE BEING NORMALISED?

Deetz (1992) agrees with Rose that experts play a significant role in fabricating individuality. However, Deetz (1992: 17) extends this argument by suggesting that the corporate sector has come to overshadow the state in controlling and directing individual lives and in influencing collective social development. Corporate decisions about the shape of work, pay structures, what is produced and internal practices have a profound effect on the way in which people live. Deetz draws on the work of Habermas (1984, 1987) on colonising activity and de-institutionalisation to analyse the ways in which corporate life and the norms produced within the corporate form is extending into the non-work aspects of our lives. Such colonising activity refers to the process of extending corporate values into non-corporate institutional forms that make up society; for example, family, government, religion, the media and educational institutions. Activities carried out in these non-corporate institutions begin to support the corporate world and, in doing so, reproduce pro-corporate ideology and practices which increasingly become the dominant way to think about and organise society, including determining which values, attitudes and behaviours ought to be normalised.

As discussed in Chapter 3, governments increasingly subsidise the corporate sector through pro-corporate legislation and by interpreting the public good in terms of economic development and stability. The implication of this is a power shift from (elected) governments to the (unelected) corporate form. This power shift also represents a shift in the location of where social norms and values are decided, as corporate work processes, practices and codes of conduct become translated and embedded in desirable social behaviours, attitudes, norms and values. Deetz (1992) argues that, within this system, disciplinary power acts to ensure that our day-to-day experiences and conduct reinforce the normalisation of pro-corporate ideology.

This colonising process as expressed by Habermas and Deetz extends to educational institutions as students receive education that prepares them for occupational roles rather than providing education that enhances critical reflection, autonomy and preparation for their life role as citizens (Braverman, 1974; Clegg and Dunkerley, 1980). This shift in the function of education represents a shift in the values and legitimacy granted to the corporation. The curriculum becomes aligned with corporate needs, grades translate to mastery of material required to be learned, research becomes aligned with corporate problem-solving, and practices internal to educational institutions come to mirror corporate values. The combined effect is to teach students material that supports corporate needs and practices that will be useful in the corporate world.

While educational curriculum, practices and processes have changed over the years, the economic and pro-corporate focus remains. This is particularly evident in a World Bank report where Fasih (2008: 8–9) argues that 'Education plays a central role in preparing individuals to enter the labor force and in equipping them with the skills needed to engage in lifelong learning experiences … [and importantly that the] role of education needs to be seen in a broader macroeconomic context to ensure that education contributes to the growth of a country's economy.' The explicit link made between education, individualism and economic growth is further supported in the discursive shift from educating students to take on lifelong employment in a single vocation or organisation to preparing students for lifelong employability in any number of organisations. Such a shift both acknowledges and normalises, but does not question, the changes in the employment market typified by insecurity and flexibility.

## LEARNING RESPONSIBILITY EARLY

Peter loves his school. He enjoys his friends and his teacher. He does well at most things. Even at eight years old, Peter knows that it was a struggle for his parents to meet the many costs associated with his being at this great school. Although it is a publicly funded school, it seems that very often he needs to bring money to school to pay for something on top of the costly school uniform, the technology and sports fees, and the annual school camp. His parents know, however, that all these activities would improve Peter's chances to do well in life. The teacher announced that today the class would be focusing on careers. The teacher explained that a career was what you wanted to do when you grew up. A large stack of magazines was placed on the big table Peter shares with some of his classmates. They each had a lovely sheet of strong white paper on which to glue pictures they could cut from the magazines of all the things they desired. Soon each child's paper was indeed a work of art. Peter looked at the two on each side of himself. Jenny's page was covered with girly things! He saw dresses and jewellery, make-up and hand-bags. He also saw she had some images of families in lovely houses and children playing on beaches in far-away places. On his other side, Mickey had covered his page in fabulous looking cars, motorbikes and horses! Horses! How Peter would love to have a horse. He had hoped to get one for his birthday but even as the wish formed in his mind, he knew that his parents could never afford such a gift. His own picture was made up of farm pictures, farm trucks, farm houses, farm animals and farm families. He would love to be a farmer. He would have to earn a lot of money before he could buy a farm! He would need a job! Luckily, the teacher announced that next week the class would look at what kinds of jobs would help the children reach their goals. Peter already knew what he needed to do! Selling farm tractors would surely get him to his dream! Trojan Tractors were big in his little town. Often on his way home from school he peered into their sales yard. YES! That is what he would do. He would become a salesman for Trojan Tractors.

The early shaping of education to meet the employment needs of employers denies children and wider society the enhancement of the potential of the full human being. Literacy and numeracy in infants has driven both the preschool markets and afterschool acceleration programmes. Governments participate in this downward pressure on the age of children starting school by urging parents to send their children to pre-schools and by broadcasting the educational achievements of those children who attended these in contrast to those who did not. Narrowly defined career-focused post-primary programmes of education are the norm everywhere. Limited time on political orientations or unnoticed institutional orientated curricula inhibit the development of more critical skills that enable deeper considerations about the implications of current corporate practices and alternative methods of organising society. Such an education helps develop and reinforce hegemonic value systems as discussed in Chapter 2. The provision of education that focuses directly or indirectly on corporate needs helps to domesticate individuals and citizens to pro-corporate ideology as the only ideological form (Braverman, 1974). Through schooling, children learn to accept the particular way that work is organised and are already equipped with a particular set of understandings about work and their place within it prior to entering the labour market. Similarly, business schools reproduce corporate ideology through curriculum design (Clegg and Dunkerley, 1980); thus, the newly trained manager comes equipped with a commitment to notions of profit maximisation, efficiency and effectiveness – critical reflection is rarely offered.

Habermas's (1987) analysis of the colonisation of the lifeworld and the process of deinstitutionalisation becomes particularly fruitful in understanding how our personal and family values and norms might become aligned with those of the organisation, and how family and community subsidise the corporate world. In Hancock and Tyler's (2009) edited collection, *The Management of Everyday Life*, contributors show that the managerial discourse of rationality and efficiency has entered into areas as intimate as sexuality (Tyler, 2009), drug and alcohol use (Wray-Bliss, 2009), health (Hughes, 2009), managing sleep (Hancock et al., 2009), family management (Hochschild, 2009) and how to manage our homes, to name but a few. Of interest here, perhaps, is Hochschild's (2009: 95) critique of the 'Family 360' programme designed by the management consultant group LeaderWorks to measure corporate executives' performance in their family lives. The programme is based on the 'Management 360' performance review of corporate executives' effectiveness. In the 'Family 360' version, however, members of the family are interviewed, and the consultants offer a myriad of advice and how-to tools to facilitate the executive to interact more efficiently with their family.

Increasingly, even the very structure of family and community involvement is affected by the extension of systemic rationality and economic centrality into the lifeworld (Moss Kanter, 1989; Deetz, 1992). Indeed, one significant trend has been the declining birth rates in industrialised nations since the 1960s. Preston (1986) presents a compelling argument that changing social values have seen a movement away from the family unit as being a meaningful and mean-ing-giving institution. Instead, he suggests that the spread of individualism is implicated in declining birth rates, as both men and women are insisting 'per-haps more than ever before, on finding our true selves independent of any cultural or social influence, being responsible to that self alone, and making its fulfilment the very meaning of our lives' (Bellah et al., 1985: 150, as cited in Preston, 1986: 187).

An economic analysis of declining birth rates highlights the increased cost of living and downward pressure on the wage levels of many workers (see Chapter 4) as affecting decisions around the number of children. Decreased birth rates among tertiary-educated women have also been recorded in a num-ber of countries, including Sweden (Persson, 2010), Britain (Whitehead, 2009) and the United States (Abma and Martinez, 2006). This particular cohort of women has student debt to repay and often enters professions and pursues careers associated with cultures of long working hours. Thus, decisions about whether to have children are becoming embedded in career decisions. For some, the time dedicated to developing their careers means that they delay having children for too long. The consequent reduction in birth rates has become of interest to a number of developed nations, including Australia and Germany, whose governments are now concerned about the flow-on effect on their ageing populations. Community participation, too, is being reshaped around working time. The extension of the working day for some reduces available time to participate in volunteer community activities (Deetz, 1992), while under-employment and unemployment are associated with community withdrawal, increased crime and reduced volunteer activity (Ehrensal, 1995; Uchitelle and Kleinfeld, 1996; McBride, 1999).

Corporate ownership of the media has a direct impact on advertising, programming and news presentation (Herman and Chomsky, 1994). The dominant ideology presented in the media supports the needs of a dominant elite, corporates and governments. News is filtered. Its shaping marginalises dissent and presents the views of governments and dominant interest groups to the public. Advertising campaigns that aim to sell products also offer images of preferred lifestyles which are presented as '*the* social good' (Deetz, 1992: 34, emphasis in original); consumption that favours corporations is seen as good. Personal identity becomes shaped by media messages and expressed through purchasing decisions. The disciplinary effects of purchasing behaviour are more deeply explored in Chapter 7.

The 2011 focus on the 'Murdoch' media empire reveals the extent to which corporate ownership of the media can and does shape governments and societies (Doward, 2012). Moreover, as the Murdoch case unfolded, arrests and corruption charges were laid associated with phone tapping, as well as with bribing police and other law enforcement personnel. Moreover, Deetz's (1992) assertion that news presented in the media is filtered, and marginalises dissent, is apparent in the coverage of protests against globalised capital and corporate greed as discussed in Chapter 3. The protesters in the late 1990s and early 2000s (e.g., in London, Seattle and Genoa) were framed as violent and anti-capitalist. In his media coverage, John W. Schoen (2011), senior producer of msnbc.com, described the early days of the 'Occupation Wall Street' sit-in protest in this way: 'It's messy. It's disorganized. At times, the message is all but incoherent.' Such framings detract from the deeply embedded concerns that the protesters against the World Trade Organization (WTO) and the more recent sit-in protesters (which began in New York on 29 September 2011 and spread to other nations) have with respect to the global sociopolitical economy, corporate bail-outs and high unemployment.

Moreover, government response to these citizen acts of resistance has varied. The use of riot police to disperse crowds was witnessed throughout the campaigns against the WTO and G8 meetings during the late 1990s and early 2000s, while local governance bodies have sought legal redress and issued eviction and trespass notices to campaigners in the sit-in movement. The protesters in the 'Occupy London' sit-in, for example, were evicted from outside St Paul's Cathedral on 28 February 2012 in this manner. These examples illustrate two things: first, there are moments and spaces of resistance to sociopolitical framings; second, that once these are defined as abnormal (or anti-capitalist or violent or disruptive), those holding hegemonic power are willing and often able to gain the use of the government apparatus to assert their position of power.

Colonisation of the lifeworld is supported through the process of de-institutionalisation of primary institutions, such as family and religion. Diverse cultural values weaken. Individuals increasingly turn to 'experts in subjectivity' for guidance on how to create meaning for and about themselves. Unwittingly re-institutionalisation occurs but in a subtle form, a form in which the institution that commands our fealty is 'the economy' enacted through the necessary participation in 'the market'. Participation in 'the market' is the means to life. The responsibility to make it in 'the market' is individualised to ever greater degrees. Along with Rose (1988), Deetz (1992) maintains that the expert, the counsellor and the trainer play particular roles in the fabrication of identity, but the identity offered is a differently produced identity from that of previous epochs. It is at this point of seeking guidance that de-institutionalisation of other forms of social order particularly supports colonisation of the lifeworld by neo-liberal ideals. Advice given reinforces dominant ideology that supports particular behaviours and values that are supportive of the corporate world. The experts within the corporate context have a particular role in creating norms and fabricating identity in contemporary society that supports the needs of corporations and, in particular, multinational corporations. As such, corporate life extends into the very heart of how individuals come to structure their identity, their lifestyles and their life choices (Hancock and Tyler, 2009).

## DRESS FOR SUCCESS

Jake and Uma were required to attend a job-skill class as part of the conditions of receiving their unemployment cheque. The course was kind of fun. The tutor was pretty cool. Together they crafted CVs that could be used in their (required) job hunts. They practised interview techniques. On the last day of the course, there was to be a role play. The tutor would be the interviewer and each course member would have a turn at practising their presentation for a potential job. The tutor gave some clear last-minute instructions for the next day's class. 'Be sure to wear appropriate clothes and shoes. Make sure your hair is neat and tidy. Remove those studs from your tongue and eyebrows!' What to wear? The boys in the class had a scheme! They pooled their money and bought a full dress suit from the local charity shop and six neck ties. Much fun was had as they changed clothes between role plays – pinning the pants on the thin guys, changing the tie for each interviewee just for effect! The girls had a different idea. Uma's mother was part of a Church social service committee. She knew they had a wardrobe of clothes

*(Continued)*

*(Continued)*

that were lent out to jobseekers. They would go there! Indeed, each of the girls in the class found some corporate-looking clothes. Thank goodness the kind ladies in the Church were there to help them. When the day came for a real job interview, they would know where to go because, as the tutor had told them, the clothes they generally felt good in would be a disadvantage in the competition for scarce jobs. It was nice pretending for a few hours that maybe they could one day become a well-paid executive and prance around in a cool suit, wear great shoes, and drive a fancy car. Meanwhile, back in the real world …

The implication of the human relations theorists as 'experts in subjectivity' in the shaping and disciplining of workers in the form of HRM is where we now turn our scrutiny.

# HRM: HUMANISING THEORY OR CORPORATE HEGEMONY?

The origins of human relations theory are often traced to Mayo and the Western Electric Hawthorne studies conducted between 1927 and 1932 (Clegg and Dunkerley, 1980). Mayo argued that scientific management techniques, while enabling workers to earn an income and satisfy material and economic needs, ignored fundamental social needs. These unmet social needs, Mayo argued, led to power and control problems manifesting as absenteeism, turnover and worker strikes. Mayo linked this to an inherent problem of scientific forms of control, leading to a reduction in the social skills of workers (Clegg and Dunkerley, 1980). The Hawthorne experiments further established an apparent link between work groups that had developed social skills, management style and productivity. That is, productivity and satisfaction were deemed to increase when workers felt that they had input into decision-making and when they believed managers were interested in them. Moreover, through these experiments, Mayo identified the notion of formal and informal organisational structures. The formal structure was typified by official managerial rules and the informal structure was characterised by the social interactions of workers within groups. One role of management, then, was to ensure that informal organisation relationships complemented the achievement of formal organisational goals (Clegg and Dunkerley, 1980).

One outcome of these studies was the emergence of human relations theory. One fundamental assumption embedded in much human relations theory is that human beings have a full range of needs and that many of these needs can be met through work design. A number of the more popularised human needs theories found in management textbooks include Maslow's 'hierarchy of needs' and Hertzberg's 'two-factor theory'. Similarly, a number of specialist disciplines have developed with the focus of researching work and workers with the aim of improving the efficiency and humanisation of work. These specialists include occupational and industrial psychologists, vocational guidance officers, ergonomic designers and organisational behaviouralists (Rose, 1999).

By the 1970s, traditional Tayloristic practices had begun to incorporate considerations of job rotation and job-enrichment measures (Ingraham and Lutz, 1974) and notions of employee 'empowerment' in an attempt to improve measures of 'job satisfaction'. During this time, an emerging debate questioned deskilling and direct control as forms of control, and terms such as 'responsible autonomy' began to enter the workplace discourse (Jones, 2000). Although the argument invariably centres on meeting employee needs, the focus of the humanisation project remains on increasing organisational productivity and profit, complete with methods to measure employee productivity.

Miller and Rose (1998) argue that the humanising efforts of the Human Relations School focused on three areas that helped gain managerial control through worker compliance. First, workers began to be understood as having a personal life outside work, which could interfere with their productive capacities. Attempts were made to align the needs of workers with the needs of organisational goal achievement. Second, the informal organisational structure came under scrutiny from experts as needing to be managed to ensure that the relationships between workers, their colleagues and managers became focused on organisational goal achievement. Third, viewing workers as productive machines with family lives meant that departures 'from specified norms in a worker's home and personal life could henceforth be seen to have possibly disruptive effects on his or her work performance' (Miller and Rose, 1998: 53). Workers, through their mental capacities and private lives, have become the concern of managers, experts and politicians as a means to improve organisational and societal efficiency. And, as noted above, new ranges of specialists (e.g., occupational and industrial psychologists, and so on) have developed to improve efficiency and the humanisation of work (Rose, 1999). Such a growth industry has come under criticism from sociologists as being 'no more than servants of power, engaging in the manipulation of workers in their attempts to adjust them to exploitative working conditions' (Rose, 1999: 57).

## THE COLOUR OF EMANCIPATION

'The color of your clothing is very important' [said Teacher Fu to the girl in his class who said she wanted to be a sales assistant]. 'Now I will tell you what kind of character people will think you have when you wear different colors. Please write it down: Red represents enthusiasm. Orange represents

*(Continued)*

(Continued)

excitement. Yellow represents brightness ...' Teacher Fu covered a lot of ground that day. He gave tips on how to build confidence. '*Practice boldly expressing yourself. Walk into the room like you own it.*' (Chang, 2008: 178–9; emphasis added). Dress for [Job] Success is becoming a global phenomenon!

The techniques that have emerged under humanising projects, while treating workers as having a subjective capacity as opposed to being an extension of the automation process, have not alleviated the conditions that scientific management techniques imposed on workers (Rose, 1999). Workers still lack knowledge of the work process, there is a continued gap between the salaries of workers and managers/owners, workers are still subject to being managed, and the rationale of profit for owners still applies (as evidenced in this book so far). Critics of the humanisation movement argue that changes to date have not done anything for workers except to entrench them further into exploitative relationships, while at the same time legitimising those relationships. While work redesign, such as job enrichment, job rotation and so on, appears to give workers greater control over their working lives, many commentators argue that humanisation efforts primarily focus on increasing productivity through gaining worker compliance (e.g., early critiques were offered by Clegg and Dunkerley, 1980; Miller and Rose, 1998). In this sense, Clegg and Dunkerley (1980: 135) argue that the Human Relations School produced 'a highly developed ideological apparatus of normative control, of hegemony, for the management of organisations'; they go on to say that, from this perspective, the 'Human Relations School has significance not as a body of scientific findings of highly dubious nature, but as part of the apparatus whereby organizations attempt to impose and maintain control of production' (Clegg and Dunkerley, 1980: 135).

A Foucauldian analysis would suggest that the human relations discourses can be seen as another aspect of the 'panoptic gaze'. The individual turns the gaze upon the 'self' and becomes a self-regulating 'being' within the system, being taught how to redefine structural inequalities and inequities as stories of celebrating life's journeys. Rose (1999) suggests that these new forms of control ignore the inherent power imbalances within capitalist work relationships. Rather, the focus of the new field of experts has been to collude with management in creating subtle ways to bring about worker compliance by adjusting the worker to the demands of the organisation. Under the human relations perspective, worker discontent, as manifest in strikes, absenteeism, low productivity and so on, can be explained by poor adjustment between workers and their conditions of work, and, as such, can be alleviated by realigning workers through various psychological techniques or interventions by various experts (Rose, 1999). As such, Rose argues:

> The apparent discovery of a fortunate coincidence between personal contentment of the worker and maximum efficiency and profitability for the boss is merely yet another dissimulation of the fundamental conflict between capital and labour. By concentrating upon theories and techniques that would sell it to managers, the psychological expertise of production has inevitably adopted a managerial perspective. (Rose, 1999: 58)

The ideological work on organisation theory makes readily available packages of individuals ready to take up uncritically the hegemonic perspective that reproduces the institutional logics of capitalism, that of the rational orientation of business run by non-owners. While management schools equip potential managers with an introduction to rational thought, managerial techniques and attitudes for managing uncritically on behalf of owners, internal organisational practices have also developed to reinforce alignment between the behaviour of individual members and the needs of capital. In this sense, managers not only learn to manage workers, but also learn to manage themselves in ways consistent with the needs of capital.

While much of the focus in this chapter has been on the atomisation of human beings in the competition for life, it is to the selective call to our human interrelatedness that we now direct some closer attention. We are all part of a team, a team that may be controlled by the possibilities and pace of technology, the pressure of peers, the decline in conditions of service and the acceptance of job loss if need be to save the firm, the industry, the nation or the global economy. But when it comes right down to it, the team will expel an individual if such expulsion is deemed important for the survival of the team, the department, the firm, the industry or the economy as a whole (Barker, 1993). Experiential exercises have demonstrated to us that this is a response to pressure to economise spontaneously and uncritically implemented by aspiring managers in our classes. How can this be explained? For this, we turn to the subtle metamorphoses of Taylorist and human relations ideas into the contemporary form of human resources management (HRM).

The Hawthorne experiments that led to the formation of the Human Relations School of Thought have been criticised on a number of accounts: in particular, the research design, the sample groups used, poor analysis and reporting of research results and the lack of appropriate control groups (Clegg and Dunkerley, 1980). Re-analysis of the original research results dispute the apparent relationships between managerial interest, worker input, job satisfaction and productivity. Despite this, these experiments continue to be cited as making a significant contribution to the understanding of work and workers, and to the development of the human relations discipline, the beginnings of industrial psychology and sociology, and of human resource management.

Much of this research has come to inform the development of the academic discipline and practice of HRM, which incorporates the traditions of labour process and industrial relations, organisational psychology and human capital. HRM practices have come to include involvement in recruitment, retention, succession planning, induction, training, remuneration, performance management, industrial relations and collective bargaining. Deetz (2003: 24) writes that

HRM 'is clearly in the culture and meaning business, its focus is on the production of a specific human being with specific self-conceptions and feelings.' Citing Jaques (1996), Deetz (2003) suggests that the notions of 'free contract' and 'social relations', and our ideas about our personal identity as 'manager', 'secretary' or 'worker', are corporate productions and reproductions that need investigation. Such investigations into organisation-wide practices central to HRM considerations have come to include a critical organisational development, change management, organisational structure and design, and restructuring and downsizing (Youndt et al., 1996; Huselid et al., 1997). So, is HRM a new and more humane coordination of people in the production of goods and services than we have portrayed so far in the book?

Bolton (2011: 74) suggests that HRM is different from the earlier incarnations of employee control as these earlier ways:

> did not have such high expectations of their employees, and they had a limited perception of the capabilities of organisational actors. Most importantly though, managers may have wished to enlist (or at least tame) the energies of the informal work group it was never assumed that such energies would become an integral part of the formal organisation in the way that they have for HRM.

In reviewing the work of Townley (1994), Pfeffer (1998), Thompson (2003), Sewell (2005) and Legge (2006), Bolton comes to the conclusion that contemporary HRM might be thought of as:

> part of a general move towards a more flexible capitalism. Most clearly of all this is represented in the observation that over the past three decades, despite economic growth in most developed countries and huge investment in HR practice, we have seen reported increases in job dissatisfaction, work intensification, hours worked, job insecurity and economic and social inequality. (Bolton 2011: 78)

# CONCLUSION

The forms of control inherent in what are portrayed as flexible work practices have become entrenched at the macro, organisational and individual levels of organising self and others. The notion of flexibility is deceptive, however. While money can be moved around at the click of an icon, and workers can be made redundant or moved to distant places at the stroke of a pen, finding, keeping and changing jobs to meet personal aspirations appears a much less fluid reality for most people on the globe. The discourse of the flexible firm initially provided a point of conflict between the Keynesian worker mentality and the individualistic mentality required under flexible forms of work. The solution to overcoming this conflict was to domesticate citizens to strive for individual 'utopia' over communal well-being by becoming flexible individuals. The tools used to naturalise these aspirations include discourses of human resource management: the boundaryless organisation; self-shaping career orientations; and limited engagement with spiritual and diversity values. The uncritical embedding of these ideas is becoming increasingly prominent in career studies and management education and practice. Inkson and colleagues (2012: 335) write that, while career studies are pushing in innovative directions, they have 'failed adequately to define their concept, have overestimated agency and underestimated institutional effects, have neglected and derided organizational careers, and have assumed the predominance of careers where the evidence says otherwise'.

> ## TALK BOX
>
> Today most people usually think of slavery in terms of history classes they have taken, or movies they have seen. The fact is, modern slavery is just as real, just as brutal, and just as inhuman as any history book. Modern slavery controls, and in some cases claims, the lives of millions of people across the globe. (Abolition Media, 2013)

Slaves are people bought and sold on markets. They are not free to leave their owners. Wage slaves may be equally bound. Wage slavery may be achieved overtly or surreptitiously. Why should we care? Should we act to ensure that exploitative working conditions are completely eradicated? Notice the various forms of reasoning in your response. Can you distinguish ethical from pragmatic considerations? If living wages and safe working conditions were the right of all workers and the duty of all employers, what might be the consequences? What may be the consequences of not doing so?

# NOTE

1 New Zealand has been a leader on many fronts: signing a treaty with indigenous peoples to assure their sovereignty; the first to grant women the vote; a widespread, deep and speedy commitment to neo-liberalism in the 1980s. Currently, the head of the UNDP is the immediate past prime minister of New Zealand, Helen Clark. Clark both oversaw a period of rapid liberalisation in New Zealand and signalled a later recognition of its social cost. She now heads the world's most powerful 'development' agency. Are the lessons learned in New Zealand about the effects of economic liberalization being noted globally?

# ADDITIONAL RESOURCES

Bauman, Z. (2004) *Identity*. Cambridge: Polity.
Bolton, S. and Houlihan, M. (2007) Beginning the search. In S. Bolton and M. Houlihan (eds), *Searching for the H in HRM*. London: Palgrave. pp. 1–18.
Fromm, E. (1942) *The Fear of Freedom*. London: Routledge and Kegan Paul.

Grey, C. (1994) Career as a project of the self and labour process discipline. *Sociology*, 28 (2): 479–97.

Hall, D.T. (1996) *The Career is Dead – Long Live the Career: A Relational Approach to Careers*. San Francisco: Jossey-Bass.

Levitt, T. (1958) The dangers of social responsibility. *Harvard Business Review*, September–October: 41–50.

Miller, P. and Rose, N. (1988) The Tavistock programme: the government of subjectivity and social life. *Sociology*, 22 (2): 171–92.

Mintzberg, H. (1975) The manager's job: folklore and fact. *Harvard Business Review*, 53 (July–August).

Peppers, C. and Briskin, A. (2002) *Bringing your Soul to Work: An Everyday Practice*. San Francisco: Berret-Koehler.

Rose, N. (1989) Calculable minds and manageable individuals. *History of the Human Sciences*, 1 (2): 179–200.

Sennett, R. (1998) *The Corrosion of Character: The Personal Consequences of Work in the New Capitalism*. New York: W.W. Norton.

Sennett, R. (2008) *The Craftsman*. New Haven, CT: Yale University Press.

# REFERENCES

Abma, J.C. and Martinez, G. (2006) Childlessness among older women in the United States: trends and profiles. *Journal of Marriage and Family*, 68 (4): 1045–56.

Abolition Media (2013) Modern slavery statistics (http://abolitionmedia.org/about-us/modern-slavery-statistics; retrieved 8 September 2013).

Atkinson, J. (1984) Manpower strategies for flexible organizations. *Personnel Management*, 16: 28–31.

Barker, J. (1993) Tightening the iron cage: concertive control in self-managing teams. *Administrative Science Quarterly*, 38 (3): 408–37.

Bellah, R.N., Madsen, R., Sullivan, W.M., Swidler, A. and Tipton, S.M. (1985) *Habits of the Heart: Individualism and Commitment in American Life*. Berkeley, CA: University of California Press.

Bolton, S. (2011) Critical human resource management. In M. Tadajewski, P. MacLaran, E. Parsons and M. Parker (eds), *Key Concepts in Critical Management Studies*. London: Sage. pp. 74–82.

Braverman, H. (1974) *Labor and Monopoly Capital: The Degradation of Work in the Twentieth Century*. New York: Monthly Review Press.

Carson, K.D. and Phillips-Carson, P. (1997) Career entrenchment: a quiet march toward occupational death? *Academy of Management*, 11 (1): 62–75.

Chang, L.T. (2008) *Factory Girls: Voices from the Heart of Modern China*. London: Picador.

Clegg, S. and Dunkerley, D. (1980) *Organization, Class and Control*. New York: Routledge.

Crane, G. (1999) Imagining the economic nation: globalisation in China. *New Political Economy*, 4 (2): 215–32.

Deetz, S. (1992) *Democracy in an Age of Corporate Colonisation: Developments in Communication and the Politics of Everyday Life*. Albany, NY: State University of New York Press.

Deetz, S. (2003) Disciplinary power, conflict suppression and HRM. In M. Alvesson and Willmott, H. (eds), *Studying Management Critically*. London: Sage. pp. 23–45.

Doward, J. (2012) Murdoch media empire engulfed in scandal as Scotland Yard's net spreads. *Guardian*, 11 February (www.guardian.co.uk/media/2012/feb/11/rupert-murdoch-media-empire-scrutiny; retrieved 8 September 2013).

Ehrensal, K.N. (1995) Discourses of global competition: obscuring the changing labour processes of managerial work. *Journal of Organizational Change Management*, 8 (5): 5–16.

Fasih, T. (2008) *Linking Education Policy to Labor Market Outcomes*. Washington: World Bank (http://siteresources.worldbank.org/EDUCATION/Resources/278200-1099079877269/547664-1208379365576/DID_Labor_market_outcomes.pdf; retrieved 10 September 2013).

Foucault, M. (1976) *The Will to Knowledge: The History of Sexuality*, vol. 1, trans. R. Hurley. Harmondsworth: Penguin.

Foucault, M. (1977) *Discipline and Punish: The Birth of the Prison*, trans. A. Sheridan. Harmondsworth: Penguin.

Garsten, C. and Grey, C. (1997) How to become oneself: discourses in subjectivity in post-bureaucratic organizations. *Organization*, 4 (2): 211–28.

Gramsci, A. (1971) *Selections from the Prison Notebooks*, trans. Q. Hoare and G. Nowell-Smith. London: Lawrence and Wishart.

Habermas, J. (1984) *The Theory of Communicative Action*, vol. 1: *Reason and Rationalization of Society*. Cambridge: Polity Press.

Habermas, J. (1987) *The Theory of Communicative Action*, vol. 2: *The Critique of Society*. Cambridge: Polity Press.

Hancock, P. (2009) Management and colonization in everyday life. In P. Hancock and M. Tyler (eds), *The Management of Everyday Life*. Basingstoke: Palgrave Macmillan. pp. 1–21.

Hancock, P., and Tyler, M. (eds) (2009) *The Management of Everyday Life*. Basingstoke: Palgrave Macmillan.

Hancock, P., Williams, S.J. and Boden, S. (2009) Managing sleep? The colonization of everyday/night life. In P. Hancock and M. Tyler (eds), *The Management of Everyday Life*. Basingstoke: Palgrave Macmillan. pp. 74–93.

Harvey, D. (2006) Neoliberalism and the restoration of class power. *Economics and Political Weekly*, 16 September: 2294–300.

Herman, E.S. and Chomsky, N. (1994) *Manufacturing Consent: The Political Economy of the Mass Media*. New York: Pantheon.

Hiscock, G. (2012) *Earth Wars: The Battle for Global Resources*. Singapore: Wiley and Sons.

Hochschild, A. (2009) Through the crack in the time bind: from market management to family management. In P. Hancock and M. Tyler (eds), *The Management of Everyday Life*. Basingstoke: Palgrave Macmillan. pp. 95–108.

Hughes, B. (2009) Managing health in everyday life. In P. Hancock and M. Tyler (eds), *The Management of Everyday Life*. Basingstoke: Palgrave Macmillan. pp. 56–73.

Huselid, M.A., Jackson, S.E. and Schuler, R.S. (1997) Technical and strategic human resource management effectiveness as determinants of firm performance. *Academy of Management Journal*, 40 (1): 171–88.

ILO (International Labour Organization) (2010) *Global Wage Report 2010/11: Wage Policies in Times of Crisis*. Geneva: ILO.

Ingraham, A.P. and Lutz, C.F. (1974) Managing positions – the key to effective organization, compensation, and productivity. *Human Resource Management*, 13 (2): 12–21.

Inkson, K., Gunz, H., Ganesh, S. and Roper, J. (2012) Boundaryless careers: bring back boundaries. *Organisation Studies*, 33 (3): 323–40.

International Biosciences (2013) DNA testing (www.ibdna.com/regions/UK/EN/?pa ge=DNATestingAndPersonality; retrieved 8 September 2013).

Jaques, R. (1996) *Manufacturing the Employee: Management Knowledge from the 19th to the 21st Century*. London: Sage.

Jones, O. (2000) Scientific management, culture and control: a first-hand account of Taylorism in practice. *Human Relations*, 53 (5): 631–53.

Legge, K. (2006) Human resource management. In S. Ackroyd, R. Batt, P. Thompson and P. Tolbert (eds), *The Oxford Handbook of Work and Organization*. Oxford: Oxford University Press. pp. 220–41.

Lynch, M. (1985) Discipline and the material form of images: an analysis of scientific visibility. *Social Studies of Science*, 15: 37–66.

McBride, S. (1999) Towards permanent insecurity: the social impact of unemployment. *Journal of Canadian Studies*, 3 (4): 13–30.

Miller, P. and Rose, N. (1998) Governing economic life. In C. Mabey, G. Salaman and J. Storey (eds), *Strategic Human Resource Management*. London: Sage. pp. 46–57.

Moss Kanter, R. (1989) *When Giants Learn to Dance: Mastering the Challenges of Strategy, Management and Careers*. London: Unwin.

Persson, L. (2010) Item 5 – Constructing assumptions for fertility: data, methods and analysis. Trend reversal in childlessness in Sweden. United Nations Statistical Commission and Economic Commission for Europe, Conference of European Statisticians, Statistical Office of the European Union (Eurostat), Statistics Sweden.

Pfeffer, J. (1998) *Competitive Advantage through People*. Cambridge, MA: Harvard University Press.

Preston, S.H. (1986) Below-replacement fertility in industrial societies: causes, consequences, policies. *Population and Development Review*, 12 (suppl.): 176–95.

Rickards, J. (2011) *Currency Wars: The Making of the Next Global Crisis*. London: Penguin.

Rose, N. (1988) *Governing the Soul: The Shaping of the Private Self*. London: Free Association Books.

Rose, N. (1990) *Governing the Soul: The Shaping of the Private Self*, 2nd edn. London: Routledge.

Rose, N. (1999) *Governing the Soul: The Shaping of the Private Self*, 2nd rev. edn. London: Free Association Books.

Schoen, J. (2011) Familiar refrain: Wall Street protest lacks leaders, clear message (www.unibaker.com/occ_wallstreet_5_protestunorganizes_msnbc.php; retrieved 8 September 2013).

Sewell, G. (2005) Nice work? Rethinking managerial control in an era of knowledge work. *Organisation*, 12 (5): 685–704.

Thompson, P. (2003) Disconnected capitalism: or, why employers can't keep their side of the bargain. *Work, Employment and Society*, 17 (2): 359–78.

Townley, B. (1994) *Reframing Human Resource Management*. London: Sage.

Tyler, M. (2009) Managing under the covers: lifestyle media and the management of sexuality in everyday life. In P. Hancock and M. Tyler (eds), *The Management of Everyday Life*. Basingstoke: Palgrave Macmillan. pp. 23–38.

Uchitelle, L. and Kleinfeld, R. (1996) The downsizing of America. *The New York Times*, 3 March.

Whitehead, T. (2009) One in five women stays childless because of modern lifestyle. *The Telegraph*, 25 June (www.telegraph.co.uk/news/uknews/5637417/One-in-five-women-stay-childless-because-of-modern-lifestyle.html; retrieved 8 September 2013).

Wray-Bliss, E. (2009) Over the limit: the management of drug and alcohol use. In P. Hancock and M. Tyler (eds), *The Management of Everyday Life*. Basingstoke: Palgrave Macmillan. pp. 39–55.

Youndt, M.A., Snell, S.A., Dean, Jr., J.W. and Lepak, D.P. (1996) Human resource management, manufacturing strategy, and firm performance. *Academy of Management Journal*, 39 (4): 836–66.

# 6 GENDER, RACE AND CLASS DIVERSITIES IN THE WORKPLACE

## Learning Objectives

To gain a growing understanding of the attractiveness of diversity management (DM) and the degree of emancipation this can deliver in the context of a wider and deeply embedded, competitive, market-orientated institutional logics, in this chapter we will:

- compare and contrast notions of equality, equity and fairness;
- examine the doctrines of equal employment opportunities (EEO) and affirmative action (AA) and their limitations;
- examine the emancipatory claims of diversity management.

## CRITICAL CONCEPTS

Programmes of *equal (employment) opportunities* (EEO) and *affirmative action* (AA) are hard-won institutional responses to evidence of prejudice, racism, sexism and other forms of institutional discrimination that belie the claim for universal participation and empowerment of both neo-liberal and democratically orientated societies. This response has been overshadowed by a discourse of *diversity management* (DM).

# EQUALITY, EQUITY AND DIVERSITY MANAGEMENT

[C]omparative findings suggest that members of Western, educated, industrialized, rich, and democratic societies ... are among the least representative populations one could find for generalizing about humans ... Overall, these empirical patterns suggest that we need to be less cavalier in addressing questions of human nature on the basis of data drawn from this particularly thin, and rather unusual, slice of humanity. (Henrich et al., 2010)

Henrich and colleagues (2010) invite us to think about the populations that have been researched, and the misleading generalisations that have been drawn from such research and become embedded as knowledge or truth about some aspect of our humanity. The sampling has been taken from a very thin slice of humanity! The influence of this selection bias has gained some attention in management literature and teaching. The discussion of human diversity has found a place in most textbooks for students who aspire to manage other people. What remains problematic, however, is the still deeply embedded preconceptions about 'normal people' from which many management theories have taken their shape.

Much of the empirical work that underpins model-making for theories in organisation behaviour or human resource management, for example, was conducted on populations of workers that were most readily accessible to the researcher. Researchers themselves were most likely to be Western-trained academics, often white and male, rarely openly gay, and most likely to have been trained in one of the positivist sciences. Workers or workforces were the objects of their research. The personal particulars of the people they studied might or might not have been deemed important to the researcher. In the case of the famous Hawthorne studies, gender blindness might be an apt description of the researchers' considerations (Bendl, 2008; Emandi, 2012). Needless to say, this resulted in some significant biases in the generalisations of research findings and their applications to the management of employment.

We concur with, but do not rehearse in this chapter, the claims that are now well supported in the literature that race, sex, sexual orientation, age, religion, levels of physical (dis)ability and even perceived physical attractiveness make a difference in terms of how people are treated and what individuals may anticipate as possible or not (Byrne, 1971). Their (self)-perceived identity, too, will have an impact on the opportunities and the hurdles they experience and the power they (believe they) can muster to manifest their hopes, to meet their responsibilities and to access and protect their human rights to the means with which to generate a flourishing life.

The intentional distinction between the words 'work' and 'paid employment' has been discussed in previous chapters. In this chapter, we explain our emphasis on this distinction more fully. We revisit the use of these words when we reconsider the unpaid work that subsidises the economic measures we are expected to see as the indicators of global well-being. The way this discussion plays out in typified areas of unjust organisational discrimination is where we now refine our focus. Who gets to be employed, how and under what conditions are increasingly challenged when it seems that people categorised *in one way* appear to have more or less access to the jobs of influence and high rewards or when categorised *in another way* may find themselves relegated to insecure, unsafe, low-paid and dirty work. We examine more closely the influences that may foster or inhibit the equal opportunities that are assumed to be a necessary dynamic in neo-liberal markets and in the organisation of Western democratic nations more generally. We suggest that the equal employment opportunities (EEO) and affirmative action (AA) programmes have been overshadowed by a discourse focused on diversity management (DM), a discourse that is attractive because it appears to make good business sense. What if EEO and AA approaches to demonstrable inequality of outcomes result in some form of proportional representation of diverse people in all occupations and in all institutional positions of the system? Has justice been served?

# WORK AS A UNIVERSAL HUMAN RIGHT AND DUTY

Access to employment is codified as a universal human right in the United Nations Universal Declaration of Human Rights, the International Labour Organization Convention on Equal Pay and Discrimination, and the United Nations Convention on the Elimination of All Forms of Discrimination against Women (CEDAW). The redefinition of work as a human right not only raises issues in employment contexts, but is now so closely associated with the form of development being imposed on people the world over that we have reason to reconsider these instruments of emancipation in a more critical light. A broad-brush picture drawn from global statistics would suggest that in the global economy white men hold a disproportionate number of the well-rewarded jobs. Women from non-white gene pools, if they reach the labour market at all, hold a disproportionate number of the insecure and low-paid jobs. The old, the frail, the diagnosed disabled and increasingly the young seem also to have difficulty attaining secure, safe and well-paid employment. A finer grained examination will show some variation in this pattern, but not sufficiently so to dismiss the depiction of this disparate access to employment as invalid. While in Chapters 4 and 5 we examined the diverse ways in which human populations experience employment, and perhaps become defined by (in)access to employment, in this chapter we look more closely at how the diversity of human beings is managed to systemic benefit.

Historically, characteristics of the scope and design of many jobs assumed the unencumbered, white, able-bodied, male employee as the standard against which all others might be assessed. This is changing. There are two significant lines of reasoning about this change that need closer attention: (i) there will not be enough white males to hold all the jobs that need doing; and (ii) work, now redefined as a universal human right, must not only *be* accessible to all human beings, but it is being made *the duty* of almost all people to secure such employment as the most legitimate way to achieve a livelihood. Efforts to manipulate the relationship of diverse people with the ever-changing needs of the global economy, as discussed in Chapters 3, 4 and 5, has generated some significant differences in outcomes in distinctly patterned ways. Where these patterns are suspected to be the result of discrimination, both neo-liberals and more radical theorists agree that action is needed. Not all agree on what those actions should be. EEO programmes have proliferated for several decades. Their necessary corollary, AA, is often demonised. The issues of unequal inclusion and exclusion, however, seem intractable. Explanations as to why these EEO and AA approaches have not achieved their projected employment outcomes have been framed by some as 'the wrong focus' and by others as 'historically incomplete'. We have argued elsewhere that these approaches to diversity management have been allowed to be marginally successful in order to dissipate dissent and to ensure hegemonic integrity (see, for example, Humphries and Grice, 1995; Gatenby and Humphries, 1999a, b, 2000; McNicholas and Humphries, 2005; Humphries and Verbos, 2012).

Questioning the efficacy of equal employment commitments is among the more difficult exercises for students of management. Such programmes seem so enlightened to their advocates and so necessary to their enactors. How can they be deemed so pernicious to their critics? The critique of EEO and AA programmes can be vociferous – but for many different reasons. In Chapters 3 and 4 we examined the systemic changes in the global political economy and the significant impact of these changes on the structure, location and conditions of paid employment. We argued in those chapters that the changes we have examined contribute to the disparate outcomes in terms of who gains access to paid work and the level of remuneration associated with such employment. That disparate employment outcomes are experienced by particularly vulnerable groups within the global economy; for example, women, minorities, migrant workers and indigenous people. We now examine the rhetoric of equality (of opportunity) as it is shaped, supposedly in the interests of such vulnerable people.

The measurement of livelihoods, primarily framed in income terms, demonstrates radical disparities among nations, among individuals within nations, and among employees within and across occupations. The generation of an outcry by some against such disparities makes good sense – in a way. One proffered solution embedded in the philosophical positioning of neo-liberalism, as well as in policy initiatives promoted by the World Bank, the International Monetary Fund, the International Labour Organization, the OECD, the United Nations and many governments throughout the world is that all people must become more actively engaged in paid employment. The view that access to paid employment is a means to achieve social justice and to relieve poverty, as well as being a fundamental human right, are embedded in a number of United Nations and International Labour Organization conventions generated from the United Nations Universal Declaration of Human Rights endorsed in 1948 (see www.universalrights.net/main/creation.htm). These values are made explicit or implied in the constitutions of various democratic jurisdictions and are increasingly espoused in many corporate mission statements, particularly, but not only, by those corporations explicitly committed to the United Nations Global Compact introduced in Chapter 1.

A call to focus on local or distant poverty and the attractiveness of market remedies to alleviate this poverty is a good place to start thinking about the connection made between the notions of emancipation and paid employment. It seems such a reasonable connection to people who have long assumed its validity. Demonstrating that some people are living on less than a dollar a day (or below a specific poverty line determined in a particular jurisdiction) invites justification for (further) economic development of a particular Western capitalist type and pressure for the poor or poorly paid to improve their circumstances through paid employment – no matter what non-monetary riches such development may undermine or what the cost of this 'work' on offer may be. Women and men, people from various ethnic affiliations, experience efforts for their development differently. In the global economy, it is white men who continue to hold a disproportionate number of the most lucrative and influential jobs. White women have made some inroads into such careers. In general, a patterned outcome holds firm.

People jostling for jobs in our own communities – economic refugees subletting mattresses in Russia's basements in a desperate attempt to send money home to their dependents in Central Asia; Greek farming families pressured off their small landholdings by the stroke of a policy pen to make room for the more 'efficient' agri-businesses; South Americans looking north for livelihoods; seasonal workers whose opportunities are framed by politically controlled economic aspirations; and rural peoples flushed into cities to provide the labour for the booming or struggling industries – are diverse in many ways, but they also have much in common. Within each context, gender, age, race and so on, will have a specific manifestation. The patterns of their struggles suggest to critical theorists that their situation is systemically generated and the shaping of their situation goes well beyond anything they can be held personally responsible for. The eradication of almost all other forms of achieving a livelihood and the vagaries of where employment is to be found constitute a systemic pressure to search for, accept and remain engaged in employment – no matter how grim the conditions of work.

Advice on how to do so is prolific in the literature. Dani Monroe (2013) is a recent example of an expert in explaining the relationship of diversity and organisational change to the bottom line, the value of the hidden talents of their workforce, and the importance of resourcefulness, resilience and resolve. According to the publisher's promotional material, through Monroe's book, managers will 'learn to recognise *and mine* some key, fundamental leadership traits that are essential for a competitive business' (emphasis added). The way such mining plays out has diverse consequences. This invites closer scrutiny by liberals and radicals alike. The rhetoric of equal rights to participation and inclusion – a conceptualisation of equality framed as 'equal (employment) opportunity' (EEO) – is purportedly the insurance that all will have the opportunity to compete and be rewarded based on merit, two of the implied values of capitalism we question in this book. The outcomes of employment are demonstrably unequal. That this inequality takes specific patterns wherever the capitalist mode of development is undertaken invites an examination of potential systemic discrimination and selective privilege, dynamics deemed unacceptable in a meritocracy.

## THE CIRCLE OF PRIVILEGE AND RESPONSIBILITY

Professor Jones has enjoyed her time in Hong Kong. Initially, she was angry at her husband, Ted, for taking a posting so far from her family in Germany. Now she was glad she had conceded. Here in Hong Kong they were able to secure two good maids to look after their children, to ensure the house was spotless, food cooked, and the car was cleaned. With domestic responsibilities reduced to supervision, she had been able to complete her PhD and gain significant research experience at the local university. Now Ted had taken a job in China and she was pleased to have scored a position as professor, a position well above the rank she might have achieved in Germany. In China, they would need only one maid. Which one could she most easily take with them? Which one would be most easily discarded? Both, she thought, had been lucky to have had time in her household. Both had improved their English. Both had been able to keep in touch with their families because of the generous phone allocations she had provided for them. Perhaps she could let them decide. After all, both were now in a better position to improve their circumstances than they were before she hired them.

Despite a significant challenge to the integrity of this blunt categorisation, we are each defined as either male or female. Even though biological sex and social(ised) gender categories are of much greater diversity than this two-option category suggests, census and employment forms are examples of where we must all affiliate with one identifier or the other. This is a further example of the confessing of identity we introduced in Chapter 5. Space constraints mean that we cannot cover all forms of discrimination in employment in this chapter. Thus, seemingly biologically determined but socially defined gender differences are the main thread of diversity discussions in this chapter – with the added emphasis that women and men, of course, are not 'homogeneous categories'.

Race, class, religion, sexual preferences, age, physical strength, intellectual agility, geographical location, number of dependants and so many other aspects of their being affect a person's ability to engage in paid employment. The race of privileged women also needs scrutiny because those who have experienced racism have been writing about white privilege for decades. From their worldview, it is self-evident that white people have directly and indirectly benefited from historic and contemporary processes of colonisation and institutional racism. Came (2012) reviews the emerging field of whiteness studies that seeks to make whiteness visible. She calls on a landmark essay on the subject by McIntosh (1988) who describes white privilege as a collection of unearned assets, an invisible weightless knapsack of white privilege that has special provisions such as: 'maps, passports, codebooks, visas, clothes, tools and blank checks' that can be cashed in at any time. McIntosh (1988: 1) explains 'whites are taught to think of their lives as morally neutral, normative, and average, and also ideal, so that when we work to benefit others, this is seen as work which will allow "them" to be more like "us".' In examining privilege, McIntosh and Came both maintain that it is necessary to confront the myth of meritocracy, the realisation that certain doors are opened and closed for people through no virtue of their own (Came, 2012: 88).

# CREATING FAIR EMPLOYMENT

## Paid Employment as a Fundamental Human Right

Access to decent paid employment is deemed a fundamental human right within the United Nations Universal Declaration of Human Rights (1948), by the International Labour Organization and in the United Nations Convention on the Elimination of All Forms of Discrimination against Women (1979, CEDAW). For example, Article 23 of the Universal Declaration of Human Rights states that everyone has the right to work of their own choosing, protection from unemployment, to fair and safe working conditions, equal pay for equal work, and pay levels that ensure 'for himself [sic] and his family an existence worthy of human dignity' which is to be supplemented by social protection if necessary. Moreover, Article 24 stipulates that 'Everyone has the right to rest and leisure, including reasonable limitation of working hours and periodic holidays with pay' (www.un.org/en/documents/udhr/).

The right to equal remuneration for equal work of equal value between men and women is further codified and more clearly defined in Article 1 of the International Labour Organization's Equal Remuneration Convention 100 (1951) where equal pay is to be based on rates 'of remuneration established without discrimination based on sex' (ILO, 1951). The International Labour Organization's Discrimination (Employment and Occupation) Convention 111 (1958), Article 1, defines discrimination in employment as: 'any distinction, exclusion or preference made on the basis of race, colour, sex, religion, political opinion, national extraction or social origin, which has the effect of nullifying or impairing equality of opportunity or treatment in employment or occupation' (ILO, 1958). Of the 183 ILO member nations, Conventions 100 and 111 have been ratified by 168 and 169 members respectively (ILO, 2011). More recently, a number of ILO conventions have been signed that seek to address discrimination in employment in a number of areas; for example, on the basis of sexual orientation, age, ethnicity, disability, indigenous status, parental status, including pregnancy, and marital status (ILO, 2007).

The United Nations CEDAW specifically addresses the persistent discrimination experienced by women in the political, social and economic realms. The focus of the CEDAW is to extend fundamental human rights that have been codified in various United Nations' documents and conventions to women by promoting equality of treatment between men and women in all areas of life. Embedded in the CEDAW is the recognition that discriminatory practices against women are perpetuated through legal, cultural and religious practices. The CEDAW also recognises that women's reproductive role has an impact on their access to employment. Article 11 of the CEDAW specifically focuses on eliminating gender discrimination in paid employment and incorporates many features embedded in the Declaration of Human Rights and in a number of ILO conventions. In Article 11, work is deemed to be 'an inalienable right of all human beings' (United Nations CEDAW, 1979).

As of October 2011, there were 187 parties to the CEDAW. To secure this right, Article 11 promotes equality of opportunity and treatment between men and women in all areas of the employment process. This begins with enabling women to freely choose work which is meaningful to them, through to applying the same criteria in the selection, training, job evaluation and promotion processes, and ensuring equal pay for work of equal value, job security, paid sick leave and access to safe work environments, and social security in times of sickness, unemployment and retirement. How most people do not experience such freedom is discussed in Chapters 4 and 5. We assume that this must then be an aspirational position. Much energy, however, is going into achieving equal representation of women and men at all levels in all occupations. Such activity *is*, by definition, affirmative action. Opinions vary about what shape such action might be allowed to take. Perhaps most controversial and perhaps most effective are the instigation of mandatory quotas.

## Anti-discrimination and Quota Legislation

To engage with any equalising activities is to engage with *affirmative action*. For many neo-liberal idealists, this is to corrupt the free workings of 'the market'.

### DISCIPLINING THE QUOTA QUEEN

Lani Guinier served as Professor (and Chair) of the Afro-American Studies Department at Harvard University. In April 1993, President Bill Clinton nominated Lani for the position of Assistant Attorney General for Civil Rights. In the process of selection, President Clinton was informed that her interviews with senators were not going well and he was urged to withdraw the nomination (Geoff, 2012). Lani was branded a 'Quota Queen' – the kiss of death for any political career. By affiliation, she would become a career impediment for Clinton and his supporters. President Clinton took the advice of his elected officials and withdrew her nomination.

Despite the influential ideological preference for non-intervention in the free market as the arbiter of merit and outcomes, many nations have implemented minimum anti-discrimination and various forms of equal pay legislation as a means to redress the differentiated outcomes experienced by certain groups in society (Bell, 2007; ILO, 2011; Shore et al., 2011). Examples include the United Kingdom (Wells, 2003), the United States (Kohl et al., 2005), New Zealand (Harcourt et al., 2005) and European Union member nations (Lawson and Gooding, 2005).While such legislation differs around the world, it typically reflects the demographic features identified above. That is, the target groups or aspects identified in anti-discriminatory legislation have come to include women, people with disabilities, religious affiliation, sexual orientation, age, political affiliation, HIV/AIDS status, ethnicity, nationality and race (ILO, 2011).

Some countries – for example, Spain (ITUC, 2009) and Norway (Casey et al., 2011) – have extended anti-discrimination legislation to include quotas for women board membership. Hole (2010) reports that the implementation of a quota system in Norway has improved women's participation on boards from 7 per cent in 2003 to 38 per cent by 2008. Other nations – for example, New Zealand (Casey et al., 2011), Australia and Germany (ILO, 2011) – have minimal anti-discrimination legislation that underpins exhortations to voluntary development of internal policies to redress disparate employment outcomes between women and men. Increasingly visible is the rising concern about high and growing levels of youth unemployment and its gendered expression. Some analysts suggest that the class divide that has been the concern of Marxists and the gender divide that preoccupies feminists should be broadened to examine the intergenerational struggle for the means of life. The law as it stands everywhere and the policy responses that are emerging seem not to be stemming the rise in youth disaffiliation in Europe – with its attendant risks to social stability. While some organisations have implemented particular processes to achieve compliance with anti-discrimination legislation more recently, there is a different type of willingness to develop diversity strategies because employment of 'the best person for the job' regardless of their biological characteristics is deemed to make good business sense, an issue we now turn to.

# MORPHING EEO AND AA INTO 'DIVERSITY MANAGEMENT'

Embedded in the business case for greater achievement of workplace diversity is a recognition that significant changes in the demographic composition of the workforce and customer base have occurred in recent decades. One source of this change is through global outsourcing of business activities in terms of the location of goods and services provision and the development of global markets as discussed in Chapters 3 and 4. In turn, this globalising process has significantly changed the ethnic, religious, language and nationality features of workforces and customer bases (Watson et al., 2009). Increased migration patterns have had similar effects on the demographic features of more localised communities, workforces and customer bases (ILO, 2010). In addition, many localised labour forces have been affected by an exponential growth in the number of women in the labour market (Lee et al., 2007) and, in many countries, by ageing workforces (ILO, 2011). Youth unemployment has reached a level so high in various places that calls for urgent interventions are amplifying, particularly in Europe where such calls are motivated at least to some extent by fears that youth, left in such dire circumstances, may be increasingly attracted to neo-Nazi-style, right-wing groups.

These changes in the demographic make-up of communities, labour forces and customer bases have some commentators arguing that diversity management takes on new meanings involving cross-border interactions between managers and workers with different backgrounds, cultures and languages (McVittie et al., 2008; Watson et al., 2009). In this environment, Ashkanasy and colleagues (2002) conclude that emotional intelligence and diversity management skills are required to be efficient, to retain customers and remain competitive. These types of discussions, now well embedded in some areas of management education and practice, might cover such concerns as, for example, the appropriateness of employing men in early childhood education or as assistants in women's underclothing retail. Equally controversial is the idea that bringing more women to the tables of power would enhance the likelihood of more peaceful and just negotiations (Myers, 2013). These kinds of examples rely on complex and inappropriate stereotyping.

At the organisational level, diversity management is offered as a solution to improve organisational performance and productivity in light of the demographic changes (Richard, 2000). In support of this view, a number of reports show that companies with women board members achieve profits that are higher than industry averages (*Catalyst*, 2004; Rosener, 2009). Applied to the national level, Goldman Sachs chief economist Tim Toohey reported that closing the gap between male and female workforce participation rates in Australia, and increasing women's participation rate in non-traditional, male-dominated and growth industries, would boost the economy by $180 billion (Ferguson, 2011). Applied to other nations, Toohey estimated that such an increase in women's participation rate would lead to GDP rises of 10 per cent in the United States, 20 per cent in Italy, 12 per cent in Germany, 11 per cent in Britain and 8 per cent in Sweden.

A number of explanations are offered as to why workforce diversity leads to improved productivity and profits. One argument embedded in human capital theory is that effective diversity management widens the potential pool of candidates, leading to hiring more skilled and qualified individuals (Meier et al., 1999; McVittie et al., 2008). A flow-on effect is the creation of diverse workgroups, who, it is argued, can draw upon their individually unique talents, skills and abilities reflective of their backgrounds. In doing so, such groups are believed to make better and more innovative decisions because they are less susceptible to 'group think' (McVittie et al., 2008).

A more recent analysis of why workforce diversity improves organisational performance and profits is tightly linked to the increased ethnic diversity within communities and customer bases resulting from globalisation and migration. The ILO (2011) estimates that workforces are made up of as much as 8–20 per cent of ethnically diverse workers. We note but will pass over the observation that all women have ethnicity and that this statistic vindicates the claim of white blindness we have made earlier. From this pragmatic perspective on ethnic diversity, it is argued that customer attraction, service and retention are enhanced by ensuring a match between the demographic composition of the workforce and that of the surrounding community (Andrews et al., 2005). Jackson and colleagues (2003) argue that there is a significant body of similarity-attraction literature that confirms people prefer to engage with those similar to themselves. Put another way, people have an aversion towards engaging with others who are perceived as dissimilar to themselves. Paradoxically perhaps, a heterogeneously diverse workforce enables the maintenance of homogeneous relationships between demographically similar employees and customers. It is this homogeneity in the relationship that is believed to enhance customer attraction, retention and service because of the comfort experienced by dealing with someone who shares a similar background, language or culture. Indeed, Andrews et al. (2005) conclude that a mismatch between workforce ethnic diversity and the demographic composition of the community had a negative association with organisational performance. Ashkanasy et al. (2002) suggest that matching workers and customers is particularly important in service organisations, as shared understandings enable service workers to understand and respond to customers. In turn, performance is said to improve because of increased customer loyalty and retention, and customer attraction through word-of-mouth advertising (Anderson et al., 1994; Wangenheim and Bayón, 2007).

## BANKING ON GOOD DIVERSITY MANAGEMENT

Sheeba and her friend Marcus have worked at the same bank for some years. Their path up the professional ladder has been pretty similar. Now, however, a very senior job has become available in marketing. Sheeba and Marcus both want the job very much. The manager, Su, who is to make the decision, is facing a quandary. On the one hand, Sheeba has shown a great sensitivity to the cultural diversity of the community this bank serves. Marcus, however, is a man. Many of the bigger clients the bank wants to attract show a significant preference for dealing only with men. No one has spelled this out to Su. He just knows this in his gut, a gut feeling no doubt well informed by the subtle and not so subtle jokes that are exchanged at the swanky professional club he drinks at. On balance, it may be best to go with Marcus. Sheeba's personal capacities to challenge his decision are probably not as solid as those of Marcus. That in itself is worth a consideration. Sheeba, after all, has been comparing notes with Marcus in the tearoom about the plans each has to start a family – and that too is worth a thought.

While a number of scholars assert links between workforce diversity and increased productivity and profits, as discussed above, evidence of such a relationship in empirical research is a mixed bag (McPherson, 2008). For example, in their meta-analysis of 63 studies, Jackson et al. (2003) found limited and inconclusive evidence to support the claim that ethnic workforce diversity increases organisational performance. This conclusion was supported by Jehn and Bezrukova (2004). Others highlight that there may be a negative relationship between organisational performance and workforce diversity. Williams and O'Reilly (1998) show that ethnically diverse workgroups can experience miscommunication, conflict and poor cohesion, leading to lower group and, therefore, organisational performance. Richard (2000) points out that this might be so because effective diversity management requires supportive organisational structures and strategies. Shore et al. (2011) also suggest that such negative results might be partially explained by the initial emphasis of diversity strategies which focused on increasing the proportions of target groups within organisations, with little emphasis placed on integrating and including them within the organisation. They propose that it is timely for diversity management strategies to move beyond a preoccupation with numbers and move towards developing inclusive strategies that enable the valuing of diverse input.

# EEO, AA AND MANAGING DIVERSITY

Combined, equal employment opportunity (EEO), affirmative action (AA) and the more recent diversity management (DM) provide the legal, philosophical and practical frameworks aimed at achieving a diverse workforce and avoiding costly challenges to discriminatory practices. Moreover, the philosophical and practical methods associated with these three approaches are advocated as mechanisms to help comply with anti-discrimination legislation, by some groups seeking to achieve human rights and fairness through access to paid employment (e.g., ILO, 2011), as well as by those who view diversity management as a means to enhance business performance.

AA has often related specifically to legislated quota systems and, as an approach, has its roots in the United States, though, as noted above, it has been adopted more recently in a number of jurisdictions as a means to enhance the entry of women into senior leadership positions (Burgess et al., 2009; ILO, 2011). While variations can be found, definitions of EEO typically embed many of the human rights issues apparent in the Declaration of Human Rights, the CEDAW and the ILO conventions discussed above. For example, such definitions include notions of eliminating explicit or implicit barriers throughout all aspects of employment, including recruitment, selection, training, pay and rewards, career development and promotion to ensure that decisions throughout the process are based on individual merit and fairness. By doing so, EEO, then, is deemed a means to enhance an individual's ability freely to choose work that is of interest to them. Similarly, many definitions make explicit links between EEO and the business case presented above, by promoting the proposition that an individual's ability to choose work of interest that reflects their skills to personal productivity will enhance motivation, loyalty, commitment and organisational performance.

A number of nations combine a legislative approach with a voluntarist approach to achieving workforce diversity. For example, some countries specify a limited range of target groups, or apply anti-discrimination legislation to specific sectors or to specific organisations based on, for example, size (Burgess et al., 2009; Dyer and Hurd, 2011). Organisations or sectors that are not specifically covered by EEO or AA legislation may be encouraged to adopt practices that enhance worker diversity. This approach is most closely aligned with the notion of managing diversity (Burgess et al., 2009). Thomas (2001) suggests that while anti-discrimination legislative approaches provide the entry of target groups into the workforce, managing diversity practices provide the means within which to enhance the productivity and development of the newly created diverse workforce. In many ways, this reflects the view of Burgess and colleagues (2009) that the management of diversity is more closely aligned with the business case, and Shore and co-workers (2011) who argue that, while the initial focus of diversity was to increase target group numbers in non-traditional fields of employment, the task now is to include and value diversity within the organisation.

Regardless of whether codified in law or taken up as a voluntary initiative by organisational leaders, there are a number of practices that have been recognised and promoted as facilitating the achievement of equal employment outcomes and effective diversity management. Topical among these are the development of work–life balance initiatives, many of which focus on various forms of flexibility around start and finish times of work and the location of jobs. More long-standing initiatives include sexual harassment and bullying policies, and the development of informal and formal mentoring and networking relationships (Tremall and Nierenberg, 2006). However, despite the significant and sustained interest in enhancing EEO at the level of the United Nations and at national and organisational levels, disparate employment outcomes continue based on gender, ethnicity, race, religion, sexuality and so on (ILO, 2011).

# EXPLAINING DISPARATE EMPLOYMENT OUTCOMES

Research continues to show that a number of organisational practices continue to affect the allocation and rewards associated with work, and how workers are treated within the organisational context. For example, women and minorities are still more likely to be hired into positions that are not linked to formal (and informal) career paths. Women continue to experience discrimination surrounding maternity and are more likely to experience sexual harassment in the workplace (ILO, 2011).

Structural explanations look beyond organisational practices to consider why disparate outcomes continue. For example, women still perform the majority of the unpaid work in the home which directly affects their ability to participate in paid employment on an 'equal footing' to men. The structural explanation also highlights the connection between globalisation, changes in economic and political policies and the low wages attributed to the jobs held primarily by women. In the global economy, women feature as the low-wage workers in manufacturing and services, and even where women compete directly in the same domain as men, their wages are often much lower than their male counterparts (see, for example, recent publications by the OECD, the United Nations, the ILO, or your own nation's income statistics). The current structure of employment divides workers globally through outsourcing specifically to less-expensive but appropriately skilled labour. Women have been particularly vulnerable in this process, as employment has shifted globally to where the cheaper, often female labour force can be sourced.

Combined, these structural considerations provide evidence to support the argument that patriarchal values are embedded in, produced and reproduced within the global economy. Moreover, the way that paid and unpaid work is structured, organised, allocated and rewarded acts to produce and reproduce traditional male-breadwinner/female-caregiver roles within the home, regardless of how couples might prefer to organise themselves and their families. Because men are more likely to be paid more, couples may by necessity divide their work load to maximise the income to the family, and by doing so reproduce the structural constraints that affect women's ability to engage in paid employment. Thus, notions of freedom of choice to make individual decisions with regard to employment, and to be rewarded according to merit achieved on an apparent level playing field, become more myth than reality, but a myth supported by what might appear at face value to be rational choices made by well-informed individuals and by organisational work–life balance initiatives aimed at enhancing women and men's working lives.

## MEET THE TEACHER

Jesse is a teacher. This week it is 'meet-the-teacher' week at her school. On these days, Jesse will be at school from 8 a.m. to 8 p.m. Her own little daughters, Ella (8) and Rebecca (5), will be free from their class from 1 p.m. for two afternoons that week. The day before the first 'meet-the-teacher' day, Jesse's friend found her in her classroom looking anxious and upset. An administrator had just delivered a set of documents that required her to provide new measurements of children's achievements to complete quality assurance documentation urgently required by the Principal for a funding application. The documents appear to have little to do

*(Continued)*

*(Continued)*

with the good teaching of children. The school, however, could certainly do with the extra funding the Principal is seeking. In the interests of the children, Jesse believes that she had better complete the forms. She realises that this week she would be at school for an additional two evenings and also parts of the weekend to cope with the backlog of work. Jesse misses her children and her children miss her. At home, the laundry is building up. Housework has been put aside for precious time with Ella and Rebecca. It all seems so huge! Jesse cannot afford to work part-time. Her Mum would love to help her, but she has her own job issues to contend with, including an intercity commute to manage her job and other family commitments, commitments that include some care for her own increasingly frail mother. Jesse wishes she, Ella and Rebecca could visit their grandmother more often. There just is not the time to do so. Is *this* what the liberal feminists Jesse had admired in college had intended to achieve?

Underpinning the discussion of employment are particular definitions and (de)valuations of paid and unpaid work. Work is recognised in the United Nations Universal Declaration of Human Rights and the CEDAW as an inalienable human right. A definition and valuing of paid and unpaid work can be found in the United Nations National Accounting System. Paid work is valued according to the dollar amount this work contributes to national economic and financial wealth, and is recorded in gross domestic product figures. In contrast, unpaid work – for example, that which is done in the home, including raising and nurturing children – is defined as not contributing to the financial wealth of a nation, and hence is deemed of little or no value (Waring, 1999). These definitions and values of paid and unpaid work are embedded in the WTO, the IMF and the World Bank, as well as OECD policy initiatives, and can be discerned in many national-level legislative frameworks, as well as being manifest in social and economic policies. Importantly, GDP figures help determine budget allocations; moreover, by these definitions, the majority of women's work the world over is not accounted in GDP figures, and hence much of women's contribution to society is ignored by their governments, and, as a result, by proxy, men's contribution is deemed more valuable to society.

From a critical perspective, an analysis of the assumptions embedded in the way work is defined, structured, allocated and rewarded not only helps to highlight which particular set of meanings and practices have become taken for granted and common sense, but, importantly, how those meanings shape, produce and reproduce power relations within society. Developing this line of reasoning, we argue that the philosophical underpinnings of EEO and AA provide a liberal solution to a fundamentally neo-liberal problem. That is, at the philosophical level, EEO and AA advocates focus on the individual and the removal of all artificial barriers preventing such individuals, regardless of race, gender, ethnicity, parental status and so on, accessing the employment of their choice and that which they are capable of performing. This focus on individuals and paid employment is in harmony with the neo-liberal philosophical position that individuals ought to be responsible for looking after the self through paid employment, and, again, regardless of race, gender, ethnicity, parental status and so on. However, as part of a greater commitment or subjugation to neo-liberalist ideals, many nations have withdrawn their legislative as well as philosophical support for full employment policies achieved by legislation or policy pressures. Market-orientated rules governing employment relationships, including enabling offshoring, as discussed in Chapters 3 and 4, prevail. As a set of initiatives, EEO or AA policies and practices cannot create employment, but having such policies and practices in place gives the appearance that disparate employment outcomes can be attributed to individual success and failure in the market. Such an approach ignores the systemic practice of vulnerable groups drawn in and pushed out of employment along with boom–bust cycles (Burgess et al., 2009) and the growing power of business to determine the conditions, location and reward associated with work within the global economy.

# CONCLUSION

The sense of duty to find and maintain employment for one's personal survival and the care of one's dependants is a fabricated necessity that is easily manipulated by the powerful to serve their interests. The vast array of values and beliefs, of personal and group identities, of desirable skills and attitudes, of geographical locations, and of access to power are just some of the diversity considerations to be managed. Despite claims to valuing diversity, through the imposition of a kind of mono-cultural, instrumental and functional notion of humanity, workers are generally treated as atomised labour widgets in patterns of employment devised to provide flexibility for the system's changing needs. Many are held entranced by a delusional metaphor of the self-actualising man (and some kind of enabling woman who probably also needs a job). Even very self-aware and self-directed people can be challenged, re-configured and re-harnessed to the interests of 'globalisation'.

EEO and managing diversity have been depicted in this chapter as a neo-liberal solution to a neo-liberal problem, that of shifting the emphasis from employment as a fundamental and inalienable human right to that of an individual responsibility. In the context of a global economy, based on patriarchal and neo-colonialist values and underpinned by structural unemployment, EEO and managing diversity, embedded with merit principles, shift the responsibility of obtaining employment and the blame of not obtaining employment onto individuals and therefore abdicate responsibility from governments to address structural and social inequalities to the individual.

## TALK BOX   STEPPING IN 'GOOD OLE BOY POOH'

From an email conversation in 2012 between two professional women, each in an institution with explicit EEO and anti-discrimination policies:

'I stuck my foot in some "good ole boy pooh" this week! I went to the worst presentation I have ever seen given by a candidate for a job in our department. In the supposedly confidential feedback process we were required to contribute to, I said as much. I was told by the colleague whose office is next to mine that my opinion was totally inappropriate. My comments were obviously forwarded to him, and probably to the job candidate too. It turns out that they are friends! I might as well paint a target on my back. It will be open season on me if he gets the job – or maybe even more so if he does not! It is so ugly. And here I am fretting over it and emailing you about what a mess I have made when I should be getting my next project out. So this is how unqualified males get hired over more qualified minorities or women!'

- Does the 'danger' in the story hinge on the gender of the three main characters?
- Are you aware of similar incidences where an under-qualified 'in-group' member achieved employment?
- What are the implications from (i) a human rights perspective; (ii) an EEO perspective; (iii) an AA perspective; and (iv) a business case perspective?
- How much energy, distraction and demotivation are generated by various forms of discrimination at work, in education and elsewhere?

## Tricky Questions

- Organisational behaviour texts tell us that, in selection interviews, decisions are often made in the very first few minutes of an interview. What dynamics may be at play in those early minutes?
- Researchers in management education have found that the same piece of written work assumed to be written by a male attracts higher scores than if the work has been attributed to a female. What does this indicate for all aspects of careers in management, politics and media, in particular, but in other careers as well?
- 'Passing for' and 'coming out' are two terms used by people who, through certain biological features, can 'pass for' members of the dominant group. 'Coming out' (or being 'out-ed') has significant career implications. Can you find examples of courageous people who 'came out' to 'call out' those who are part of a repressive regime of discrimination, subtle or covert? What were the consequences of their actions? Examples may include the US military 'Do not ask' policies.
- In a system that is competitive, does not have room for all, but is the only or main means to a livelihood, what does/should happen to those for whom there is no room?

- Structural unemployment is deemed by some to be a necessary condition for employment flexibility. If 'equality' or even 'proportional representation' is deemed to have been achieved within the current structural environment (e.g., those in paid employment reflect personal identity characteristics in proportion to their presence in the composition of the community) what would we have achieved? How do 'ousted' groups/individuals take care of their survival needs?
- What would have to occur to achieve the human rights and social justice principles inherent in the ILO position on access to paid employment? What concerns does this position not adequately address?

# ADDITIONAL RESOURCES

Berg, N. and Lien, D. (2002) Measuring the effect of sexual orientation on income: evidence of discrimination. *Contemporary Economic Policy*, 29: 394–415.

Humphries, M.T. (2011) The bully in the workplace. In J. Marques, S. Dhiman and J. Biberman (eds), *Stories to Tell your OB Students*. New York: Palgrave-Macmillan. pp. 60–2.

Jackson, S., Brett, J., Sessa, V., Cooper, D., Julin, J. and Peyronnin, K. (1991) Some differences make a difference: individual dissimilarity and group heterogeneity as correlates of recruitment, promotions, and turnover. *Journal of Applied Psychology*, 76: 675–89.

Keough, L.J. (2006) Globalizing 'postsocialism': mobile mothers and neoliberalism on the margins of Europe. *Anthropological Quarterly*, 79 (3): 431–62.

Komisar, L. (2013) At the end, Betty Friedan broadened her vision (www.thekomisarscoop.com/2013/03/at-the-end-betty-friedan-broadened-vision/; retrieved 10 September 2013).

Pines, A.M., Lerner, M. and Schwartz, D. (2010) Gender differences in entrepreneurship: equality, diversity and inclusion in times of global crisis. *Equality, Diversity and Inclusion: An International Journal*, 29 (2): 186–98.

Sacks, J. (2002) *The Dignity of Difference: How to Avoid the Clash of Civilisations*. London: Continuum.

Thomas, A. and Humphries, M.T. (2011) Alternative futures filling the empty signifier with the rhetoric of emancipation: drawing women into the market – a case in point. Paper presented at the 7th International Critical Management Studies Conference, Naples, 11–13 July.

Waring, M. (1995) Who's counting? Marilyn Waring on sex, lies and global economics, dir. T. Nash (www.nfb.ca/film/whos_counting; retrieved 14 September 2013).

# REFERENCES

Anderson, E., Fornell, C. and Lehmann, D. (1994) Customer satisfaction, market share, and profitability: findings from Sweden. *Journal of Marketing*, 58 (3): 53–66.

Andrews, R., Boyne, G., Meier, K., O'Toole, Jr, L. and Walker, R. (2005) Representative bureaucracy, organisational strategy, and public service performance: an empirical analysis of English local government. *Journal of Public Administration Research and Theory*, 15: 489–504.

Ashkanasy, N., Hartel, C. and Daus, C. (2002) Diversity and emotion: the new frontiers in organisational behavior research. *Journal of Management*, 28 (3): 307–38.

Bell, M.P. (2007) *Diversity in Organizations*. Mason, OH: South-Western.

Bendl, R. (2008) Gender subtexts: reproduction of exclusion in organizational discourse. *British Journal of Management*, 19 (1): 50–64.

Burgess, J., French, E. and Strachan, G. (2009) The diversity management approach to equal employment opportunity in Australian organisations. *Economic and Labour Relations Review*, 20 (1): 77–93.

Byrne, D. (1971) *The Attraction Paradigm*. New York: Academic Press.

Came, H. (2012) Institutional racism and the dynamics of privileges in public health. PhD thesis, University of Waikato, Hamilton, New Zealand.

Casey, C., Skibnes, R. and Pringle, J.K. (2011) Gender equality and corporate governance: policy strategies in Norway and New Zealand. *Gender, Work and Organization*, 18 (6): 613–30.

*Catalyst* (2004) The bottom line: connecting corporate performance and gender diversity. *Catalyst* (www.catalyst.org/knowledge/bottom-line-connecting-corporate-performance-and-gender-diversity; retrieved 10 September 2013).

Dyer, S. and Hurd, F. (2011) Gendered perceptions of corporate restructuring and community change in a single industry town. *NZ Sociology*, 26 (1): 68–88.

Emandi, E.M. (2012) Conflicting views of women in Hawthorne. *Gender Studies*, 12 (2): 147–56.

Ferguson, A. (2011) A call to get more women working. *The Age* (www.theage.com.au/national/a-call-to-get-more-women-working-20110826-1jem1.html; retrieved 10 September 2013).

Gatenby, B. and Humphries, M.T. (1999a) Defining careers. *International Career Journal*, 2 (3/4).

Gatenby, B. and Humphries, M.T. (1999b) Exploring gender, management education and careers: speaking in the silences. *Gender and Education*, 11 (3): 281–94.

Gatenby, B. and Humphries, M.T. (2000) The more things change, the more they stay the same: reconstructing gender through women's careers. *Australian Journal of Career Development*, 9 (1): 45–53.

Geoff, K. (2012) Susan Rice: This Decade's Lani Guinier. The Root (www.theroot.com/blogs/blogging-beltway/susan-rice-lani-guinier-sisters-witch-hunt; retrieved 28 September 2013).

Harcourt, M., Lam, H. and Harcourt, S. (2005) Unions and discriminatory hiring: evidence from New Zealand. *Industrial Relations*, 44 (2): 364–73.

Henrich, J., Heine, S.J. and Norenzayen, A. (2010) The weirdest people in the world? *Behavioral and Brain Sciences*, 33 (2–3): 61–135.

Hole, A. (2010) Government action to bring about gender balance (www.20-first.com/406-0-a-personal-account-of-the-quota-legislation-in-norway.html; retrieved 10 September 2013).

Humphries, M.T. and Grice, S. (1995) Equal employment opportunity and the management of diversity: a global discourse of assimilation? *Journal of Organizational Change Management*, 8 (5): 17–33.

Humphries, M.T. and Verbos, A. (2012) Decoupling equality, diversity, and inclusion from liberal projects. *Equality, Diversity and Inclusion: An International Journal*, 31 (5/6): 506–25.

ILO (International Labour Organization) (1951) *Equal Remuneration Convention No. 100.* Geneva: ILO.

ILO (International Labour Organization) (1958) *C111: Discrimination (Employment and Occupation) Convention, 1958 (No. 111)* (www.ilo.org/ilolex/cgi-lex/convde. pl?C111; retrieved 28 September 2013).

ILO (International Labour Organization) (2007) *Equality at Work: Tackling the Challenges.* Geneva: ILO.

ILO (International Labour Organization) (2010) *Global Wage Report 2010/11: Wage Policies in Times of Crisis* (www.ilo.org/wcmsp5/groups/public/---dgreports /---dcomm/---publ/documents/publication/wcms_145265.pdf; retrieved 10 September 2013).

ILO (International Labour Organization) (2011) Equality at work: the continuing challenge. Global report under the follow-up to the ILO Declaration on Fundamental Principles and Rights at Work. International Labour Conference 100th Session. Geneva: ILO.

ITUC (International Trade Union Confederation) (2009) *Gender In(equality) in the Labour Market: An Overview of Global Trends and Developments.* Brussels: ITUC.

Jackson, S., Joshi, A. and Erhardt, N. (2003) Recent research on team and organisational diversity: SWOT analysis and implications. *Journal of Management*, 29 (6): 801–30.

Jehn, K. and Bezrukova, K. (2004) A field study of group diversity, group context, and performance. *Journal of Organizational Behavior*, 25 (6): 703–29.

Kohl, J.M., Mayfield, M. and Mayfield, J. (2005) Recent trends in pregnancy discrimination law. *Business Horizons*, 48 (5): 421–9.

Lawson, A. and Gooding, C. (eds) (2005) *Disability Rights in Europe: From Theory to Practice.* Oxford: Hart.

Lee, S-H., McCann, D., Messenger, J.C and International Labour Organization (2007) *Working Time around the World: Trends in Working Hours, Laws and Policies in a Global Comparative Perspective.* London: Routledge/Geneva: ILO.

McIntosh, P. (1988) White privilege: unpacking the invisible knapsack. Working paper 189. *Peace and Freedom*, 10 (2): 1–2 (www.areteadventures.com/articles/white_ privilege_unpacking_the_invisible_napsack.pdf; retrieved 10 September 2013).

McNicholas, P. and Humphries, M.T. (2005) Decolonisation through critical career research: Maori women and accounting. *Australian Career Development Journal*, 14 (1): 30–9.

McPherson, M. (2008) *Diversity and Equality: Evidence of Positive Business Outcomes and How to Achieve Them. A Review of the Literature.* Auckland, NZ: Equal Employment Opportunities Trust.

McVittie, C., McKinlay, A. and Widdicombe, S. (2008) Organizational knowledge and discourse of diversity in employment. *Journal of Organizational Change Management*, 21 (3): 348–66.

Meier, K., Wrinkle, R. and Polinard, J. (1999) Representative bureaucracy and distributional equity: addressing the hard question. *Journal of Politics*, 61 (4): 1025–39.

Monroe, D. (2013) *Untapped Talent: Unleashing the Power of the Hidden Workforce.* Basingstoke: Palgrave Macmillan.

Myers, D.D. (2013) Viewpoint: what if women ruled the world? *BBC News Magazine*, 8 March (www.bbc.co.uk/news/world-21661744; retrieved 10 September 2013).

Richard, O. (2000) Racial diversity, business strategy, and firm performance: a resource-based view. *Academy of Management Journal*, 43 (2): 164–77.

Rosener, J. (2009) Women on corporate boards makes good business sense (www.womensmedia.com/lead/87-women-on-corporate-boards-makes-good-business-sense.html; retrieved 10 September 2013).

Shore, L.M., Randel, A.E., Chung, B.G., Dean, M.A., Ehrhart, K.H. and Singh, G. (2011) Inclusion and diversity in work groups: a review and model for future research. *Journal of Management*, 37 (4): 1262–89.

Thomas, R. (2001) From affirmative action to affirming diversity. In *Harvard Business Review on Managing Diversity,* pp. 1–32. Boston, MA: Harvard Business School.

Tremall, S. and Nierenberg, S. (2006) 'Blending in' vs. 'sticking together': women of color use differing strategies for informal networking, catalyst study finds (http://catalyst.org/media/blending-vs-sticking-together-women-color-use-differing-strategies-informal-networking; retrieved 10 September 2013).

United Nations CEDAW (1979) United Nations Convention on the Elimination of All Forms of Discrimination against Women (www.un.org/womenwatch/daw/cedaw/text/econvention.htm#article11; retrieved 10 September 2013).

Wangenheim, F. and Bayón, T. (2007) The chain from customer satisfaction via word-of-mouth referrals to new customer acquisition. *Journal of the Academic of Marketing Science*, 35 (2): 233–49.

Waring, M. (1999) *Counting for Nothing: What Men Value and What Women are Worth.* Toronto: University of Toronto Press.

Watson, B., Spoonley, P. and Fitzgerald, E. (2009) Managing diversity: a twenty-first century agenda. *New Zealand Journal of Employment Relations,* 34 (2): 61–76.

Wells, K. (2003) The impact of the Framework Employment Directive on UK disability discrimination law. *Industrial Law Review*, 32 (4): 253–73.

Williams, K. and O'Reilly, C. (1998) Demography and diversity in organisations: a review of 40 years of research. In B.M. Staw and L.L. Cummings (eds), *Research in Organisational Behavior*, 20: 77–140. Greenwich, CT: JAI Press.

# 7 CONSUMER CULTURE, COMMODITIES AND CONSUMPTION

## Learning Objectives

In this chapter, we will:

- explore the framing of people as consumers who buy goods and services, identities and (delusional) security;
- examine the shifting sands of implied consumer influence on the processes of production and consumption;
- review the arguments that endorse the potential of consumer sovereignty and its limitations;
- re-visit the influence of Karl Marx on our analysis of commodity fetishism and consumer sovereignty;
- invite reflection on the contribution of ethical consumption in a broadened sense of responsibility to self, others and the planet.

## CRITICAL CONCEPTS

*Consumerism* is a disciplinary force harnessing diverse individuals and heterogeneous populations to the interest of the market. We reconceive *consumer sovereignty* as a form of *commodity fetishism*. The idea of individual and perhaps even organised consumer influence on the processes of production and consumption globally are posited as a necessary but not sufficient influence for change on the prevailing institutional logics of capitalism.

## CONSUMER SOVEREIGNTY

'The more you have the more you want' (Žižek, 2008; quoted in Tadajewski et al., 2011: 54)

Žižek (2008) argues that consumer culture draws people into a never-ending cycle of desire and incomplete fulfilment. These desires are to be met through purchases of goods and services in markets that exploit us not only as workers but also as consumers. Ironically, argues Bauman (2007), 'a precondition for becoming a subject of consumerism is that we must become an object to be consumed ... [in] ... selecting goods and services that are loaded with lifestyle values and meanings (i.e. they are cool, sexy or chic) in the process of identity construction ... [C]onsumption is our reward for working in jobs we don't like' (cited in Bradshaw, 2011: 55–6). We become subject to the seductive power of desire and we remain entrapped in the conditions of production that promise to provide the income we need to satisfy our desires.

Among the many ways in which our humanity may be conceived and constructed, the 'human as consumer' is the topic of this chapter. We examine the shifting sands of implied consumer responsibility, how these are in service to various ideals, and we review the arguments that endorse the potential of consumer sovereignty and its limitations. We re-visit the influence of Karl Marx on our critical appreciation of commodity fetishism and consumer sovereignty and invite a reflection on the contribution of ethical consumption in a broadened sense of responsibility to self, others and the planet. From a critical perspective, consumer capacity to influence the 'what' and the 'how' of production and consumption requires continuing investigation and invigoration. Do consumers have the power to influence the processes and politics of production? Are all consumers equal? What is consumed? Are we consuming our own future, the future well-being of our children and cannibalising the future of others in the ways in which we live? These are some of the hard questions that have motivated the shaping of this chapter.

# CONSUMER CONTROL

Control of diverse individuals and of heterogeneous populations concerned many of the critical theorists we introduced in Chapter 2. They examined what systemic or personal constraints on freedom could be justified for the common good. We argue, in this chapter, that control is largely achieved in contemporary Western societies through the intensification of consumer markets, a hyped-up form of commodity fetishism (Munro, 2011). Controlling consumption is one path still open to governments for the control of populations. Consumption at times can be portrayed and punished as wasteful, the morally reprehensible actions of a spendthrift. Consumption can also be promoted as a duty to ensure the money-go-round continues to go round. Populations can be exhorted to follow one or other extreme en masse. Segments of populations can also be directed or attracted to specific products or services through the skilful match of buyers and sellers – as the apologists for sub-prime mortgages have demonstrated, education ministers know well how to exploit, and the growth in commercially orientated care for the elderly would indicate. In each case, the consumer is trusted to know what they need, and to make responsible purchasing decisions.

The framing of people as consumers is a precondition for their assumed willingness to buy goods and services, identities or (delusional) security through their perceived freely earned (but still centrally controlled) purchasing power. Particular lifestyles, dreams and identities are marketed through sophisticated advertising campaigns. The achievement of those lifestyles, dreams and identities is portrayed simply as a matter of buying the right products, engaging the trendy leisure activities, decorating your home in the latest fashions, and dressing yourself in recognisable and admired brands. Contemporary critical theorists view this behaviour as emanating from a deluded belief that supposedly free-market opportunities allow us to shape, earn and influence our status in life. Consumerism, they suggest, is a seductive arm of the ever-tightening grip of capitalism on our psyches. Under these conditions, overt control is not needed to march most people to their jobs. The discipline is internalised and motivated by the requirement to purchase the necessities of life and the fripperies of egos.

The forms of disciplinary measure once used by the state to organise whole populations associated with the industrial era are now not needed to control most people. These means of control are now reserved for the specific members of the population who cannot be controlled through 'the market'. These folks may include the poor who cannot purchase sufficient goods and services to participate in the social order of the day or those who are not sufficiently seduced into legitimated and normalised market-society attitudes. These folks may include those who persist in bad eating habits and become an expense item in health budgets. They may be those who engage in criminal behaviour and drain resources through the justice system (Seidman, 2008). The state may purchase the goods and services from the private for-profit or not-for-profit segments of 'the market' for the control, discipline, subjugation and domestication of such persons. The state can use the psyche services, as we described them in Chapter 5, to guide people to accept these services. For some, the courts can require such acceptance in a process of normalisation that, if all else fails, may result in incarceration.

# FRAMING CONSUMERS

Like many other such concepts, the integration into our everyday language of the phrases of consumerist society, such as consumption (as the flip side of production), consumer influence, consumer sovereignty and the like, facilitates insight into some dimension of human behaviour, while obscuring the complexities of, or deflecting attention away from, others. The framing of people as 'consumers' is certainly a phenomenon worthy of our attention. Having been framed as people whose needs are best served by markets, such consumers can now be pressured to spend or save depending on the policy preferences of the government of the day or the marketing skills of the producers and distributors of goods and services. In their recording of consumer spending as a percentage of GDP, for example, governments who attempt to stimulate the economy through increased consumption are interested in what researchers can tell them about consumer behaviour (Ward, 2009). Information gathered about the human consumer is also of interest to business leaders for whom the link between sales and business survival is paramount (Neilson and Paxton, 2010). Once so framed, researcher information not only provides snapshots of purchasing behaviour, but also the means by which marketing specialists can set to work on manipulating such consumers. The observations of consumer researchers can be rallied to endorse behaviours to be amplified by skilled marketers to ensure that the preferred market choices are made. These choices can be observed and recorded by consumer researchers as consumer preferences and used by subsequent marketers to accelerate the desired purchasing behaviour. A virtuous circle is thus deemed to be created.

High-income earners with new-age tendencies are likely to spend some of their money on soul-enhancing products and services. These soul-enhancing characteristics of products and services are, for the wealthy, apparently to be found in everything from cosmetics to cars. For the poor in so-called developed nations, extracting money from their already overly stretched budgets includes the skilful building of new needs: cars to get to jobs or to bolster depressed identities or to assuage gadget envy; televisions or iPods as a means of recreation or connection to the 'real world'; electricity or gas from privatised utilities to cook or keep warm; imported cheap clothing and toys from giant importers to make the budget go further; the cheapest food items on the supermarket shelves leading to the necessary purchase (sometimes by the state) of the insulin and other medicines needed to cope with the outbreak of epidemics associated with inadequate diets, and so on.

## FOOD: FADS, FATS AND FATE

The cancer-inducing effects of the industrialised hydrogenation of fats (in much of the food on supermarket shelves) are being recognised by many regulatory bodies. For example, products using such a process have been highly regulated in Denmark since 2003. Heart disease plummeted in this nation. As we can see from the thriving of the tobacco industry in many places in the world, however, not all governments are as willing to regulate to remove dangerous products from markets. 'Let the customer decide/beware' is the mantra. Even where ingredients in food items are supposed to be labelled, it would take a very sophisticated shopper to understand the diverse types of fats in a product and their effects on health. Hydrogenated fats make for cheaper foods. They may be reported as vegetable fats – and thus thought to be healthy. 'The dirty word is "hydrogenation" not "regulation"', says Wayne Brittenden (2013). Surely a blasphemy in the cathedral of neo-liberalism.

Creating and intensifying consumer demand as a means of development in communities that have been relatively cash free to date is an issue we return to several times in this book. Education is a good example of consumerism that we have in common as writers and readers of this book. Among the many examples is the universalising need to find the fees to school the children to be qualified to seek the jobs that the economy may or may not provide in order to buy the things they need to live and to pay the fees to educate their children so that they may find the jobs to buy the things they need to live and to pay the fees to educate their children … and so on. A virtuous circle in the prevailing capitalist institutional order is created and maintained as a normalised cycle of work and investment in the hope of future work!

This normalised, even naturalised, cycle deepens the idea of education as an industry with customer needs to satisfy. It deepens the logic of 'the market' on our psyche. Education comes to be seen as a personal purchase, a consumer good, be it purchased in a village school or in an urban university: the immediate interests of students and parents or of those state beneficiaries for whom the state has plans, and in whom they have a vested interest. Increasingly, boards and advisory groups drawn from industry are invited to help shape the products to be purchased. For subsistence communities, numeracy and literacy skills are also needed for children to become 'job ready'. Elsewhere, science and technology, management and marketing qualifications, for example, are valued. The product, a certification of desirable standards attained, can be sold to future employers. These employers will, in turn, pay wages, with which the employees can purchase goods and services, consumption that keeps the cycle going. For those who find themselves locked out of this cycle, however, despite their best efforts to participate, and despite sacrificing much in order to be included, this may feel more like a vicious circle, a dance of disaster they are forced to dance. Graduates in Italy, Greece and Spain are notable because of the huge numbers now unemployed despite their commitment to higher education. The same pattern, however, is occurring elsewhere, if somewhat more subtly. It is not always obvious that a taxi driver or a barista may be a qualified lawyer or engineer. But it is not only the privileged tertiary graduates who are part of this particular circle of production and consumption of education intensifying the world over.

For those deemed to be the poorest on Earth, consumerism is promised to be part of their salvation. Interest in the 'bottom-of-the-pyramid' opportunities has demonstrated that remote villagers will purchase shampoo in small sample sachets rather than large bottles, a luxury that will soon become a necessity. Many such new consumers or their governments may need to purchase more water to rinse the suds away. This consumption is portrayed as good for them, and for the economy – and not least for the producers of the goods. Not on the balance sheet of these companies will be the devaluing and loss of traditional hair-cleaning methods, the deflection of the dollars spent here from other household needs, and the cost of the disposal of the packaging. In another example of consumer creation, vast amounts of pure water are being converted to unhealthy sugary drinks. Water (assumed pure) is sold in plastic bottles for which consumer demand seems endless. This demand can be fuelled by fear for those whose domestic water supply has been compromised. The demand can be fuelled by marketing messages that imply that the people who drink sugared drinks or water from plastic bottles will have enhanced joy in their life, improve their status among their peers or uplift their soul. For them, bottled water is a *must have*. This reinforces the view that humanity is a vast pool of producers and consumers and that *all and only* that which passes through the market is to be seen as valuable (Waring, 1999). This is the kind of encroachment of the prevailing capitalist institutional logics on our lifeworld that we discussed in Chapter 2.

# BEING (MADE) RESPONSIBLE CONSUMERS

Thinking of people as rather one-dimensional consumers (albeit with exploitable niched characteristics) appears all pervasive in the marketer's mind-set. What it means to consume and what the act of consuming achieves, however, have become invested with multiple meanings, meanings that can be harnessed or manipulated to various ends or galvanised for strategic intent. For example, throughout the early 1900s, American and European consumers were constructed as moral agents who, through their purchasing, would lift their nations to higher spiritual and cultural planes (Dixon, 1999). Indeed, some argued that a nation's progress and civilisation could be explicitly linked to the number of wants developed (Johnson, 1910, cited in Ward, 2009: 204–5). Consumption has been linked to the achievement of happiness (Hudson and Hudson, 2003), as the means to lift a nation out of recession (Ward, 2009) and as a path to achieving personal goals and solving problems through proper consumption (Murphy, 2000). Consumers have thus become a site for political struggle and are called on to exercise their influence as consumers responsibly. Through consumption decisions, consumers are assumed to be able to transform alienating and destructive production practices, address environmental concerns and enhance the well-being of all.

Through what has recently been termed political or ethically inspired consumerism, politicised consumers are urged to base their purchasing decisions on their sense of responsibility to wider society (Carrington et al., 2010). Their purchasing decisions are thus moved beyond issues of quality and price to include a social or ethical dimension based on, for example, their personal values, political beliefs, ethical positioning or principles (Harrison et al., 2005; Neilson and Paxton, 2010). Political and ethical buying or boycotting decisions have come to include considerations for the environment, the critique of labour practices, concerns about food safety and the promotion of organic food production, the support of fair trade and a heightened critical awareness of the country of origin (Allen and Kovach, 2000; Hudson and Hudson, 2003;

Carrigan and Pelsmacker, 2009; Yani-de-Soriano and Slater, 2009; Neilson and Paxton, 2010). For those ethically or emotionally affected by the cruelty of mass caging of hens for egg production, for example, buying eggs laid by free-ranging hens seems a simple decision – if they are available, and if they are affordable in the household budget. Similar choices may be made on environmental or human rights dimensions. This ethical purchasing is having a significant impact on markets. Consumer markets may be extended to ethical investment opportunities, opportunities to buy into assumed collective ownership and control of production. Where such choices can be made, political and ethical consumers make explicit links between personal purchasing and boycotting decisions with political outcomes in the wider society (Micheletti, 2003; Young, 2003; Neilson and Paxton, 2010). Ethical consumerism is a growing and exploitable aspect of globalisation. It is a fairy tale in which the customer is king – but beware! The king may (yet prove to) have no (substantial) clothes!

# CONSUMER SOVEREIGNTY: ENACTING POLITICAL AND ETHICAL CONSUMERISM

*Consumer sovereignty* is a term coined by Hutt in 1936 (see Reekie, 1988) and is linked to classical and neo-classical economic theories (Slater, 1997). Consumer sovereignty is generated from the premise that 'consumers exert ultimate control over the economy' as their purchasing decisions dictate the activities of producers (Reekie, 1988; Saving, 2006: 107). This position is often historically associated with a limited reading of the work of Adam Smith who, like Hutt (1936), argued that consumer dictates within a *laissez-faire* marketplace would ultimately result in 'efficient production, better and cheaper products, social progress, and increased general welfare' (Denegri-Knott et al., 2006: 955). In this line of reasoning, general welfare is based on the utilitarian principle of utility maximisation. Increased universal happiness and social welfare are deemed to be achieved through an individual's pursuit of their personal interests in the market (Hansen and Schrader, 1997). Adam Smith had much more to say about moral obligation, however, but this discussion seems to find less favour in the economic argument of neo-liberals.

Consistent with its parent doctrine (the free-market economics as discussed in Chapter 3), consumer sovereignty is embedded with the assumptions that consumers have sufficient information and power to make rational and optimal purchasing decisions within the context of a competitive marketplace (Hansen and Schrader, 1997; Saving, 2006). Political and ethical consumers, advocates of consumer sovereignty and classic economic theorists hold the belief that consumer purchasing decisions are explicitly linked to active participation in democracy and, therefore, democracy is explicitly linked to free-market capitalism (Saving, 2006). From this perspective, purchasing decisions are widely viewed as an everyday vote through which consumers elect the sort of society they wish to live in (Brinkman, 2004; Neilson and Paxton, 2010). Taken together, advocates of consumer sovereignty argue 'that aggregate of well-informed autonomous consumer agents possess greater power than individual producers' (Denegri-Knott et al., 2006: 955).

Numerous examples do suggest that concerted consumer' activism may lead to producers and governments responding to citizen concerns as expressed through purchasing or boycotting behaviour and various other mass demonstrations of opinion (Kotler et al., 2005; Denegri-Knott et al., 2006; Jaffe and Gertler, 2006). Some examples include the Greenpeace 2001–2003 Stop Esso Campaign (involving coalitions between Friends of the Earth and other consumer groups), the Free Burma campaign against Pepsi, and animal rights activist and rainforest protection campaigns against McDonalds (Denegri-Knott et al., 2006). Governments have introduced consumer protectionist legislation in response to mass consumer demonstrations and activism and specific business practices (Rothchild, 1998; Sirgy and Su, 2000; Kotler et al., 2005). Examples of this include requirements to use tamper-proof packaging, controls over the level of additives in packaged foods and the accurate listing of their ingredients. Individuals at all levels of society might feel motivated to contribute to such active decision-making.

## ETHICAL MOTIVATION

Toni was delighted with her new promotion to purchasing officer for Wholefoods Ltd. She loved working for this company which took such a strong stand on whole-of-supply-chain purchasing. The ingredients used in their products, the sources of energy used in their processes, the ways waste is disposed of, and the conditions of work for every person employed on the supply chain are all certified as ethically managed. The canteen at work uses locally grown produce and coffee is sourced from fair-trade suppliers. In this context, she believed it would be very appropriate to replace the fleet of company trucks with bio-fuelled vehicles. She was surprised to be refused permission to do so. Later that month, a board member of Wholefoods Ltd hosted a staff seminar that demonstrated the worrying outcomes of turning ever more fertile farmland over to the production of crops for fuel rather than for human consumption. Toni thought hard about what to do. She felt out of her depth for the responsibilities she felt she had. She would begin by taking up some postgraduate studies in sustainability. She soon learned that sugar plantations and other bio-fuel crops were taking up increasing tracts of arable land. Indigenous peoples and small farm-holders were being dislocated from their homes and livelihoods in order that consumption can continue. 'How can we balance human desires, justice and environmental responsibility?' wonders Toni.

When we purchase anything, we are engaging in a complex set of relationships that include relationships of production, distribution and disposal. While this may be most explicitly demonstrated through the purchasing of goods, it is also a dynamic we can think about in terms of our purchase of services. The production and purchase of financial products might be a good example. Banks, for example, may pressure a mortgage owner to take out life or house insurance that becomes important in times of catastrophes such as earthquakes, other 'acts of God' and under the actions of unscrupulous financiers. The entwining of the perceived requirement to purchase insurance products that purport to protect against every possible eventuality is adding pressure to already cash-strapped families – such families who, in times of their greatest need, may still be cast to the charity or mercy of strangers, even as they may hope for some revival of the mutuality of care by communities. Most people on Earth must find employment to purchase the necessities of life, necessities of life that have themselves been converted to commodities to be purchased. To purchase the necessities of life, people find they need jobs. From what perspective might this interrelationship be seen as a virtuous or a vicious circle?

## SPREADING THE FOOD AROUND

'Use-by dates', we all know, are merely a guide for safe consumption. Often, items may be fine (for the poor) long after their recommended expiry date and can be donated to grateful recipients. This is just one of the many ways we can make the food supply go further. Governments might even be willing to foot the bill for transport and distribution if the food is to be used as part of their aid commitments. 'Dumpster diving', too, is a way that food budgets can be extended. Another growing entrepreneurial response to creating edible food and useful compost is to make better use of waste from supermarkets. Are these win-win solutions for the over-stocking or under-consumption of mass food production? Do these create a virtuous circle or perpetuate a vicious circle? Surf the Internet and find many great examples of everything from providing meals to homeless shelters to 'pop-up' restaurants to make a point.

Verbos and colleagues (2011) draw our attention to the wisdom of indigenous people whose ideas of a virtuous circle are somewhat different from those of the prevailing capitalist mentality. Their wisdom, however, is very difficult to manifest in practice within and beyond indigenous communities in the face of the widespread normalisation of Western institutional logics. Many indigenous communities the world over have been driven into various forms of isolation for which their remedy for future survival, it seems, is to enter the market and compete with the rest of humanity for the goods and services they need to survive. For many, this has encouraged the commercialisation of much that might otherwise have remained sacred. Holding back what is not (to be) for sale becomes increasingly difficult. For some, participating in fair-trade schemes is one way to protect themselves from the harshest ravages of markets, even though these markets are not huge. Fair-trade sales, for example, increased by 47 per cent in 2007 (Fairtrade Foundation, 2008). Fair-trade or alternative trade has the explicit agenda of improving the social and environmental conditions and living standards of low-income developing nations, and making the production process visible at the point of sale (Hudson and Hudson, 2003). Despite the exponential growth in fair-trade sales in 2007, the highest average per capita spending was £14.25 (US $ 23.34) recorded in Switzerland (Fairtrade Foundation, 2008). Fair-trade goods account for only 1 per cent of global trade (Siegel, 2009). Hudson and Hudson (2003: 423) conclude that '[a]lternative trade can only become a genuinely transformative movement if it reaches a much broader segment of the population.'

Market researchers demonstrate that particular demographic features and social background status appear to be linked to the current segment of ethical and political consumers. These features include experiences of trust, gender, education levels, income levels, where one lives (including at the national, rural and suburban levels), exposure to information, work ethic and the extent of one's social capital (Carrigan and Pelsmacker, 2009; Mørkbak and Nordström, 2009; Lee et al., 2010; Neilson and Paxton, 2010). In their attempts to understand and expand the ethical and political market segment, market researchers, drawing on intention–behaviour modelling, constantly reveal an intentions gap between consumers' expressed interest in ethical consumption and their actual purchasing behaviour (Carrigan and Attalla, 2001; Belk et al., 2005; Futerra, 2005; Mayo and Fielder, 2006; Auger and Devinney, 2007). Futerra (2005) suggests that while 30 per cent of respondents report an intention to purchase ethically, only about 3 per cent actually do so. Carrington and colleagues (2010: 142) argue that much of this market research is methodologically flawed, as many intention–behaviour models rely on self-reporting and assume 'perfect and constant conditions without considerations of environmental or social settings, thus oversimplifying the complex translation of purchase intentions and actual buying behaviour'.

## CHEAP FLIGHTS AND HUMAN RIGHTS

Hidden in the bargains to be found on budget travel are the cost-cuttings that airlines must find to make these journeys ever more attractive and affordable to ever more people. In 2009, businessman David Cancion got caught up in a scuffle. He found himself in a Chinese prison. Here, he experienced significant torture. He witnessed contemporary slavery and forced labour under conditions of gross human rights abuse. He believes that the cheap ear-plugs he was forced to make in this prison would have found their way to regular airline carriers we all use. No airline contacted has been able to say definitively that their ear-plugs are not manufactured by slave labour. In searching for best deals in travel, holidays, cars, gadgets, clothes or food preferences, we cannot always know what dynamics we are participating in. Does this absolve us from responsibility? (TVNZ, 2013)

We suggest that as well as just not knowing the details of commodity production, there are any number of practical barriers and philosophical limitations embedded in the notion of consumer sovereignty. These include the price barriers that get in the way of making such decisions and the unequal power arrangements that influence perceptions of need and value. It is to these issues we now turn.

# PRICE BARRIERS TO TRANSFORMATIVE CHANGE THROUGH CONSUMPTION

We have discussed many of the issues that might affect participation in democracy through consumption choices. For example, in Chapter 3, we drew attention to income inequality within and between nations, and changes to the structures and conditions of paid employment and the extent of, and pressures on, discretionary income. Enacting consumer power through a vote-with-the-dollar is perhaps a luxury for the rich and not such a feasible option for ordinary people residing in rich and poor countries alike. Mintrom (2003) comments on the fragility of the market as a space for enacting transformative change when he suggests that:

> [because] markets accord more choice and hence more power, to the affluent, they often serve to perpetuate rather than arrest social inequality and social injustices … [to] the extent that wealth derived from market activity can be transformed into political power, markets seriously encroach on the notion of political equality that is 'the moral foundation of democracy'. (Dahl, 1998: 178, cited in Mintrom, 2003: 55)

Believing that one is engaging in democracy through personal purchasing decisions is being challenged as ethically fraught. While consumers argue that they have the right to vote with their dollars, they may not necessarily have the skills, qualifications and expertise to appreciate fully the implications of their consumption choices, argue Hansen and Schrader (1997). Nowhere is this made so pertinent as in the genetic engineering debates or in discussions about whether to pay for (through user-pay fees or taxes) compulsory or voluntary inoculations for one's own children in the interests or otherwise of all children. Reducing democracy to the use of the dollar as a vote also denies all other non-consuming stakeholders and citizens access to the decisions about how they may wish their society to be managed (Sirgy and Su, 2000).

Instead, ethical considerations embedded in consumer sovereignty are frequently limited to the examination and challenge of infringements between individuals through a violation of existing laws; that is, between consumers and suppliers or between consumers and consumers (Hansen and Schrader, 1997; Rothchild, 1998). Moreover, some consumers have been found to use existing laws to engage in mischievous and fraudulent claims against businesses or fellow consumers (Yani-de-Soriano and Slater, 2009). The limits of ethical considerations within the utilitarian consumption framework have some calling for a move away from consumer sovereignty and its 'rights-based' assumptions towards an amplification of greater consumer as well as producer responsibility (Hansen and Schrader, 1997; Yani-de-Soriano and Slater, 2009). We next focus on a consideration of the extent to which consumers have been argued to have more power than producers.

# THE (MORE?) POWERFUL PRODUCER AND THE (PRE)-FABRICATED CONSUMER

In contrast to Adam Smith's proposition that consumers dictate economic activity through their purchases, Schumpeter argued that it is producers who initiate economic exchange and control the market, and that it is consumers who 'are educated by him [sic] if necessary; they are, as it were, taught to want new things, or things which differ in some respect or other from those which they have been in the habit of using' (Schumpeter, 1911/1999: 65; cited in Korthals, 2001: 202). Ward (2009: 218) demonstrates the instrumental role of marketing activities in the United States, between 1880 and 1930, in developing new wants to be transformed into needs, and, in particular, through fabricating the notion of the affluent and propertied consumer as a respected/envied individual. This image not only served the profit motives of a free-market society but was also drawn upon by producers and sellers to decide 'what products to manufacture, what images to associate with those products, where to sell those products – and to whom' (Ward, 2009: 218).

## RESTORING THE SOUL

Gill was pretty exhausted. She had been hard at it for weeks facilitating a compromise between the purchasing division of her Dairy Industry Collective and a local environmental group with links to much more powerful environmental lobbyists. The purchasing department had come to an agreement not to import more palm products for cattle-fodder if the environmental activists would not get in the way of the industry's application for more irrigation rights in the next round of council negotiations. After all, the cattle need to be fed. Grass was better than imported palm-based fodder even if it did channel irrigation water away from the few small communities in the district. They would barely notice the loss, so long as there was no drought. The negotiations had been gruelling. Gill was pleased to notice an advertisement for an affordable package deal for a spa holiday in a romantic-looking Asian holiday resort. It was not long before she was reading the local newspaper by the very pool she had seen in the advertisement that prompted her choice. She was discomforted and a little annoyed to read that an NGO was planning to mount a protest against the resort owners and their enabling councils for their disproportionate access to fresh water needed for the local market gardens. Was there to be no peaceful, guilt-free enjoyment of her hard-won earnings? (see Red, 2004)

Media images and messages are deemed to be a powerful source for shaping self-identity, self-image and meaning (Klein, 2000; Hudson and Hudson, 2003; Denegri-Knott et al., 2006; Jaffe and Gertler, 2006; Ward, 2009; Yani-de-Soriano and Slater, 2009). Embedded in this argument is the idea that consumerism and consumer culture are created through the use of manipulative advertising and marketing techniques which, for example, exploit consumer insecurities and vulnerabilities, entice over-consumption, exaggerate products through packaging design, and sell particular notions of lifestyle (Yani-de-Soriano and Slater, 2009). Knights and colleagues (1994) suggest that the concept of 'need' embedded in market research is essentialist and individualistic: 'need' is conceived as an essential feature of the individual psyche, something that can be measured and acted upon. Producers can exercise power through marketing, advertising and selling campaigns to induce consumers to believe that they, in fact, have these needs which can be met through purchasing certain products or accessing particular services. They point out the irony in at first conceiving need as an essential feature of the psyche, and then validating such needs by socially constructing reality. In this sense, consumerism becomes understood as 'the doctrine that the self cannot be complete without a wealth of consumer goods' (Murphy, 2000: 636).

Consumer culture is deemed to be fabricated by more powerful marketers, producers and advertisers, who shape meaning and purchasing behaviour. The consumer becomes alienated by cultural messages and comes to see fabricated wants and needs as their own. Purchasing, then, is an act of buying status symbols that enhance the fabricated self-identity and projects a particular self-image within the public domain (Yani-de-Soriano and Slater, 2009). More so, when viewed as manipulative, all marketing and advertising campaigns might be received with scepticism and mistrust (Hudson and Hudson, 2003; Carrigan and Pelsmacker, 2009), affecting consumer willingness to buy products that might very well lead to improved working conditions, a cleaner environment or safer food. However, de Certeau (1984) suggests that even when considered as culturally oppressive, consumers can engage in subversive tactics to resist the strategies of more powerful producers, marketers and advertisers by adapting or evading the fabricated meanings to meet their own needs.

The discursive analysis of consumerism draws upon Foucauldian framings of disciplinary power and knowledge. In Chapter 5, we discussed the operationalisation of the concepts of disciplinary knowledge-power and the panoptic gaze (Foucault, 1970, 1976, 1977, 1980), as well as technologies and techniques of the self, and the gaze of the expert (Miller and Rose, 1988, 1998; Rose, 1988). Applied to consumerism, purchasing decisions are deemed to be an outcome of repeating patterns of (producer) objectification and (consumer) subjectification. Producers, advertisers and marketers make objectified truth claims and offer normalised images not only of their goods and services, but also of lifestyle choices, and even of spiritual enlightenment. Consumers subject themselves to these externally normalised truth claims when they respond to the disciplinary power by willingly acting upon the self and purchasing the goods or accessing the services offered (Denegri-Knott et al., 2006: 961). From the discursive analysis, consumer power is evident when consumers actively participate in changing the power-knowledge base and the normative and discursive structures of the marketplace, resulting in transformations in the power-knowledge base and new truth claims (Denegri-Knott et al., 2006).

Critics of the transformative potential of consumer sovereignty are not without their own critics. Denegri-Knott and colleagues (2006) suggest that such views oversimplify consumer culture as repressive and culturally authoritative, creating passive consumers and threatening active citizenship. In contrast, the discursive interpretation of market activity posits that what occurs in the marketplace is a co-creative and interactive process between consumers and producers. The discursive approach denies that either consumers (as is argued within consumer sovereignty) or producers (as argued within cultural frameworks) have ultimate power to determine and shape meaning in market activities. Instead, 'the wills of consumers and producers turn out to be far more overlapping, mutual and interdependent than commonly recognised' (Kozinets et al., 2004: 671).

## KNOWLEDGE SPEAKS TO POWER: FILMMAKER ACTIVISTS

Frank Poulsen was interested in the supply chain that allowed him his mobile phone. His investigation culminated in the film *Blood in the Mobile*. In this film, we can see young boys who say they spend many long hours in the mines of the Congo. Nokia, a signatory to the Global Compact, is believed to source raw materials from these mines. Poulsen took his movie to Nokia to ask them if they could explain their participation in this form of mining. The company responds: 'We are doing all we can.'

Check out:

- www.nokia.com/global/about-nokia/people-and-planet/strategy/strategy-and-reports/ (retrieved 10 September 2013).
- www.hs.fi/english/article/Filmmaker+urges+Nokia+to+shoulder+more+responsibility+over+human+rights+in+Congo/1135261683446 (retrieved 10 September 2013).
- http://news.cnet.com/8301-13579_3-57520121-37/digging-for-rare-earths-the-mines-where-iphones-are-born/ (retrieved 10 September 2013).

All manufacturers of electronic gadgets have an insatiable need for the minerals necessary for the products we choose to buy. Is it sufficient to concern ourselves with segments of the supply chain when the cumulative effects of our personal consumption may be the root of the danger?

Attractive as it might seem to abide by the theories of a conscious form of co-creation by consumers and producers, Jaffe and Gertler (2006: 143) argue that consumers do not have, and are systematically deprived of, the information, knowledge and analytical frameworks needed to make informed decisions, let alone contest the truth claims of more powerful producers. Instead, they argue that, along with labour, consumers have been systematically deskilled as an outcome of industrialised production processes. Skills and knowledge once taught in the home, and used to sustain family, are no longer deemed to be productive activities, but acts of consumption. These skills range from the growing and preparing of food to the care of the young, old and infirm. As more people shift their productive activities from the home to the public domain, these traditional skills and knowledge are no longer handed down through the generations and are lost. This, then, can become an ever-intensifying process of lost skill, market remedy, need for income to support market purchase, and the subsequent loss of time to develop or use domestic skills. Ever more people are under ever more pressure to purchase the goods and services required to sustain themselves through what is available in the marketplace. Information, too, is increasingly externally sourced from the public domain, much of it filtered by editors employed by privately owned news media corporates and through advertising campaigns or new experts in subjectivity. Jaffe and Gertler (2006) locate the process of deskilling consumers in the deskilling of labour within the production process, and, in particular, to what Marx termed commodity fetishism.

# COMMODITY FETISHISM AND CONSUMER SOVEREIGNTY

Marx located commodity fetishism within the commodity production process (Hudson and Hudson, 2003; Jaffe and Gertler, 2006). Through commodity production and exchange, Marx contended that people come to understand social relations as relations between the products of their labour; that is, 'relations between things, rather than relations between people' (Hudson and Hudson, 2003: 413). As workers engage in commodity production and the intrinsic and creative aspects of work are removed from the production process, 'work becomes a means to an end ... rather than a means in itself' (Hudson and Hudson, 2003: 416): to earn money in order to consume. Value is accorded to the commodity produced, and not to the social relations of production. By according value to the product, exploitative social relationships inherent in the production process become obscured; social relationships become reified as relationships between things; and the capacity for political social action and resistance is reduced (Allen and Kovach, 2000: 226).

Satisfying emotional needs moves from engaging in social relationships and is transferred to engaging in self-interested consumption of products exchanged in the marketplace (Jaffe and Gertler, 2006). While the purchase of sex may be seen as the extreme example of this case, complex dynamics arise when we purchase the services of others to care for our children, our elderly and our frail, or when young people must accumulate expensive clothes and accessories to fulfil a sense of personal well-being. Emotions can come to be expressed through purchases and are thus readily exploitable. 'Mother's Day' and 'Father's Day' are perhaps fun days to show appreciation to parents deserving of such respect. Festivals with their roots in various religious orientations, such as the Christian Christmas and Easter, are also great marketing opportunities. Even in economic hardship, parents can be persuaded to part with cash to prove to themselves, their children and all onlookers that they care about their kids. These festivals have become market opportunities at times desperately needed by retailers to counter otherwise difficult economic climates. How stuff is made, transported or disposed of is often not top of one's mind at these times.

The commodity production process, according to Marx, detaches workers from consumers; their only point of contact is through the thing that has been produced. Because of this detachment, Hudson and Hudson (2003) suggest that it is unlikely that many workers are concerned about the well-being of an anonymous and faceless consumer. They are unlikely ever to know whether the end consumers are satisfied with their purchases. So, too, it is unlikely that consumers (who themselves are workers embedded within the commodity production process) consider the working conditions, pay levels and working hours of workers (Hudson and Hudson, 2003; Fleetwood, 2008). As part of the hegemonic 'consumer is king' discourse, purchasers may come to see low-priced goods as bargains and extended shopping hours as outcomes of enlightened responsive shopkeepers, instead of an expression of low wages and unsocial working hours (Fleetwood, 2008). Workers, then, in their roles as consumers, are embedded in exploitative production practices. The detachment between workers and consumers and their co-involvement in the exploitative commodity production processes is exacerbated within the globalised commodity production process. De-fetishising commodity production requires the reclaiming of social relationships in the production process and making the production relationships evident to the consumer at the point of sale (Allen and Kovach, 2000; Hudson and Hudson, 2003). More intensive advertising campaigns, labelling and certification demands could facilitate this process.

The extent to which the transformative ideals espoused by critical theorists can be achieved through consumer sovereignty is a contested domain. On the one hand, there is strong evidence that concerted consumer campaigns have resulted in producers changing aspects of the production process and governments enacting legislation. In this line of reasoning, power is assumed to reside in the coordinated efforts of a number of groups working together to effect change. Even where this can be seen to be the case, this power of a few does not come without a dark side. These coordinated acts, in part, have been facilitated by communication technologies that enable information to be spread globally – at least, to those who have access to such technologies. While we might value the achievements of some such groups, we might equally be disturbed by the disproportionate power of a few to influence what may or may not become possible for the rest of the population and the pressures brought to bear by a few on the natural, social or political environment – through their purchasing power rather than some other means of influence.

On balance, we argue that there are limits to the extent to which hegemonic power can be challenged through individualised purchasing decisions to bring about the transformative ideals of critical theorists. Denegri-Knott and colleagues (2006: 964) point out that the cultural and discursive accounts of consumer empowerment show little sign of redressing the power imbalance between consumers and producers; instead, they suggest that any sense of empowerment derived from these approaches appears to be 'self-illusory and contrary to the spirit of social and critical theory'. Similarly, Johnston (2002) contests the extent to which a counter-hegemonic movement, relying on existing hegemonic discourses of the supposedly empowered individual, can effect sociopolitical change. This approach rests with the belief that democracy can be enacted simply through purchasing the right products in the domain of the market, obscuring the political origins of the power imbalance. Political decisions determine wage levels, environmental standards and working conditions; as such, redressing power imbalances resulting from these decisions requires a political response (Hudson and Hudson, 2003).

Exert your influence through your spending power? By all means! Do not assume, however, that it is a robust enough response to effectively address the issues we are tackling in this book. Consumer sovereignty does not address issues of income inequality, managed information campaigns that have as one aim the fabrication of desires or wants and proffered lifestyle choices, the deskilling of workers or consumers, or the geographical distance between consumers and producers. Instead, the doctrine of consumer empowerment rests with the idealised starting point that equality exists in the marketplace, where producers and consumers meet to make fair exchanges.

Finally, ethical and political consumerism and consumer sovereignty advocates do not address the environmental issues or working condition considerations that arise from over-consumption. Instead, these approaches rest on the belief that simply buying differently will have an effect on over-consumption (Johnston, 2002). Carrigan and Pelsmacker (2009) acknowledge that the 2007 recession saw a reduction in consumer spending. Ironically, they note that one outcome of reduced spending has been the achievement of many of the ideals expressed by ethical and political consumer advocates; that is, people buy less, trade down and repair rather than replace. One unintended outcome of such decisions, of course, is that this reduction in purchasing also ripples into further job losses and spirals into poverty for many at the sharp end of this cycle – for so long as such 'cycling' is intrinsic to the system of production and consumption/trade and exchange that we appear to be unable or unwilling to change.

Is consumer pressure an effective channel for change? *Non modo sed etiam*! Not only but also! It may be a necessary but it is not a sufficient force for change. The 'not only but also' approach may need to serve us until we have a better idea. From those who have the courage to press for influence, the transformations needed to the issues we tackle in this book will require more than an ethically considered choice of coffee brand, the selection of gifts from social entrepreneurs on distant websites or the ability to buy fuel-efficient cars manufactured through quality-assured conditions of production. More or different?

'The market', we have argued in previous chapters, is purported by its neo-liberal advocates to be the best means to enhance our emancipation – whether as producers or consumers. The doctrine of consumerism is well embedded in the neo-liberal ideology of human freedom. When examined through the lens of critical theorists, however, the idea of consumption as the best path to freedom contains a kind of paradox. These theorists observe that desires created by marketers can shape consumers who can then be exploited. Advertisers, for example, frequently present people who drink Coke as beautiful, healthy and fun. The idea that to drink Coke is to be part of a Western and therefore desirable life is a powerful marketing strategy. Who would *not* want to be beautiful, healthy and fun! The rapid uptake of Coke in cash-strapped villages, impoverished neighbourhoods and luxury locations the world over will attest to this idea. It is too bad that the production and consumption of such drinks is a significant contributor to the killing of people and the degradation of the planet. Drinking Coke, Pepsi and their ilk cannot ever fulfil aspirations to good health! The combined impact on health and planet of the production, waste, recycling and disposal of plastic bottles of (sugared) water may still be more than Earth can bear. It is to this issue that we turn our full attention in Chapter 8.

---

**TALK BOX**

Astounding technological advances suggest that the world is getting smaller by the second. I can see the capitalistic elites rubbing their hands in glee as international trade legislation relaxes and the race for wealth reaches fever pitch. My question is: ethically, I am against the principles behind globalisation, but in reality I have to feed, clothe, educate and entertain my kids, house my family and live a full and satisfying life. My subscription to globalisation by being a dedicated consumer impedes my ability to think credibly on the subject – true or false?

Have you ever considered your personal impact as consumer as part of a wider political-economic system?

- What products do you buy?
- Where are they manufactured?
- Under what conditions are the products made?
- How are they disposed of when you have finished with them?
- How far do you conceive your personal purchasing decisions as an act of:
  o Attempted market influence?
  o Personal sovereignty?
  o Image building?
  o Necessity?

If you did want to become more conscientious about your purchasing decisions:

- What might you purchase differently?
- How would you become informed about the products you regularly buy?
- What prevents you from gaining full information about the current products you buy?
- What 'realities' do you contend with that prevent you from making different purchasing decisions?
  o Price?
  o Location?
  o Lack of time?
  o Lack of information?
  o Lack of assurance that your small decisions will lack assurance that they will have a significant impact?

# ADDITIONAL RESOURCES

Baudrillard, J. (1998) *The Consumer Society: Myths and Structures*. London: Sage.

Bloch, P. and Banerjee, S.B. (2001) An involvement perspective on environmentally conscious consumption. *Journal of the Australian and New Zealand Academy of Management*, 7 (2): 1–19.

Goodall, J. (2006) *Harvest for Hope: A Guide to Mindful Eating*. New York: Wellness Central.

O'Shaughnessy, J. and O'Shaughnessy, N. (2002) Marketing, the consumer society and hedonism. *European Journal of Marketing*, 36 (5/6): 524–47.

Siegal, L. (2009) Is buying fair-trade a waste of money? *Observer Magazine*, 22 February: 59.

Tutu, D. (2010) Foreword. In K.D. Moore and M.P Peril (eds), *Moral Ground: Ethical Action for a Planet*. San Antonio: Nelson Trinity University Press.

# REFERENCES

Allen, P. and Kovach, M. (2000) The capitalist composition of organic: the potential of markets in fulfilling the promise of organic agriculture. *Agriculture and Human Values*, 17 (3): 221–32.

Auger, P. and Devinney, T.M. (2007) So what consumers say matter? The misalignment of preferences with unconstrained ethical intentions. *Journal of Business Ethics*, 76: 361–83.

Bauman, Z. (2007) *Consuming Life*. Cambridge: Polity Press.

Belk, R., Devinney, T. and Eckhardt, G. (2005) Consumer ethics across cultures. *Consumption, Markets and Cultures*, 8 (3): 275–89.

Bradshaw, A. (2011) Consumer culture. In M. Tadajewski, P. MacLaran, E. Parsons and M. Parker (eds), *Key Concepts in Critical Management Studies*. London: Sage. pp. 54–7.

Brinkman, J. (2004) Looking at consumer behavior in a moral perspective. *Journal of Business Ethics*, 51 (2): 129–41.

Brittenden, W. (2013) Wayne Brittenden's counterpoint, 31 March (www.radionz.co.nz/national/programmes/sunday/audio/2550660/wayne-brittenden's-counterpoint; retrieved 10 September 2013).

Carrigan, M. and Attalla, A. (2001) The myth of the ethical consumer: do ethics matter in purchase behaviour? *Journal of Consumer Marketing*, 18 (7): 560–78.

Carrigan, M. and Pelsmacker, P. (2009) Will ethical consumers sustain their values in the global credit crunch? *International Marketing Review*, 26 (6): 674–87.

Carrington, M.J., Neville, B.A. and Whitwell, G.J. (2010) Why ethical consumers don't walk their talk: towards a framework for understanding the gap between the ethical purchase intentions and actual buying behaviour of ethically minded consumers. *Journal of Business Ethics*, 97 (1): 139–58.

Dahl, R.A. (1998) *On Democracy*. New Haven, CT: Yale University Press.

de Certeau, M. (1984) *The Practice of Everyday Life*. Berkeley, CA: University of California Press.

Denegri-Knott, J., Zwick, D. and Schroeder, J.E. (2006) Mapping consumer power: an integrative framework for marketing and consumer research, *European Journal of Marketing*, 40 (9/10): 950–71.

Dixon, D.F. (1999) Some late nineteenth century antecedents of marketing theory. In P. Cunningham and D. Bussiere (eds), *Marketing History: The Total Package*. Lansing, MI: Michigan State University. pp. 17–29.

Fairtrade Foundation (2008) Global fairtrade sales increase by 47%. Press release (www.fairtrade.org.uk/press_office/press_releases_and_statements/may_2008/press_office/press_releases_and_statements/april_2008/press_office/press_releases_and_statements/april_2008/global_fairtrade_sales_increase_by_47.aspx; retrieved 11 February 2008).

Fleetwood, S. (2008) Workers and their alter egos as consumers. *Capital and Class*, Spring: 31–47.

Foucault, M. (1970) *The Order of Things*. New York: Random House.

Foucault, M. (1976) *The History of Sexuality*, vol. 1: *The Will to Knowledge*, trans. R. Hurley. London: Allen Lane.

Foucault, M. (1977) *Discipline and Punish: The Birth of the Prison*. Harmondsworth: Penguin.

Foucault, M. (1980) *Power/Knowledge*. New York: Pantheon.

Futerra, S.C.L. (2005) *The Rules of the Game: The Principles of Climate Change Communication*. London: Department for Environment, Food and Rural Affairs.

Hansen, U. and Schrader, U. (1997) A modern model of consumption for a sustainable society. *Journal of Consumer Policy*, 20 (4): 443–68.

Harrison, R., Newholm, T. and Shaw, D. (2005) Introduction. In R. Harrison, T. Newholm, and D. Shaw (eds), *The Ethical Consumer*. Thousand Oaks, CA: Sage. pp. 1–10.

Hudson, I. and Hudson, M. (2003) Removing the veil? Commodity fetishism, fair trade and the environment. *Organization and Environment*, 16 (4): 413–30.

Hutt, W.H. (1936) *Economists and the Public*. London: Jonathan Cape.

Jaffe, J. and Gertler, M. (2006) Victual vicissitudes: consumer deskilling and the (gendered) transformation of food systems. *Agriculture and Human Values*, 23 (2): 143–62.

Johnson, J.F. (1910) The new economics and the marginal consumer. *Printers' Ink*, 15: 42–3.

Johnston, J. (2002) Consuming a global justice: fair trade shopping and alternative development. In J. Goodman (ed.), *Protest and Globalization: Prospects for Transnational Solidarity*. Annandale, Australia: Pluto Press. pp. 38–56.

Klein, N. (2000) *No-logo*. London: Flamingo.

Knights, D., Sturdy, A. and Morgan, G. (1994) The consumer rules? An examination of the rhetoric and 'real'. *European Journal of Marketing*, 28 (3): 42–54.

Korthals, M. (2001) Taking consumers seriously: two concepts of consumer sovereignty. *Journal of Agricultural and Environmental Ethics*, 14 (2): 201–15.

Kotler, P., Wong, V., Saunders, J. and Armstrong, G. (2005) *Principles of Marketing*, 4th edn. Harlow: Pearson Education.

Kozinets, R., Sherry, J.F., Storm, D., Duhachek, A., Nuttavuthisit, K. and Deberry-Spence, B. (2004) Ludic agency and retail spectacle. *Journal of Consumer Research*, 31 (3): 658–72.

Lee, M., Pant, A. and Ali, A. (2010) Does the individualist consume more? The interplay of ethics and beliefs that governs consumerism across cultures. *Journal of Business Ethics*, 93: 567–81.

Mayo, E. and Fielder, A. (2006) I will if you will. *Consumer Policy Review*, 16 (4): 148–55.

Micheletti, M. (2003) *Political Virtue and Shopping Individuals, Consumerism and Collective Action*. New York: Palgrave Macmillan.

Miller, P. and Rose, N. (1988) The Tavistock Programme: the government of subjectivity and social life. *Sociology*, 22 (2): 171–92.

Miller, P. and Rose, N. (1998) Governing economic life. In C. Mabey, G. Salaman and J. Storey (eds), *Strategic Human Resource Management: A Reader*. London: Sage. pp. 46–57.

Mintrom, M. (2003) Market organizations and deliberative democracy: choice and voice in public service delivery. *Administration and Society*, 35 (1): 52–81.

Mørkbak, M.R. and Nordström, J. (2009) The impact of information on consumer preferences for different animal food production methods. *Journal of Consumer Policy*, 32 (4): 313–31.

Munro, R. (2011) Identity. In M. Tadajewski, P. MacLaran, E. Parsons and M. Parker (eds), *Key Concepts in Critical Management Studies*. London: Sage. pp. 138–42.

Murphy, P. (2000) The commodified self in consumer culture: a cross-cultural perspective. *Journal of Social Psychology*, 40: 636–47.

Neilson, L.A. and Paxton, P. (2010) Social capital and political consumerism: a multilevel analysis. *Social Problems*, 57 (1): 5–24.

Red, E.P. (2004) Hype over oil palm potential. *Business World Online*, 24–25 September (www.aseanfood.info/Articles/13004772.pdf; retrieved 10 September 2013).

Reekie, D.W. (1988) Consumers' sovereignty revisited. *Managerial and Decision Economics*, special issue: 17–25.

Rose, N. (1988) *Governing the Soul: The Shaping of the Private Self.* London: Free Association Books.

Rose, N. (1996) *Powers of Freedom: Reframing Political Thought*. Cambridge: Cambridge University Press.

Rothchild, J. (1998) Making the market work: enhancing consumer sovereignty through the telemarketing sales rule and the distance selling directive. *Journal of Consumer Policy*, 21 (3): 279–313.

Saving, J.L. (2006) Consumer sovereignty in the modern global era. *Journal of Private Enterprise*, 22 (1): 107–19.

Schumpeter, J. (1911/1999) *The Theory of Economic Development: An Inquiry into Profits, Capital, Credit, Interest and the Business Cycle*. Oxford: Oxford University Press.

Seidman, S. (2008) *Contested Knowledge: Social Theory Today*. Oxford: Blackwell.

Siegel, L. (2009) Is buying fair trade a waste of time? *The Observer*, 22 February.

Sirgy, M.J. and Su, C. (2000) The ethics of consumer sovereignty in an age of high tech. *Journal of Business Ethics*, 28 (1): 1–14.

Slater, D. (1997) *Consumer Culture and Modernity*. Cambridge: Polity Press.

Tadajewski, M., MacLaran, P., Parsons, E. and Parker, M. (eds) (2011) *Key Concepts in Critical Management Studies*. London: Sage.

TVNZ (2013) Kiwi a 'slave' in Chinese prison, 31 March (http://tvnz.co.nz/sunday-news/kiwi-slave-in-chinese-prison-video-5390956; retrieved 10 September 2013).

Verbos, A.K., Gladstone, J. and Kennedy, D.M. (2011) Native American values and management education: envisioning an inclusive virtuous circle. *Journal of Management Education*, 35 (1): 10–26.

Ward, D.B. (2009) Capitalism, early market research, and the creation of the American consumer. *Journal of Historic Research in Marketing*, 1 (2): 200–23.

Waring, M. (1999) *Counting for Nothing: What Men Value and What Women are Worth*. Toronto: University of Toronto Press.

Yani-de-Soriano, M. and Slater, S. (2009) Revisiting Drucker's theory: has consumerism led to the overuse of marketing? *Journal of Management History*, 15 (4): 452–66.

Young, I. (2003) From guilt to solidarity: sweatshops and political responsibility. *Dissent* (spring): 39–44.

Žižek, S. (2008) *For They Know Not What They Do: Enjoyment as a Political Factor*. New York: Verso.

# 8 SUSTAINABILITY AND ECOLOGICAL RESPONSIBILITY UNDER CAPITALISM

## Learning Objectives

In this chapter, we invite you to reflect critically on:

- the naming and framing of Earth as a 'resource' and the associated imputation of meaning and value;
- the responsibilities that are assumed based on the views that we hold about Earth;
- the possibility that Earth has a life-force intentionality distinct from but entwined with human existence;
- the processes of, and the extent to which some are prepared to defend, 'a way of life' – even at the (unsustainable) cost to Earth and many of her creatures;
- the transforming of the human relationship with Earth and all of her creatures;
- instrumental ethics in contrast to relational ethics in leadership for change.

## CRITICAL CONCEPTS

*Critical theorists* make a distinction between *deep* and *shallow ecological thinking* in concerns about *sustainability* and in the human relationship with *anima mundi*. *Ecosophy* generated from an Earth-orientated *teleology* invites a more radical *ontology* and *epistemology* than is currently popular.

## MANAGING FOR ECOLOGICAL RESPONSIBILITY

Rising sea levels, salination of once rich arable soil, intensifying climatic events and the extinction of crucial links in the chain of life are brought to our attention on a regular basis by scientists, concerned citizens and by nature itself. While the entwined exploitation of people and planet has been our main focus to this point in the book, how we collectively and individually exploit Earth is the question to which we now turn our specific attention. Who speaks for Earth? Does Earth have her own voice? Can we hear her? Just as a more complex image of humanity is needed for a more ethical and sustainable process of trade and exchange, so, too, we may need a more complex notion of Earth and our relationship with her. We each need to breathe the air, drink the water and eat the foods that are intrinsically woven into the circle of life. The framing of thinking about Earth in the prevailing institutional logics in terms of 'resources for use' in the 'competition for life' fuels dangerous outcomes generated from the very meanings we have invested in our understanding of ourselves, our relationship with others and with Earth who sustains us.

The interests of critical management scholars in how human identities, organisations, work and values are shaped, endorsed and policed are threaded through this book. How power, control, dependency, responsibility, emancipation, fear or love is invested in the social fabrications of any era or geographical location is the concern of those focused on meaning-making. While neo-liberals continue with their project of atomising individuals and framing their life's opportunities in a dangerous game of competition for life's necessities, critical management scholars call for a different wisdom. They explore and expose how, in a specific time or place, such meanings may be imposed, negotiated or challenged, how these may serve dominant interests or how they may be used to open opportunities for new ways of thinking and acting. As indigenous peoples situated on land, water or minerals now coveted by corporate interests strengthen their resistance to exploitation, they are challenged to hold on to ancient views of themselves as children of Mother Earth with a duty of care in a way that is operable in the contemporary context. The seductive invitation to partnership with states and corporations holds interesting transformational potential for both.

Reflections on these dynamics are equally vital for examinations of the meaning invested (or 'vested') in Earth. These are ontological and epistemological examinations. Naming and imputing purpose and value are importantly linked. The purposes to which Earth has been harnessed are teleological considerations. Is Earth better thought of as 'a resource' or as a 'living being'? What we can know is that the assumptions we make affect the activities we will condone or challenge. The justification of the meaning we give to Earth and the way we use her is the work of epistemology. Simply put, epistemology, in the context of environmental concerns, is the study of the justifications we use explicitly or implicitly for thinking of Earth as we do. Examining the human relationship with Earth and all her creatures is the focus of this chapter. Imposing a self-serving identity on Earth may be as arrogant as the objectification and subjugation of one living creature to another – be that as labour, pet or food.

The morphing in human understanding of Earth from a living being to an inanimate thing to be exploited for material gain is a relatively new Western idea that holds many aspects of Western capitalist logic in place and vice versa. Those who do not wish to accept the way in which people, Earth and all her creatures have been turned to resources useful for profit maximisation, growth of the economy, the firm or their personal bank balance as their main/sole reason for being, point to the dangers of the very foundations of prevailing ideas and their normalisation in everyday practice. How we each relate to Earth is a vital part of this exploration. How we see our part in the circle of life is deeply entwined in how we engage with ideas of sustainability, in how we view environmentalism, in what we might call an eco-crime, and in what alternative ways of being we might think encouraging.

In this chapter, Mufasa's jungle wisdom is brought to the consideration of the growing concern with, complexity of, and conflicting opinions about contemporary environmental conditions and their trajectories. We invite a reflection on the diverse analyses of the state of the environment and the specific remedies associated with each to illustrate the very different ways we humans think about ourselves and about our relationship with Earth. We explore the example of the management of water to demonstrate our critique of commodification and marketisation of the necessities of life, particularly when the process is framed in the prevailing neo-liberal capitalist mentality being intensified the world over in the processes of globalisation we discussed in Chapter 3.

## MONSANTO AND MISLEADING ADVERTISING

In 2012, the Dutch Advertising Code Commission (DACC) found that Monsanto had misled the public in claiming that the poison Roundup does not persist in the soil, and does not reach the groundwater despite Monsanto's own research indicating

*(Continued)*

*(Continued)*

that Roundup is an endrocrine disruptor, a neurotoxin, a reproductive toxin and is linked with some forms of cancer. Rather than addressing these issues, Monsanto argued that its product had passed the scrutiny of various regulatory bodies. 'Thus "regulation" has become a convenient shield for industry to hide behind. It means that industry does not have to address evidence against its products directly but can simply point to regulatory approvals as a way of divesting itself of responsibility for toxic effects.' The complaint was brought to the DACC by the NGO Gifsoja and the Corporate Europe Observatory and Pesticide Action Network. Gifsoja commented on the ruling: 'Monsanto is still trying to keep up appearances that Roundup is a harmless substance … while [it is] very harmful to humans, animals and the environment'. (Earth Open Source, 2012)

It may well be the case that, in many instances, it is difficult to show a direct link between specific chemical and diverse outcomes in the health of individuals or natural habitats. Even more difficult to establish are the interactions of various chemicals and other toxins in the wider environment and in combination with perhaps other vulnerabilities in individuals and species. Does this mean that corporations who produce or use the chemicals can distance themselves from expressed concerns about them? The rise of human respiratory problems, epidemics in cancers and diabetes, the incidence of deformed babies, and so many more indicators that have been difficult to pin to a specific cause, would suggest that these may be attributable to the combination of poisons and pollutants in the toxic soup we ingest every day in so many ways. The cost of proving specific connections between pollutants and specific production processes and taking legal action can be daunting. Managers in organisations deemed to pollute, and managers of organisations that challenge such actions, are both working at the sharp end of these issues. We suggest that their tussles are a necessary but perhaps insufficient response to our environmental crisis. If substantial, life-enhancing transformations are to be invented, it may be that we need to revisit our ontological assumptions about Earth and our relationship with her.

Growing awareness of the complexity of the impact of human activity on environmental outcomes invites the consideration of a more elaborate notion of responsibility than the currently fashionable sustainability agenda or espoused concern with supply-chain security discourses we have discussed in previous chapters. Equally inhibiting to a thorough review of our relationship with Earth are the overly simplified limitations of role-specific responsibilities. We include in our thinking not only the powerful corporates and their immediate suppliers, but also the smallest of component manufacturers, service providers, food producers and consumers, coffee growers and drinkers, and parents and grandparents, teachers and lawyers, accountants and judges, and disciplinary professions and policing occupations of all kinds. All must be responsible for what happens on and to Earth as each of us is vulnerable. We depend on each other for our own well-being and that of our children's children. But how can we begin to make sense of the claims and counter-claims of the various voices in the debates about environmental responsibility?

# RESPONSIBILITY FOR SUSTAINABILITY (OF LIFE)

The significance of human effects on the environment and the entwining of this with issues of poverty, global insecurity and the arms race were brought to global public attention in a highly graphic way in the documentary *An Inconvenient Truth* and the continuing work that has been generated from this production. The programme *24 Hours of Reality* is just one example of the kind of education and activist engagement we can, each of us, become involved with. This documentary, of course, is not the only or perhaps even the best example of its kind, but it is an example that has had wide public attraction and impact. In this chapter, and on the companion website, you will find many more discussion starters, links to corporate positions on the environment, examples of activist groups and ideas about environmental responsibilities to learn about. Our examples are only a sliver of what is now so easily accessible for consideration.

## SEEING THE FIRES DOES NOT STOP THEM

'The GEONETCast will help us to take the pulse of the planet' writes Moulden (2008). However, knowing the fires are burning, inhaling the smoke, needing to keep children home from school so that the palm trees can be planted has not stopped the burning to date.

In June 2013, the smoke drifting into Singapore from forest burn-offs in Indonesia to make yet more room for yet more palm tree plantations closed schools and generated a warning that all but the most healthy people should stay indoors. One newly arrived expat, anticipating a privileged life in Singapore commented, 'I did not come here to lock myself into my apartment!' She was thinking very hard about a way to curtail her contract with her employer – or to figure out how, if there were to be health complications in her family, how the company might be held to account.

We are merely pointing towards the tip of an iceberg of concerns and creative actions peeking through the surface of an ocean of apparent trust or complacent compliance with corporate or state reassurance that best practices are being followed, that treaties and voluntary commitments are being honoured, and that all will be well in the future. We are not as confident! We are of the view that every person must take stock of their part in the intensification of harm to Earth and take responsibility for her restoration.

More focus than ever is being directed to corporate and state contributions to environmental damage and to the suffering they are believed to cause Earth and all her creatures. Corporations are taking note because claims that are upheld may result in expensive restitution and immeasurable damage to the corporate image and to the political security of governments. Even a claim that does not gain legal standing can entail costly defence. The once externalised costs of clearing up debris on Earth and in the stratosphere, the mopping up of spills from oil-wells, coal mines and nuclear plants, and the disposal of toxic waste and scrapped technologies are now increasingly brought to the accounting ledgers. The evidence for this can be seen in the greater attention given to 'triple bottom-line' accounting mechanisms, and the raft of corporate reports claiming greater transparency of environmentally and socially affective activities.

Environmental sustainability and responsibility for managing ecosystems have become a central platform for consideration of corporate responsibility and thus fall within the obligation of every manager in a supply chain. We include in our thinking all those people making decisions at the level of governance to the actions or non-actions of the most distant contractor, purchaser or household manager, and, as we discussed more fully in Chapter 7, the consumer decisions each of us elect or are compelled to make. (Not) packaging or (not) purchasing onions or lemons in plastic nets are simple decisions for producers and consumers – one choice can influence the other. Whether to require multiple paper copies of documents or to support electronic recording may be directly in our control. Whether we opt for more energy derived from fossil fuels or from renewable sources, such as sun or wind, seems more out of our direct reach – and yet they impact upon us directly. Is democracy up to the task of responsible governance of the issues we cannot tackle alone? Would a market-mentality serve justice better? Are these the only two options (in combination or alone) for organising our humanity and our relationship with Earth?

Words like eco-management, environmental responsibility, greening and sustainability have become much more visible in management education. Their growing visibility and the greater recognition of their complexities suggest that being informed about them as managers is important. A robust engagement with the potential of governments to be subservient to corporate interests or directive in the assertion of corporate responsibilities is also increasingly recognised in management education and research. Our part as consumers, employees, parents, teachers or students also runs deeper than the state, corporate or industry media invite us to think about. It takes a significant commitment to reflection on the part of individuals to contemplate the interrelatedness of our lives with the life of Earth and her relationship to the constellations of the universe. Such reflection, however, is what Socrates calls a duty of all citizens (Ober, 2003).

Being more aware of, and explicit about, the complexity of our multiple positioning (as employers, employees, customers and parents, interwoven into our notion of citizen) is itself a political action and invites us to think about a sense of responsibility that transcends the prevailing (economically orientated) utilitarianism that underpins the institutional logics that are being intensified globally. Despite the growing influence of environmental activists on how our organisations are to be managed, there still appears in the general population much concurrence with arguments based on purported economic necessity for destructive practices, significant indifference by some, or hopeless and paralysing despair with the status quo by others. Perhaps we each respond in a number of these ways across the diverse range of environmental issues, and differently so as we come under diverse pressures over time. What is more damaging to the environment, for example: the use of disposable diapers or the production, transport, cleaning and disposal of reusable cloth nappies? How can we possibly know? What information can we trust? Few of us can claim perfect consistency between our espoused values and our actions at all times. Much of what we believe about ourselves, as we have discussed in Chapter 5, can be shown to be intrinsically interwoven with a sense of self that is affected by a myriad of influencers – in which not only overt but also covert processes and powers of socialisation, education and media manipulations are at play.

Uncertainty and inconsistency of insight and commitment, however, should not hold us back from requiring an ever-deepening sense of responsibility from ourselves and each other. We may be required to meet or circumvent the environmental standards set for our industries in our place of employment. We may be the ones making purchase and disposal decisions for our households. We may act to ensure the well-being of Earth for her own sake. Sometimes this is easy to see and do. At other times, it may be easy to see but harder to do. Often we may not know what to do for the best. Each action or non-action will benefit from a greater critical engagement with their potential impacts. We take our critical position in this chapter for the sake of all those whose health and well-being are now being undermined by the current environmental situation, a situation deemed only to become more serious unless radical changes are made to the way human beings think about themselves and shape their relationship with Earth. Thus, in this chapter, we think particularly about the effects of our actions on our grandchildren's grandchildren – the seven generations many indigenous peoples urge us to be responsible for. A big ask? A big task? Is this a path of reasoning with horizons too far off to provide motivation to act now? Indeed, it may feel that way. Regardless of the horizons we recognise – near or far – all are relevant. We are all vulnerable to misinformation, deflection or derailment from an intention to care. We will each know of people who have suffered health concerns that may be linked to the polluted soup we call our environment. We may have a passion for a species of life that is under threat as a result of aggressive economic development. We may be concerned about the water we surf on, swim in or drink. What we can be sure about is that all are connected in the web of life – and this message is no longer the call of eco-geeks! From the early activities of the Sierra Club to the increasing membership of green parties, environmentalists are a growing influence in many parliaments across the world. Environmentalism is a growing challenge to neo-liberalism at the doctrinal level.

Environmentalism could be seen as a movement or a faith attracting ever more devotees – and critics. Climate change prophets and sceptics each carry opportunities for the manifestation and amplification of selective interests. Not all priests proclaim the same gospel. Not all devotees wield the same influence. Claims of corporations about the sustainability of their processes abound. They attract scientists to work on promising inventions. They indulge the promises of engineers who are working on technical solutions from porous concrete to lighter weight, more fuel-efficient aeroplanes and unpiloted stealth bombers to protect our way of life. From strategists setting corporate direction to account-ants who invent methods to disclose, redistribute or conceal the costs of such new entities as carbon credits and quotas of all kinds – all are busy with their work. Technical inventions, we have argued throughout this book, are not restricted to mechanical inventions. Legal and social fabrications abound. Management specialists who recruit, select, train and reward their staff, and communication experts who tell the stories, are all creators or operators of what Foucault calls 'technique' – the disciplinary processes we have introduced in Chapter 5. All of us who eat, play, build, travel, vote, don't vote, do or don't have jobs, affect the state of the environment – much of this effect circum-scribed or constrained by systemically endorsed interests.

The student demonstrations in London in November 2011 were ostensibly raising a protest against rising fees. Implied in their protests, and many citizen uprisings around the world, are concerns about greater corporate and political influence on curriculum development, police control of student demonstrators, concerns about greater military presence at universities, and wider concerns about the controls over minds and actions that are important to this chapter because state and corporate notions of sustainability and responsibility for the ecosystem appear to overshadow the concerns of many others. The right to be free to educate our minds and to express our views (and the duty to do so) is one of those long-held icons of democracy. For many philosophers, it is the defining condition of a moral person who can be held to account for their actions.

# FREE TO BE MORAL – OR MORAL TO BE FREE

Actions, whether attributed to corporations, states or NGOs, are *all* actions of people. The people directing the actions may be obscured from view by the artificial instruments of a corporate entity or the muffling effects of the separa-tion and curtailment of responsibility ascribed to role-specific duties. How far does the idea of merely following orders justify destructive actions? Formal contexts when individual actions are carried out on behalf of others require management. Such management requires managers to be conscious of their part in the process if they are to be considered as ethical beings, a precondition for which, as we discussed in Chapter 1, is freedom. All other positions are merely conditions of compliance and raise the very questions of authority this book is concerned with.

Commercial, entrepreneurial or state investors, NGOs, lobbyists or activists may work for or against corporate or state authorities when they perceive these to be environmentally damaging. Disrupting such authorities is seen by some to be a duty. The same action might be viewed by one person as an act of courage and leadership and another as an act of vandalism. We will introduce you to some eco-warriors on the companion webpage for this chapter. The exacerbating pressure for all humanity to be somehow linked to the global economy is represented by critics as serving the interests of a few but cloaked in the mystical garb of economic growth, a cloak purported to be, but yet to prove, beneficial to all. What do you think about this? Does this critique of the harnesses of the corporate form to the interests of a few and as risk to Earth condemn the corporate form? Think about the eco-guerrillas who uproot the crops which they believe to be dangerous. Think about the activists entering penned poultry and pig barns. Think about the people drawing attention to the powerful interests attempting to control the flow of information, be that about military or commercial matters or about environmental concerns that range from gambling on future food prices or the diversion of water to commercial interests over private needs to the displacing of people from lands and locations that appear desirable to investors under the guise of promising greater efficiency in food or forest production, water distribution or energy generation and flows. But is it the corporate form that is the demon?

Anita Roddick's use of the corporate form in the shaping of the Body Shop stands as an example of how a creative and courageous leader used her commercial strength to draw public attention and activist commitment to influence political and environmental atrocities. The publicity generated by the Body Shop (and like-minded activists) about the activities of Shell Oil in Ogoniland did not save the lives of those who brought these activities to light in the global political arena however. Nor does Shell's current claim to leadership on environmental matters redeem all those in authority who did not act to save them. The cumulative effects of the activities of courageous leaders, such as Anita Roddick, have no doubt intensified pressure on corporations and states to pay attention to their polluting activities. In the environmental field – from the production and distribution of food and water to cosmetics and defence technologies – all have environmental implications. All are 'managed' by a massive cohort of managers. How are they being educated? If we reflect on the work of Rose (1988) on the governance of the soul that we introduced in Chapter 5, we could rethink the influence of such academies as the School of the Americas as not only the overt inculcation of power and service to power expressed in military expertise. We could also think of their graduates as mercenaries that defend the interests of the already powerful – at times against their own fellow citizens.

Taking this logic further, we could re-view uncritical business education as the tacit facilitator of this selective channelling of power and wealth. Security experts, from strategic planners to thugs, can be employed to ensure compliance to the preferred behaviours of the landowners. For some, licensed security firms will provide insurance that no 'undesirables' can enter spaces such as malls, gated communities and corporate campuses (Miller, 2013). For others, even formal policing might be experienced as a form of thuggery. See, for example, what happened at an organic farm in Texas in August 2013 (Balko, 2013; Gummow, 2013). From a critical orientation, these look and feel much like modern feudal strongholds, as communities that generate lords and serfs, jesters and hand-maidens. All are enchanted by the myth of their genesis. They are modern-day Camelots with networks that are more powerful than ever were the interconnected royal households of Europe.

Many of the issues of power differentials in the organisation and management of our lives raised in this book come into play in the web of organisations through which we organise our humanity as a whole and our relationship with Earth. The United Nations ranks among powerful global influencers on environmental matters and is perhaps a body that has the interdisciplinary depth needed to attract specialists and invite generalist responsiveness. Their engagement with global organisations such as Greenpeace, and with faith-based organisations of all kinds, was demonstrated in the controversial Copenhagen meetings of 2010 (Hurd and Humphries, 2010). Arms of the United Nations specifically focused on the environment link with the arms devoted to responsible investment, good governance and so on. The Declaration of the Rights of Indigenous Peoples is of particular interest in this consideration as the United Nations has declared their rights to sovereign control over their destinies – destinies which include a relationship with Earth that is conceived in radically different ways from the instrumental, exploitative views underpinning Western rationalism. All these activities of the United Nations include streams of development that are of specific interest to those in business schools who have committed to the Principles for Responsible Management Education (PRME), as discussed in Chapter 1. The behaviour of the United Nations itself, however, has come under scrutiny in a suspected link between the flushing of their waste and the cholera epidemic in Haiti (Lee, 2011). While this is an extreme and overt case of behaviour that may be isolated and addressed, we invite much greater scrutiny of the connection of other arms of the United Nations – NATO, the World Bank and the IMF – in the shaping and controlling of the future of humanity and our relationship with Earth.

All organisations in the web of human life and our relationship with Earth require management. There is much good work to be done through bodies such as the various arms of the United Nations, our governmental institutions, our corporations and our NGOs. Whether these bodies ultimately manifest justice and redemption or are harnessed to the hegemonic project(ion) of neo-liberalism is not one we might think of as 'time will tell'. Levy (2011: 112–13) alerts us to a question by Hajer (1995) who asks:

whether ecological modernisation is 'the first step on a bridge that leads towards a new sort of sustainable modern society' or whether it is a 'rhetorical ploy that tries to reconcile the irreconcilable only to take the wind out of the sails of "real" environmentalists' ... Mobilising the language and practices of environmentalism, leading business sectors can sustain their hegemonic position, construct alliances with key environmental groups in society and marginalise radical environmentalists calling for deeper structural change and cultural transformation in the [prevailing] social and economic order.

The work of *vigilance* should not be minimised. We might pay closer attention to what we have done or not done to contribute to the shaping, influence and authority of various influential bodies, and what we might still do. This requires us to be alert and critical – not as a form of nay-saying that leads to paralyses, as discussed in Chapter 1, but in the dedication of critical energies to think deeply about what we do and not do, what we expect or allow others to do on our behalf, and why. This takes creativity, courage and tenacity.

# ECO-WARRIORS AND US

The extensive damage to the nuclear plants caused by the earthquake and tsunami in Japan in 2011 is an example of the global impact of local management decisions of many kinds. For whom, why and for what nuclear energy is the chosen option entails layers of decisions and management. These decisions involve states, financiers, insurers, scientists, media specialists and technicians of all kinds – all managed in the myriad of support activities from ensuring that the necessary ICT is reliable and secure to the provision of toilet paper and pay cheques for everyone from the executives to the cleaners.

Restoration and future care of the environment must also draw on the labour of many. This, too, invites some critical reflection. Who gets to risk their health to clean up after an accident has deep implications for the shaping and control of work discussed in Chapter 5. Who gets to make decisions in the future of the choice, ownership and distribution of energy in the boardrooms of corporations, finance houses and re-insurers of the world is discussed more fully in Chapter 9. What happens to the harbingers of future wisdom, particularly when they have felt the need to amplify their concerns in radical action, does not only depend on the views of prosecutors and judges. They, too, are products of their times. The oil spill in the Gulf of Mexico and the stranding of the Greek cargo ship *Rena*, which released oil and cargo into New Zealand's near shore seawater, are contemporary examples that are repeated the world over. They are not always reported. They are our modern-day Bhopal, *Exxon Valdez* and Chernobyl. Owners, directors and managers are not always as openly contrite as Diamantos Manos, owner of the *Rena*, appeared to be (Manos, 2011).

The long-term impacts on the lives of people and on Earth of events from Bhopal to *Rena* are still not fully addressed. The study of these examples indicates that corporates have invested much in defending their presumed or legally invented rights and many have frustrated environmentalists, employees and protesters by resisting responsibility. The countless hours of work contributed by hundreds of volunteers to remove manually the large patches and minuscule globules of oil from beaches and birdlife around the Gulf of Mexico and the New Zealand shoreline are only the most visible tip of the mobilisation of people, trained to do the job safely and effectively, not to spread the contamination. People were fed. Politics and media releases were managed. The clean-up efforts stand as a further testimony to the human capacity to act responsibly, collaboratively and without the assumed competitive, self-serving motivations attributed to humanity by the advocates of neo-liberalism under critique in this book.

From the waste-disposal issues of nuclear power generation to the much less obvious but perhaps equally risky flushing of hormones, chemicals and pollutants that each of us pours down our own domestic drains, to the widespread tolerance of industrial and agricultural processes, the use of heating and ventilating many of us seem to take for granted, the pollutants of travel, the surfacing of Earth with impervious materials, the destruction of ecosystems to support our energy requirements, we are all implicated in the abuse or the restoration of Mother Earth by our day-to-day choices and actions. Many of the graduates from management and law schools become the technicians who corporations employ to ensure that the needs of the business are met, first and foremost. Managers must manage the processes and the public perception of these processes. Accountants must provide the explanations of what is included in the costing of pollution, insurance, clean-ups and future liabilities. They make decisions about the illumination or fudging of subsidies. Lawyers are trained and paid to challenge or defend the activities of accused polluters in court cases that need clear causal evidence of the specific detrimental effects of particular processes in order for damages to be considered actionable.

While a supply-chain orientation may be useful in exposing demonstrable guilt, we argue that such a system of detection and prosecution will never be robust enough to meet the needs of a flourishing Earth. Denial of causal relationships and competition over whose rights should prevail are entwined with the interconnectedness of financial investments of states, insurers, pensions and profits. Greater traction in stakeholder theory, for example, has invited wider groups of interests to be considered in corporate and government decisions. In the case of Bolivia, Earth herself is given stakeholder rights. As attractive as stakeholder theory may be, however, the theory has some hard-to-get-over limitations. Competition for whose rights should prevail entails a conflict mentality that weakens its effectiveness (Weiss, 1995). Might these issues be better addressed through a prioritisation of a focus on responsibility rather than rights as suggested by Desmond Tutu in Chapter 1? To do so, we suggest, aspects of our leadership may need a mind-shift of Copernican dimensions! Who would take the responsibility to achieve such a mind-shift? The myriad of creative activities in eco-restoration projects suggests that the talent and the will exists in many communities – but that the forces that are being used to subjugate these energies also need our closest scrutiny and action.

Responsibility for the ecosystem is ours because it is ours. How we organise to enact this responsibility falls rightly into the realm of management education. We are individually and collectively responsible, and we individually and collectively will suffer or thrive, depending on how we manage the environment through our actions as managers, as consumers and as citizens. The expense and energy devoted to denying the causal effect of this or that process, or negotiating compensation for proven harm, do not of themselves transform toxic environments to thriving ones or prevent the further poisoning of air, water and land. And this anomaly in the strategy for sustainability is of crucial importance to every human being, every species on this Earth, and Earth herself. We are, as Mufasa knows, all connected in the great circle of life. The tolerance of polluting processes that may cause a yet-to-be-conceived baby to be deformed is not only a potential cost in pain and in expense, but an indictment of our potential as ethical beings. We each have a part to play in what we do, and what we fail to do, to address the serious environmental issues that confront humanity. The future is seeded in the actions of the present. Our individual and collective conscious and conscience must break free of the enclosures of our minds that have allowed the current situation to manifest or that inhibit new, creative and transformative responses from flourishing. In the next part of this chapter, we invite a deeper exploration of concerns about the environmental situation by inviting a reflection on life itself – embodied in seed, nurtured by water – both gifts of nature that have been appropriated and commodified, commercialised, sold and fought over, and may become the means by which we destroy the very life they generate.

# COMMODIFICATION OF WATER AND SEED: ENCLOSING LIFE

It is said that our bodies are made up of over 90 per cent water. The impacts of dehydration and rehydration can be seen in people who are in acute need of water whether they be hard-out athletes, critically ill people or victims of droughts, desertification and groundwater pollution. The power of water to restore life is evident in the rapid revival of a wilted Peace Lily with just a little water. It is visible in the power of the ocean in collaboration with robust sealife to restore water quality to desecrated coastal areas. Undeniably, water is necessary for all life. Water 'is able to combine with more substances than any other molecule and, flowing as water, sap and blood, it is the creator of the myriad of life forms on this planet … Ultimately their needs and their continuing health are as important as ours, and we neglect them at our peril' (Coates, 2001: 2–3).

The concern about the state of, and our attitude to, water expressed by Callum Coates is reiterated in the scientific literature associated with the technical purity of water, in Western organisational and political literature concerned with its management and control (often for commercial purposes), the needs of all people (and all species) to clean drinking water (increasingly cast in a 'rights'-based discourse), and now, emerging in the consciousness of the West, through the wider consideration of an ethos upheld by many indigenous peoples, the need (and the right) of Earth to her own hydration. At the deepest levels of consideration, water is life. Water is energy and has a destiny – as have all energies of the universe. Yet, in keeping with trends throughout the history of Western capitalism, the commodification of anything with (potential) commercial value applies to water also. Its destiny is harnessed to the interests of selectively privileged human beings, captured and fought over, serving the few at the expense of the many.

## FISHING THE ATLANTIC

The collapse of the Canadian Atlantic fisheries illustrates how government support for the expansionist motivations of private investors in fisheries often results in society at large being long-term losers. The profits from capital-intensive, hi-tech, industrial-scale fisheries are privatised by investors during the boom years, while the costs of such irrational economic behaviour are socialised for years after the crash. In Canada's case, a two-billion dollar recovery bill may only be a part of the total long-term costs. The human costs to individuals and desperate communities now deprived of meaningful and sustainable employment are staggering. The trauma suffered by some 40,000 workers and their families in Newfoundland cannot be measured in dollars and cents. (Greenpeace, 2009)

Vandana Shiva uses the concept of 'enclosure' (the limitation of freedom and the curtailment of diversity) to illustrate the impact of the globalisation of trade in the capitalist form intensifying the world over, particularly on the lives of the poor (Shiva, 1997). Modelled on the early enclosures of land in the UK (see, for example, *The Cheviot, the Stag, and the Black, Black Oil*: Pantheon, 2011), contemporary enclosures include the acquirement of land for private use, the formulation and selling of 'quotas' (be they fish, trees or carbon credits) and the culmination of this mentality in the capture and sale of knowledge, not only as we think of the intellectual property of mechanical inventions and stored in organisational techniques, but also as stored in the very genetic code of life. The knowledge and power embryonic in a seed is a great example to explore in this regard.

# SEED: THE CODE OF LIFE

Vandana Shiva teaches us about the concepts and impacts of enclosure and capture through the story of seed. A seed is life. A seed is nature. A seed holds all the knowledge of the 'plant-to-be'. A seed can thrive in favourable conditions or its fruition can be stunted, distorted or deformed. A seed can be manipulated by scientists with or without the backing of financiers and powerful interests. Shiva argues that, today, the knowledge and potential in seeds have been captured, enclosed in rules of ownership and use, and turned into commodities on which investors can gamble. Futures trading must be one of the more sophisticated gambling uses we are asked to accept as a legitimate mechanism of trade and exchange. The specifics of this story, the story of seed, is a story that entails the appropriation of seed from the original owners (peasant farmers) or their substitutions (new generations of contractors to corporate controlled growers), for processing in a cycle of appropriation and institutionalised dependency called free trade – a form of trade that is anything but free. Shiva argues that the process is controlled from start to finish by the giant corporations causing havoc, devastation, illness and death for many, while enriching the lives of few people. Shiva tells the enduring story of the commodification, sterilisation, patenting and re-issue of seed through the mechanisms of the trade system increasingly articulated as corporate neoliberal capitalism being intensified globally as discussed in Chapter 3. The story of seed, as Shiva tells it, is part of a bigger story about enclosure and the control of human, animal and plant reproduction. It is a story that is finding resonance among many activists for change.

## PLANTING FOR PEACE, POVERTY OR PROSPERITY

Wangari Maathai, a Kenyan environmentalist, began a movement to re-forest her country by paying poor women a few shillings to plant trees. Dr Maathai, one of the most widely respected women on the continent, wore many hats: environmentalist, feminist, politician, professor, human rights advocate. In 1977, she founded the Green Belt Movement which has planted more than 30 million trees in Africa and has helped nearly 900,000 women earn an income, while inspiring similar efforts in other African countries. She led the charge against a government plan to build a huge skyscraper in one of central Nairobi's only parks. The proposal was eventually scrapped. Not long afterward, during another protest, Dr Maathai was beaten unconscious by the police. She served as a member of parliament and as an assistant minister on environmental issues until falling out of favour with Kenya's new leaders and losing her seat. In 2004, she became the first African woman to win a Nobel Peace Prize. In 2008, after being pushed out of government, she was tear-gassed by the police during a protest against the excesses of Kenya's well-entrenched political class. 'Wangari Maathai was known to speak truth to power', said John Githongo, an anti-corruption campaigner in Kenya, who was forced into exile for his own outspoken views. 'She blazed a trail in whatever she did, whether it was in the environment, politics,

*(Continued)*

whatever.' In presenting her with the Peace Prize, the Nobel committee hailed her for taking 'a holistic approach to sustainable development that embraces democracy, human rights and women's rights in particular' and serving 'as inspiration for many in the fight for democratic rights'. Dr Maathai received many honorary degrees, including an honorary doctorate from the University of Pittsburgh in 2006, as well as awards, including the French Legion of Honour and Japan's Grand Cordon of the Order of the Rising Sun. In her Nobel Prize acceptance speech, Dr Maathai said that the inspiration for her work came from growing up in rural Kenya. She reminisced about a stream running next to her home – a stream that has since dried up – and drinking fresh, clear water. 'In the course of history, there comes a time when humanity is called to shift to a new level of consciousness,' she said, 'to reach a higher moral ground. We are at a time when we have to shed our fear and give hope to each other. That time is now'. (Gettleman, 2011)

# WATER: THE FLOW OF LIFE

The story of seeds, plants and the reproduction of life is also the story of water. To illustrate this point, we take water as our example for illustrative purposes through two explanatory sections:

1. Water! Captured, commodified, commercialised and contested
2. Remedies: rights, responsibilities and the resurgence of the spirit(ual) in accessing water

## Water! Captured, Commodified, Commercialised and Contested

Hard-to-process ideas are sometimes better learned from stories. David Boje (2008) provides many examples that can demonstrate the value of 'storying' to management students. We recommend that you browse his website for stories about Ronald McDonald and of the manufacturing processes of the many ingenious characters and gadgets to be found in McDonald's Happy Meals. Water must surely be a feature of these stories – from the growing of pasture in regions cleared of rainforests in order to meet the increasing preference for beef burgers and the supply of sugary drinks to the flushing of waste from factories.

In an example of a story specifically related to water, Susan George (1999) has crafted an evocative, semi-fictional report of an all-too-real (but fictitious) think-tank set up to protect capitalism from the growing crisis of water quality and access. By invoking the laws of diminishing returns, she illustrates the accompanying expansionism implied in an ontological commitment to growth as an indicator of progress (George, 1999: 108). *The Lugano Report* is written to alert a sleeping world of impending crisis. The story is based on dossiers of factual material. Fresh water, the report notes, 'is increasingly in short supply, and competition, not to say open warfare to secure it, is heating up between nations as well as between agricultural, industrial and individual users (George, 1999: 108–9).

> In the Chinese countryside, in spite of its disproportionately favoured position, tens of millions of peasants in the Northern provinces already suffer chronic water shortages ... Other countries, from Mexico to Algeria, are similarly affected. Waste and poor management contribute markedly to scarcity but absolute physical constraints bind ever more tightly. (George, 1999: 109)

What are some of the indicators of the shortages and maldistribution of access to water leading to conflict? George (1999: 109) writes:

> Aquifers are drying up. Fossil water under the US Great Plains is already half depleted. Once fertile land in Texas, Israel and India has been abandoned for want of ground water. In the former USSR, where the Aral Sea was drained in order to irrigate cotton, close to 3 million hectares have turned to salt deserts and can no longer be farmed ... from the Aral Sea fiasco to many of India's previously high-yielding Green Revolution areas, salt build up is common and destroys fertility. In the Sahel, at the behest of the World Bank, land once carefully tended under communal ownership has been privatised at bargain prices. Cheap land, the proximity of rivers and easy credit for irrigated rice growing have attracted get rich merchants using makeshift, no-drainage irrigation systems that can ruin tens of thousands of hectares in a season or two ...

Even a cursory examination of formal, scientific and statistical information shows this story to be more a trustworthy sketch of reality than a prophetic call.

The prior commodification of water is a prerequisite for the claim that private ownership and control of water is the most efficient means of managing water. While this is a highly contentious position, this concept has been well integrated into water management instruments. Among these are the powerful interests represented at the World Economic Forum at Geneva where privatised interests expressed through property rights were being furthered through the ever more popular rhetoric of public and private partnerships of all kinds. In this case, shared responsibility:

> for the management of watersheds from mountain ranges to coastal areas will improve the quantity and quality of water for business, populations, and the environment. (José María Figueres, Senior Management Director at the World Economic Forum, quoted in GreenBiz Admin, 2003)

> Reliable access to fresh drinkable water is one of the most important and fundamental issues for many communities ... I am pleased that Alcan can bring to bear its 101-year experience with the management of watersheds and water resources to enhance the availability of this precious resource ... (Travis Engen, President and CEO of Alcan Inc., quoted in GreenBiz Admin, 2003)

For Alcan's investors, distributors and customers, the commodification of water was already a given. What is being contested is merely the share or control of access and responsibility for security. A decade on, and we can see the trajectory of this conversation as history – and, as we do, become implicitly or explicitly embroiled in its future developments.

Characteristic of the 'capture', 'enclosure', 'commodification' and 'privatisation' of many of nature's energies, water, in capitalist economies, is now considered as a marketable resource. The articulation of water as a resource (rather than a gift or even the life-blood of nature) has been seized upon by some theorists concerned with the environmental costs of production. The threat to water as the source of life is being increasingly articulated as urgent. In this form of reasoning, the use of water in production is to be calculated into the costs of production widely conceived: transport, use/irrigation technologies, pumping and plumbing, and clean-up and flushing costs, for example. Meanwhile, others – potential distributors or managers of water, for example – are engaged in prioritising their rights to water as a source of income, or to honour a serious commitment to a perceived stewardship mandate. For many indigenous peoples, their ability to action their perceived guardian responsibilities for Earth is increasingly reliant on their capacity to access and argue through an ownership discourse, usurping great amounts of energies and funds in a form of reasoning that, in itself, runs counter to their preferred way of being in the world. Indigenous peoples are becoming increasingly active in stakeholder discussions (Humphries and Hurd, 2011) and vulnerable to ever greater state, police and military control – as exemplified in a number of the cases we explore on the companion webpages for this chapter.

### Warring over Water

Vandana Shiva opens her book *Water Wars* (2002) with a now famous claim made by the then Vice President of the World Bank in 1995: that future wars will be fought, not over oil as in the twentieth century, but over water. Shiva's response to this claim is that this cannot be read as a prediction of the future but as a description of what is already happening (Shiva, 2002: iv): 'as paradigm wars (conflicts over how we perceive and experience water) and traditional wars, fought with guns …' (and money). For a growing group of people this (threat of) war is exacerbated by the ownership and control of water by the few, protected and fuelled in their endeavours by the new trade rules, enabling a few to control the necessary life source for all humans, plants, ecosystems and Earth herself. This form of trade, in which water is both a means and a product, exemplifies the globalisation of neo-liberalism.

According to Shiva (2002), this system is a system of theft. It is a system that systematically encloses, captures, commodifies and exploits increasing aspects of nature (land, water, air, space and DNA), the social (relationships, knowledge, spirituality), the socio-biological (health, culture, human and social reproduction) and so on. Once established as legitimate, these commodities are traded at the global, national and community levels. Such trade may take many legal and illegal forms, and each form carries with it particular opportunities, risks and consequences. Diamonds, ores, logs and metals are just some material examples. Their harvesting, transport and conversion to marketable good are all water dependent. Owning and controlling water thus offers a significant market opportunity and, as such, will require a battalion of functionaries to serve these opportunities obediently.

A critical management orientation might respond to (i) the dangers of a commercialisation of water and (ii) Shiva's claim that water has been stolen, by exposing the shortcoming of the former and the extent of the latter if universal access to water is to be valued. Those with a more critical orientation may choose to work with those seeking to develop ideas of water stewardship that recognise our common dependence on access and quality. Examples of such scholarly activism can be seen in the work of Elinor Ostrom, awarded the 2009 Nobel Memorial Prize in Economics for her contribution to just water management (Tabarrok, 2009).

We invite two levels of moral enquiry:

1. The (il)legality of the processes currently assumed as good governance.
2. The ethical basis of the privatisation of water (a form of acquisition that might be considered a form of legitimised piracy).

There are many arguments that seek to tidy up the game of water management and control. These might be recognised in the work of numerous 'ethical' water companies. Among these are those who argue that, although the game has its dangers, it is the only possible game and we must learn to play it safely and put into position support systems for those who are excluded or hurt. Others argue that this remedial approach is a risky deflection of creative energy from seeking real alternatives.

If the current situation over the intensification of access to water through the market mechanisms are not to escalate what needs to happen? Two common responses are:

1. A rights-based solution dependent on a legalistic or socially binding articulation of rights, attribution of interests and responsibilities, and conflict resolution.
2. A modality based on a cosmological awakening, calling on a deep ecological ethic dependent on individual commitment (Rothenberg, 1993), and implemented by individuals and communities using whatever instruments they have at hand so long as these be non-violent.

As the population of the world continues to expand so too will the need for water. For increasing numbers of people on the planet, this water must reach the cities – for drinking, washing and flushing. Where water is sourced, for cities or rural areas, how it is channelled and managed, will provide a rich case-study for generations of management students to come. That these managers must be environmentally orientated there is no doubt.

How this environmental orientation is to be framed is always an open and contested question. Critical management education has much to contribute to the consideration of the latter, and there is nothing as practical as a good question asked close to home!

## Looking Close to Home

We introduced the unconscious or unwitting implication in various exploitations in Chapter 1 as a contemporary expression of what Hannah Arendt calls 'the banality of evil'. Insofar as our collective behaviour knowingly or unwittingly kills people through the destruction of their livelihoods, through the pollution of air and water that kills and maims, it might be argued, we have the conditions of genocide (Humphries, 2007). Whether the prevailing modes of trade and exchange systemically injure and kill is the question we raise in this chapter. We now critically review the idea that greater attention to human and environmental rights will provide the balance of power in accessing the many life-sustaining needs of humanity and the planet, and we introduce two more radical (or complementary) framings: (i) an ethic of responsibility, and (ii) an opening of a spiritual channel for an energy named love.

## Remedies: Rights, Responsibilities and the Resurgence of the Spirit(ual) in Accessing Water

Below we introduce three approaches that differ from a pure market orientation to water governance, restoration and protection:

1. Legalistic or socially binding rights-based approaches entailing an expensive and complex organisational machinery.
2. A prioritisation of responsibilities with challenges of who should take up such responsibility and how.
3. A Gaian approach to ecology and democracy.

We devote most space to the Gaian approach as the one perhaps least visible in management education, but perhaps the approach with the most radical potential.

## Rights-based Approaches

The World Economic Forum, in association with the United Nations Environment Program (UNEP), has launched a water initiative to create public–private partnerships to improve the management of watersheds:

> Public opinion appears to be clear about the urgent need to protect water resources. According to the results of a Gallup International survey, more than half the world's population believes that access to clean drinking water should be added to the list of basic human rights even if additional taxes would be required to ensure universal access. (Environmental Media Services, 2003)

The rights-based approach finds some exercise also in a special edition of *Resurgence* (2002, no. 214: 3) in which 'Earth Democracy' and 'Earth Justice' is posited to engage with the rights-based approach characteristic of the United Nations. We have discussed the downsides of the articulation, enforcement, protection and competition for the prioritisation of rights. We wonder whether there is more traction to be had by prioritising a focus on responsibilities rather than rights.

## Prioritising Responsibilities over Rights

Human beings are part of a 'woven universe' which is balanced and integrated in ways that are still far beyond human knowledge. Given the growing appreciation that human well-being is interdependent with Earth systems, a redefinition of responsibility is needed in order to extend personal responsibility in the present to collective responsibility for the future, argue Hoskins et al. (2011). The work of the Response Trust (2013) in the Pacific is focused on water harvesting, restoration and governance. As they have been going about their work, they have come across two very interesting and contrasting examples in neighbouring villages. Both villages are able to harvest sufficient water for their own needs: one is seeking entrepreneurial ways to on-sell; the other is willing to on-send but only if no one is making a profit. The overlaying of a prioritisation of responsibility as the predominant orientation of the governance and management of water invites deep reflection on how water is ontologically conceived. While market-driven relationships between humans have been argued to leave much to be desired if they are to be considered through any number of ethical frameworks, the human relationship with Earth certainly opens new vistas of thought if water is deemed a living relation.

## Gaian Ontology, Earth Democracy and a (Re)vital(ising) Ecosophy

The limitations of a rights-based approach to the governance and management of water and the hope invested in an orientation to responsibility are taken further by Satish Kumar (see the rich sources edited by Kumar at www.resurgence. org/magazine/issues.html). In inviting a more spiritual consideration of our being, he calls for a reconsideration of the many spiritual ideas secreted in myths and metaphors. It is not unusual to find many creationist stories that make Sky and Earth our first parents. Earth is our Mother and the source of life to whom we will return. There are a number of variations of this story in human history. In Hesiod's divine genealogy, for example, Gaia (the deity Earth) was the first parent. She mates with Uranus and gives birth to the Titans, the first generation of gods. Thus, even the patriarchal Greeks began their cosmology and creation with a female image (Bolen, 2001: 17). Christianity has posited a male creator – but still one who breathes life into matter – and shaped the male and female forms as intrinsic to the continuing process of creativity. It is in Christianity, however, that the female in the form of Eve is initially vilified but curiously redeemed in the portrayal of Mary, mother of Jesus. What are the creationist stories that inform your communities? What are the implied relationships between Earth and her creatures? Regardless of the mythical figures in each story, water is both vital to life and given a spiritual dimension in most parts of the world. It is only in Western economics that water is secularised, commoditised and diminished to its market value.

The whole world does not concur in the morphing of meaning from 'source of life' to 'market commodity'. Much of the world, however, is being pressed to comply with it. We are seduced or disciplined into believing that the privatisation of water is the most efficient and fair means for its distribution. Many hundreds of thousands of managers are being educated to manage the harnessing, marketing and selling of water. Many managers, accountants, financiers and insurers are involved. Of these, some are mandated to keep clean the water that they are made responsible for, others to purify the water that has become contaminated. PR specialists manage campaigns to promote and protect politicians and corporates. Activist groups manage programmes and projects that attract their passion. Each will have an explicit or implied idea about water: commodity, source of life or living entity.

Understanding their view of water is an important ontological exercise for all those who anticipate that the management of water will, in some way, be a part of their responsibilities. This responsibility may be framed as the person signing off the cheque for family water consumption or the boards of governors directing the sourcing and securing of water for their industries, corporations or nation-states. Can a deeper ecological orientation bring us to an ecosophy that may draw on the prevailing pragmatic, instrumental, rights-based approaches to environmental responsibility and call for a spiritual transformation of humanity closer together? As this ecosophical approach is at least explored in the management literature, we devote a little more space to its explanation and our link to the management fields. An ecological approach consistent with a Gaian approach to ecology and democracy entails a deep individualised ecosophy; a 'connect' with indigenous ontologies in which Earth is a Living Being who humanity needs more that she needs us, who requires respect for the gift of life she affords, demonstrated through a relationship of love – a relationship hard to argue for in materialistically oriented worldviews.

# ECOSOPHY, ECOLOGY, *ANIMA MUNDI* AND ME

I believe in three doctrines [says Irish Poet Yeats] ... (1) That the borders of our minds are ever shifting, and that many minds can flow into one another ... and create or reveal a single mind, a single energy. (2) That the borders of our memories are as shifting and that our memories are part of one great memory of Nature herself. (3) That the Great Mind and Great Memory can be evoked by symbols. (cited in Ronsley, 1977: 111)

The invitation to reflection on the concept of Gaia allows for connections between interest in social justice, economic sustainability and environmental stewardship. Chaos and chaordic theories of organisation in Western science are examples of how developments in physics may be ontologically much closer to the understandings of indigenous people the world over. The universe as a self-organising entity is explored in the work of Lovelock, Swimme and Berry. These ontological studies provide for a cosmological perspective of the *anima mundi* expressed through the Gaian deity and can be seen in the expression of all life – from the energies of rocks releasing gasses to the myriad expressions of animal and human life. The myth of the Garden of Eden may symbolise a memory of wholeness forgotten with the eating of the fruit of the tree of knowledge, drawing us into time and consciousness and now continuing to live inside us as the impulse to remember the state of union before dismemberment in time, for the memory persists in echoes and glimpses that cannot be explained and will not go away.

Water, as 'source of all life', has been associated with fertility and with a variety of 're-birth' rituals. Responsibilities for the relationship among all the creatures of Earth, framed as stewardship, or as rights for their use, and rules for their protection, distribution and care, are expressed in all human communities and, according to cosmologists, artists and mystics of all cultures, deeply expressed through the energies of the universe, the expression of *anima mundi*. Examples in the West include the work of the Irish poet Yeats, and perhaps mystically, the teachings of Jesus Christ to be found in the Gnostic Gospels of Thomas (the Doubter):

Cleave a (piece of) wood, I am there

Lift up the stone and you will find me there.

(Baring and Cashford, 1991: 545)

Expressed as *anima mundi* and as the 'Great Memory' by Yeats, as the Collective Unconscious by Jung and as the 'Sacred Hoop of the World' by Black Elk, renewed thoughts about our relationship with Earth and with each other may come from many sources of reasoning. These may include the Akashic records and Plato's knowledge as recollection (Baring and Cashford, 1991: 545–6). For many educated in the Western rationalism of business schools, these ideas may be too far-reaching or too far-fetched for any practical application. Where might we look to assure our rational minds that we have not lost the plot?

# GAIA MEETS SCIENCE MEETS GAIA

The peoples of the earth are being brought to the common table by the march of time.

Rakato Te Ragaiita

The Ancient People all agree on one thing: we are in the period of the Great Shift.

Christine Page

Page (2003) encourages us to become alchemists of the spirit and recognises many levels of awareness that may move humanity towards our energetic essence (2003: 14) – the vibrating energy source we know as consciousness. This is the energetic union with other sentient beings (2003: 30). She argues that the world as we know it is crystallised light or vibrating energy that 'has become organized into a particular configuration by the frequency of our consciousness or intention' (2003: 24). There is increasing convergence among the deep spiritual thinkers of animistic cultures, the major world religions, the findings of new cosmologists, mathematicians, scientists and of healers of many kinds. The ways of thinking evoked by the imaginary of *anima mundi*, as a life with a destiny of her own, appears in direct contradiction to the scientific traditions that now prevail. This way of thinking was thought to have been eliminated by the political and technical arms of the Enlightenment thinkers. The replacement of a spirit-filled world with one focused on a positivist materialism was achieved by the selective applications of the work of such thinkers as Bacon, Galileo, Descartes and others. Now a link is being forged between ancient cosmologies and emerging branches of physics. Page (2003) reviews the work of Fritz Popp who argues that wherever light travels, it takes on the memories of its experiences (2003: 38–9). Wehr (2002) invites us to reconsider photons as angels. At the densest form of light (materiality), when we eat food that still has a life force present, the light body of our DNA receives information for our well-being. Biophotons are articulated as messengers of consciousness. In the 1970s, for example, an experiment was carried out where two blood samples within glass containers were placed a little distance from each other. To one was added an agent that caused it to produce antibodies. Within moments, the second blood sample produced the same antibodies even though it had no contact with the original agent. However, when an opaque wall was placed between the containers, there was no cross-communication between the samples, strongly suggesting that light was the primary messenger of information (Wehr, 2002: 41).

Rupert Sheldrake's theory of 'morphic resonance' proposes that something learned by a particular species in one part of the world facilitates learning in another. This radically changes the interpretation of the world as inhabited by self-contained isolated units (Baring and Cashford, 1991: 670–80). It is from these radical ideas that critical management scholars can invite hope that the catastrophes projected from the current trajectories are not prophetic but cautionary and instructive.

Page (2003) argues that we exist within an ocean of undifferentiated potential or consciousness known as 'quantum hologram', a form of awareness being recognised by magneto-encephalograph recordings (2003: 6). These measurements record high-energy frequencies thought to be linked to extrasensory perception and intuitive insight. This energy becomes organised into patterns/ forms through the power of our intention or thought. The more conscious our intention, the more pure the form that is created. When we bring an idea into manifestation, we generate energy. We limit ourselves, however, to unconscious or poorly designed efforts, motivated by insecurity and short-term goals and limited long-term planning. But, she argues, we are being guided to a global consciousness that will bring greater peace. Rather than this wrinkle in the debate strengthening a case for the closed systems of deterministic evolutionary thinkers, a new way of understanding choice and learning emerges. From these scientific traditions, it is now possible for Bruce Lipton, a cellular biologist, to say that:

> [despite] the fact that for the past 50 years science has maintained that our fate was pre-programmed in our genes, it is now emerging that our external universe, internal physiology and more importantly our perception directly control the activity of the genes. (Page, 2003: 38)

It would seem that when we choose to invest a situation with love rather than fear, with hope rather than despair, we can change the energy waves, and with them the biological and/or social outcomes. These explanations may quicken in us a new interest in understanding the logics of cloisters dedicated to prayer and the contribution of those who meditate as a form of achieving peace not only in the soul of the meditator, but the world at large. What types of management education might be needed for such responsiveness to be normalised? Is the interest in the study of spirituality that is emerging in the Academy of Management and elsewhere a step in the right direction or an example of the further co-option and neutering of potentially powerful ways of thinking about our humanity? Is it a further deflection from the significant responsibility we each have to *be critical* or a timely caution about the interests being taken in spirituality in a context where water, body parts and life itself are deemed to be mere commodities at the beck and call of profit?

The shift in consciousness being called up by ancient peoples through their modern-day incarnations, psychics, mystics and scientists of many varieties is thought by some to be a manifestation of a shift by Earth, a vital being in her own right. Page argues that Earth 'is raising her frequency to join with other planets so that our solar system can take its place in the greater scheme of the galaxy and the Universe' (2003: 1–2). She argues that we have a choice, as individuals and as communities, to ease and facilitate this transition or not. Regardless, she argues, the transition is taking place. It does not need human approval. In this line of reasoning, Earth does not need humanity in the way humanity needs Earth. She may yet shrug us off!

Baring and Cashford (1991: 681) see as evocative the images of the new sciences. They review Bohm who argues that the 'Three dimensional world that we see is enfolded in an unmanifest implicate order', which is its ground. This ground is also called the 'holomovement', whose movement is a folding and unfolding, emphasising 'the unity of unity and diversity' and the 'wholeness of the whole and the part'. Once a vision of life as an organic whole is accepted in principle, humanity becomes in one sense a co-creator with nature, insofar as it can foster or ignore or destroy its identity with nature, for nature ultimately depends on the kind of consciousness we bring to bear on it. Remembering this knowledge, humanity can assume that original creative delight in nature as the greater form of itself. In the language of mythology, this is the sacred marriage of goddess and god. Baring and Cashford (1991: 251) conclude with the words of Chief Seattle:

> Will you teach your children what we have taught our children? That the earth is our mother? What befalls the earth, befalls the sons of the earth. This we know: the earth does not belong to man, man belongs to the earth. All things are connected like the blood which unites us all. Man did not weave the web of life, he is merely a strand in it. Whatever he does to the web, he does to himself.

If the Gaian deity is posited as the archetype of life, and her fruit in humanity can be expressed through the pantheon of creation expressed in the infinite generation of species, then Jung has much to tell us about the way in which rationally trained minds are likely to respond to a re-arrangement of human society based on Gaian principles. Fear, leading to denial, deflection, dismissal and destruction has been evident in the historical banishing of Gaia in the reach of the Enlightenment. This was expressed as witch killing in Europe (Burke, 1985; Bolen, 2001: 58) and the elimination of traditional spiritual leaders and healers in the indigenous cultures within the reach of European colonisation. But fear can also be a useful response. If faced with courage, there is nothing more galvanising for a parent than the fear that the water and food we provide for our children are unsafe and that the global unrest generated from the system of their production that we are supposed to trust is the source of violence. It requires a creative response if the tentative emergence of Gaia is not to release a violent response far outweighing the violence we now do to each other and to Earth in our grasp for water and the life-bearing processes it underpins.

Let us imagine that a Gaian water ethic will be established in this world and that the wisdom of the ancients might rekindle a sense of the holy preciousness of water. Unless such understanding overtakes humankind in the next few decades, and is acted upon, we threaten the very existence of the extraordinary and singular blue planet: Planet Water (Sale, 2003: 36). Using Gaian philosophy as a guide for thinking shifts our view from seeing water as a resource to be plundered and warred over, to the flow of our own source of life. We diminish it at our peril.

Beginning with the story of seed, or water or any of the commodifications discussed above (land, water, body parts, DNA, and even ideas in the form of commoditised intellectual property), allows us to deepen our understanding of the processes of creation, harvesting, manufacture, commodification, privatisation, consumerism and associated waste disposal to describe insight into their control and the price of that control. A critical management orientation invites investigations into the way that such control is exercised and managed, who is affected and how. With such a critical orientation, we can examine examples 'close to home' that may affect us and those who are dear to us. Corporations, entrepreneurs, states and NGOs are providing many examples and opportunities for innovation (see, for example, *Big Ideas for a Small*

*Planet*: www.sundancechannel.com). For some people, passion for the well-being of Earth may invite (perhaps tentative) forays into the deep ecology offered as an ethic of human survival through an improved relationship with Earth and all her creatures. Such an ethic may be framed in capitalist apologetics or perhaps generated from a more pragmatic utilitarianism that seems more commonplace in individual and corporate decisions (see www.justiceharvard.org/). Neither ethical framework may be far-reaching or robust enough for the issues at hand. Such passion may draw some into an exploration of the spiritual and cosmological consideration of Earth as *anima mundi*. While such an approach to a relationship with Earth is not news for indigenous peoples the world over, and spoken with consistency and increasing scientific support among a number of Western disciplines and theologies, this is a very new and unsettling development for many of us brought up to believe that Earth is a kind of mine, mill-pool or playground for our personal use; for those of us who believe Earth to be a set of materials to convert to 'resources' to claim and own, to exploit or sell as suit our personal desires. To think we cannot be otherwise is to relapse into a form of hopelessness which is a state of being serving the status quo – and not befitting a moral being. Such a tame or domesticated view of the future as an inevitable march of history is rejected by Freire (1994), who sees it as a view shared by reactionaries and revolutionaries of many kinds 'in which there is no room for authentic hope' (Freire, 1994: 101).

# HOPE! A SPIRITUAL VIRTUE AND A PRAGMATIC NECESSITY

We must not only increase public awareness about the challenges the world is facing in relation to water, but we must also change the way the water issue is perceived: from being a driver of conflict to being a catalyst for collaboration. (Klaus Topfer, UNEP Executive Director, quoted in GreenBiz Admin, 2003)

Vandana Shiva's stories of water and of seed are stories of resistance, of resurgence and of a deep commitment to an alternative future to the one associated with the meliorated trajectory of the corporate colonisation of our lifeworld, as Habermas (1990) and Deetz (1992) would express the current processes of economic predominance over social process and moral constraint. This inversion of economic principles and permissions from their direction *by* people to the direction *of* people by economic principles was noted by Polanyi (1957) as the first time this phenomenon has appeared in human history. Many are calling for its reversal. Competition is now posited as the motivational force deemed most productive in the neo-liberal worldview we introduced as the prevailing institutional knowledge in Chapter 1. Sometimes that motivation is linked to a shallow understanding of the work of Charles Darwin. 'Survival of the fittest' is perniciously harnessed to arguments that justify the failure of firms through competition, unless, of course, they are 'too big to fail' – as discussed in Chapter 3. Earth cannot sustain the continued pressure of this ideology.

Environmental considerations in this chapter have been focused on Earth and her vessels, her skin and her coverings, and the web of creatures that sustains the life of all. We hope we have illustrated that the environment cannot be considered without taking account of the social, political and economic environments, and, for some, the realms of angels, ancestors and light-bearers of all types. These need to be seen as one and the same, rather than discrete realms. All require management. All require a different management education from the one that has serviced these realms to date. We are challenged to imagine management as an art that does not universalise values, or that does not pit one set of interests against others to the point of destruction and even death. Who is to be responsible for crafting and certifying such an education? In the next chapter, we tackle the vexed issue of (good) leadership.

---

## Tricky Questions

Coral reefs are on course to become the first ecosystem that human activity will eliminate entirely from Earth, a leading United Nations scientist claims. Professor Peter Sale (2011) says this event will occur before the end of the present century. This means that there are children already born who will live to see a world without the beauty of coral.

- What are the important functions of coral reefs in the global ecosystem?
- What about marshlands, water-tables, oceans, rivers and streams?
- What would their loss mean to people who live close by these water features?
- What would their loss mean to people in your region of the world?
- What are the responsibilities of managers who manage the industries with direct impact on the reefs and/or other water features?
- What about the responsibilities of managers today, whose decisions which impact upon the environment will affect the lives of many close by and in distant regions, people alive now and people yet to be born?
- What difference would it make when we think of Earth as a 'living entity' rather than a 'resource to be mined'?
- How do various spiritual traditions explain the human relationship with Earth?
- The book of Genesis gives two images for human relations with Earth:

  1 dominion over (Genesis 1.28)
  2 stewardship of (Genesis 2.15)

- What are the implications of each of these interpretations? How would such actions differ if Earth was understood as a 'living relation'? How does this question illustrate the work of cosmology, ontology, teleology and epistemology initiated in Chapter 1?
- The insights of quantum physics are bearing witness to the wisdom of Mufasa – and the many spiritual traditions that venerate the 'circle of life'. If all is (nothing but) pulsating energy, what transformational potential might be found in this way of thinking?

---

## TALK BOX   SAVE THE LORAX – SHUN THE STUFF

'For more than forty years, the Dr Seuss classic [*The Lorax*] has been a clarion call for reducing consumption and promoting conservation. But the book's eloquent environmental message is being crushed by the film's slew of corporate cross-promotions.'

'The Lorax, who once spoke for the trees, now speaks for corporations. While he once warned how rampant greed and consumerism destroyed the Truffula Trees, he now sells Truffula Chip Pancakes at IHOP. The Lorax, who taught a powerful lesson about the fragility of ecosystems by describing the fate of the Brown Bar-ba-loots, Swomee-Swans, and Humming-Fish after their forest was destroyed, now welcomes consumers-in-training at Target, Pottery Barn Kids, and Whole Foods. His image is emblazoned on Seventh Generation diapers and packages of YoKids Yogurt. He's marketing HP in classrooms. And he's promoting Target, Comcast Xfinity, and more through online Lorax advergames and sweepstakes.'

*'As the real Lorax said,*

*UNLESS someone like you*

*cares a whole awful lot*

*nothing is going to get better.'*

(Golin and Linn, 2012)

# ADDITIONAL RESOURCES

Banerjee, S.B. (2004) Managing sustainability. In S. Linstead, L. Fulop and S. Lilley (eds), *Global Organizational Behavior and Management: A Critical Text*. London: Palgrave. pp. 151–81.

Beaver, R. (2013) Sacred seven grandfather teachings (http://ronniebeaver.myknet. org/; retrieved 12 September 2013).

Bello, W. (2002) *Deglobalization: Ideas for a New World Economy*. London: Zed Books.

Egri, C.P. and Pinfield, L.T. (1996) Organizations and the biosphere: ecologies and environments. In S.R. Clegg, C. Hardy and W. Nord (eds), *Handbook of Organisation Studies*. Newbury Park, CA: Sage. pp. 459–83.

Hines, C. (2000) *Localisation: A Global Manifesto*. London: Earthscan.

Lovelock, J. (2009) *The Vanishing Face of Gaia; A Final Warning*. Melbourne: Allen Lane.

Scanlon, T.M. (1998) *What We Owe to Each Other*. Cambridge, MA: Harvard University Press.

Sessions, G. (ed.) (1995) *Deep Ecology for the 21st Century: Readings on the Philosophy and Practice of the New Environmentalism*. Boston: Shambalah. Shiva, V.

(2011) *Earth Democracy* (www.youtube.com/watch?v=UOfM7QD7-kk; retrieved 12 September 2013).

Verbos, A.K., Gladstone, J. and Kennedy, D.M. (2011) Native American values and management education: envisioning an inclusive virtuous circle. *Journal of Management Education*, 35 (1): 10–26.

Whiteman, G. and Cooper, W. (2000) Ecological embeddedness. *Academy of Management Journal*, 43 (6): 1265–82. (http://www.youtube.com/watch?v=mF0dR1 XCNYQ&feature=youtube; retrieved 13 January 2014).

# REFERENCES

Balko, R. (2013) Texas police hit organic farm with massive SWAT raid. *Signs of the Times*, 18 August (www.sott.net/article/265078-Texas-Police-hit-organic-farm-with-massive-SWAT-raid; retrieved 4 October 2013).

Baring, A. and Cashford, J. (1991) *The Myth of the Goddess: Evolution of an Image*. London: Viking.

Berry, T. (2002) Rights of Earth: recognising the rights of all living beings. *Resurgence*, 214: 28–9.

Boje, D.M. (2008) *Storytelling Organizations*. London: Sage.

Bolen, J.S. (2001) *Goddesses in Older Women: Archetypes of Women over Fifty*. New York: Harper Collins.

Burke, J. (1985) The day the universe changed; worlds without end … (www.youtube.com/watch?v=7IH4iLhhL7k&list=PLCAED13C2CAFF5BE4&index=1&feature=plpp_video; retrieved 12 September 2013).

Coates, C. (2001) Water: the unifier of life. Paper presented at the Alliance Workshop 'Interbeing', Bangalore, South India, 19–23 June.

Deetz, S. (1992) *Democracy in an Age of Corporate Colonization: Developments in Communication and the Politics of Everyday Life*. Albany, NY: State University of New York.

Earth Open Source (2012) Monsanto ad claiming Roundup safety is misleading: Dutch commission, 31 December (www.nationofchange.org/monsanto-ad-claiming-roundup-safety-misleading-dutch-commission-1357003021; retrieved 4 October 2013).

Environmental Media Services (2003) Private sector takes action to improve watershed management. *APEC-VC Korea*, 12 June (www.apec-vc.or.kr/?p_name=newsroom&sort=NW&gotopage=744&query=view&unique_num=367; retrieved 12 September 2013).

Freire, P. (1994) *Pedagogy of Hope: Reliving the Pedagogy of the Oppressed*. New York: Continuum.

George, S. (1999) *The Lugano Report: On Preserving Capitalism in the 21st Century*. London: Pluto Press.

George, S. (2002) Another world is possible. *The Nation* (www.tni.org/george/articles/awip.htm; retrieved 12 September 2013).

Gettleman, J. (2011) Wangari Maathai, Nobel Peace Prize Laureate, dies at 71, 26 September (www.nytimes.com/2011/09/27/world/africa/wangari-maathai-nobel-peace-prize-laureate-dies-at-71.html?pagewanted=all&_r=0; retrieved 11 September 2013).

Golin, J. and Linn, S. (2012) Save the Lorax: shun the stuff. *Common Dreams*, 1 March (www.commondreams.org/view/2012/03/01-12; retrieved 11 September 2013).

GreenBiz Admin (2003) Private sector takes action to improve watershed management. *GreenBiz*, 5 June (www.greenbiz.com/news/2003/06/05/private-sector-takes-action-improve-watershed-management; retrieved 4 October 2013).

Greenpeace (2009) The collapse of the Canadian Newfoundland cod fishery, 8 May (www.greenpeace.org/international/en/campaigns/oceans/seafood/understanding-the-problem/overfishing-history/cod-fishery-canadian/; retrieved 11 September 2013).

Gummow, J. (2013) Massive SWAT team raid destroys organic farm. *Salon*, 20 August (www.salon.com/2013/08/20/massive_swat_team_raid_destroys_organic_farm_partner/; retrieved 4 October 2013).

Habermas, J. (1990) *Moral Consciousness and Communicative Action.* Cambridge, MA: MIT Press.

Hoskins, T.K., Martin, B. and Humphries, M.T. (2011) PRME as an ethic of relationality. *Electronic Journal of Business Ethics and Organization Studies* (special issue).

Humphries, M.T. (2007) Denial and the dance of death. Paper presented at the 23rd EGOS Colloquium. Beyond the Waltz – Dances of Individuals and Organization. Stream: Genocide, Individuals, and Organisations. Choices, Actions and Consequences for Contemporary Contexts. Vienna.

Humphries, M.T. and Hurd, F. (2011) The PRME: emancipator or oxymoron in the muddied waters of responsibility for life. Paper presented at the First Cr3 Conference, Hanken School of Economics, Helsinki, 9–10 April.

Hurd, F. and Humphries, M.T. (2010) Bringing faith to the master's table: Windsor Castle, Copenhagen, and the discourse of organisational/environmental spirituality. Paper presented at the 9th International Conference on Organizational Discourse: Crises, Corruption, Character and Change, Amsterdam, 14–16 July.

Lee, M.R. (2011) As Linkin Park joins UN on energy citing Haiti, no cholera or BofA coal answers. *Inner City Press* (www.innercitypress.com/linkin1park110811.html; retrieved 11 September 2013).

Levy, D. (2011) Environmentalism. In M.Tadajewski, P. MacLaran, E. Parsons and M. Parker (eds), *Key Concepts in Critical Management Studies.* London: Sage. pp. 108–13.

Manos, D. (2011) *Rena* ship owner 'deeply sorry' for oil spill. (www.youtube.com/watch?v=pcZSLPG3t44; retrieved 11 September 2013).

Miller, S. (2013) Spies and thugs for hire. *Open Salon*, 30 June (http://open.salon.com/blog/stuartbramhall/2013/06/30/spies_and_thugs_for_hire; retrieved 4 October 2013).

Moulden, J. (2008) *We are the New Radicals: A Manifesto for Reinventing yourself and Saving the World.* New York: McGraw Hill.

Ober, J. (2003) Gadfly on trial: Socrates as citizen and social critic. In A. Lanni (ed.), *Athenian Law in its Democratic Context* (Center for Hellenic Studies Online Discussion Series). Republished in C.W. Blackwell (ed.), D'mos: Classical Athenian Democracy (A. Mahoney and R. Scaife, eds, The Stoa: a Consortium for Electronic Publication in the Humanities; www.stoa.org/projects/demos/article_socrates?page=5&greekEncoding; retrieved 10 September 3013).

Page, C. (2003) *Spiritual Alchemy: How to Transform Your Life.* Essex: C.W. Daniel.

Pantheon (2011) *The Cheviot, the Stag, and the Black, Black Oil* (www.pantheon theatre.co.uk/2001/cheviot; retrieved 11 September 2013).

Polanyi, K. (1957) *The Great Transformation*. Boston: Beacon Press.

Response Trust (2013) Responsibility. Responses to new challenges: charter for universal responsibilities (www.response.org.nz/responsibility/; retrieved 12 September 2013).

Ronsley, J. (1977) *Myth and Reality in Irish Literature*. Ontario: Wilfred Laurier Press.

Rose, N. (1988) *Governing the Soul: The Shaping of the Private Self*. London: Free Association Books.

Rothenberg, D. (1993) *Is it Painful to Think? Conversations with Arne Naess*. Minneapolis, MN: University of Minnesota Press.

Sale, K. (2003) Planet Water: what we need today is a 'water ethic'. *Resurgence: A Time to Heal*, 219 (July/August).

Sale, P. (2011) *Our Dying Planet*. Berkeley, CA: University of California Press.

Shiva, V. (1997) The enclosure of the commons. *Third World Network* (www.twnside. org.sg/title/com-cn.htm; retrieved 11 September 2013).

Shiva, V. (2002) *Water Wars: Privatisation, Pollution, and Profit*. London: Pluto Press.

Tabarrok, A. (2009) Elinor Ostrom and the well-governed commons. *Marginal Revolution*, 12 October (http://marginalrevolution.com/marginalrevolution/2009/10/ elinor-ostrom-and-the-wellgoverned-commons.html; retrieved 11 September 2013).

Wehr, G. (2002) *Jung and Steiner: The Birth of a New Psychology*. Great Barrington, MA: Anthroposophic Press.

Weiss, A. (1995) Cracks in the foundation of stakeholder theory. *Electronic Journal of Radical Organisation Theory*, 1 (1): 1–15.

# 9 STUDYING LEADERS AND LEADERSHIP CRITICALLY

## Learning Objectives

In studying leaders and leadership critically, we can:

- ask if widespread compliance, tolerance, concurrence or trust in the leadership of capitalism is well placed;
- think about leadership studies within management education as a necessary or controversial inclusion;
- focus on how, in management education, leaders are recognised, selected and profiled, and how these profiles generate and inspire commitment to the prevailing institutional logic, values and goals;
- ask 'leadership for what?' in order to generate broader questions about 'good' leaders and leadership from the critical management studies orientation we are developing in this book.

## CRITICAL CONCEPTS

*Leaders* and *leadership* cannot be conceived without *followers*. The inclusion of leadership in management education is examined. We note the *paradoxical* preoccupation with attempts to maximise the impact of attractive leaders from within or outside the organisation who can harness the energies of followers. We are more interested in the paradoxical harnessing of both to *power*. Why paradoxical? *Critical leadership studies* is introduced to examine what it is to harness leaders and followers to serve the prevailing institutional logics of capitalism.

## STUDYING LEADERS AND LEADERSHIP CRITICALLY

Can management education generate leaders or inspire a form of organisational leadership that will generate critical engagement with and beyond the immediate needs of an individual's career interests, the needs and aspirations of a particular employer, or the development of particular industries and services? Can such an approach to leadership challenge and change the assessment and conduct of narrowly conceived notions of efficiency and the maintenance or intensification of a particular way of being that we have referred to as the institutional logics of capitalism or the *Zeitgeist* of the times? Can a more critically orientated education in leadership and management ensure generations of graduates willing and able to contribute to the transformation of the prevailing imperatives? To do so requires the belief that change is possible. This book assumes exactly that.

In the context of business schools, issues of leadership are often focused on corporate leaders such as Richard Branson, Bill Gates and Steve Jobs. However, studying leadership critically invites us to think well beyond the realms of corporate contexts. Hitler's sway over the people of Germany and Colonel Gaddafi's control of Libya provide dramatic examples of effective leadership and skilful management by these men and their administrations and by those who ultimately overthrew them. There are many more examples of effective leadership: Mahatma Ghandi's resistance to the British Raj; Mikhail Gorbachev's influence on the changing directions of Russia; Wangari Maathai's movement to re-forest her country through the Green Belt Movement; Nelson Mandela's leadership in the transformation of South African Apartheid; and Margaret Thatcher's influence on the direction of the UK, are amongst those we can learn from. Each person demonstrates leadership. All have required good management of their leadership and of the institutionalisation of their ideas for enduring impact. Their values and goals were not shared by everyone within their realms, yet they were able to command sufficient follower allegiance for significant periods. Resistance to their ideas took many forms and the legacies of their leadership and its resistance are varied. Barack Obama's leadership is worthy of close scrutiny. As president of the US, he is a man much admired and much to be feared as he makes good his promise to assure that America will remain 'number one' in the world (Pardo, 2011; Deen, 2012). What makes for effective leadership? Is effective leadership the same as trustworthy leadership? How do we recognise leaders and their potential to motivate and guide populations?

In this chapter, we invite reflection not only on the dramatic examples of leadership, but also on the everyday examples of the leadership and management of the organisations that collectively make up the dynamics of capitalism and democracy: of large and small businesses, of social enterprises, of government and community organisations, nations, cities, villages and families. All are groupings of people who must manage their collective activities. All provide the possibility for generating, nurturing or resisting leadership. All provide context in which emancipation and flourishing might be encouraged or inhibited, where compliance might be required, or where exploitation might be uncovered and transformed. The examples you might study are as varied as the people, places and epochs that draw your attention.

# LEADERS AND LEADERSHIP

Whether you find yourself interested in the power of charismatic leadership or drawn to the ethics of servant leadership is not what is at stake in critical management studies. How and towards what outcomes the paymasters and their managers practise their leadership can be argued to be of interest to all stakeholders. Where such leadership leads is what generates the real questions of interest in critical management studies. Is a decision, or a requirement, to follow a leader always a free and informed act of consent? Managers are paid to manifest the interests of their employers. Do they have an obligation of obedience and loyalty to their leaders? How have our discussions on the shaping of selves and places of work in the previous chapters prepared us for thinking about such questions? What of the sophistication of leaders who draw us so deep into their interests and their views of the world that we think we are acting of our own accord? What of the shaping of fear and need by skilful media that makes us vulnerable to the remedies of heroes?

Who are the leaders we admire? How can such leaders be attracted and controlled in the interest of the firm, the industry or the nation? What effects do they appear to have on their followers? Do followers have an impact on the shaping and effectiveness of the leader? What risks do marketers take when they brand their organisation or product through popular sporting heroes such as Tiger Woods or Lance Armstrong whose personal choices subsequently become corporate liabilities? What of the credibility of leaders whose decisions in private life bring public disgust and tarnish institutional credibility? We need not look further for practical examples than the widespread sex scandals associated with the various churches, as parish leaders and their 'higher-ups' deny or deflect responsibility for the abuse of many of their loyal followers. The leadership of these and other institutions who see themselves as a moral vanguard is compromised when their representatives in the field fall short of acceptable behaviour. This is illustrated through the widely condemned participation of UN staff in the trafficking of women (see Owen, 2011) and in the perhaps unintentional pollution of water associated with a cholera outbreak in Haiti (Lall and Pilkington, 2013). The behaviour of staff is one matter; the institutional response is another.

Behind the questions about specific leaders and their forms of leadership is a deeper, largely unanswered question: are leaders born or made? John Kenneth Galbraith frames this as a question of pinpointing the 'essence' of leaders. For him, an essential characteristic of leaders is their courage to address the uncertainties of their times (Heathfield, 2013). Some of our examples above show that, by their very status and influence, leaders can bring opportunities for the achievement of great good or widespread harm.

Questions about the nature and consequences of leadership have been enduring. The Western academy that informs much management education has been hard at work on these questions. In this context, the work originates largely in the positivistic research generated from the US after the Second World War on the coat-tails of its perceived contributions to victory in this war, and to the restoration of the many places devastated by it. The focus has been on how the understanding of leadership so effective in winning this war might be harnessed to improving organisational efficiency or effectiveness framed largely in financial returns. These heroic notions of leadership are coming under increasing review even in mainstream management education. Do the questions now asked in management education go deep enough, however? Are these questions alerting us to the possibility that we may be duped into believing that we are on a trajectory to enlightened human development and environmental restoration through the intensification of neo-liberal principles and the imposition of democracy worldwide? We briefly review the controversy about the inclusion of leadership studies within management education, and some of the perspectives on leadership typically included. The main focus of the chapter, however, is on the questions that might be generated from more critically orientated perspectives. The emergence of critical leadership studies is one area of the academy where related research is being encouraged.

## LEHMAN BROTHERS: FROM LEADERSHIP TO BANKRUPTCY – AND PAIN FOR MANY

On 15 September 2008, the venerable investment banking firm Lehman Brothers filed for bankruptcy protection after the Federal Reserve and the Treasury Department pointedly refused to bail the company out, and no other Wall Street firm was willing to step into the breach. It was the largest bankruptcy ever in the US, but the really big news was what happened afterwards. First came a financial panic that threatened to shatter the global capitalist order; then came an unprecedented, and expensive, effort by governments on both sides of the Atlantic to patch things up (Fox, 2009).

What were the real costs of this case? Who led? Who followed? Who led the exposure? Who listened? Who suffered unfairly? Who will lead the restoration of trust in the financial system? Will such trust be deserved or is there a risk that such trust in the current system of capitalism (no matter how amended) is misplaced – no matter how sincere the leaders may be? Who are the thought-leaders for a more radical review of 'the system' and who are following in their wake? How can we assess the potential answers to such questions when even the most expert in leadership studies, economists, organisational theorists and ethicists cannot give us definitive answers about the shaping and effectiveness of leadership, let alone its moral compass. Where do such questions direct our attention?

Critical leadership studies is an emerging field, and we demonstrate how the issues of leadership and followership considered from such a perspective may usefully inform a more critically oriented management education.

Klaus Schwab, founder of the World Economic Forum, argues that there has been widespread loss of trust in the very veracity of the current form of capitalism and its leadership. Schwab, now famous for initiating the meetings of powerful leaders in Davos, believes that the established leadership models are not up to the job of guiding the world out of its current mess. In attending the opening event of the 2012 meeting, he said:

> Capitalism, in its current form, no longer fits the world around us ... We have failed to learn the lessons from the financial crisis of 2009. A global transformation is urgently needed and it must start with reinstating a global sense of social responsibility ... Many people have lost trust in leadership and increasingly perceive life primarily in terms of hardship. The question is: what can we do and what should we do? (Allen, 2012)

According to Schwab, a new system of leadership would share more power, encourage greater religious tolerance and create more sustainable jobs, while removing income inequality. These are radical aspirations. How would they be played out? How can we trust the system that explicitly endorses a dynamic of competition even where this dynamic can be shown to destroy freedom and even kill those who get in the way? The questions of trust asked in the management literature appear to remain at a more superficial level. We will deal with some of the practical implications of lost trust in leadership before we return to the deeper questions of the trust we are asked to vest in capitalism and in democracy as leading humanity to freedom, security and peace.

# THE COST OF TRUST LOST

- Toyota was once an icon of the car industry. After a series of vehicle recalls, the reputation of the company was seriously damaged.
- The Roman Catholic Church dealt inadequately, in the eyes of many, with allegations of sexual abuse by clerics.
- Nike and Gatorade, sponsors of golf celebrity Tiger Woods, saw as much as $12bn wiped off the value of their shares in the wake of the sex scandal around Mr Woods.
- The EU countries, the European Commission and the IMF had to build an unprecedented financial package after financial markets lost trust in Greece, Portugal and Spain. (European Leadership Platform, 2010)

In the opening decades of the twenty-first century, business leaders, especially bankers, appeared to have lost their public status. Of course, Toyota and the Roman Catholic Church are not the only institutions needing to recover their leadership credentials. Might the unfortunates who have been named to wear this badge of untrustworthiness be more instructively seen as examples of the systemic failure of humanity to invent and manifest social and economic frameworks that are respectful of all people and planet and a leadership that endorses this? There are signs that a greater number of people are willing to ask such questions. Our concern in this book is with the potential of management education to contribute to this awakening and, in this chapter particularly, to explore the potential of a more critically focused leadership studies. Behind our engagement with the literature sits a question about the dynamic of 'being led' by not only the skilful and well-resourced media experts but also those with leadership qualities associated with spiritual leaders. The philosopher-cum-mystic Lao-tsu is an example:

> To lead people, walk beside them … As for the best leaders, the people do not notice their existence. The next best, the people honour and praise. The next, the people fear; and the next, the people hate … When the best leader's work is done the people say, 'We did it ourselves.' (Lao-tsu, see Heathfield, 2013)

Does Lao-tsu make a virtue of manipulation? When applied to the processes of self-management in organisations that will easily expel you at its convenience, such surreptitious leadership may be the ultimate form of hegemonic control. Mindless followership, of leadership in 'good business', 'workplace change', 'the management of diversity', 'technological remedies to environmental crises' or 'invitations to consumption' may be as dangerous as following leaders into religious zealotry, self-serving wars or corporate raiding. Not to be at risk of such brainwashing requires a disciplined mind.

A disciplined mind is not the same thing as a subjugated mind. Yet, as we have argued throughout this book, the contemporary discipline of populations as a form of subjugation through the co-option of spirit, body, culture and community to a narrow notion of development might be very difficult to notice. How embroiled are we all in the processes and practices that serve the interests of the few at the expense of the many and puts at risk the planet that sustains us? Is it possible to be led or to be managed, or to be controlled by an idea, a worldview, a *Zeitgeist*? Can we retain notions of ourselves as decent people when we reject or diminish personal responsibility for the cumulative outcomes of individualised preferences, choices and self-actualisation associated with the dogmatic imposition of neo-liberalism? These questions raise deeper questions about our trust in, or abrogation of responsibility for, the systems by which we organise our humanity. The most widespread of these systems intensifying globally are the systems of capitalism and democracy and the focus of this book.

The idea of leadership and management, of following or of merely participating more or less mindlessly, are as entwined together as they are implicated in notions of power and control of the past, the present and the future. How the relationships of leaders and managers with those they lead or manage manifest in practice is of vital significance to individuals in their organisations and their wider communities. How the cumulative effects of these relationships form the world of the future has implications well beyond the well-being of present generations. How we each navigate our lives, balancing opportunities for ourselves and the care of those we love or have been given responsibility to care for, how we understand the effects of our way of being on the system of life cannot be taught as an equation to be repeated in an exam. It requires the cultivation of emancipated minds and social contexts that celebrate their expression – be that in the place of work, the home or the wider context we call civil society. The shaping and discipline of our economic activities, we argue, must be led by such minds – not the reverse. Should such considerations be part of management education? Some suggest that leadership and governance ought to be treated as discrete fields of study. Not all agree.

# STUDYING LEADERS AND LEADERSHIP IN MANAGEMENT EDUCATION: WHAT'S THE FUSS?

Most texts prescribed for management students will include a section on leaders and leadership. John Kotter is a much-quoted researcher on management and leadership. He had this to say about the relationship between leadership and management:

> Successful corporations don't wait for leaders to come along. They actively seek out people with leadership potential and expose them to career experiences designed to develop that potential. Indeed, with careful selection, nurturing, and encouragement, dozens of people can play important leadership roles in a business organization. But while improving their ability to lead, companies should remember that strong leadership with weak management is no better ... The real challenge is to combine strong leadership and getting strong management and use each to balance the other. (Kotter, 1990/2011: 37)

As the repercussions of the financial crises of the first decade of the twenty-first century continue to ripple out, the leadership and management of some of the most trusted organisations in the capitalist world are now under the microscope. Bankers, investment brokers and financial advisers of many kinds are under deep scrutiny, as are law-makers, the governors of institutions, the formal bodies that are mandated to assure professional practice or quality of production or process and the teachers (or systems of education) who have educated the generation of leaders who appear to have got the world in such a predicament. Educating a more responsible leadership has become intrinsic to the call for greater corporate social responsibility.

Henry Mintzberg is another prominent voice in the management academy. With the origins of this most recent and continuing financial crisis initially attributed largely to bad practices in the US on his mind, he had this to say:

America has much rebuilding to do, beyond bailing out its largest, sickest companies. Many businesses will have to be restored as communities, which to my mind means from the middle out, not the top down. Being an engaged leader means you must be reflective while staying in the fray – the hectic, fragmented, never-ending world of managing ... (Mintzberg, 2009)

The origins and implications of the crises for finance coming to light towards the end of the first decade of the twenty-first century will continue to exacerbate the crisis facing humanity if we allow it to be so. This latest crisis for finance, however, did not start with and will not end through remedial activities in America alone. The global reach of Western ways of thinking and doing that we have examined closely in this book are deeply implicated and they are under increasing scrutiny. In our adaptation of Thornton and colleagues (2012), we call these prevailing ways of thinking and doing as the institutional logics of the system of globalisation we refer to as neo-liberalism. One response to this crisis is to patch up the system of thinking so it can continue as one would repair a broken vehicle for which there seems to be no replacement. Another response would be to turn our minds to whether a completely new way of being might yet be invented. Such possibilities must be generated by leadership in ideas and perhaps different leaders for their dissemination. These ideas may come from anointed leaders or leading minds anywhere in the universal thought-scape. How would we recognise such ideas as 'good ones'? How would such ideas be brought into consideration and managed into practice? Even the most creative ideas will not manifest into reality without effective leadership and sound management.

With the notion of the necessary interdependence of leadership and management in mind, this may also be the place to cast our mind to the notion of governance, the consideration of which, like leadership, has been given a realm of its own in the academy and in practice. It has become common wisdom to separate the functions of governance from those of management. This separation invites a reflection on the mindlessness of managers (as employees) and of employees (in general) as feeling obliged or constrained merely to implement the directives of their governors – be they politicians, boards of directors or trustees or a business owner. Where and under what conditions would we tolerate such control over our lives? The newest entrants to armies are required to obey mindlessly, and so up the ranks, so that when an instruction from the leader is sent – all will obey. Scope to interpret the means of doing so is entirely dependent on rank. Are the employees of the world (managers included) merely to be thought of as foot soldiers, cannon fodder, expendable privates in the army of the powerful? It is to these questions that the work of critical leadership and management studies and the study of the leadership and responsibilities of governors bring transformational insight.

## ASSESSING A UNION LEADER: PERSPECTIVE IS EVERYTHING

Andy Stern '(mis)leads' the Service Employees International Union (SEIU). Critics charge that:

> the president of SEIU, Andy Stern, is leading the union into becoming a business union, where the union and the bosses that they face try to work out a common approach. This is different than the way unions have made gains throughout history. Class struggle unionism is what workers need, where the union recognizes that the workers and the capitalists have different interests, fights hard for the workers' felt and urgent needs, and negotiates the best contracts possible based on the current strength of the workers. (Iosbaker, 2008)

Stern's leadership is seen quite differently by others:

> Under Stern's leadership, the SEIU commonly bullies and pressures companies into signing agreements to make SEIU the representative of their employees. If a company resists joining the union, Stern and his political, media and activist allies conspire to launch corporate campaigns aimed at breaking down that resistance through what they term the 'death of a thousand cuts'. In such campaigns, the cabal of attackers harasses and disrupts company activities, sends vicious emails and letters to stockholders, intimidates customers, stalks and frightens employees, files baseless lawsuits, and plants false stories with media allies to smear the company's reputation. These pressure tactics are often successful in bringing companies into SEIU's fold. When this occurs, all of their employees are required to join the union. SEIU prefers this arrangement (which Stern calls 'Union Democracy') because, in times past, a large percentage of workers who were given a choice voted against joining the union. (Ponte, 2004/2012)

Whose perspective of Stern's leadership would you trust? Why?

Taking at face value that participation and inclusiveness is an intrinsic value of democratic societies, that autocratic leadership and blind followership is inconsistent with espoused notions of universal emancipation, and that emerging imbalances of power require institutional remedies, why should businesses, governments, unions, churches or any collective activity be entitled to control the behaviour of its members – overtly or, as we have explored much more closely in this book, through the myriad of ways compliance is surreptitiously achieved? Does being paid give the paymaster the right to command and expect fealty and silence – no matter what? Karl Marx assumed not: 'workers of the world unite' is not just an empty slogan as those paying attention to Andy

Stern's leadership of the Service Employees International Union (SEIU) would recognise and the politicians in southern Europe are struggling to control. Investment banks, business owners and governments (who can give directions to police and sometimes armies) have not refrained from exerting overt and covert power when compliance or hegemonic control of workers breaks down. In previous chapters, we have given many examples of both forms of control. The hanging of Ken Saro-Wiwa and his fellow activists and the shooting of miners at the Lonmin Marikana site in South Africa could be seen as two examples of the system defending itself with violence. The more subtle breaches of trustworthiness by leaders of the prevailing order are more difficult to expose.

## SIDEWALK LEADERSHIP: CHALKING UP RESISTANCE

*San Diego*: 'Activists are standing behind a North Park man charged with 13 counts of vandalism for using chalk to scribble anti-bank slogans on city sidewalks. Dozens gathered Saturday outside the Hall of Justice to protest the prosecution of Jeff Olson' (ABC 10 News, 2013). Some citizens are angry that tax-payer money is being squandered on what seems like a very trivial offence. The court systems everywhere are jammed with unheard cases of much dire consequences. Our judges are mandated to keeping order. Whose order(s)?

The contest and the context of the struggle to find greater balance in the relationships of justice, including those within employment, have a fraught and sometimes bloody history. Skilful leadership has been intrinsic to the transformation of the conditions of employment in both directions – for and against the improvement of the conditions of service in the capitalist system. To make a difference to the issues we have raised in this book thus requires good leadership and sound management, no matter whether the people are deemed leaders or managers, or where in the system they are located. But whether such leaders and managers are born to lead or manage, or whether anyone can be trained to lead or manage, has been an enduring question with few reliable answers. Whether one believes leadership and management can and should be considered as two sides of the same coin or not, leadership is an appropriate topic of investigation for those studying management. How such leadership is recognised, encouraged and rewarded are just some of the applications researchers and writers have attended to – whether they have recorded anything but their own projections is a matter to which we will return.

# RECOGNISING LEADERS

The leadership literature in management education covers a range of assumptions that can be considered separately or together: (i) leaders are born not made; (ii) leadership is a generic quality of people and can be nurtured in anyone.

## Leaders are Born not Made

This proposition invites the questions:

- How do we recognise (naturally gifted or divinely anointed) leaders in all their variety?
- How can an organisation benefit from their potential by ensuring their leadership style is compatible with the community to be led?
- How can we attract such leaders to the organisation, motivate and retain them, while also making sure that they lead in the desired direction?

## Leadership is a Generic Quality of Individuals

If potential leadership and followership are qualities of people (just like the potential to walk upright, learn to count or to think deductively), given the right encouragement desired leadership behaviour can be instilled or trained into a person. This proposition invites the questions:

- Can the specific characteristics of desirable leadership be isolated and trained into employees?
- How can we identify people who have more of such leadership potential than others?
- How can a person be trained to be a leader, yet be controlled to ensure the security of the employing organisation?

Each way of thinking about leadership has provided a large volume of empirical research. The preferred theory is often illustrated by an example of a person who appears to embody it. It is inspiring to read stories of heroes who have led people through struggles and adversity to victory or success – often against all odds. A lot of research hours have gone into isolating the specific characteristics of such recognised leaders and to try to understand what characteristics they may have in common. Goleman (1996/2011: 1), for example, reports that the most effective leaders are alike in one crucial way. He reports that all have a high degree of what has come to be known as 'emotional intelligence'. This intelligence may be exhibited in a wide range of personality traits. Drucker (2004/2011) brings a note of caution to the appeal of attractive personalities. He writes that leadership is not just a magnetic personality:

> as that can just as well be a glib tongue. It is not 'making friends and influencing people', that is flattery. Leadership is lifting a person's vision to higher sights, the raising of a person's performance to a higher standard, the building of a personality beyond its normal limitations. (Drucker, 2004/2011: 23)

Drucker's observations appear to support the finding that personality traits may not be the defining factor of a leader. While the leaders he worked with were 'all over the map in terms of their personalities, attitudes, values, strengths, and weaknesses', it was their behaviours that were the notable hallmarks of their leadership. Two of these behaviours related to ensuring that they were well informed, four were about converting knowledge into effective action and the last two 'ensured that the whole organization felt responsible and accountable' (Drucker, 2004/2011: 24).

Conceptualising and categorising leadership traits and behaviours (born or bred), and matching those with assumed personal demonstration of these traits (perhaps modified with situational considerations), is a big industry. The disciplinary effects of this science of leadership in system-preserving power lie in the very way the concepts and constructs are generated. A nice fit can be sought. Typical of all such investment (of money and meaning) assumes that these findings can be put into some equation with similarly identified characteristics of followers. Add the characteristics of the context, and spin the calculator, to produce a recipe for some desired outcome: productivity, happy workplaces, faith in the economy. The many disagreements and contradictions in the findings of positivist researchers should alert our critical attention to such truth claims.

Although still very prevalent in the way in which organisations seek to find and nurture leaders, the shortcomings of this type of research can now be found in a number of regular management texts. The feminist author Marta Calas (2013), for example, brought attention to the way in which concepts of leadership had been framed in very masculine and heroic terms. These terms were recognised, valued and promoted at the expense of more feminine and collaborative qualities. The debate initiated by Calas opened new opportunities for some women either by exposing to view the leadership traits apparently valued by organisations so that they could be emulated, or by finding opportunities in organisations more willing to engage with what were soon to be dubbed 'feminine leadership styles'. From this development, we now have the varied images of 'Iron Ladies', 'Queen Bees' and 'Office Wives and Mothers' to set alongside the many other images of leadership in management texts.

From the critique of the post-Second World War preoccupation with heroic male leaders, new genres of leadership studies were generated. It opened the possibility of considering the many styles of leadership that might be harnessed to achieve the desired outcomes – some of which appear more compatible with gendered, cultural or religious stereotypes than others, some of which are more sensitive to time and place than others. Students of leadership can now be asked to recognise, compare and contrast the dynamics and impact of many leadership styles, the supposed effects of context and history, and how the harnessing of each of these forms of leadership in the service of institutional aspirations can be assessed as effective. What thus came out of the early challenges to narrow notions of leadership, and the way leadership energies might be harnessed to institutional aspirations, was a more malleable notion about the qualities of leadership, about where they might be found and about how they might be deployed and enhanced.

The realisation that leadership can take many forms and is intrinsically connected to organisational management has had significant impact on the extent to which the various leadership qualities could be harnessed to institutional control. The feminine traits, for example, came to be seen as more compatible with the employee empowerment movement because women were (stereotypically) seen as (naturally) more inclusive and less hierarchical. Through harnessing their more collaborative practices, hierarchies could be reduced – as could the expense of layers of management. The pyramid of power and control (and of career opportunities for some) could be reduced.

Foucault's notions of power as more diffuse are harder to detect. Despite Foucault's critique of hierarchical power, power remains disproportionately vested in the top – or at the core – if we use Atkinson's (1984) model of workplace change presented in Chapter 4. There we demonstrated that collaborative, relational leadership styles, whether practised in factories or service organisations, were soon harnessed to serve the preservation of the status quo by having employees discipline themselves and their peers to ensure corporate targets were met. What were promoted as employee empowerment schemes, and served for a while to open career opportunities for women, could soon be demonstrated to be an active attack on the power of unions.

As the effectiveness of a more feminine style in leadership and management became evident, men were increasingly encouraged to reach for their feminine side in their range of leadership qualities. The realisation that leadership traits might be learned, enhanced, spiritually guided or implanted seems to settle the apparent(ly false) nature/nurture divide: some women could and did measure up on heroic indicators, and many men could exhibit the qualities once assumed to be feminine and turn them to good career advantage. In the management of institutions, leadership orientations seem to be a matter of recognising and grooming values and their expression to meet the interests, preferences and needs of employers – be that in Richard Branson's entrepreneurial world or in traditional bureaucracies that still define large institutions such as universities, hospitals, government departments and many factories.

John Kotter (1990/2011) implies that leadership qualities are quite universal and open to training and development. The literature based on assumptions such as these is vast. It entails the selection of the qualities to be recognised and how these can be enhanced. Leadership studies of this type found in management education include the naming and measuring of qualities, traits or characteristics of people who are recognised as leaders and the people, situations and outcomes that such qualities, traits and characteristics might influence. Typical focus in management education is concerned with identifying the characteristics of leaders/leadership and of followers, matching styles with context, recognising nascent leadership potential and instilling or enhancing particular leadership qualities in employees (as managers or team-members). There are many examples of management textbooks that review leadership in or of organisations, and much more material of this kind is now easily found online. More serious students of leaders and leadership can tap into the specialist journals on the topic. These, too, are readily available online to students enrolled in university-based management programmes. A plethora of books on leadership, its significance to organisational success, how to be a leader, or how to know or develop them, can be found in any good general bookshop or airport book stand. Leadership remains a topic of interest within management studies and beyond.

The *Harvard Business Review* undertook a search of the leadership material and provides a *10 Must Reads on Leadership* (2011) for aspiring leaders. It has selected 'only the most essential readings ...'. This little volume provides a good sketch of the history and emergence of interest in leadership as an essential topic for management studies. 'Leaders looking for the inspiration that big ideas provide, to accelerate both their own growth and that of their companies, should look no further ... [providing] timeless advice that will be relevant regardless of the ever changing business environment...'. These articles will (purportedly) inspire the reader to a leadership that will:

- Motivate others to excel
- Build team self-confidence
- Provoke positive change
- Set direction
- Encourage smart risk-taking
- Manage with tough empathy
- Credit others for your successes
- Increase self-awareness
- Draw strength from adversity

(*Harvard Business Review's 10 Must Reads on Leadership*, 2011: cover blurb)

There are 19 named authors in this book. Sixteen of these are men; three are women. We cannot see the ethnic origins of each author, but the list of their institutional affiliations include ten US/UK-based universities, a UK and a US consulting firm and a former New York Citigroup executive. Harvard is perceived as a leader in the publishing of material read the world over as 'authoritative' with significant influence on what is generated as knowledge to be taught about leadership.

According to the thread of the literature on leadership that begins with the supposition that anyone might be called on to be a leader, and that we can each, to a greater or lesser extent, carry such responsibility when the need arises, managers are expected to show leadership in a variety of ways. So are team leaders and individuals in all kinds of situations. In this broadened way of thinking, leadership is not so much vested in a rather unique person. It is seen as an inherent quality of humanity. Can we trust the data?

# POSITIVIST DELUSIONS OR SCIENTIFIC ALCHEMY?

The search for simple causal relationships between certain types of people and the successful implementation of ideas or practices has been a hallmark of management education. It would be most useful if ideas about cause and effect could assure predictable outcomes in the management of people and processes of production and consumption. At first glance, it may seem that science has been leading us in that very direction. Studies of effective leaders in or of organisations, the effective team leadership in the processes of production, the market-morphing effects of leading brands in industry development, and industry, sector or stakeholder leadership in local, national and international realms of interests are examples of the way leadership has become entwined in management education. Rather than uncritically supporting the positivist project of seeking ever tighter predictability and control through assumed understanding of the complex combinations of people and contexts reduced to a ready reckoner, we are more interested in how the science is used to create reality. Many studies support the general project of educating a class of people to see themselves as leaders or as managers of organisations, investing in them, measuring their attributes and matching them with contexts. Other groups of people are reminded that their purpose in life is to do the menial work of society, to accept peripheralisation or even permanent redundancy (see Figure 9.1).

**Figure 9.1**   Delusional leadership

*Source*: Black (2013).

We represent a reminder of our station in life not as a self-fulfilling prophecy but as a subtle tolerance of the discipline of hierarchical societies in which the exclusion of some is justified in the doctrine of merit. A further complexity we find in the existing literature entails the debates about whether leadership and management of business can lead or learn from leadership or management as it has been developed in and for other sectors or vice versa. There are many examples with local impetus and impact, driven by entrepreneurs or policy-makers seeking to redress the urgent situations in their country, city, neighbourhood or family. Their motivation may be the poverty of the people around them, the quality of water or soil on which they must depend, or some personal experience of injustice or injury. These kinds of controversies invite new lines of reasoning – but lines of enquiry that are remarkably similar in their mind-set. Our very preoccupation with overly simplistic causality and the rush to impose best practice based on the most convincing currently popular story may be short-changing the creativity of humanity.

Pertinent to the orientation of this book are the discussions about the extent to which business leaders *should* be encouraged to lead to remedy the many issues facing humanity. It is in this field that we see the burgeoning work of various global (and local) responses by business leaders, activists, innovators and investors. An example of this can be found in the work of Richard Branson: *Screw It! Let's Do It!* (2006) and *Screw Business as Usual* (2011). Of the many popular examples of business leadership, Branson is amongst the most explicit about the systemic impacts of capitalism and our responsibility to remedy the situation. Capitalism (albeit in a modified form) will 'fix it'. Branson has strong views on leadership and has invested much in the promotion and support of those people, ideas and practices he believes will make a difference. For him, intuition in spotting a leader and opportunities to support potential leaders to practise leadership has become his mission. He reports that he does not need a scientific method to support his selection or his management style and gives many examples of successful enterprises generated from a spur-of-the-moment decision. For most businesses, this is not how the selection and assessment of leaders and managers is conducted. Much scholarly work and expensive research has been undertaken to understand the many supposed dimensions of organisational leadership and management, their unique or entwined characteristics, and the purported effects of the combination of leadership and management styles and situational factors. Whether one believes that the research findings reflect reality, or are somehow complicit in making reality, is a matter for ontological and epistemological enquiry. The contrasting of the early and late work of Wittgenstein explains this distinction most explicitly. So what kinds of orientation to leadership and management do those institutions mandated to teach leaders and managers display?

# TEACHING LEADERS, MANAGERS AND FOLLOWERS

After the collapse of Lehman Brothers in 2008, trust in financial institutions vanished. Trusted leaders in the finance industry scrambled for self-preservation. Some saw the focus on these few extreme cases as both an opportunity and a deflection from much more echoed, deeply seated, systemic issues with the system of capitalism. Whether there ever was widespread trust in any form given to capitalism and democracy and their leadership is a moot point for their advocates, leaders and apologists. Countless of sometimes bloody protests against their various incarnations are recorded in history. Leading capitalism has always and everywhere entailed the subjugation or transformation of dissent. Where overt consent cannot be gained, dissent must be harnessed, managed or destroyed. Thus, how we educate for leadership has relevance to programmes of management education. How the institutions that provide this education model their principles of leadership and management is also important.

In *Leadership by Design*, Bogue (1994) identifies the ideals that are essential to successful leadership in colleges and universities. Bogue explains that values shape a leader's realities. He suggests that leadership is a conceptual, moral and performing art form built on ideas and ideals as well as on solid philosophical and empirical foundations which are perfected in practice. Given that this idealisation is now more than 20 years old, and the graduates of such schools have been the leaders and managers of a world now thought to be at the brink of crisis, it seems pertinent to question the direction of their education and its effect.

Earlier in this book, we introduced the United Nations Global Compact as one example of more collective action towards leading a transformation in business practice and outcomes. In management education, the work of the Centre for Business as an Agent of World Benefit (BAWB) of Case Western University may also be viewed as an example of leadership, whose activities include the profiling of organisational leaders and of connecting leaders in business, research and teaching to transformational change. There is no shortage of examples of leaders and leadership attempting to change the conditions of social, economic, political and environmental distress assumed to be systemically related to the system of trade and exchange we know as contemporary capitalism in its many variations, but – up to the time of writing – predominantly driven by selectively applied rules of neo-liberalism.

Whether the rise of China, India or Indonesia as leaders on setting the rules for compliance on any number of issues will eclipse the leadership of the US and Europe is too early to tell. As we write, China's refusal to pay carbon tax in the European Emission Trading System is feared to result in a trade war. While concern about the production of nuclear power is amplifying the world over, France and the UK are leading new developments in this field. Countless science and industry leaders will see this revitalisation as great opportunities to lead in the science, economics and safety of harnessing nuclear energy and so will leaders in construction, engineering and waste management. To what extent will the leaders convinced otherwise be able to have an impact on investment in research education and job opportunities to generate attractive alternatives? If one was convinced of the urgency of either position (the need for some form of nuclear power to sustain our way of life – or the risk of nuclear dependency on our way of life), would this justify some form of manipulative leadership to ensure the desired followership, the invisible leadership of Lao-tsu for example?

# THE CHALLENGE ISSUED BY THE LEADERS OF THE PRME

How can we – as universities and business schools – provide the future generation of leaders with the knowledge and competencies needed to create sustainable development? (PRME, 2012)

In their promotion of the Principles for Responsible Management Education (PRME), Muff and colleagues (2013) call for a return to ethics and human development in the heart of economic activity.

Leadership is the art of directing the human dimension of the company: developing, motivating, empowering employees and giving sense to their work through values that are meaningful to them. Leadership rests on moral authority – and it is through this authority that values are disseminated throughout a company. Ethics give meaning to a corporation's actions: it guides its decisions and their implementation. In a more positive way, ethics also give a sense to economic progress in a global and long term perspective and makes it serve true development of a work-force. In order to do this we need a new type of leader as the 'sense maker' and as an 'architect of the corporate conscience'. Such responsible leaders thereby commit to an ethical approach. (Muff et al., 2013: 20–1)

Muff et al. (2013: 9–10) and the World Economic Forum at Davos are seeking to lead 'the great transformation' of capitalism. Indeed, difficult questions are being asked about the ethics of what Branson (2011) calls 'business as usual'. These are questions that are in some ways as old as the hills and almost universal in human memory. How *may* we engage with each other and with Earth who sustains us? In whom and in what do we vest trust and authority to guide and manage our personal and collective well-being? For whom and for what are we individually and collectively responsible? Muff et al. (2013: 10) provide a guiding vision:

We may imagine a reality where economic growth has been decoupled from ecosystem destruction and material consumption, and has been reconnected with societal wellbeing. Imagine all the stakeholders working towards the global common good – the greatest possible good for the greatest numbers of individuals. Imagine a society that has redefined the notion of prosperity and successful lifestyles, as well as the basis of profit and loss, progress and value creation. Imagine the world in a peaceful state, caring about environmental impacts, as well as societal wellbeing – and respecting differences in cultures, thought and behavior. Imagine global citizens translating these differences into sources for personal growth and enrichment. All of these factors together become what future economists may call a *sustainable economy*.

Who do we recognise as leaders in the expression of these questions in our times? Who do we ignore? Why and with what consequence? And who are the thought-leaders in any era and locality? How well educated are their potential followers? Does the implication of 'following' assume individual moral insecurity? In following the directive of Muff and her co-authors to achieve 'the greatest possible good for the greatest numbers of individuals' are we at risk of accepting the necessary sacrifice of some for the benefit of the many? Has the UN's vision for universality been derailed by a call for the most benefit to 'the many'? Certainly, this has been the force at work in the justification of saving corporations and whole nations by relegating to the periphery of society those who are no longer desirable in a workforce. There is no doubt that fear experienced as explicit or deeply buried insecurities give leaders (and managers) the power to offer remedies for the way forward. From Hitler to Gaddafi, from Mother Teresa to Bill Gates, from Rupert Murdoch to Ban Ki-moon, we see examples of leaders and their followers. The PRME is a global influence intent on transforming management education. How do we assess the impact of these leaders on people and planet? How we resist or follow, remove or endorse them is not just a question for macro-political consciousness. It requires close attention to who we recognise as leaders in the moment-by-moment actions in our own lives, how we view leadership and influence in our own activities. Are the calls to enlightened consciousness and invigorated conscience with which we began this book a sign that the tide is turning on the exploitative institutional logics now under question well beyond the once limited group of critical theorists?

# SPIRITED OR SPIRITUAL LEADERSHIP FOR THE FUTURE

Among the most recent developments in leadership studies are those that come from a greater recognition of the challenges to the mechanistic orientation of Western science. The trend has a focus on the (re)inclusion of spiritual dimensions of leadership which, in the most developed version of this genre, are generated by cosmological, teleological, ontological and epistemological challenges to the mechanistic orientations of Western management research, education and practice. Simply put, this development invites much deeper questions of 'who are we?', 'why are we here?', 'what do we believe is real?' and 'how do we know what we are getting?', than is typically given time in programmes largely devoted to socialising management students to seek mechanical answers to instrumental questions to do with serving organisational ends – i.e. management as it is taught 'in the main'.

Attention to the impact of deeply held values brings us to the most recent inclusions of more spiritually informed notions of leadership in Western management research and education. Is it that people marked for, recognised as, or groomed for leadership are instilled with values that serve their institutional attractiveness – or is there something in their spirit that needs merely the opportunity to emerge and shine? The emergence of interest in spiritual leadership, transcendental leadership, and more such, is an interesting turn in the study of leadership and management. It is increasingly common to see values for leadership expressed from belief systems other than the capitalist/military command and control model, adapted perhaps by a slightly enlarged notion of leadership characteristics and situational complexities. Will such a turn in the discourse bring forth a different, perhaps wiser, more human, more ecologically sound leadership?

We would venture to comment that the above threads within leadership studies are important to understand by students *of* management as well as students being trained *for* management. Whether we think people are born to be leaders, born as leaders, find themselves treated as leaders or can be educated, encouraged or required to be leaders; whether we think certain situations will generate particular types of leaders and that we can scour the horizons for their arrival; whether we think the most compelling understanding of social dynamics is to be found in the effects of various leader/follower relationships – are fascinating lines of enquiry. There are many scores of books that take one position or the other or opt for a middle way; i.e., nature provides the potentiality, but socialisation, education and training shape this potential.

Many management texts and training programmes provide inspirational and instructional material with cultural or industry-specific variations that assume leadership can be taught or enhanced. Textbooks will typically describe each proposition that a theory is based on and then rehearse the criticisms of the theories. Sometimes, this level of criticism is devised to privilege one theory over another, particularly if there is a training module to be attached to it. The interest in 'women and leadership' over the past two decades is a good example. A liberal response to the observation that women are not equally or even proportionally represented in leadership and management of organisations, across occupations or in the governance of local, national and international institutions, has led to decades of research and training intended to change this. Apart from some high-profile examples of female inclusion in leadership and management, the overall picture remains one of inequality, inequity and, for many, systemic exploitation or exclusion the world over. Popular women in leadership programmes have not equalised the representation of women and men in employment, but they have been intrinsic to encouraging women to see their identities and salvation as being met increasingly through their participation in the labour market and to strive for inclusion and achievement.

Understanding leadership studies at this level of critique is useful. It moves attention towards generating a more critical management education about leadership, but this is not the full point of critical management studies. Critical management scholars may find it more important to ask: who is leading us where? What are the effects of their leadership on shaping or achieving the aspirations of the followers? What are the broader effects of their leadership on the lives and, perhaps, identity of their followers and on issues well beyond the boundaries of their organisation? Sporting heroes abound. Political dynamics are also played out in the leadership of sport. At the end of March 2013, Paolo Di Canio agreed to a two and a half year deal to become the new manager of Sunderland Football Club in the UK. Di Canio is a self-proclaimed fascist. He is reported to have supported anti-racism campaigns. He is not a racist. Sunderland's director David Miliband said: 'in the light of the new manager's past political statements, I think it right to step down.' Miliband also quit his position as shadow foreign secretary to take up a post in New York City as the head of a charity. The former politician's comments about Di Canio are a quick attempt to distance himself from a politically volatile situation (Harris, 2013). Both Miliband and Di Canio would be recognised as leaders in their field. What can we say of their followers? Certainly, the rising influence of the neo-fascists is causing concern and may well become the motivator for the political leadership of democracies to address the levels of unemployment, particularly of increasingly alienated youth. Corporate leaders may or may not share their concern. A new war or the subjugation of rebellious segments of the population can provide good business opportunities. Wars can also mop up many unemployed.

Greater interest in indigenous knowledge in management education raises a new range of considerations to view. In the larger cosmological vistas of many indigenous peoples, leaders may be born as part of a lineage of leaders, their destiny set in a cosmology rejected by Western rationalism. Yet, was the birth of Jesus also not foretold in the stars? The successor to an incumbent Dalai Lama is not chosen from a template of supposed leadership traits, but from a belief that the incumbent is a reincarnation of the line of leadership that descends directly in a line of leaders who are considered to be the manifestation of compassion, Avalokite vara (www.dalailama.com/biography/from-birth-to-exile). These explanations of leaders as mandated and energised from spiritual realms are difficult to accommodate in a Western rational paradigm of positivist science.

> ## RUPERT SHELDRAKE: HERO OR HERETIC (OF SCIENCE AND POLITICS)
>
> Rupert Sheldrake, once Cambridge biochemistry don, is one of the brightest Darwinians of his generation, a researcher at the Royal Society, a Harvard Scholar and a Fellow of Clare College. He is a leader in his field. But he expressed opinions that the institutions of power could not tolerate. His first book *A New Science of Life* (1981) was deemed 'a book for burning' by the editor of the journal *Nature*, Sir John Maddox. What Sheldrake called into question then, and does to this day, is the very assumptions that the assurances of science may prove to be delusions. He came to realise that consciousness is much richer than physiologists can account for: 'A lot of our old certainties, not least neoliberal capitalism, have been turned on their head.' Yet we still allow the economist to lead social thought. How strange is that?

It would seem from this genre of leadership research that more 'mystical forces' are often at play. This takes our thoughts to the emerging interest in the spiritual dimensions of leadership, perhaps most explicitly developed by Senge and co-workers (2008) and exemplified in the work of Joseph Jaworski. In 1980, Jaworski, an expert in transformational leadership,

> founded the American Leadership Forum, which focused on promoting civic leadership in the United States. In 1990 he joined the Royal Dutch/Shell Group in London to head their team of scenario planners. While there he radically altered the way the company looks at scenarios. Under his tenure Shell began to focus not only on predicting futures, but on creating better ones. Upon returning from London, Mr. Jaworski joined the Board of Governors at the MIT Center for Organizational Learning and co-founded the Society for Organizational Learning. (Arlington Institute, 2007)

The Royal Dutch/Shell Group has provided us with numerous examples of corporate entwinement with social, political and environmental outcomes. They claim leadership on many fronts. Are Ken Saro-Wiwa and his fellow protesters to go into history as villains or heroes, saints or sinners? Might they be reconceived as the redeemer that has allowed Shell to claim a position of leadership in the world, a position sanctioned by its inclusion in the list of corporations that manifest the United Nations Global Compact? We revisit this idea in Chapter 10. We turn first to the speech given by Saro-Wiwa in his address to the court – surely the place of moral leadership in any jurisdiction.

> My Lord,
>
> We all stand before history. I am a man of peace, of ideas. Appalled by the denigrating poverty of my people who live on a richly endowed land, distressed by their political marginalization and economic strangulation, angered by the devastation of their land, their ultimate heritage, anxious to preserve their right to life and to a decent living, and determined to usher to this country as a whole a fair and just democratic system which protects

everyone and every ethnic group and gives us all a valid claim to human civilization, I have devoted my intellectual and material resources, my very life, to a cause in which I have total belief and from which I cannot be blackmailed or intimidated. I have no doubt at all about the ultimate success of my cause, no matter the trials and tribulations which I and those who believe with me may encounter on our journey. Nor imprisonment nor death can stop our ultimate victory. (Saro-Wiwa, 1995)

Saro-Wiwa and eight other men (the *Ogoni Nine*) paid for their moral stand with their lives.

The connection of Royal Dutch/Shell to this travesty of justice invites a close scrutiny of leadership, collaboration and courage. The story differs depending through whose experience the story is told or with whose eyes it is read. It would be shallow, however, to discuss the perceived misdeeds of corporations without examining the web of enablers that are part of their stories or to consider their espoused commitments to greater environmental care, commitments often expressed by increasingly high-profile relationships between corporate leadership and environmental activists at global, regional and local levels. To understand the story of corporate impact on the environment, and our complicity in it, is told is to invite the work of David Boje into our enquiries.

David Boje is a pioneer among critical management educators. He demonstrates the power of human creativity by his skilful use of the theories of Mikhail Bakhtin in his teaching to suggest that any situation is open to transformation to a different trajectory if we have the courage to make it so. Boje (1995, 2003) demonstrated this point by creating powerful role plays that are halted before we can know the ending. Participants and audiences are then invited to think up (and play out) a conclusion. The stunning diversity of endings is a testimony to the human imagination. The relatively uniform outcomes of institutional exploitation are a sad indictment of our courage! Perhaps it is the embeddedness of the mechanical logic of systems thinking that needs attention. It is the knowing of human power to create that brings us to the work of Margaret Wheatley and like-minded thinkers. Wheatley was thrown into the public spotlight in 1992 with the publication of *Leadership and the New Science*, a ground-breaking look at how new discoveries in quantum physics, chaos theory and biology challenge our standard ways of thinking in organisations. It showed how our reliance on old, mechanistic models stands in the way of innovation and effective leadership.

A survey of Western leadership research would suggest that much of this mechanistic model of leadership still prevails – perhaps at our collective peril, as Rupert Sheldrake asserts. While management textbooks and countless examples on the Internet describe the many directions leadership research and related practice has taken, of much greater interest, to the purpose of this book, is the ends rather than the means of leadership. Self-awareness and self-development are seen as key elements of a leader's character. A vast industry has emerged to encourage such development in students of management and employees of organisations. We recommend that this seemingly universal statement is taken under advisement – bearing in mind the many dictators who have led millions to their death in pursuit of their own ends – enabled by a followership that has pointed to what Hannah Arendt has called the 'banality of evil'. Whether ensuring that the trains run on time to endear the German people to a Hitler – or whether we collectively abandon millions of people to fight for survival on an inhospitable employment market in systems not afraid to demand personal sacrifice and direct abandonment – is a question for leadership and for management, for all those formally charged and the rest of us who have the wit, the right and the means to change the course of history. Both examples can illustrate the impact of effective leadership and sound management. Such good leadership and sound management require robust education. The Nazi movement understood this well – instilling its values in a youthful population almost imperceptibly. The cumulative effects of the leadership and management of capitalism, intensifying globally, appears to have embedded a similar societal tolerance or blindness to the controlling, empire directives of this system. Despite the many exemplars of courageous and creative alternatives, these together appear not to have gained enough traction to turn humanity from what increasing numbers of thought-leaders are calling a crisis of survival. A radical re-think is required. It is to such issues we now turn.

## LEADERSHIP TO/FOR WHAT?

We have it in our power to begin the world over again.

Tom Paine, *Common Sense*, 1775

In the study of leadership, styles and contexts as conducive to achieving organisational outcomes have dominated the management literature. Less under scrutiny until recently has been the impact of institutional aspirations framed as a duty to maximise profit (within the boundaries of the law) as dictum for all, as spelled out by Milton Friedman and his ilk, and the effectiveness of leaders in making this happen. The preoccupation of leadership studies with the 'means' is being eclipsed with questions as to the 'ends'. The greater interest in corporate social responsibility and the necessity of attention to sustainability redirects our attention to where prevailing leadership is taking us. Certainly, corrupt leadership, unethical leadership as defined by the system, has found prominent media coverage – and has fuelled public debate, protester passion and educational self-examination.

Being able to predict the impact of particular leadership styles on particular followers in particular circumstances and their combined impact on organisational outcomes would be a handy management tool. And the search for such definitive combinations continues. However, it is argued that this is a unique field of studies and does not belong in the field of management studies. Rather, such discussions belong in the field of governance studies. This distinction is made visible in practice by those who advocate for the clear separation of responsibilities between governance and management. In the hierarchy of responsibilities, this means, in theory at least, that boards of governors lead and must take responsibility for the actions of their corporations. Corporations cannot act (because they are not people). Certainly, they cannot be sent to jail. This then means someone must be held to account for the people they employ and mandate to act on their behalf. But who are boards of governors accountable to? Do they lead in the full sense of the word or are they in service to a paymaster who sets the agenda, the code of ethics and the standards of tolerable behaviour? This does bring to mind the question of who this paymaster may be.

Given the entwinement of pension funds in corporate investment decisions, given the notion of the customer as an investor of sorts, given that voters elect their politicians, and given that the duties of 'public servants' employed by civil society are to serve the public, there is room to think deeply about the responsibilities we each have for the outcomes of the corporate bodies we create, mandate and send out upon missions of various types. This brings to the table a level of personal responsibility to assess and discipline our leaders and managers, peers and workmates – and ought to mandate an education of managers that goes well beyond an instruction in domesticated, uncritical service to an economic agenda of corporate or GDP growth, maximisation of profit for shareholders or national accounts, or keeping the world safe for capital(ism) at the expense of the lives of the most vulnerable, and Earth who sustains us all. Thus, in this chapter, we see the study of leadership, organisational mandates and the expression of power, control and discipline of leaders and managers as at least as important as the study of employee control and discipline, consumer behaviour and environmental responsibility. It entails a holistic notion of ethics that must reach well beyond the confines of the organisation's formal boundaries and beyond being vested only in its leaders and executives.

But this, too, is a controversial issue. If there is strength to our analysis of the domination of a market logic that appears to override all other considerations, can we trust the call for greater involvement of corporations in changing the course of human action on the issues we have raised in this book? Can such corporate leadership, vested in specific leaders or in the employee body as a whole, be trusted to act in the interests of all and for Earth as a living being rather than a mine of minerals, a pond of water, and a pool of people that must be 'sustainably managed' with corporate, industry or market interests determining what such sustainability would look like? How does the study of leadership and management woven together bring light to such a question? The United Nations Principles for Responsible Management Education urge management educators to contribute to:

> thought leadership globally ... in order to develop a new generation of business leaders capable of managing the complex challenges faced by business and society in the 21st century ... Any institution which is willing to integrate corporate responsibility and sustainability in a gradual but systemic manner is welcome to join the initiative. (www.unprme.org/)

What examples are available to us? Schumacher College (2012) offers this:

> The emerging field of ecological facilitation and leadership looks to healthy, dynamic ecosystems for guidance in approaching change. Such bio-mimicry provides a logical and instinctive starting point for new leadership towards a sustainable world. This approach takes facilitator-leaders beyond self-interest and the individualistic and organisation-centred concerns which have dominated recent decades. It suggests that we broaden our concept of 'self' and 'organization' to encompass the larger interdependent systems such as the natural systems and cultural forces to which we are compellingly connected.

Examples of corrupt or inadequate leadership and governance are of interest to us in this book. They provide us with particularly dramatic illustrations of the systemic effect of particular ways of doing business and their wider consequences. Countless hard-working people have lost jobs, homes, relationships and lives because of the corrupt leadership of some – be they particular people or whole industries. But who was witnessing? Who was challenging? Who was calling these dangerous leaders or ineffectual governors to account? Some of them still claim that they have done nothing wrong and that they cannot be prosecuted as they acted within the law as they understood it. Some are astounded that they are being accused. These are important questions to be addressed in the reconsideration of how capitalism is practised. We dig a little deeper in this book. It is the more subtle weavings of this capitalist spell that has enchanted the world that this book has sought to explore.

How far would we need to 'reinvent' notions of self and other, corporate activity and responsibility, for the Schumacher image to be manifest in reality globally? In the final chapter, therefore, we revisit the contribution of critical management studies as supporting a reflective pedagogical process to serve the calls for a greater engagement with the big issues facing humanity rather than the training of functionaries who will either obey or resist, depending on their orientation – and whose obedience or resistance must be managed in the interest of the security of a system that does not serve all equally well. In Chapter 10, we introduce our reading of 'subaltern studies' as a radical response to any notion of compliance or assimilation that might draw us into (mindless) enactment of the capitalist system and thus our embroilment in the suffering of others and in the destruction of Earth. We revisit the concepts and issues we have raised throughout this book to consider how far studying management education critically could contribute to such a vision.

## TALK BOX

Small, with grey hair and now 70 years old, Raffaella Ottaviano is not the most likely looking heroine. But there was a moment when she confronted the Camorra – the formidable Neapolitan mafia. She made a stand, and launched a movement to drive the gangsters out of her community.

It all began when some Camorra men walked into Mrs Ottaviano's clothes shop on a street in Ercolano, a town on the outskirts of Naples. 'You know why we're here', they said. They had come to demand what's known as 'il pizzo' – protection money …

For generations, the Camorra has extracted payments from shopkeepers, and bar owners and other small businesses in Ercolano and all across the region.

But Mrs Ottaviano decided that she would not hand over her money. 'Listen, please be kind and get out immediately, I have no intention of paying', she said, remembering her exchange with the men. And they said, 'But do you realise what you're doing?' And I said: 'I'm not interested. Just get out!'

The Camorra has been described as Italy's most bloody and ruthless mafia. And very often its victims chose to say nothing … But Mrs Ottaviano broke the silence. She went to the police, and from photographs she identified the men who came to her shop. Soon they were arrested, and Mrs Ottaviano needed protection. 'For a year and a half, I was alone with the policemen, who never left me', she said. But gradually, other shopkeepers in Ercolano began to follow her lead and refuse to pay the Camorra.

There were just two or three at first, and then a few more. But they would meet secretly and eventually they formed an association with the help of the local council. That was back in 2006. And in the years since, their movement has grown in size and strength and determination … More than 80 businesses now refuse to pay the Camorra – and all the time more join her … But even now, does Raffaella worry that the Camorra might exact violent revenge for her defiance? 'I am calm', she says. 'I don't even wonder about that. I wouldn't be able to live otherwise.' There is no more fear now. We are all united. We couldn't go on like that. 'We must fight the Camorra. Not just with talk, but with action – with action.' (Johnston, 2012)

## Tricky Questions

- Who can lead the world to security for all and restoration of the planet?
- What does management education teach about leadership in this regard?
- How would we recognise, enhance and encourage such leadership?
- Can state leadership service their (total) citizenship, at least as is espoused in democratic nations?
- How can citizens hold their elected leaders to account?
- Do the public protests against the austerity measures imposed on the people of Greece have the power to lead the world to question the prevailing economic powers in Europe and beyond?
- Has the Occupy Movement morphed into a global force to be reckoned with?

*(Continued)*

- Will the democracy offered by the courageous resisters to despotic leadership in the Middle East bring peace and prosperity to the people? Has it done so for all Americans, Europeans and other places where democracy and capitalism have been practised together?
- Is good leadership to be thought of only or mostly in terms of the power of a person to garner a followership regardless of the project?
- Does the concept of leadership go beyond the visible actions of a leader to the ways such leaders are recognised or formed, chosen and disciplined by the followers?
- How are followers educated to assess the merits and impact of those they choose or are required to follow?

# ADDITIONAL RESOURCES

Bolman, L. and Deal, T.E. (2011) *Leading with Soul: An Uncommon Journey of Spirit*. San Francisco: Jossey-Bass.

Chapman, A. (2000–2012) John Adair's action centred leadership: a model for team leadership and management. *Businessballs.com* (www.businessballs.com/action.htm; retrieved 14 September 2013).

Fairhurst, G.T. and Cooren, F. (2009) Charismatic leadership and the hybrid production of presence(s). *Leadership*, 5: 1–22.

Gibney, A. (dir.) (2005) *Enron: The Smartest Guys in the Room* (www.imdb.com/title/tt1016268/; retrieved 14 September 2013).

Marshall, J., Coleman, G. and Reason, P. (2011) *Leadership for Sustainability*. Sheffield: Greenleaf.

Myers, S. (2012) Leadership and management: what is the difference? (www.teamtechnology.co.uk/leadership-basics.html; retrieved 14 September 2013).

Straker, D. (2003–2012) Leadership vs. management. *Changing Minds.org* (http://changingminds.org/disciplines/leadership/articles/manager_leader.htm; retrieved 14 September 2013).

Zoller, H.Z. and Fairhurst, G.T. (2007) Resistance leadership: the overlooked potential in critical organization and leadership studies. *Human Relations*, 60: 1331–60.

# REFERENCES

ABC 10 News (2013) Rally held to show support for Jeff Olson, man charged in chalk vandalism case. *ABC 10 News*, 30 June (www.10news.com/news/rally-held-to-show-support-for-jeff-olson-man-charged-in-chalk-vandalism-case-06292013; retrieved 14 September 2013).

Allen, M. (2012) WEF seeks to rewire global leadership. *Swissinfo*, 18 January (www.swissinfo.ch/eng/specials/world_economic_forum/WEF_seeks_to_rewire_global_leadership.html?cid=31956150; retrieved 14 September 2013).

Arlington Institute (2007) Joseph Jaworski. *The Arlington Institute*, 26 April (www.arlingtoninstitute.org/Joseph+Jaworski; retrieved 14 September 2013).

Atkinson, J. (1984) Manpower strategies for flexible organizations. *Personnel Management*, 16: 28–31.

Black, A. (2013) Letter to a young social entrepreneur: the poor are not the raw material for your salvation. *Pioneers Post*, 10 April (www.pioneerspost.com/comment/20130410/letter-young-social-entrepreneur-the-poor-are-not-the-raw-material-your-salvation; retrieved 14 September 2013).

Bogue, E.G. (1994) *Leadership by Design: Strengthening Integrity in Higher Education*. San Francisco: Jossey-Bass.

Boje, D. (1995) Stories of the storytelling organisation: a postmodern analysis. *Academy of Management Journal*, 38 (4) 997–1035.

Boje, D.M. (2003) Theatrics of leadership; leaders as storytellers and thespians, 16 August (http://business.nmsu.edu/~dboje/teaching/338/theatrics_of_leadership_links.htm; retrieved 14 September 2013).

Branson, R. (2006) *Screw It! Let's Do It!* London: Virgin Books.

Branson, R. (2011) *Screw Business as Usual*. New York: Penguin.

Calas, M. (2013) Faculty profile. Isenberg School of Management (www.isenberg.umass.edu/management/Faculty/Profiles/Marta_Calas/; retrieved 14 September 2013).

Deen, T. (2012) US lifestyle is not up for negotiation. *Inter Press Service*, 1 May (www.ipsnews.net/2012/05/us-lifestyle-is-not-up-for-negotiation/; retrieved 14 September 2013).

Drucker, P. (2004/2011) What makes an effective executive? In *Harvard Business Review's 10 Must Reads on Leadership*. Boston: Harvard Business Review Press. pp. 23–36.

European Leadership Platform (2010) Regaining trust. Annual Leadership Conference, Noordwijk aan Zee, 30 September (www.felconference.info/; retrieved 14 September 2013).

Fox, J. (2009) Three lessons of the Lehman Brothers collapse. *Time*, 15 September (www.time.com/time/business/article/0,8599,1923197,00.html#ixzz1o0lHBk9q; retrieved 14 September 2013).

Goleman, D. (1996/2011) What makes a leader? In *Harvard Business Review's 10 Must Reads on Leadership*. Boston: Harvard Business Review Press. pp. 1–22.

Harris, C. (2013) Paolo Di Canio appointed manager of Sunderland; David Miliband resigns in protest. *World Soccer Talk*, 31 March (http://epltalk.com/2013/03/31/paolo-di-canio-appointed-manager-of-sunderland-david-miliband-resigns-in-protest/; retrieved 14 September 2013).

Harvard Business Review (2011) *Harvard Business Review's 10 Must Reads on Leadership*. Boston: Harvard Business Review Press.

Heathfield, S.M. (2013) Inspirational quotes for business and work: leadership. *About.com* (http://humanresources.about.com/od/workrelationships/a/quotes_leaders.htm; retrieved 5 October 2013).

Iosbaker, J. (2008) Andy Stern's *A Country that Works* and the struggle in SEIU (book review). *Fight Back! News*, 8 March (http://www.fightbacknews.org/2008/03/sternbook.htm; retrieved 14 September 2013).

Johnston, A. (2012) Naples' Camorra faces resistance from businesses. *BBC News Europe*, 21 February (www.bbc.co.uk/news/world-europe-16932130; retrieved 24 February 2012).

Kotter, J. (1990/2011) What leaders really do. In *Harvard Business Review's 10 Must Reads on Leadership*. Boston: Harvard Business Review Press. pp. 37–56.

Lall, R.R. and Pilkington, E. (2013) UN will not compensate Haiti cholera victims, Ban Ki-moon tells president. *Guardian*, 21 February (www.theguardian.com/world/2013/feb/21/un-haiti-cholera-victims-rejects-compensation; retrieved 14 September 2013).

Mintzberg, H. (2009) The best leadership is good management. *Business Week Magazine*, 6 August (www.businessweek.com/magazine/content/09_33/b4143068890733.htm; retrieved 14 September 2013).

Muff, K., Dyllick, T., Drewell, M., North, J., Shrivastava, P. and Haertle, J. (2013) *Management Education for the World: A Vision for Business Schools Serving People and Planet*. Cheltenham: Edward Elgar.

Owen, J. (2011) UN sex-trafficking whistleblower feted in film. *The Independent*, 23 January (www.independent.co.uk/arts-entertainment/films/news/un-sextrafficking-whistleblower-feted-in-film-2192045.html; retrieved 14 September 2013).

Pardo, N. (2011) Made in America: Obama maps a future for manufacturing. *PTC: Product Lifecycle Stories*, 9 September (http://blogs.ptc.com/2011/09/09/made-in-america-obama-announces-jobs-act/; retrieved 14 September 2013).

Ponte, L. (2004/2012) Quoted in 'Death by a thousand cuts'. *The Devil at our Doorstep*, 22 May (http://devilatmydoorstep.wordpress.com/2012/05/22/death-by-a-thousand-cuts/; retrieved 14 September 2013).

PRME (2012) The challenge. *PRME*, 25 February (www.unprme.org/news/index.php?newsid=198; retrieved 14 September 2013).

Saro-Wiwa, K. (1995) Ken Saro-Wiwa's final address to the military-appointed tribunal. *Earth Island Journal*, 11 (1): 25 (see also http://en.wikisource.org/wiki/Trial_Speech_of_Ken_Saro-Wiwa; retrieved 14 September 2013).

Schumacher College (2012) Ecological facilitation: a gritty and creative approach to leadership (course) (www.schumachercollege.org.uk/courses/ecological-facilitation-a-gritty-and-creative-approach-to-leadership-2; retrieved 14 September 2013).

Senge, P., Scharmer, O., Jaworski, J. and Flowers, B.S. (2008) *Presence: Human Purpose and the Field of the Future*. New York: Currency Doubleday.

Sheldrake, R. (1981) *A New Science of Life: The Hypothesis of Formative Causation*. London: Blond and Briggs.

Thornton, P.H., Ocasio, W. and Lounsbury, M. (2012) *The Institutional Logics Perspective: A New Approach to Culture, Structure, and Process*. Oxford: Oxford University Press.

Wheatley, M.J. (1992) *Leadership and the New Science: Learning about Organization from an Orderly Universe*. San Francisco: Berrett-Koehler.

# 10 REFLECTIONS ON SELF, OTHER AND ORGANISATIONS

---

## Learning Objectives

To review our capacity to:

- assess the ideas of critical management studies for their usefulness in the interpretation of the prevailing institutional logics;
- reflect on how far you believe individual responsibility for universal and planetary well-being extends;
- consider whether managers have a specific duty to consider responsibilities beyond compliance with employer directives;
- assess the value of a holistic, activist education for yourself.

---

## CRITICAL CONCEPTS

*Critical management studies* encourages us to examine the *taken-for-granted* in relation to ideas about *hegemonic control, transformation* and *emancipation*. We have focused on the growing *influence of corporations*, but we recognise the *interdependencies* of small and big enterprises, governments, NGO organisations and individuals in the *fabrication of systems* and *discourses* of perceived *reality* and thus ideas about possibilities. We have paid close attention to the *prevailing institutional logics* that are being challenged from within and by a focus on *the systems or the discourses* through which we organise our humanity. Our very *identities* are entwined. To challenge the logic with which we make sense of ourselves is *soul* work. The *coercion* of the human *spirit* to the interests of the *powerful* is an extension of *managerial* interest to *control* people, materials and processes in the interests of their task masters. *Imperialist dynamics* that may be at work are a contradiction to the ethos of *universal freedom*, the aspiration of Western liberals. Contradictions and paradox are opportunities to challenge and transform hegemonic control. How activist can we be?

# REFLECTIONS

The classroom remains the most radical space of possibility in the academy. (bell hooks 1994: 12)

In her reflections on her career as a teacher, bell hooks writes: 'I have been most inspired by those teachers who have had the courage to transgress the boundaries that would confine each pupil to a rote, assembly-line approach to learning' (1994: 13). She suggests that to teach in a manner that respects the souls of students, it is essential that teachers provide the necessary conditions whereby learning can most deeply and intimately begin. This is radical stuff! It may be too presumptuous and even dangerous to think that we as teachers and students can exercise the enhancement of souls through management education. Yet, it would seem that our souls are wide open to exploitation. We appear not to notice or to tolerate the harnessing of human soul-aspirations to the sale of products, the harnessing of human and environmental energy, and the control of others in the pursuit of profit or growth. Who has not seen an advertisement that associates the purchase of a particular brand of car, skin products or a holiday with the liberation of the soul!

Subtle and not so subtle co-options of new age, soul-orientated aspirations are woven through clever marketing campaigns for everything from health-destroying, sugar-laden drinks to ego-enlarging cars or gadgets. Government, NGO or corporate recruitment projects are increasingly designed to attract employees and funders who may want to be associated with goodness, sustainability or spiritual enlightenment as aspects of personal success – however these may be defined in a given community at a given time.

Recruitment agencies and marketers do not spend their significant resources on futile campaigns. They know what sells. Public relations and communications experts are skilled at sensing potential resistance to corporate greed or destructive or inhumane practices. They are expert at deflecting attention away from damaging analysis. They know how to assuage the human conscience when destructive corporate activities hit the media. Media editors must manage the sell-power of a spectacular corporate disaster for their publications and the risk of losing corporate advertising income if they point the finger too effectively. The attempts of experts to affect our consciousness and conscience (or soul) in system-supporting lifestyles and work habits are calculated.

The effects of marketing campaigns on behaviour and even identities cannot be dismissed as random or accidental by-products of a commitment to efficiency. It may be reasonable to assume, then, that active emancipation of our spirit is a necessary aspect of a good education. It may be critical to demand an education that prepares us to contribute to the transformation of evil and to enhance the good – those contestable notions we discussed in Chapter 1. For this reason, we round off this book with a reflection on management education as soul work.

In this chapter, we review the concerns of critical scholars about the outcomes of the prevailing economic paradigm that is disproportionately influencing all other ideas of social organisation. We re-examine the prevailing discourses of corporate responsibility (CR) and sustainability for their potential to address the issues we have canvassed in this book. We signal the emerging interest in 'conscious capitalism' for its expressed hope and for the risk that its uncritical uptake becomes the most subtle hegemonic defence of capitalism yet devised. We revisit the Kantian ethics implied in this book to contrast these with the instrumental ethics of economic rationalism. We wonder whether such ethics have more chance of enactment under the conditions of 'conscious capitalism' or whether uncritical indulgence in these discourses distracts us from a more robust critique. We conclude by providing two theoretical perspectives that may keep us on our critical edge in order to invigorate the decolonising potential of the future development of our humanity: an adaptation of subaltern studies and an introduction to radical human ecology as potential fruitful developments of the critical scholarship now a little more frequently found in the academy.

# EDUCATION AS SOUL WORK

Activities that maintain life, health, culture and legacies occur the world over. These activities may or may not be called work. Much of this activity in various epochs, regimes and regions of the world has been and remains exploitative and harnessed to benefit the powerful. Capitalist endeavours have been no different in this regard. There is a significant mandate to challenge such exploitation wherever liberal ideals of democracy and emancipation are promulgated. Capitalist and democratic ideologies are both posited on principles of emancipation, inclusiveness and fairness. In neo-liberal contexts, this emancipation is to be achieved in and through paid employment. As authors of this book, we too are part of this 'workforce'. With terminal degrees, three of us are in secured jobs, three of us are women, all of us are white. All four of us have many publications to our names in our various fields of interest. We have achieved the trust of a significant publisher to bring this book to print. We are acutely conscious of our privilege, particularly when we write about the exclusions of many people from the organisations that are deemed to provide access to income and thus implied well-being and security. After all, this has been so for at least three of us. There is no doubt that, as teachers, we work hard. There are many people, however, who work a lot harder for a lot less income than we do. Many are not as secure(d) as we are. Some may not want to be.

We, as authors, have strong opinions about many things. We do not assume that our insights and concerns are universally shared. As demonstrated in this book, we are clear that Western thinkers have been influential in shaping the very ideas about people and planet that are being globalised. This may not remain the case. As we write, it looks as if China and India may become more influential global players in the future than the US and Europe combined. White, male, heterosexual and functionalist ideas, however, will still seep almost imperceptibly into much of our own work. That we have not been able to transform our text entirely is partly to do with our own immersion in the prevailing institutional logics. There is much we do not notice. There is also much we do notice, but accept or tolerate as the pragmatic domestication of our writing. It is a conscious and managed domestication that permits us to remain active in the realms of management education. We are conscious that what we think can be said and heard in a text for management students is coloured by context. This selective domestication is a form of self-management exercised universally – sometimes consciously, sometimes intuitively, and sometimes dangerously unconsciously. It is a process that shapes what can be said or heard in cathedral, mosque or synagogue, at the dinner table, around the cooking fires, or in a football locker room. It is a common form of discipline in management education. Domestication is achieved by the instigation and policing of rules and a response to their perceived effects on our lives.

All social contexts have domesticating rules. But strong as the rules are, they are still only and always a set of ideas and values. They are conceptual inventions that are woven into social fabrications and routines. They are formalised as the institutions of any community or society. They become the institutional logics that underpin the taken-for-granted of a time and place. As such, they are open to change. Their transformation is always an option. If the issues we have raised in this book about the systemic harms of capitalism are valid, we have it in our power to change the institutional logic that we live by. Some people are more passionate, courageous or desperate than others to achieve such change. Where do you fit?

## BETTER DEAD

The requirement to accept the austerity measures imposed on the people of Greece has seen a raft of protests that appear to have no impact on the policy-makers of Greece. In April 2012, Dimitris Christoulas, a 77-year-old retired pharmacist, shot himself in the head outside the Greek parliament. In a suicide note, he said he preferred to die rather than to scavenge for food. Reuters (cited in *The Waikato Times*, 7 April 2012: D1) restates the conservative newspaper, *Eleftheros Typos*: 'the act was filled with "profound political symbolism" that could shock Greek society and the political world and awaken their conscience' – but has it? (Margaronis, 2012)

Many people are calling for a change not only to the rules of capitalism but to the ideals and values that are informing the institutional logics that we have explored in this book. We can all make a contribution to this change by radical and courageous acts or by seemingly less dramatic acts. We can all participate by engaging differently in conversations at a given time or place. Such engagement can be achieved by consciously changing the words we use, the policies we craft and the level and types of discipline and domestication we tolerate in our freedom to shape a way of being that is hospitable to all and that ensures that the very Earth who is home is in good shape for our children's children (Maori TV, 2013).

As authors of this book, we see the analytical strengths of critical management studies particularly in the exposure of the subtle use of power and the diverse processes of domestication and subjugation of individuals and populations. Critical management scholars bring a diversity of perspectives that broaden the range of questions that can be probed by teachers and students of management and the ways in which these can be explored. The scholarship and the associated teaching endorse calls to uphold higher-order human ideals of responsibility to articulate and achieve justice, emancipation and environmental restoration. But critical management studies is not without some significant challenges, not least of which is making the insights of its scholars understandable, attractive and motivational, while not overly simplifying or overly generalising their perspectives. In seeking to benefit from the diversity of perspectives available in this way of thinking, there is a risk that the work of critical management scholars is not seen as a cohesive and reliable body of knowledge. This lack of a single voice may undermine a trustworthy path to transformations in our way of being human increasingly articulated as necessary and even urgent. Regardless of these challenges, we see the field as growing in significance in the academy. More wide-reaching and intensifying critiques of neo-liberalism are being articulated. Calls for or against its change or even abandonment need close attention by contemporary management students. A position on the matter takes not only rational analyses but an arousal of the spirit.

# THE PSYCH-SCIENCES AND DOCTORS OF THE SOUL

The insights of psychoanalysts have been ancillary to both mainstream and critical knowledge as developed in business and management schools. We suggest that is due to the continued attractiveness of a narrow form of behavioural and functionalist approach to psychology that has informed the management and organisational disciplines for the best part of a century. From the discourse of the self-actualising, self-serving, competitive individual central to the worldview of the liberal economists, to the behaviourally, attitudinally and now spiritually controllable employee of the organisational behaviourists, the functionalist rhetoric and mechanistic logic of Western dualism has reigned almost supreme. Psychoanalysts have led us to the study of the effect of the unconscious on the maintenance of the personal and collective expressions of our humanity.

Critical theorists describe apparently invisible structural injustices as conditions of hegemony. A combination of these insights with our respective views of institutional, personal and interpersonal expressions of power and control may contribute not only to an explanation but also towards the transformation of society in ways that address the significant issues facing humanity. We are interested in the way in which a confluence of our understanding may help not only to explain but to transform the functionally constructed manager and employee living in a form of personal and collective denial, existing under conditions of hegemony that work against personal and collective emancipation. *How might critical theorists move our analytical strength into transformational energies?* How can we hope to pay attention to this call when we are distracted and deflected by all manner of psycho-tricks!

Psychoanalysts have a means of inviting us to auto-gnosis: auto-gnosis is about the knowing of self. It entails self-reflection as a necessary part of the transformation we must attend to if the values we purport to uphold are to manifest in practice. This is a different response to concerns about personal integration into the system from the assimilation ones we explored in Chapters 5 and 6 as the various therapeutic forms of guidance or psychological treatment designed to subjugate individuals to adapt, adjust and even to thrive in the system as it is. If a more radical perspective is entertained, we can see that personal adjustments to an ever-intensifying system are not the radical changes they purport to be. They may be better viewed as being system-preserving remedies. When taken together with the myriad ways we all engage in the system, which has a range of devastating and dangerous outcomes blindly accepted by some and widely tolerated by many, the conditions of the colonisation of our lifeworld are established and maintained by our engagement with it. Gramsci (1971) might call this the conditions of hegemonic control. Numerous critical theorists have posited that such control is never watertight. Such a position would deny the hope for and possibility of change. Histories of courageous acts of transformation indicate that conscious influence for change is possible. All prevailing systems of truth come with conditions of paradox and contradiction. The prevailing institutional logics we have tackled in this book are no different in that regard. Seo and Creed (2002) have shown the transformative potential of taking contradictions and paradoxes. It is with this view in mind that we revisit Habermas's concern, outlined in Chapter 2, about the colonisation of the lifeworld, so accessibly expressed in the work of Deetz (1992), and knit it into the critical pedagogy of this book.

# COLONISATION OF THE LIFEWORLD BY A LIMITED AND LIMITING ECONOMIC RATIONALITY

*The ruling class has the schools and press under its thumb. This enables it to sway the emotions of the masses.*

Albert Einstein (1879–1955)

In this book we have invited reflections on how the attitudes and actions of managers and employees through and beyond their formal jobs have implications beyond the boundaries of employment. We did so by introducing some key concepts of critical theory and by providing links to places where these ideas are more fully explained. These concepts provide analytical tools that enable the asking of different kinds of questions of all aspects of our social world. They allow us to enquire into how we manage our individual opportunities and responsibilities and how, through these actions, we contribute to the collective well-being and security and how we might feel about that. A de-reified understanding of an organisation's rules, codes and practices would be evident when we realise that these are the fabricated outcomes of people making countless decisions based upon their particular understanding of the efficacy of the rules and the rights of corporations and governments. Such understanding is a deep realisation that the organisations to which we affiliate ourselves, or to which we are harnessed, are entities that exist only as a conglomeration of humanly fabricated and sanctioned rules-for-being. Organisations, such as governments, corporations and their rules and codes of practice, in this way of thinking, then, are historical social constructions, fictive entities or social fabrications that carry with them interests and power, as we discussed in Chapter 1. They are figments of the human imagination, and because of that they can be changed – no matter how entrenched they are 'as things' or 'reality' and no matter how hard and how dangerous it is to expose them for what they are: the preferences of some imposed on others – a travesty of Kantian ethics.

There is always an opportunity to offer new ideas to replace those that support and justify processes that may be deemed unethical, destructive or unsafe when given a more critical analysis – no matter how seemingly dense the hegemonic influences at play. In any example where rules become things, and the things are made into systems, and the systems are so normalised we come to take them for granted (as 'natural' even), we can see the extension of the idea of false consciousness by including the notion of a reified consciousness. That is, reified consciousness is manifest (or incarnated) when we no longer recognise that rules, codes and customs are historically specific and created, imposed and tolerated by enough people to give them their seeming materiality. We forget or choose not to remember that we can remake the rules and change our practices. This will require us to think outside the boxes we have been trained to think in. It requires transdisciplinary education. How might Earth be part of this education?

# RECAPPING THE STORY

Some of the influential thinkers who have generated a number of the key ideas that provide a useful backdrop for understanding management critically were introduced in Chapter 2. To contextualise the issues we raise in this book, we provided an opening discussion about globalisation. This discussion continued throughout the book by taking a closer look at various aspects of this way of organising our humanity and its management. The changing dynamics of (paid) work was chosen as the next big focus of attention, as, particularly in the study of management, this is where much of the specific action takes place. However, as authors, the placing of this chapter was a hard call for us to make. After all, we argue that the shaping of work, workplaces and workers is integrally related to the way we are invited or required to think of ourselves as people (as students, employees, managers, consumers, parents and citizens). These ideas appear to be institutionally given, and outline what we believe may yet be possible.

The very idea of being a person, an individual, in the contexts of shaping and being shaped through our engagement with or entwinement in various forms of organising is developed as a kind of symbiotic relationship in Chapter 5. Markets, firms, industries, communities, homes and nations are the formal ways in which we enact our values and interests. All imply management of self and others. From a critical perspective, the processes of globalisation, workplace and wider social organisation, and intentional or unintentional institutional influences on the shaping of identities, may create challenges to assumed democratic values within and beyond specific places of work or occupational groupings. These are usefully made problematic when we wish to understand and perhaps change the ways these influences shape or uphold often hidden power relationships. Chapter 6, focused on diversity management, provided a great opportunity to explore how the management literature has coped with human diversity, justification for the management of inclusions and exclusions through the allocation or withdrawal of rewards, and the harnessing of perceived productive diversity to organisational ends.

In the face of undeniable inequity or destructive behaviour, or in the light of perhaps unintended unjust or injurious consequences, a number of ideas for systemic change have been offered in the theories and practices of contemporary capitalism. We have invited the consideration of the extent to which efforts to effect change may preserve rather than challenge the values under question. Our examples include how paid employment is conceived and experienced as the most important form of work, how human diversity is attended to in the management of organisational outcomes, the extent to which the idea of consumer sovereignty embeds and does not challenge the consumption society, and the market-led remedies to growing environmental concerns. These responses to the issues facing humanity might be more accurately read as systemic adaptations that ensure that unequal power and opportunities are preserved. We left the chapter on leadership till very late in the book. As well as inviting thought about the extent to which management and leadership are to be considered in the same book, we have positioned the chapter in order to think about the potential of 'good leadership for good outcomes' – however problematically these are to define and no matter how broad we are willing to make our canvas of concern.

Concerns about the mass starvation of children, the environmental implications of desertification, the tussle over the corporate grip on fossil fuels, water and minerals, the tensions over the control of labour, and the destruction of food chains in the preservation of an abstract notion of economic growth sometimes seem far removed from our daily working lives and consumption habits. When we cannot but acknowledge the seriousness of the issues facing humanity, it may be tempting to give into feelings of futility. It may also be tempting to assume that people more powerful than us have solutions to the issues facing humanity. It may be reassuring that leaders in various aspects of society have universal well-being in mind. They are certainly good at claiming so. This book invites a much more personal responsibility in the small and large opportunities to be the difference you may wish to see in the world.

On the chapter-specific companion website we have provided numerous examples, study notes and illustrations of situations and actions that are open to many different kinds of insights, analyses and responses by any of us who have the capacity to read this book and with access to the Internet. To assess whether the analyses we present in this book are useful, whether the claims made by those leading calls for action in one direction or another are valid, and whether the remedies offered are robust contributions to the transformations needed to ensure universal inclusiveness and environmental restoration, requires active assessment and an alert critical consciousness. Contributing to the enhancement of such critical consciousness has been a motivator for this book. We have selected the need to change our corporations as being of urgency. This can only be achieved through the actions of enlightened human beings.

# INCREASED CORPORATE RESPONSIBILITY: TRANSFORMATIONAL REMEDY OR STRATEGIC SYSTEM-PRESERVING ADAPTATIONS?

In Chapter 1, we introduced the pressure building within capitalism to recognise and change some of the destructive outcomes associated with this form of production and consumption. In various parts of the book and on the companion website, we introduced a number of the institutions, activist groups and leaders who are advocating for such change. In Chapter 9, in particular, we invited support for a greater examination of the purpose to which leadership is directed. In Chapters 1, 3 and 9 we invited a critical reflection on several institutions that are making their transformational intent explicit: the UN Global Compact and the associated Principles for Responsible Management Education (PRME) and various management educational institutions and their offspring, such as the Academy of Management and the Case Western University's Centre for Business as an Agent of World Benefit (BAWB; Fetzer, n.d.). We contrasted the remedial ideas of leaders in this realm with more radical ideas emanating from Schumacher College and like-minded educational institutions and re-thinkers of the universe such as Margaret Wheatley and Richard Sheldrake. We drew attention to the various threads of these ideas made accessible to management educators by scholars as diverse as David Boje or Peter Senge. Where have the combined efforts of all this scholarship, education and organisational commitment brought us?

The Rio+20 conference held in Rio de Janeiro in June 2012 marked the twentieth anniversary of the United Nations Conferences on Sustainable Development that began there as the Earth Summit in 1992. The preparatory documents for Rio+20 emphasised the perceived necessity for renewed attention to poverty elimination, universal inclusiveness, global security and environmental restoration. Calls such as these were once the domain of social and environmental activists and their scholarly equivalents. They are appearing ever more frequently in more mainstream management texts. There is, for example, an amplifying call to educate managers better about the direct and indirect impacts of their decisions and activities beyond the immediate concerns of their organisation or network of industries (cf. the themes for recent calls to the Academy of Management, the list of special editions produced by the *Journal of Management Education* and the many papers on various aspects of social and environmental concerns published in many specialist academic and technical journals). In the organisational disciplines, these concerns are most often expressed in the strengthening discourses of 'corporate responsibility' and 'sustainability'. The United Nations' project for the development and promulgation of PRME is a wide-reaching example of such a call.

In this book, we have raised cautions about the work of the United Nations and similar advocates of justice if this work is to be achieved primarily through market expansion, economic growth and so on. We do so that we can remain alert and ensure that these organisations do not merely provide a legitimating mechanism for the interests of a few. We emphasise, however, that there is an opportunity that the United Nations and its supporters challenge the limited and limiting instrumental ethics of Western corporate capitalism that infuse the dominant institutional logics that they may contribute to the transformation of trade and exchange, the distribution of responsibilities and rewards, so that the human community will become more inclusive and sustainable for all. We suggest that there is much wisdom to be found in the relational ethics articulated by many (but not only) indigenous peoples. The prevailing notions of time management are just one example. The projection of contemporary responsibilities to include the well-being of future generations is another. We suggest that indigenous wisdom has significant potential to contribute to radical transformation of the seemingly intractable social and environmental issues facing humanity (Williams et al., 2012). We bring the increasing assertiveness of indigenous peoples to the attention of management teachers and students to encourage an interest in, and respect for, diverse ideas as a heuristic for educating professionals who can (i) carry forward the aspirations of justice that are the hallmark of democratic societies, and (ii) contribute to the environmental restoration necessary for human survival. This suggestion is based on our view that attention to, and respect for, diverse institutional logics are desirable to prepare managers of the future to transform the hegemonic grip of the prevailing economic logic in business education and to find institutional approaches that demonstrate greater responsibility for Earth and all her creatures.

Stephens and colleagues (2008) and Young and Black (2013) add to the calls within the academy and beyond for a reduced focus on agency and economics in management education and to integrate more 'responsible' management models to address wider problems of equity, sustainability, ethics and globalisation. Evidence that such calls are being heeded lies in the increasing numbers of related courses, as well as special issues of management education journals devoted to this topic (see, for example, Jim Wu et al., 2010; Starik et al., 2010; Stead and Stead, 2010; Brower, 2011; Pless et al., 2011; Young and Nagpal, 2013). Universities and other higher education institutions are projected as key agents of change in society (Stephens et al., 2008; Sibbel, 2009). They may be argued to have a specific concurrent responsibility to make a radical contribution to the re-thinking of the issues before humanity. For Richard Branson (2011), this means a radical reformation of capitalism. Are his calls for transformation radical enough to address the issues we raise in this book or, if manifest, would we still have an economically orientated system, with all aspects of life vulnerable to the vagaries of markets?

The capitalist system has been remarkable in its resilience to critique. Open and informal resistance, violent protest and attempted renegotiations of its tenets and practices have a long and sometimes bloody history. As resistance intensified in each epoch, so too did system-preserving remedies. These remedies ranged from outright violent suppression of the resistance to greater attention to stakeholder negotiations, and sometimes seemingly radical organisational responses tackling employee empowerment and environmental responsiveness. Certainly, many management journals are celebrating contemporary flashes of enlightenment (see *Harvard Business Review on Happiness* [2012], *Journal of Management Education* special editions on poverty, on the environment, on the potential of indigenous knowledge to support systemic reform and on the PRME). Yet, seen differently, it seems that a persistent and life-diminishing thread is being strengthened – in part through the very endorsement of the rhetoric of an assumed remedy: the discourse of rights to inclusion, a discourse with a (not so subtle) colonising effect on what Deetz (1992) so insightfully calls our 'lifeworld', others might call the *Zeitgeist*, and organisational scholars might refer to as the 'dominant institutional logic'. Each articulation has some specific nuances, but all largely invite a wider reflection on the 'mood of the times', on what is taken for granted, and on what can and cannot be said, done or hoped for.

As ever fewer opportunities to generate a livelihood outside the capitalist system remain, the need, or right, or what is increasingly framed as the duty to participate in the market has become a key remedy for personal poverty and collective national and international outcomes (or perhaps a most fruitful remedy in the prevailing system-preserving hegemony). Once entwined in the markets, remedies to undeniable exploitation or exclusion of particular categories of people have been aplenty. They may initially be framed to address specific concerns, such as employee exploitation, workplace discrimination or environmental degradation, for example. Systemic repression or adaptation to such challenges diminished or deflected the potential of the critique to serve radical systemic reform. By addressing specific concerns, in even seemingly wide-reaching arenas of action, in violent or seemingly respectful ways, their potential clout as systemic wake-up calls are weakened.

Various discourses of discontent or calls for reform have been harnessed to sustain the system. These have included the now exposed ruse of 'employee empowerment' and the impotence of equal employment opportunities (EEO) to address various discriminations in employment as discussed in Chapter 6. Discourses of corporate responsibility (CR) and/or sustainability have yet to prove themselves, as we have discussed in Chapter 8. Many of these supposed remedies have shown themselves to be easily co-optable and readily harnessed to the institutional logic that supports the preservation and intensification of the capitalist system of trade and exchange that is intensifying globally. Is it reasonable to trust – or even to hope that the PRME will be less susceptible to such co-option?

Whether the PRME is used to create and intensify radical and transformational responses to these issues, or whether these principles are co-opted and massaged to ensure 'business as usual' (with some appeasing amendments), is to be determined by our actions. With their explicit focus on systemic injustice, however, specialists in critical management studies have a contribution to make in keeping collective attention on the risk of co-option of these inspiring principles and the challenge to press beyond mere system-preserving amendments.

The call to conference for the International Network for Research in Organisations and Sustainable Development (RIODD) raised some useful questions to which we posit (in italics) some tentative responses to illustrate the potential of a contribution in a critical management studies voice:

- What are the ways in which management education may implicitly foster irresponsible and unethical activities and how can it be avoided? *The ahistorical, apolitical and generally instrumental training of contemporary business schools prepares students to view management as a service primarily to the bottom line – albeit with an eye on the increasing costs and complexities of externalities but without substantial examination of their implications.*

*Institutional mandates or personal (ethical) education need to tackle these dynamics more deeply. We advocate in part for crafting and discussion of more critical polemics, poetics and aesthetics as well as rational argument as thought-provoking opportunities. We call for the greater inclusion of critical management pedagogy across all management subjects to generate the conditions of 'critical alertness' to inform and encourage action.*

- The use of critical pedagogy and ecopedagogy in teaching, e.g. Habermasian, Freirian, post-colonial, feminist or/and post-structural perspectives. *We agree, but would add that this must be accompanied by an acute and critically honed alertness to their potential co-option in systemic preservation. Pernicious harnessing of the employee empowerment discourse to weaken unions was discussed in Chapter 5. The prevalence of the liberal feminist inroads to management education is an excellent example of system-preserving co-option explained more fully in Chapter 6. While perhaps being able to claim some contribution to the selective inclusion of more women in more occupations, and while arguing that the time will amplify these relatively small achievements when globally assessed, feminists from more critical genres see the inclusion of women as systems-endorsing: more women pressed into labour markets (perhaps managed by more women), contextualised by industry standards (perhaps shaped by and certainly defended by ever more women in the PR industry), and wrapped in global policies of development also led by more women than ever. The UNDP, the IMF and Germany as the leading jurisdiction in the Eurozone are examples of women-led institutions. Yet poverty for many women is intensifying, not only for the women in regions once patronised as the 'Third World' but also for those struggling within regional anomalies to the current financial crisis. This is so in Indonesia, for example, as it is for many women in the Roar of the Celtic Tigers before them, or the countless women distressed by specific austerity measures in Greece, Portugal and Spain and those by any other name in reaches far beyond the media-feast of Greece. It is so in less dramatic jurisdictions where the pressures on many women are hidden from full view by their many forms of resilience and adaptations to financial needs and means. Common to them all are: the destruction or reshaping of local communities or their reformation along market-supporting and thus mercurial social networks; the pricing out of reach of essential products and services, including the commodification and re-channelling of water away from the irrigation of once self-sufficient communities that increasingly press women into monetary disciples deemed poor on a dollar-per-day assessment of their status; user-pay mentalities which press all ever further into an often dangerous labour market with insecure futures. In 'model democracies', it is demonstrated by the need for women (and men) to be working several jobs, commuting at great financial cost and intensifying family disruption only to find they still cannot make ends meet, and cover essential costs by increasing debt. And so it goes – back to the debt crisis – not of their making but certainly of significance to their lives be that in and among the struggling members of US society or the women eking out an existence for their families on the promises of micro-financed enterprises – the newest of remedies in the systems assimilation arsenal.*

- What views and values on corporate responsibility and ethics are promoted/tolerated in management education? *And the invitation to peers and students to be alert to this very point. Where are the boundaries of what is allowed to be said? Why? At what risk? We are deeply intrigued at the advice we have been receiving from some of the reviewers of our work not to be so extreme in our views. Management students do not like it! Perhaps it is mind-opening to put before every new entrant in a management qualification some calculations that show how many of the 20–40 per cent of young people unemployed in Greece, Italy and Spain have some kind of management or professional qualification; how many graduates of management schools in the English-speaking world are working contracts well below their educational qualifications and aspirations – and the extent of their debt that they must somehow honour; how many hardworking managers (and employees), who have committed with full integrity to their employers, still lose jobs, homes and at times their families, or their health and their hope – as evidenced in the increases in family disruptions, poverty-related illnesses, and suicides with a discernible systemic link?*

- What voices are marginalised and silenced? How are we to engage the voices that are marginalised within business discourse in the classroom? *And what responsibility do we have to ensure that these voices are not co-opted, domesticated and harnessed to systemic preservation? For this dynamic, we advocate much greater attention to subaltern studies – to a call from the 'periphery' not merely to 'be let in', but for us to learn from those who call from the margins about how these margins are created, imposed and maintained because of what this tells us about (i) who we are (as a species) and (ii) what we might yet become (as a species) should we take seriously the exposed values of universal inclusion and environmental restoration for the sustenance of all life.*

# MARKET-LED JUSTICE

Branson (2011) offers his idea of 'Capitalism 24902' as a way to remedy the ills that he acknowledges have been caused, at least in a big part, by the way in which capitalism has been directed. In *Screw Business as Usual* (2011), he provides countless examples of where businesses or particular individuals have taken a stand on an issue or matter of principle, a stand that has had positive effects on the lives of many. He draws our attention to 'philanthrocapitalism'. He is in good company. 'Philanthrocapitalism' is, of course, not new. Think about the Ford or Kellogg foundations as examples of the choices of men who could not have spent in several life-times the wealth they have accumulated. They turned their wealth to social good – but social good that reinforced and supported the world as they thought it should be. Today's examples include Bill and Melinda Gates, Warren Buffet and the many wealthy people who have significant fortunes to use in reshaping the world in ways they see fit. On the other side, the Koch brothers are affecting legal institutions through funding campaigns and pressing a radically conservative business agenda. 'The market' is seen as both 'the place' and 'the leader' for emancipation. The commitment of much smaller investors may also be harnessed through the many examples where each of us can donate to programmes of aid or invest in the financing of small entrepreneurial businesses seen as the remedy to endemic poverty the world over.

Academics, too, have become activists in this drive to ever-greater market-driven solutions to social and environmental problems. Muhammed Yunus (2007, 2010) has been acknowledged for his focus on enterprise as a way to alleviate poverty by helping the poorest people produce and consume on the market as we know it. That business can be a force for good in the world is exemplified by the Global Compact we drew attention to in Chapter 1 and in the work of the Case Western University's leadership in the BAWB programme. The idea is embedded also in the notion of corporate social responsibility (CSR) and countless examples of people who intentionally see business as a way of 'doing good' in/for the world. How such business is managed 'for good' is a very big question which we raised in Chapter 1 – a question that has taken many forms throughout this book. Much depends on how one defines 'good' – and it is for this reason that we think critical management studies in its many forms has a 'good contribution' to make to the education of managers. A structural-functionalist approach invites scrutiny of the structures and functions of an enterprise, an industry or even a person's identity. Organisational theorists with a social constructivist approach, particularly those with a focus on language, help us focus on how humanity turns ideas into reality – no less into structures, functions and roles. To leave you with some new directions for thought, we now advocate for two theories less frequently used in management education to frame different questions again, questions that may encourage new trajectories of thought and action. More attention to these theories would draw a different kind of attention to the issues discussed in this book.

# ARE WE TOO RADICAL OR NOT RADICAL ENOUGH?

In fact, it's 'business as usual' that is wrecking our planet. Resources are being used up; the air, the sea, the land – are all heavily polluted. The poor are getting poorer.

Richard Branson (2011: 4–5)

Should we subject ourselves to such a system that not only Branson depicts as destructive and degrading?

Disobedience, in the eyes of anyone who has read history, is humanity's original virtue. It is through disobedience that progress has been made, through disobedience and through rebellion.

Oscar Wilde (1891)

Given the widespread recognition that the social and environmental issues understood by many to have reached crisis proportions are systemic, there are now many calls for the reshaping of capitalism. What is hopeful about this focus on the system is that structures, functions, roles and even the very identity of managers and employees are now not to be viewed merely as functionaries in a supposedly a-moral system. The system is increasingly recognised as the outcome of our collective ideas and endeavours. Such recognition of the genesis of any system in the mind of humanity opens the potential for dramatic re-visioning, re-thinking and re-crafting. The big question, of course, is – into what?

We have introduced subaltern studies and radical human ecology as examples of theories we can look to as a way of keeping vigilant in the face of many hopeful remedies to the issues facing humanity. Through the questions generated from these theories we can ask questions about the extent to which incremental inclusion in markets of once excluded people, more robust procedures for justice within organisations, and a greater focus on sustainability can redress the colonisation of the lifeworld by the institutional logics of capitalism as is the concern of Deetz (1992). Drawing our minds back to the transformative potential of social constructivists, we are reminded that the social world is made of stories – and it is to a story we now turn to reflect on what it may mean to include all life in how we organise our humanity.

# THE WORLD AS ONE: A PARABLE

In a village far, far away people are thriving. Care for the young and old, the sick and infirm is shared with graciousness. All have homes that are warm in the winter and cool in the summer. All experience love and joy in abundance. Children are loved and sheltered from all harm. All but one little girl that is, a little girl kept in a cellar at the outskirts of the village. She cannot leave. Her physical body is kept barely alive by the regular delivery of food and water and the removal of her excrement. She cannot remember nor imagine a life that is different. The tasks of her maintenance are shared by the elders of the village and her existence is kept secret from the village children. When a village child is on the cusp of the transition from child to adult, a village elder will take that child to bring food and water to the little girl and to take away her excrement. There will be no talking till the task is done. It will then be explained that the security and joy of the village is wholly dependent on the maintenance of the status quo: the little girl in the cellar, the blissful ignorance of the village children, the transference of responsibility for her up-keep to the elders, and the responsibility of the elders to retain this order – an order in which all villagers may thrive. To be an elder means to be responsible for maintaining this order. To be an adult means to take this order for granted. To jeopardise this order would be inconceivable – or lead to instant banishment from the village to a land much less hospitable.

Parables are fables, stories told to invite reflection on some aspect of our humanity. Of course, this story does not hold up to rational analyses. It was not intended to. It is a parable. It was told as part of an invitation to teach towards a greater moral awareness of the values underpinning the predominant principles through which Western people organise themselves and seek to organise others. Perhaps this story is told in many forms in many places – as good parables often are. This one is about the principles of the economic system of trade and exchange that together are known as 'capitalism' and 'democracy'. Both declare open access to the means for human development and both purport to value universal human emancipation. Yet, despite the undeniable wealth that has been created through the application of these principles and the systemic assimilation of many previously excluded individuals and groups, there is a case to be made that it is through the uncritical manifestation of these principles that many other people are alienated, exploited and harmed. The same may be said of Earth. They are 'the little girl in the cellar'. Their precarious existence provides a conundrum for people who proclaim or aspire to be a 'just people' and part of a 'just society'.

In the telling of our version of the story of capitalism, we have, at times, dramatised for analytical effect the dimensions of the organising principles of capitalism and democracy that are often unexposed or unexplored in much that passes for management education at all levels. Building on the insight of subaltern studies, these ideas can be made more explicit yet. 'Capitalism' is personified as 'The Master' and 'Democracy' is depicted as 'His Attractive Consort'. Both are enabled by 'Patriarchy' (Thomas and Humphries, 2011a, b). Such a personification of the entities we take for granted in the fabrication of the neoliberal myth invites close attention to what may be going on in our village. This is the household we are all required to serve. It is a household from which there are few means of total escape. It is a household with a cellar big enough to hold more than just one little girl. While The Consort is dressed in the wardrobe of influence, like many a Patriarchal marriage, her influence is at best indirect and worst purely enabling. To be otherwise would risk her position and all she might hope to achieve through it – for herself and for those who she perceives of as her dependants.

If one pays close attention to the gender of the people who are sitting at the decision-making tables in the household of The Master (or 'The Market' or 'The Economy'), we can see that there are several very powerful women holding much authority, responsibility and power over the lives of many. These are almost all white women. These are nearly all women steeped in the traditions of Western liberalism. Are they harbingers of radical change or does their inclusion safeguard the values of the system? Can they be trusted to reproduce or radically reform it? The same might be asked of all the changes achieved by a greater 'respect for diversity' in employment – locally or globally and all that this has come to mean – whether this is the tacit endorsement of homophobia in Africa by diminishing calls for equal employment opportunities for homosexuals, the job opportunities for women in societies that have clear ideas about women's subjugation, or the ruse of Western capitalist societies whose purported meritocracy has not safeguarded the sustainable livelihoods of countless human beings pressed into the market to earn their living – a system, it appears, the West is willing to impose on the rest, as the best form of development known to humanity. The Global Compact, the various BAWB programmes and the ideas behind 'philanthrocapitalism', social entrepreneurship and microfinance are not radical alternatives when considered in this way. They are means to extend the reach and grip of the economic rationality that some, even Richard Branson, have firmly linked to the issues we have raised in this book.

# KANTIAN ETHICS: THE INTERRELATIONSHIP OF ALL THAT LIVES

## The Little Girl in our Cellar: A Close(r) Encounter

In this section, we return our attention to Habermas and his concerns. We ask how useful his 'communicative action' ideas are in relation to the issues canvassed in this book. This discussion is drawn into a discussion of the instrumental rationality of capitalism largely taken for granted in management education and the potential of a more relational focused ethic. To consider consciously and continually much of the world's poverty, racism, sexism and other exclusions, the continued decimation of indigenous people and their lands (United Nations, 2009) and the various (dis)stresses of people and planet that are 'systemically embedded' is challenging. Much oppression and exploitation remains largely invisible or of insignificance to many. To make the connections between the principles of the system and the outcomes of our allegiance to them in the lives of human beings requires the work of what Kirton (1997) calls 'making the invisible visible'. To do so is to invite ourselves to consider whether the outcomes we choose to examine are the unintended consequences of a basically sound system of trade and exchange or attributable to some bad decisions on the part of the sufferers.

This level of examination brings discomfort as many students will be related to people who may appear to have brought the misfortune of unemployment or poverty on themselves. A deeper discussion of their circumstances, however, will often disclose systemic influences. Even more uncomfortable is the possibility that the dire circumstances of many lives are intentional and rationally planned by third parties. Most readily at hand for discussion as examples are the current 'austerity measures' imposed to 'stabilise the system', but that will undermine the security of millions of people the world over. Some will be driven to despair.

Stress-related illness, family violence and suicide are some of the known effects of such measures. With examples such as these under the spotlight, it becomes more reasonable to re-examine the regular restructurings and outplacements that are imposed under the so-called normal workings of capitalism and, by and large, condoned as sad but necessary. These regular readjustments of (or *for)* capital no less destroy hope, life, families and communities.

From this position, students can be invited to look more closely at the consequences of otherwise apparently responsible and democratic governance of nations, as guided by the IMF and the World Bank, for the *flow on effect* on social and economic policy. We can reconsider the supposed 'collateral damage' generated by the cavalier pursuit of systemically legitimised self-interest – a breath-taking war metaphor made most explicit in the discussions of the accelerating 'currency wars' in the media as we write this book. To seek our own complicity in the generation of such outcomes is uncomfortable. Merely raising the requirement to reflect on such issues *as* systemic outcomes has been received as a (sometimes unwelcome) challenge by the students we have encountered. We have, with close colleagues, sought ways to make these challenges more interesting, more palatable, and more personally significant in the hope that they too would put their mind to the necessary transformations if their expressed ideals of justice and security for themselves, their families and the planet are to be realised.

There are now many more effective advocates framing ever more robust critiques of capitalism than there were 20 years ago. These critiques are finding their way into management education. We are in good company. We see one aspect of our task as amplifying and exploring their critiques and the remedies that flow from them. Even acknowledging the greater willingness to discuss 'sustainability' and 'justice' by many leaders, teachers and students, their eye is not often on the little girl in the cellar. Of those willing to consider her, many are still of the view that greater economic growth (albeit with more responsible management practices) will release her. Maybe more women at the strategy levels of governance, some venture, would humanise the economy. Evidence to date suggests that this is a delusion.

Humphries and Grant (2010) draw on Herman and Chomsky (1988) to help explain levels of selective (in)tolerance of inequality in explicitly democratic nations as the achievement of a form of consent. In their critique of the prevailing moral ethic, where markets can be demonstrated to be free and level, social outcomes are deemed to be just. That such a society has yet to be realised is a moot point in this line of reasoning. Put differently, 'justice', according to advocates of capitalism, is the outcome of free (but fair) market practices. This school of thought is generated from an instrumental institutional logic that finds its origins in the de-spiritualised materialism and humanism that informs much social, economic and political thinking. This view of civilisation, development and justice is being intensified the world over – yes, at times at the point of a gun – more regularly through the achievement of a naturalised logic that is limited and limiting in its scope. It is a logic that dehumanises and domesticates, a logic that has as one drastic consequence the tolerance of systemic injustice and even (premature) death. Privilege and pain might be relocated, but the basic dynamic will remain constant.

The form of capitalist practices reified as 'the market', and amplified globally, continues to require sacrifices. These sacrifices are the people whose lands are routinely confiscated, who are 'liberated' from subsistence lives to the 'freedom' of the labour market. They are domesticated to be compliant, forcibly harnessed to unsustainable life circumstances. They may live in new reservations or they may live in your street. They are the over- or un(der)-employed, drawn in or expelled, according to the economic logic of the times. Their governments may not be able or willing to underwrite their existence – even though these same governments created the conditions that serve The Master over the needs of their citizens.[1] They are the people whose alternatives are reduced or destroyed by 'the market', and whose children and elders die for want of adequate heat, food or health care. Such systemic death is no less a genocide than the outright killing of any population by a powerful elite and their functionaries (Humphries, 2007). The very ordinariness of these alienations, illness and death is the contemporary face of the 'banality of evil', a powerful phrase brought to our attention by Hanna Arendt (1994) and finding greater attention in reflections on contemporary human (organisational) behaviour (Zuboff, 2009).

We have at our fingertips a larger than ever supply of evidence to demonstrate the pervasiveness of systemic suffering. We can find countless examples that demonstrate that the suffering of others cannot be relieved without changing life as we know it for ourselves and our children. 'Development' is offered as the means for the release of the little girl in the cellar. Yet all over the 'developed world', cellars with children, displaced persons, the vulnerable and the weak are systemically entwined with the rooms and the kitchens that are the homes of the better-insulated servants of 'the system' we might now refer to as The Master's house. The world over, the destruction of alternative sources of livelihoods ensures that we must all dance to the tune called by The Master – even when it is a dangerous, life-depleting, soul-destroying dance.

Human dignity and self-respect surely must depend on the response of the rich and powerful to the poor, the weak, the vulnerable – not in the form of dignity-destroying charity or patronising compassion – but in the form of 'right-ing relationships'. The naturalised instrumental ethic that now facilitates global capitalism will not bring us to such consciousness. A relational ethic is required, one based on a transformation of the instrumentality with which we now justify and deflect attention away from death and destruction: genocide by stealth, an evil of silent complicity.

## Releasing the Little Girl from our Cellar: The PRME as Emancipation

In the recent 'crises' we have seen writ large the same disparities of old. The poor are hit hardest, the vulnerable more likely to die earlier or more painfully.

That we tolerate such repeated outcomes is a puzzle only to those who are not convinced that Gramsci got it right – the system is set up to achieve compliance – not always or only at the point of a gun, but in the collective subjugation to its principles and in the achievement of fealty to The Master. Of course, 'the system' cannot demand such fealty. It is not an intentional being. In fact, what we call 'the system' is not even a real thing. Rather 'the system' is a figment of human imagination, as is 'The Master', as depicted in our adaptation of the metaphors of subaltern studies. These characters are figments of human imagination manifest or incarnated through the processes and practices we come to experience 'as reality'. Let us tell *more* difficult, *more* confrontational stories. Let us be less quick to provide our students with a-contextual 'good news' stories. Let us credit ourselves with the capacity to live through some uncomfortable classes – and to have them reflect on their discomfort and on the discomfort suffered by many – sometimes at our direct hand – sometimes as the outcome of decisions made far beyond our apparent influence.

As authors of this book, we are teachers who have been engaged in management education for several decades. We have sought to contribute to the transformation of a broader society that we can be proud of, that we can trust to provide the conditions for thriving for all our grandchildren and theirs. Our concerns are shared by many. In expressing such concerns in our classrooms, we may bring discomfort. We maintain this uncomfortable position because we want to grow in confidence that all children and theirs will have the opportunity to thrive and that our work is a contribution to that future. We want to contribute to the organising of our collective social life so that there are no creatures in any cellars constrained from thriving so that others might.

Will the promulgation of the PRME and our personal commitment to the ideals embedded in these enhance our opportunities to do so? Will they help us to release the little girl in our cellar? Not, in our view, if these principles become the means by which we, as teachers and students, continue, by and large, to frame concerns about justice and sustainability in the prevailing market-orientated institutional logics that have colonised much of our policy and practice – well beyond the realms of trade and exchange that they may have been devised to enable. We argue that we need to make the existence of the cellar much more explicit. We need to stop averting our eyes from the little girl in our cellar. We need to commit to her release.

# CONCLUSION

For authors such as Reason (2005), Senge and colleagues (2008) and Wheatley and Frieze (2011), the current Western worldview, dominating much human endeavour with an intense and far-reaching grip on what has been thought possible, is reaching the end of its useful life. Many teachers and students recognise the need for a different approach to the instrumental management education that has been normalised for a number of generations. While individual professors continue to bring these matters to their teaching, critical management studies scholars would argue that such well-intentioned challenges have not addressed deeply enough the systemic link between the issues under review and the system that generates them. If they had, we would not see their persistence.

It is no longer radical to draw attention to the fact that, wherever a market-servicing logic has prevailed, many people are not free. Many are trapped, as is the little girl in the cellar, in jobs that do not provide sustainable livelihoods. When capital comes under stress, many are condemned to become the sacrifice we must make to save 'the economy'. The rest are required to 'tighten their belt' or to find themselves at risk of joining those in the cellar. The suffering of others is tolerated to assure the comfort of the Master and allocated privilege of the majority. The little girl of our time and place may be imprisoned by race, class, gender, act of nature or accident of birth. In times of crisis for the Master, her conditions deteriorate. Blame is variously attributed to 'the crisis', the 'over-spending population' or the 'shrinking economy'. All are suspect causal inferences. It is not that we would be so crass as to make her 'suffering as necessity' as is made explicit in the opening story. It is just that we cannot seem to find the way to release her – without fear that our own security may be compromised. Does the expression of this concern plant a seed of negativity or of hope?

## Nine Barriers to Reinventing Capitalism

*What we have before us are some breathtaking opportunities, disguised as insoluble* problems.

Amory Lovins (2011: xii)

John Elkington (2012a) reviews Amory Lovins's book *Reinventing Fire: Bold Business Solutions for the New Energy Era* (2011). Lovins argues that what gets in the way of a major shift to renewable energies gets in the way of many of the transformations needed to bring human existence to sustainability. The centennial issue of *The Wall Street Journal* named Lovins among 39 people in the world most likely to change the course of business in the 1990s; *Car* called him the twenty-second most powerful person in the global car industry; and *The Economist* wrote in 2008 that 'history has proved him right' (Elkington, 2008).

Below are Lovins's nine barriers to reinventing capitalism, as discussed by Elkington (2012a). Do these still hold true?

1. *Active or passive resistance by incumbents*: Here the key problem is that 'most organisations have an energy using and generating asset based on fossil fuels'. From the organisation's viewpoint, moving away from fossil fuels looks both 'risky and costly'. The shift to new forms of capitalism dedicated to building multiple forms of capital looks even riskier.
2. *Economics and technology*: 'The economic and technological barriers are shrinking as high-value efficiency and renewable solutions are brought to

market, but hurdles persist in some sectors.' The same is true of all major industrial sectors, energy to education, finance to food.

3. *Knowledge and culture*: Even with higher prices, 'energy is not a priority for most organisations, so many lack the knowledge, willingness, or capabilities to move away from fossil fuels.' And, too often, what is true of energy is also true of the future in general.

4. *Financing*: A key problem is that 'energy investments, often with sizeable initial investments and relatively long term paybacks, vie with others nearer a company's core priorities.' The same is true, across the economy, for governments.

5. *Value-chain complexity*: Investments in solutions in the energy sector 'often link multiple parties across long value chains, with sometimes misaligned incentives, routing costs and benefits to different parties'.

6. *Unclear value proposition*: 'Energy is energy, clean or not, so selling efficiency and renewables to undiscriminating customers can be hard.' Even governments struggle to bring their immense purchasing power to bear in support of the necessary transitions.

7. *Lack of long-term leadership*: A challenge we spotlighted in our Future Quotient work (http://futurequotient.tumblr.com/report/; www.guardian.co.uk/sustainable-business/strategy), it is an increasingly inconvenient truth that 'changing the energy strategy of a company, state, or nation requires planning and stewardship over decades – a far longer time period than profit or election horizons.'

8. *Policy and regulatory structures*: In a masterpiece of understatement, Amory and his team note that, 'some existing policies and regulatory structures impede energy transformation, so they must be changed or replaced to enable and accelerate it.' System change is easy to talk about and harder to effect than most of its champions imagine.

9. *Entanglement with partisan politics*: This is a particular killer in the US at the moment. To take just one example, congressional vacillation 'has severely damaged the US windpower industry four times and killed every sizeable domestic wind-turbine maker except GE, so China, Denmark and Germany now lead an industry which, the book notes grimly, was invented – in its modern sense – by Charles Brush of Ohio. Arguing that the fossil fuel party is now drawing to a close, Amory and his team highlight key features of the old and new energy systems. 'The old fire was dug from below', they say. 'The new fire flows from above. The old fire was scarce. The new fire is bountiful. The old fire was local. The new fire is everywhere. The old fire was transient. The new fire is permanent. And except for a little biofuel, biogas, and biomass, all grown in ways that sustain and endure, the new fire is flameless – providing all the convenient and dependable services of the old fire but with no combustion.' The sort of question Amory is likely to ask business leaders resonates strongly with the ones posed by financial analyst Jeremy Grantham: 'When your shareholders in this decade, and later your grandchildren in retirement, ask what you did to meet humanity's supreme

energy challenge, how will you answer? And when you're at work, how deeply do you discount your great-granddaughter's future' (Elkington, 2012a, b).

Should the identities on the list of his admirers raise any concerns for us?

---

### Tricky Questions

- Are we all trapped in the language games of 'the economy' – or are management students more susceptible to assimilation than other human beings?
- If all history is sealed within the power arrangements of social construction, what liberating perspectives stand outside those power arrangements and make it possible for the postmodernist to see the abuses of socially constructed power?
- To what extent do we, as management scholars, students and practitioners, deflect attention from or diminish responsibilities for systemic outcomes by teaching or applying functional competencies at the expense of ethical concern about such outcomes?

---

# NOTE

1 See, for example, the unfolding distress of the people of Cyprus, Greek citizens, outplaced people everywhere, the latest and most widely, but temporarily, covered by the media of such processes, processes that are widespread but, beyond the newsflash, largely under-reported.

# ADDITIONAL RESOURCES

Alvesson, M. and Willmott, H. (2003) *Studying Management Critically*. London: Sage.

Boje, D. (2008) Reconsidering the role of conversation: a contribution based on Bakhtin. *Journal of Organizational Change Management*, 21 (6): 667–85.

Camus, M. (2008) The hidden hand between poetry and science. In B. Nicolescu (ed.), *Transdisciplinarity: Theory and Practice*. Cresskill, NJ: Hampton. pp. 53–65.

Christensen, L.J., Peirce, E., Hartman, L.P., Hoffman, W.M. and Carrier, J. (2007) Ethics, CSR and sustainability education in the *Financial Times* Top 50 global business schools: baseline data and future research directions. *Journal of Business Ethics*, 73 (4): 347–68.

Dey, K., Hurd, F. and Humphries, M. (2011) Critical management studies (CMS) and quantum physics (QP): inviting the re-animation of (almost) every thing. Paper presented at the Organization, Identity and Locality (OIL) VII: Local

Theory ('Let's Get "Inventin"!') Conference, Palmerston North, New Zealand (www.massey.ac.nz/~cprichar/OIL%20VII%20proceedings_final.pdf; retrieved 14 September 2013).

Fougère, M. and Solitander, N. (2009) Against corporate responsibility: critical reflections on thinking, practice, content and consequences. *Corporate Social Responsibility and Environmental Management*, 16: 217–27.

Jones, C. and Munro, R. (2005) *Contemporary Organisation Theory*. Oxford: Blackwell.

Korten, D. (2009) *Agenda for a New Economy: From Phantom Wealth to Real Wealth*. San Francisco: Berrett-Koehler.

Maxton, G. (2011) *The End of Progress: How Modern Economics Has Failed Us*. Singapore: John Wiley & Sons.

O'Faircheallaigh, C. and Saleem, A. (2008) *Indigenous Peoples, the Extractive Industries and Corporate Social Responsibility*. Sheffield: Greenleaf.

Perkins, J. (2009) *Hoodwinked: An Economic Hit Man*. San Francisco: Berrett-Koehler.

Robinson, D. (2012) Universities (www.radionz.co.nz/national/programmes/sunday/audio/2513682/david-robinson-universities; retrieved 14 September 2013).

Shriberg, M.P. (2002) Sustainability in US higher education: organizational factors influencing campus environmental performance and leadership. PhD thesis, University of Michigan.

Steketee, D. (2009) A million decisions: life on the (sustainable business) frontier. *Journal of Management Education*, 33 (3): 391–401.

Stiglitz, J. (2012) *Price of Inequity: How Today's Divided Society Endangers our Future*. New York: W.W. Norton.

Stubbs, W. and Cocklin, C. (2007) Teaching sustainability to business students: shifting mindsets. *International Journal of Sustainability in Higher Education*, 9 (3): 206–21.

UNPRME (2010) The United Nations Principles for Responsible Management Education (www.unprme.org; retrieved 18 November 2010).

Wheatley, M. and Frieze, D. (2011) *Walk Out! Walk On! A Learning Journey into Communities Daring to Live the Future Now*. San Francisco: Berrett-Koehler.

Williams, L., Roberts, R. and McIntosh, A. (2012) *Radical Human Ecology: Intercultural and Indigenous Approaches*. Surrey: Ashgate.

Willmott, D. (2011) Journal fetishism and the perversion of scholarship: reactivity and the ASB List. *Organisation*, 4: 429–42.

# REFERENCES

Arendt, H. (1994) *Eichmann in Jerusalem: A Report on the Banality of Evil*. New York: Penguin.

bell hooks (1994) *Teaching to Transgress: Education and the Practice of Freedom*. New York: Routledge (http://pedsub.files.wordpress.com/2010/10/hooks-engaged-pedagogy.pdf; retrieved 14 September 2013).

Branson, R. (2011) *Screw Business as Usual*. New York: Penguin.

Brower, H. (2011) Sustainable development through service learning: a pedagogical framework and case example in a Third World context. Academy of Management Learning and Education, 10 (1): 58–76.

Deetz, S. (1992) Democracy in an Age of Corporate Colonization: Developments in Communication and the Politics of Everyday Life. Albany, NY: State University of New York.

Elkington, J. (2008) Getting companies to view CSR differently (www.sustainability.com/news/john-elkington-in-the-economist-on-getting-companies-to-view-csr-differently; retrieved 7 October 2013).

Elkington, J. (2012a) Nine barriers to reinventing capitalism. *Guardian*, 21 March (www.theguardian.com/sustainable-business/sustainability-with-john-elkington/reinventing-transforming-capitalism-barriers; retrieved 14 September 2013).

Elkington, J. (2012b) 'Your grandchildren have no value'. *Guardian*, 29 February (www.guardian.co.uk/sustainable-business/sustainability-with-john-elkington/investors-longterm-sustainable-finance; retrieved 14 September 2013).

Fetzer Institute (n.d.) Center for Business as an Agent of World Benefit, Case Western Reserve University (www.fetzer.org/resources/partners/center-business-agent-world-benefit-case-western-reserve-university; retrieved 14 September 2013).

Gramsci, A. (1971) *Selections from the Prison Notebooks*, trans. Q. Hoare and G. Nowell-Smith. London: Lawrence and Wishart.

Heathfield, S.M. (2013) Inspirational quotes for business and work: leadership. *About.com* (http://humanresources.about.com/od/workrelationships/a/quotes_leaders.htm; retrieved 5 October 2013).

Herman, E.S. and Chomsky, N. (1988) *Manufacturing Consent: The Political Economy of the Mass Media*. New York: Pantheon.

Humphries, M.T. (2007) Denial and the dance of death. Paper presented at the 23rd EGOS Colloquium Wirtschaftsuniversität Wien. Beyond the Waltz – Dances of Individuals and Organization. Stream: Genocide, Individuals, and Organisations. Choices, Actions and Consequences for Contemporary Contexts. Vienna.

Humphries, M.T. and Grant, S. (2010) In the subaltern voice (TSV): third sector researchers calling from the margins. Paper presented at the *9th International Conference of the International Society for Third-Sector Research*, Istanbul.

Jim Wu, Y.C., Huang, S., Kuo, L. and Wu, W-H. (2010) Management education for sustainability: a web-based content analysis. *Academy of Management Learning and Education*, 9 (3): 520–31.

Kirton, J.D. (1997) *Paakeha/Tauiwi: Seeing the 'Unseen': Critical Analysis of Links between Discourse, Identity, 'Blindness' and Encultured Racism*. Hamilton, NZ: Waikato Antiracism Coalition.

Lovins, A.B. (2011) *Reinventing Fire: Bold Business Solutions for the New Energy Era*. White River Junction, VT: Chelsea Green.

Maori TV (2013) *The Edge of the Earth*, Tuesday 29 January, 8.30 p.m.

Margaronis, M. (2012) Dimitris Christoulas and the legacy of his suicide for Greece. *Guardian*, 5 April (www.guardian.co.uk/commentisfree/2012/apr/05/dimitris-christoulas-legacy-suicide-greece; retrieved 14 September 2013).

Pless, N.M., Maak, T. and Stahl, G.K. (2011) Developing responsible global leaders through international service-learning programs: the Ulysses experience. *Academy of Management Learning and Education*, 10 (2): 237–60.

Reason, P. (2005) Living as part of the whole: the implications. *Journal of Curriculum and Pedagogy*, 2 (2): 35–41.

Senge, P., Smith, B., Kruschwitz, N., Laur, J. and Schley, S. (2008) *The Necessary Revolution: How Individuals and Organizations Are Working Together to Create a Sustainable World*. New York: Random House.

Seo, M.G. and Creed, W.E.D. (2002) Institutional contradictions, praxis and institutional change: a dialectical perspective. *Academy of Management Review*, 27
(2): 222–47.

Sibbel, A. (2009) Pathways towards sustainability through higher education.
*International Journal of Sustainability in Higher Education*, 10 (1): 68–82.

Starik, M., Rands, G., Marcus, A. and Clarke, T. (2010) From the guest editors: in
search of sustainability in management education. *Academy of Management
Learning and Education*, 9 (3): 377–83.

Stead, J.G. and Stead, W.E. (2010) Sustainability comes to management education
and research: a story of coevolution. *Academy of Management Learning and
Education*, 9 (3): 488–97.

Stephens, J.C., Hernandez, M.E., Román, M., Graham, A.C. and Scholz, R.W.
(2008) Higher education as a change agent for sustainability in different cultures
and contexts. *International Journal of Sustainability in Higher Education*, 9 (3):
317–38.

Thomas, A. and Humphries, M.T. (2011a) Stream 25: alternative futures filling the
empty signifier with the rhetoric of emancipation: drawing women into the market – a case in point. Paper presented at the 7th International Critical Management
Studies Conference, Naples, 11–13 July.

Thomas, A. and Humphries, M.T. (2011b) Leaders or house girls in our own land?
Sub-theme 28: Translating discourses: text, change and organization. Paper pre-
sented at the 27th EGOS Colloquium, Gothenburg University, Gothenburg,
Sweden, 7–9 July.

United Nations (2009) *State of the World's Indigenous Peoples* (www.un.org/esa/
socdev/unpfii/documents/SOWIP_web.pdf; retrieved 28 September 2013).

Wheatley, M. and Frieze, D. (2011) *Walk Out! Walk On! A Learning Journey into
Communities Daring to Live the Future Now*. San Francisco: Berrett-Koehler.

Wilde, O. (1891) The soul of man under socialism (www.marxists.org/reference/
archive/wilde-oscar/soul-man/; retrieved 7 October 2013).

Williams, L., Roberts, R. and McIntosh, A. (2012) *Radical Human Ecology:
Intercultural and Indigenous Approaches*. Surrey: Ashgate.

Young, S. and Black, L. (2013) A partnership approach to developing responsible
education. In B. Hughes and G. Avery (eds), *Fresh Thoughts in Sustainable
Leadership*. Melbourne: Tilde University Press. pp. 192–200.

Young, S. and Nagpal, S. (2013) Meeting the growing demand for sustainability-
focused management education: a case study of a PRME academic institution.
*Higher Education Research and Development*, 32 (3): 493–506.

Yunus, M. (2007) *Creating a World without Poverty*. New York: Public Affairs.

Yunus, M. (2010) Building Social Business: The New Kind of Capitalism that Serves
Humanity's Most Pressing Needs. New York: Public Affairs.

Zuboff, S. (2009) Wall Street's economic crimes against humanity. Bloomberg
Business Week, 20 March (www.businessweek.com/managing/content/mar2009/
ca20090319_591214.htm; retrieved 10 October 2010).

# INDEX

Chicago School of Economics, 70
choice *see* purchasing decisions
Chomsky, N., 95
Clancy, G., 110
class consciousness, 40
class relations, 34–5, 37, 40, 100
Clegg, S.R., 148
Coates, C., 211
Colignon, R.A., 20
collaboration, against system, 37
colonialism, 23–4, 51
colonisation, 50, 267
    by corporate sector, 140–1, 143–4, 145
commodification
    of seed, 212–14
    of water, 212, 214–18, 220
commodity fetishism, 36, 191–4
common good, 33–4, 183, 248–9
    *see also* social wellbeing
communicative action, 48–50
communism, 69
community labour, 116, 130, 144
competitive individualism, 69–70
compliance, 15, 134
    creating docile bodies, 134–5, 139
    role of government, 137
    and techniques of the self, 138–9
consciousness
    dialectic consciousness, 43
    false consciousness, 37, 267
    Hegel's self–consciousness, 33–4
    Page's approach, 222–3
    reified consciousness, 40, 267
    *see also* unconscious
consciousness-raising, 9–10, 37
consumer activism, 184
consumer culture, 177–8, 189
consumer research, 180, 186
consumer sovereignty, 183–7
    barriers to participation, 187–8
    and transformative change, 184, 192–4
consumers
    ethical/political responsibility, 182–3, 186
    framing of, 179–82
    power relative to producers, 188–91, 192–3
    relationship with workers, 166, 192
consumption
    meanings vested in, 182
    as means of control, 178–9
    transformative change through, 184,
        187–91, 192–4
contracting out, *see* outsourcing
contradiction, exposure of, 54–5, 107
control of people, 239–40
    docility and compliance, 134–5
    government role, 53, 136, 139, 179

control of people *cont.*
    market as means of, 53
    role of consumption, 178–9
    role of corporate norms, 140–5
    *see also* control of workforce; hegemonic
        control
control of work, 94–5
    *see also* organisation of work
control of workforce, 131–3
    and flexibility, 100–2, 128
    human relations theory, 147–9
    human resource management, 149–50
    and non-voluntary volunteers, 113
Convention on the Elimination of All Forms
    of Discrimination against Women
    (CEDAW), 162–3
core workforce, 102
corporate interests, 9, 141
    and state policy, 79, 83–4, 141
corporate norms, and control, 140–5
corporate responsibility, 23, 204, 207, 209–10
corporations
    free trade and outsourcing, 98, 104, 130
    power of, 22–4, 77–9, 83–4
    rise of, 77–8
    and UN goals, 23, 73–4, 76
creationist stories, 219–20
critical management studies, 31, 56
    potential contribution, 272–4
    strengths and challenges, 265
critical theory, 31–2
    contemporary thinkers, 54–5
    Frankfurt School, 41–3
    pillars of, 32–41
    postmodernism, 46–54
    and theories of unconscious, 44–5
customers
    relationship with workers, 166, 192
    *see also* consumers

De Beers, 79
de-institutionalisation, 140–1, 145
de-reification, 56
Declaration of the Rights of Indigenous
    Peoples, 75–6, 208
deconstruction, of texts, 47, 54
Deephouse, D.L., 7
Deetz, S., 140–1, 145, 150
dehumanisation of workforce, 99, 127
democracy
    Friedman's view of, 68–9
    Gaian approach, 219–20
    and neoliberalism, 84–5
    reflecting on, 277
Denegri-Knott, J., 193
deregulation of labour market, 102, 104, 128

Derrida, J., 46–7
deskilling, 99, 131, 191
developing countries
    consumerism in, 181
    imposition of neo-liberalism on, 72
development, UN principles of, 73–7
dialectic consciousness, 43
dialogue, Buber's theory of, 48
disciplinary power, 133–5
disciplinary society, 134
discipline, Foucault's theory of, 48
discourse, 17
    and consumerism, 189–90
    Foucault's theory of, 47–8
    postmodern concept of, 54
discrimination
    ILO definition, 162
    legislation against, 163–4
diversity
    recognition of, 51–2
    see also workforce diversity
diversity management (DM), 165–7, 168
docile bodies
    creating, 134–5, 139
    see also compliance
documentaries, 203
dogma, neo-liberal, 20, 64, 70, 107
domestic labour, 116, 169
domestication, 4, 264
downsizing, 106–7, 114
Drucker, P., 241–2
Dunkerley, D., 148
duty, work as, 158–9, 171

Earth
    meanings vested in, 200–1
    spiritual approach, 219–25
eco-warriors, 209–11
ecology, Gaian approach, 219–21
economics, and morals, 69
ecosophy, 220–1
education
    and consumerism, 181
    and corporate norms, 141–3
    and factory model, 13–14, 17, 136
    as soul work, 262, 263–5x
EEO see equal employment opportunities
efficiency, 92
Eichmann, A., 15
emancipation
    role of market, 19, 23, 53
    see also freedom
emancipatory moment, 43
emotional intelligence, 241
emotional labour, 115
empire, 23–4, 51

employees see workforce
employment
    concepts of work and, 92–3
    equal access to, 159, 167–8, 170–1
    as human right, 158–60, 162–3, 167
    idea of, 21
    link with freedom, 93–4, 160, 167–8, 169
    as necessity, 126
    organisation of, 96
    work that enables, 115–16
    see also work
empowerment, of workers, 101, 243
enclosure, 24, 212–13, 216
environment
    commodification of see seed; water
    spiritual approach, 219–25
environmental activism, 207, 209–11
environmental causes, donations to, 8
environmental damage, 5–6, 204, 209–10
environmental responsibility, 184, 202–3,
        204–6, 210–11
environmentalism, 205–6, 213–14
    see also environmental activism
epistemology, 200
equal employment opportunities (EEO), 159,
        162–3, 167–8, 170–1
equal opportunity, 69–70
equal pay, 162, 164
equality
    legislation/conventions, 162–4, 168
    see also inequality
ethical consumerism, 182–3, 186
ethics
    and consumer sovereignty, 187–8
    Kant, 32–3
    and leadership, 248–9
    and management, 207
    see also morals
ethnicity see race and ethnicity
experts in subjectivity, 137–8, 139–40, 145,
        147, 148
exploitation
    and American model, 63–4
    and Marx's theory of capitalism, 35
    in mining industry, 11
factory model, in education, 13–14, 17, 136
fair-trade schemes, 185–6
false consciousness, 37, 267
    see also reified consciousness
family life, 143–4
Fasih, T., 141
feminine leadership style, 242, 243
financial crisis, 62, 64, 237–8, 247
financial crisis cont.
    see also recession
financial trade, 80, 185

fishing industry, 212
flexible firm model, 102–6, 128
flexible work organisation, 100–6
  and control of workforce, 101–2, 128
  and corporate norms in education, 141
  outcomes, 109–10, 128, 129–30
  outsourcing, 103, 104, 105, 107–9
  prerequisites for, 117
followership, 236, 249
food consumption, 180, 185
food corporations, 77–8
food production, 72
Foucault, M., 47–8, 133–5, 137–8, 243
Foxconn, 117–18
Frankfurt School, 41–3
free speech, 42
free-trade agreements, 71–2, 98, 104, 127
freedom
  Friedman's view of, 68–9
  link with work, 91–2, 93–5, 99, 131, 160
  and morality, 206–9
  to choose employment, 167–8, 169
  see also emancipation
Freire, P., 225
Freud, S., 44
Friedman, M., 68–9, 102
Fromm, E., 44
Fukuyama, F., 62
functional analyses, 56
functional flexibility, 102

Gaian ontology, 219–21, 224
Galbraith, J.K., 233
Garsten, C., 139–40
gender
  categorisation, 161
  equality legislation/conventions, 162–4
  impact on profits, 165
  inequality in workplace, 168–70
  and labour market position, 158
  and leadership, 242, 243, 250–1
  and maintenance of capitalism, 273–4, 277
  and unemployment, 111
  see also women
General Agreement on Trade and Tariffs
  (GATT), 66, 71
George, S., 214–15
Gertler, M., 191
global capitalism
  corporations, 22–4
  managing, 9–12
Global Compact (GC), 23, 73, 75–6, 247
global competitiveness, 98
global economy
  and flexible firm model, 103–6
  and inequality, 169

global economy cont.
  managing, 9–12
global income redistribution, 113–14
globalisation, 9–12, 63–6
  of neo-liberalism, 70–1, 72
Golant, B.D., 7
Goleman, D., 241
governance, 238, 254–5
government agencies
  restructuring of, 104
  see also public sector
government/state
  neo-liberalism and role of, 71–2
  power shift to corporate sector, 141
  response to protest, 82, 144–5
  responsibility of, 80–1, 131, 171
  role in control of people, 53, 136,
    139, 179
government/state policy
  austerity measures, 129, 264, 278–9
  compliance, 137
  and corporate interests, 79, 83–4, 141
  neo-liberal, 71–2, 127–8
graduates, 181
Gramsci, A., 37–9, 100, 134, 266
Grant, S., 279
Greece, 264
Green, P., 84
Grey, C., 17, 139–40
Guinier, L., 163

Habermas, J., 48–50, 140–1, 143
Hajer, M.A., 208–9
Harvey, D., 126
Hawthorne Studies, 146, 149, 157
Hayek, F., 68
Hegel, G., 33–4
hegemonic control, 95, 266
hegemonic influence of corporations, 23
hegemonic power, 37, 40
hegemony, 70, 107, 134, 266
Helal, M., 15
Henrich, J., 156–7
Hertz, N., 22–3
hierarchical observation, 134–5
hierarchies, and leadership style, 243
historical context of discourse, 47–8
Hochschild, A., 143
holistic reification, 20
homeworking, 110
homogeneous relationships, 166
hooks, b., 262
Horkheimer, M., 42–3
Hoss, R., 92
Hudson, I., 192
Hudson, M., 192

human relations theory (HRT), 99, 146–50
human resource management (HRM), 127,
   149–50
human rights, and work, 158–60, 162–3, 167
Humphries, M.T., 279
Hutt, W.H., 183

I/thou relationship, 48
ideologies
   capitalist, 4
   formation of, 50
   *see also* neo-liberal ideology
ILO (International Labour Organization), 111,
   114, 162
IMF (International Monetary Fund), 66, 71,
   72, 74
immaterial labour, 115
imperialism *see* empire; neo-imperialism
income inequality, 70, 113–14, 159
income redistribution, 113–14
indigenous peoples, 200
   capitalist interest in, 74–6
   and leadership, 251
   learning from, 270–1
   participation in market, 185–6
   rights of, 75–6, 208
   as stakeholders, 216
individual responsibility, 80–1, 131, 171
individualism, 69–70, 143–4
inequality
   explaining, 168–9
   and gender in workplace, 168–70
   of income, 70, 113–14, 159
   and justice, 70, 127, 279–80
informal organisational structure, 146, 147
information technology, 10
institutional logic of capitalism, 4–6
   and concept of work, 93
   and management education, 77
   and ownership, 11–12
   in public sector, 13–15
institutional logics, 2, 4
   transformation of, 264–5
instrumental rationality, of capitalism,
   278–80
international goals *see* United Nations
International Labour Organization (ILO), 111,
   114, 162
International Monetary Fund (IMF), 64, 66,
   70–72, 74, 80, 170, 208, 235, 273, 279
International Network for Research
   in Organisations and Sustainable
   Development (RIODD), 272
internet, 10
investors, 6, 77
involuntary part-time work, 109–10

Jackson, S., 166, 167
Jaffe, J., 191
Japanese management practices, 101
Jaworski, J., 252
job satisfaction, 146, 147
Johnston, J., 193
Julian, Jr. J., 112
Jung, C., 44
justice, and market forces, 69–70, 96, 127,
   279–80

Kant, I., 32–3
Keynesian-welfare compromise, 66–7, 68
Knights, D., 32, 189
knowledge, Foucault's theory of, 47–8
Korten, D., 22–3, 32
Kotter, J., 237, 243
Kristeva, J., 50
Kumar, S., 219

labour market
   deregulation of, 102, 104, 128
   gender and position in, 158
   race and position in, 158
   *see also* outsourcing; workforce
*laissez-faire* economics, 69, 183
land enclosure, 24, 203
Landrum, N., 8, 9
Lange, D., 7
Lao-tsu, 236
Lazzarato, M., 115
leaders
   approaches to teaching, 247–8
   critical approach to, 233
   examples of, 232
   studying nature of, 233, 240–6
leadership
   approaches to studying, 233–4, 250–1
   and ethics, 248–9
   and followership, 236, 249
   and management education, 231–2, 237–40,
      243–4, 245, 250–1
   and responsibility, 255–6
   spiritual approach, 249–54
   trust lost in, 235–6, 247
leadership qualities, 241–4
leadership styles, 242–3
Lee, S., 110
legislative approach, 162–4, 167–8
legitimacy, 5, 6–8
Lehman Brothers, 234, 247
lifeworld, 50, 143–4, 145, 267
linguistic turn, 46
Lipton, B., 223
living wage, 115
logocentrism, 46–7

organisation of work *cont.*
  outcomes of flexibility, 109–10, 128, 129–30
  outsourcing *see* outsourcing
  prerequisites for flexible, 117
  restructuring and downsizing, 106–7, 114
  restructuring and unemployment, 110–12
  Taylorist, 99, 131–2
organisational flexibility, 98
organisational legitimacy, 6, 7
organisational reputation, 7
organisational rules, 39
Ostrom, E., 217
Ottaviano, R., 256–7
outsourcing
  and flexible organisation, 103, 104, 105,
    107–9
  and inequality, 169
  as means of worker control, 132
  regions targeted for, 130
  and skill, 108, 114
  and workplace diversity, 164
over-employment, 109
overtime, 113
owners, 13
ownership, 11–12
  and privatisation of water, 11, 215–16, 220

Page, C., 222–3
Palley, T., 102, 104, 113, 114
panoptic gaze, 134, 148
part-time work, 108–10, 111
patriarchy, 277
Pelsmacker, P., 193
performative labour, 116
peripheral workforce, 102, 108–9
Perkin, H., 70, 77
personality, and leadership, 241–2
personality theories, 44
philanthrocapitalism, 274–5
Phillips-Carson, P., 140
physics, 222
Pilger, J., 23–4
political consumerism, 182–3, 186
positivist analyses, 56
post-structuralism, 46
postmodernism, 46–54
power
  of corporations, 22–4, 77–9, 83–4
  Foucault's theory of, 47–8, 133–5
  hegemonic, 37, 40
  of producers and consumers, 188–91, 192–3
  shift from government to corporate, 141
power relations
  Foucault's theory, 133–4
  Gramsci's theory, 37
  in rituals of confession, 137–8

Preston, S.H., 143
price barriers, 187–8
prisons, 13–14
privatisation, 11–12, 215–16, 220
producers, power relative to consumers,
    188–91, 192–3
production
  factory model, 13–14, 17, 136
  Marx's theory, 35
productivity
  and employment, 92
  impact of diversity on, 165–7, 168
  and organisation of work, 99, 132
  and quality, 136
  and restructuring, 98
  and worker satisfaction, 146, 147
protest/dissent, 3, 10, 240
  government response to, 82,
    144–5
  media coverage of, 82–3, 144
  miners, 41
  Occupy Wall Street, 3, 38, 82, 144
  and resilience of capitalism, 271
  students, 206
  *see also* consumer activism; environmental
    activism
protesters
  media portrayals of, 82–3, 144
  reification of, 38–9
psychoanalytic theory, 44–5, 265–6
public sector, 13–15, 103
public-private partnerships (PPPs), 8
punishment, 133–4
purchasing decisions, 183–4
  constraints on, 187–8, 191

quality, and productivity, 136
quantum hologram, 222
quota legislation, 163–4, 167

race and ethnicity
  impact of diversity, 166, 167
  and labour market position, 158
  and privilege, 161–2
rationalisation processes, 50
re-institutionalisation, 145
reading, as political act, 47
recession
  of 1970s, 67, 70
  *see also* financial crisis
recruitment agencies, 262
redistribution of income, 113–14
redundancy, 106–7
regulation
  and responsibility, 202
  *see also* legislative approach

reification, 20, 35, 38–41, 191–2
    *see also* de-reification; objectification
reified consciousness, 40, 267
relations of power, 37, 133–4, 137–8
relationships, Buber's theory of, 48
renewable energies, 282–4
repatriation, 127
repression, 44, 45, 49
reputation, 7
research bias, 156–7
reservations, 24
resistance *see* protest/dissent
Response Trust, 219
responsibilities approach to water access, 219
responsibility
    of consumers, 182–3, 186
    and leadership, 255–6
    state and individual, 80–1, 131, 171
    *see also* corporate responsibility;
        environmental responsibility
restructuring, 97–8, 106–7, 110–12, 114
revolt, 50
Richard, O., 167
rights *see* human rights
rights-based approaches to water, 218–19
Rio+20 conference, 270
rituals of confession, 137–8
Rockefeller, D., 63, 85
Roddick, A., 207
Rose, N., 137, 138–9, 147, 148–9, 207
Royal Dutch Shell company, 23, 252–3
    *see also* Shell Oil

safety, at work, 97
Saro-Wiwa, K., 252
Saul, J.R., 9
Schumacher College, 256
Schumpeter, J., 188
Schwab, K., 235
scientific management, 146–7
    *see also* Taylorist work organisation
Scott, R., 104
security experts, 208
seed, commodification of, 212–14
selection bias, 156–7
self-consciousness, 33–4
    *see also* consciousness
self-disciplined individuals, 133–4, 135,
    138–40
self-help books, 139–40
self-identity, and consumerism, 189
self-management, 17, 149, 264
Service Employees International Union
    (SEIU), 239
services, purchase of, 185, 192
Sheldrake, R., 222, 252

Shell Oil, 207
    *see also* Royal Dutch Shell company
Shiva, V., 11, 55, 212–13, 216–17
Shore, L.M., 167, 168
signifiers, 46
Sillince, J.A.A., 7
Singapore, 203
Sizoo, E., 8
skills
    outsourcing of, 108, 114
    *see also* deskilling
slavery, 112–13, 151, 186
Smith, A., 69, 183
social constructions, 20–1, 39–40, 44, 267
social enterprise, 12, 106
social relations, reification of, 191–2
social systems, 2
    *see also* capitalism
social welfare, 68
    as conditional, 113
    as counter-productive, 131
social well-being
    and neo-liberalism, 19, 81
    wealth donated for, 64, 274–5
    *see also* common good
society
    as construct, 20–1
    Horkheimer's theory of, 42
soul, marketing and harnessing of, 262
soul work, education as, 262, 263–5
specialised job designs, 99
spiritual approach, 219–25, 249–54
Spivak, G., 51
sport, and leadership, 251
stakeholder theories, 8
state *see* government
Stern, A., 239
stockholders, 6
stocks/shares, origins of, 77
strategic actions, 49
structural explanations of inequality, 169
subaltern studies, 51, 274, 277
subjectification, 4, 189
subjugation, 33–4, 70, 236
suicides, 117–18, 264
surplus repression, 45
surveillance
    hierarchical observation, 134–5
    panoptic gaze, 134, 148
    *see also* monitoring
survival of the fittest, 126
sustainability, 8–9

Taylor, F., 92
Taylorist work organisation, 99, 130, 131–2,
    146–7

teaching
  of leaders, 247–8
  as soul work, 262, 263–5
  *see also* education
team membership, 149
techniques of the self, 138–9
technologies of the self, 137
temporary work, 108–9
text
  assumptions within, 46
  deconstruction of, 47, 54
Thatcher, M., 45
theory-practice relationship, 36, 40
'Third Way' ideology, 81–2
Thomas, R., 168
time
  and capitalist production, 35
  and flexibility, 100
  *see also* working hours
TINA (there is no alternative) principle, 45, 67
Toohey, T., 165
training
  and disciplinary power, 134
  *see also* education
transformational leadership, 252
transformative change
  barriers to, 187–91, 282–3
  co-opted by capitalist remedies, 271–2
  inadequate strategies, 8–9
  moves toward, 9–10, 269–71
  possibility of, 17–18, 264–5, 266
  through consumption, 182–3, 184, 186, 187–91, 192–4
trust, lost in leadership, 235–6, 247
truth, 31, 41, 46–7
  manufacturing, 20–2

unconscious, 44–5, 95
under-employment, 109–10
unemployability, 112
unemployed people, 94, 96, 129
unemployment, 102, 110–12, 128, 132
  youth, 111, 164, 165
union leadership, 239
unions, 101–2
unitarism, 42
United Nations (UN), 10, 73–7, 208, 233, 270
  *see also* UNPRME
United Nations Conferences on Sustainable Development, 270
United Nations Convention on the Elimination of All Forms of Discrimination against Women (CEDAW), 162–3

United Nations Declaration on the Rights of Indigenous Peoples, 75–6, 208
United Nations Environment Program (UNEP), 218
United Nations Global Compact, 23, 73, 75–6, 247
United Nations Universal Declaration of Human Rights, 162
universalising, 51–2
universities, and factory model, 13–14, 17, 136
UNPRME (Principles for Responsible Management Education), 10, 74, 75–6, 93, 208, 248–9, 255 281

violations and violence, 54–5
voluntarist approach to diversity, 168
volunteers, 130
  in communities, 116, 144
  non-voluntary, 112–13

wages, 35–6, 111, 114–15
  *see also* equal pay
Walling, A., 110
Ward, D.B., 188
water
  commodification of, 212, 214–18, 220
  consumption of bottled, 181–2
  importance of, 211–12
  ownership and privatisation of, 11, 215–16, 220
water access, approaches to, 218–20
wealth, use for good, 64, 274–5
Weber, M., 92
Wehr, G., 222
welfare *see* social welfare
Wheatley, M., 253
Williams, K., 167
Willmott, H., 17
women
  and birth rates, 143–4
  equality legislation, 162–4
  impact on profits, 165
  labour market position, 158
  and leadership, 242, 243, 250–1
  and maintenance of capitalism, 273–4, 277
  and part-time work, 110
  and workplace inequality, 168–70
work
  concepts of, 92–3
  control of, 94–5
  as duty, 158–9, 171
  as human right, 158–60, 162–3, 167
  link with freedom, 91–2, 93–5, 99, 131, 160
  organisation of *see* organisation of work
  paid and unpaid, 169–70

work *cont.*
    restructuring of 1970s, 97–8
    that enables employment, 115–16
    transition to employment, 96
    unconscious ideas of, 95
    *see also* employment
work-life balance, 100, 110, 168, 169–70
workforce
    control of *see* control of workforce
    dehumanisation of, 99, 127
    empowerment of, 101, 243
    flexible, 98, 100–2
    impact of flexible organisation on, 102–6,
       109–10
    meanings vested in, 126–7
    mobility of, 131, 132–3
    needs of, 146–7
    worker-customer relationship, 166, 192
    *see also* labour market
workforce diversity
    affirmative action, 159, 163–4, 167, 170–1
    and disparate outcomes, 168–71

workforce diversity *cont.*
    diversity management, 165–7, 168
    EEO, 159, 162–3, 167–8, 170–1
    impact of global processes on,
       164–5
    impact on performance and profits,
       165–7, 168
    management of, 158–9
    and research bias, 156–7
working conditions, 97, 117, 192
working hours, 35, 100, 109, 110, 113,
    144, 192
World Bank, 66, 71, 72, 74
World Economic Forum, 218
World Trade Organization (WTO), 71,
    74, 79

Yeats, W.B., 220
youth unemployment, 111, 164, 165
Yunus, M., 275

Žižek, S., 54–5, 177–8